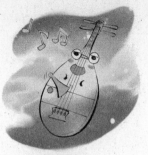

池田晃久
AKIHISA IKEDA

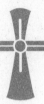

I love listening to music!

Since creating manga only requires the use of my hands and brain, no matter how busy things get, I'm always listening to music. Works out great for me.

I listen to music from the '60s and '70s, rock, funk, soul, jazz, etc. There's always music playing in my workplace. My life flows with the currents of the music I love. Creating manga sure is the life for me! (laugh).

Akihisa Ikeda was born in 1977 in Miyazaki. He debuted as a mangaka with the four-volume magical warrior fantasy series *Kiruto* in 1999, which was serialized in *Monthly Shonen Jump*. *Rosario+Vampire* debuted in *Monthly Shonen Jump* in March of 2002, and is continuing in the new magazine *Jump Square* (Jump SQ). In Japan, *Rosario+Vampire* is also available as a drama CD. In 2008, the story was released as an anime.

Ikeda has been a huge fan of vampires and monsters since he was a little kid.

He says one of the perks of being a manga artist is being able to go for walks during the day when everybody else is stuck in the office.

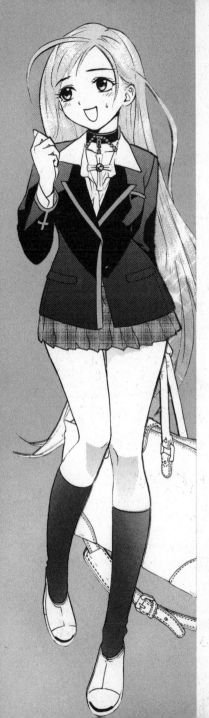

ROSARIO+VAMPIRE 5
SHONEN JUMP ADVANCED Manga Edition

STORY & ART BY AKIHISA IKEDA

Translation/Kaori Inoue
English Adaptation/Gerard Jones
Touch-up Art & Lettering/Stephen Dutro
Cover Design/Ronnie Casson
Interior Design/Ronnie Casson
Editor/Annette Roman

VP, Production/Alvin Lu
VP, Sales & Product Marketing/Gonzalo Ferreyra
VP, Creative/Linda Espinosa
Publisher/Hyoe Narita

ROSARIO TO VAMPIRE © 2004 by Akihisa Ikeda
All rights reserved. First published in Japan in 2004 by SHUEISHA Inc.,
Tokyo. English translation rights arranged by SHUEISHA Inc.

Printed in the U.S.A.

Published by VIZ Media, LLC
P.O. Box 77010
San Francisco, CA 94107

10 9 8 7 6 5 4 3 2
First printing, February 2009
Second printing, August 2009

www.viz.com   www.shonenjump.com

PARENTAL ADVISORY
ROSARIO+VAMPIRE is rated T+ for Older Teen and
is recommended for ages 16 and up. It contains
suggestive situations.
ratings.viz.com

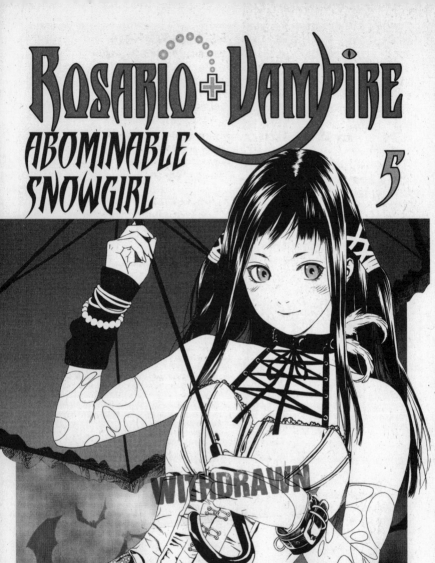

ROSARIO+VAMPIRE

ABOMINABLE SNOWGIRL

5

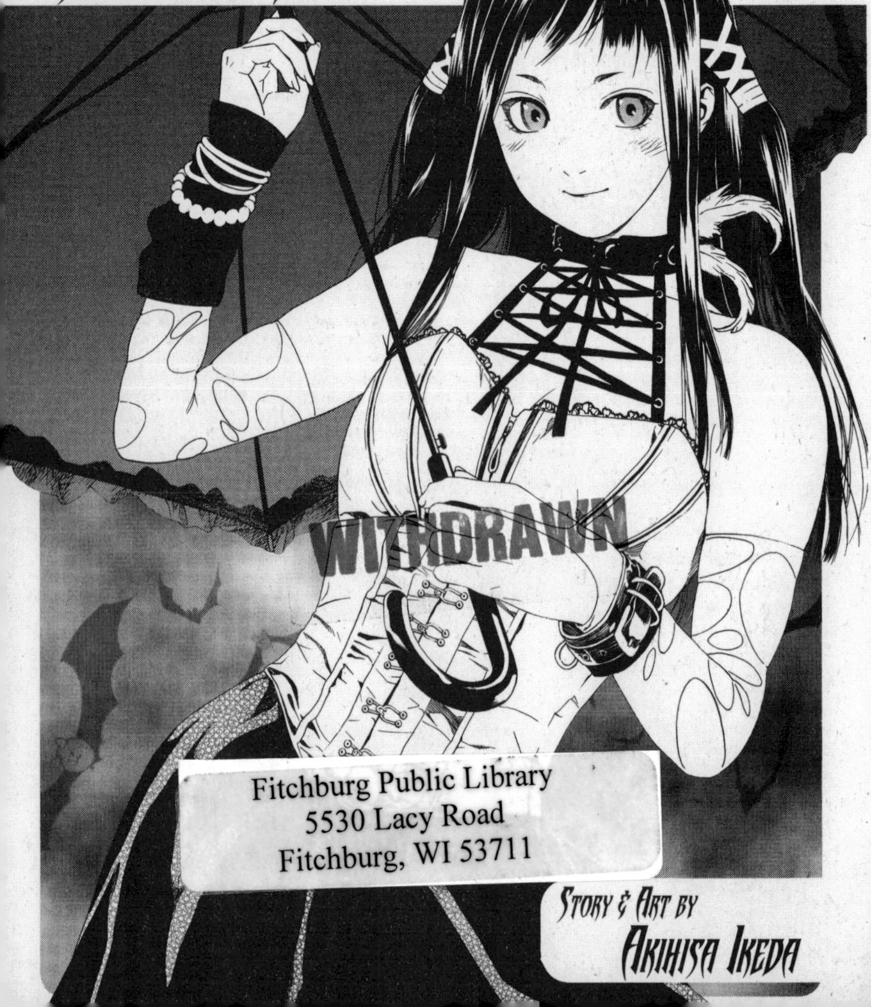

STORY & ART BY

AKIHISA IKEDA

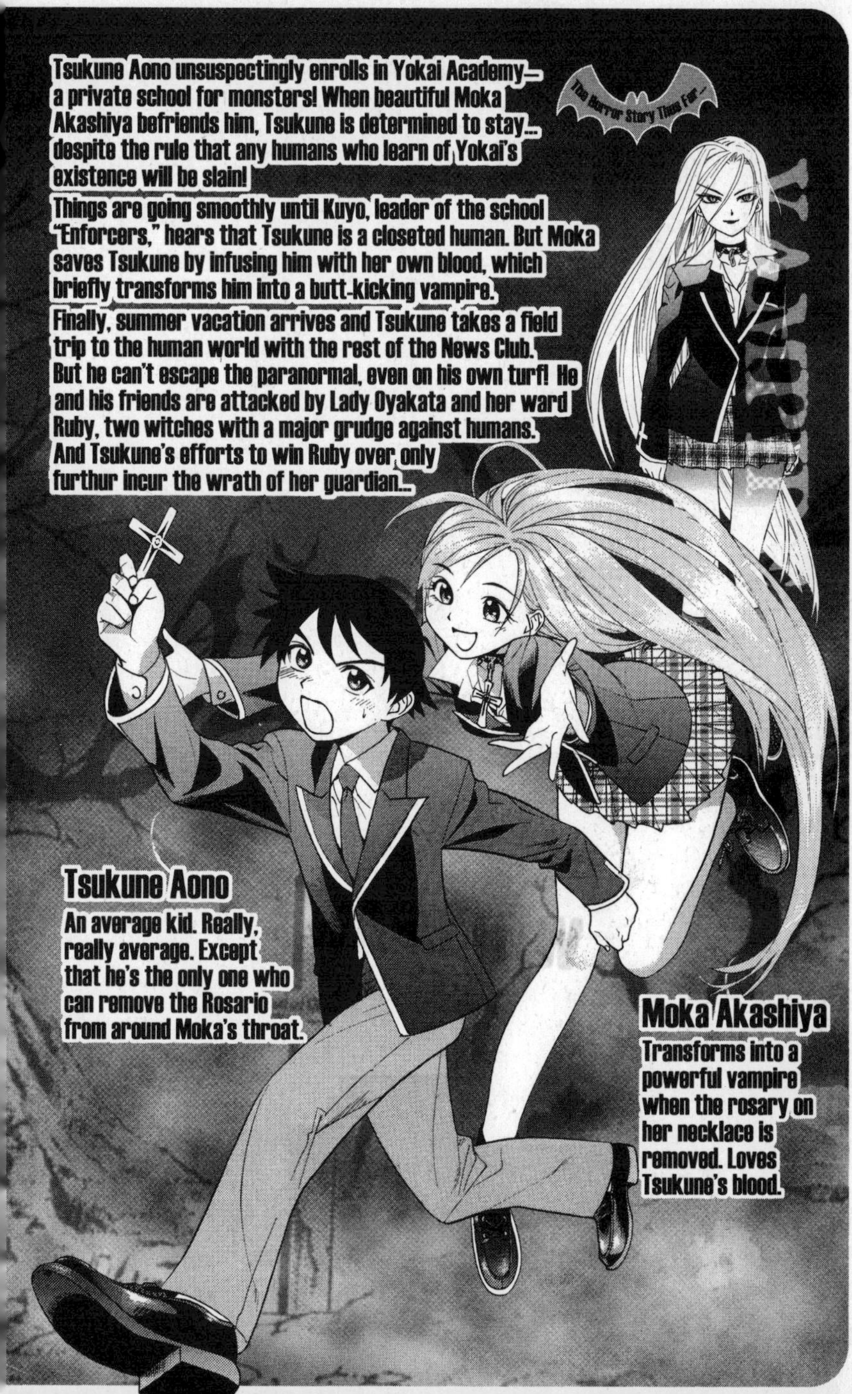
The Horror Story Thus Far...
Tsukune Aono unsuspectingly enrolls in Yokai Academy—a private school for monsters! When beautiful Moka Akashiya befriends him, Tsukune is determined to stay... despite the rule that any humans who learn of Yokai's existence will be slain!
Things are going smoothly until Kuyo, leader of the school "Enforcers," hears that Tsukune is a closeted human. But Moka saves Tsukune by infusing him with her own blood, which briefly transforms him into a butt-kicking vampire.
Finally, summer vacation arrives and Tsukune takes a field trip to the human world with the rest of the News Club. But he can't escape the paranormal, even on his own turf! He and his friends are attacked by Lady Oyakata and her ward Ruby, two witches with a major grudge against humans. And Tsukune's efforts to win Ruby over only furthur incur the wrath of her guardian...
Tsukune Aono
An average kid. Really, really average. Except that he's the only one who can remove the Rosario from around Moka's throat.
Moka Akashiya
Transforms into a powerful vampire when the rosary on her necklace is removed. Loves Tsukune's blood.

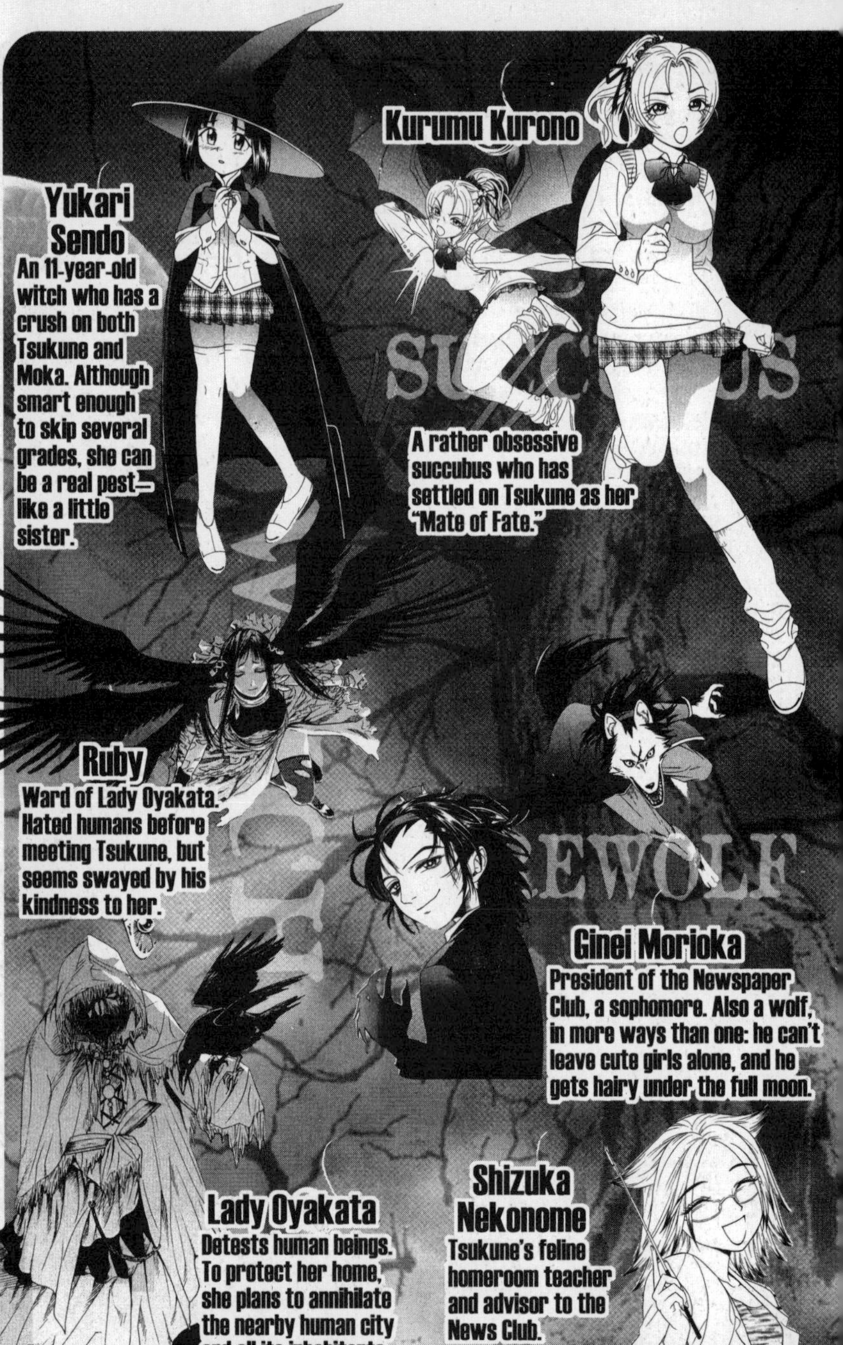
Kurumu Kurono
A rather obsessive succubus who has settled on Tsukune as her "Mate of Fate."
Yukari Sendo
An 11-year-old witch who has a crush on both Tsukune and Moka. Although smart enough to skip several grades, she can be a real pest—like a little sister.
Ruby
Ward of Lady Oyakata. Hated humans before meeting Tsukune, but seems swayed by his kindness to her.
Ginei Morioka
President of the Newspaper Club, a sophomore. Also a wolf, in more ways than one: he can't leave cute girls alone, and he gets hairy under the full moon.
Shizuka Nekonome
Tsukune's feline homeroom teacher and advisor to the News Club.
Lady Oyakata
Detests human beings. To protect her home, she plans to annihilate the nearby human city and all its inhabitants.

CONTENTS

Volume 5: Abominable Snowgirl

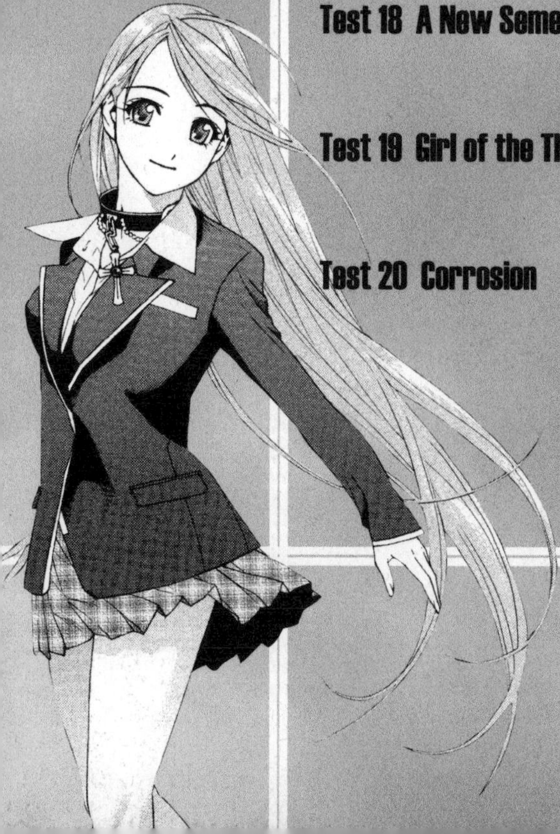

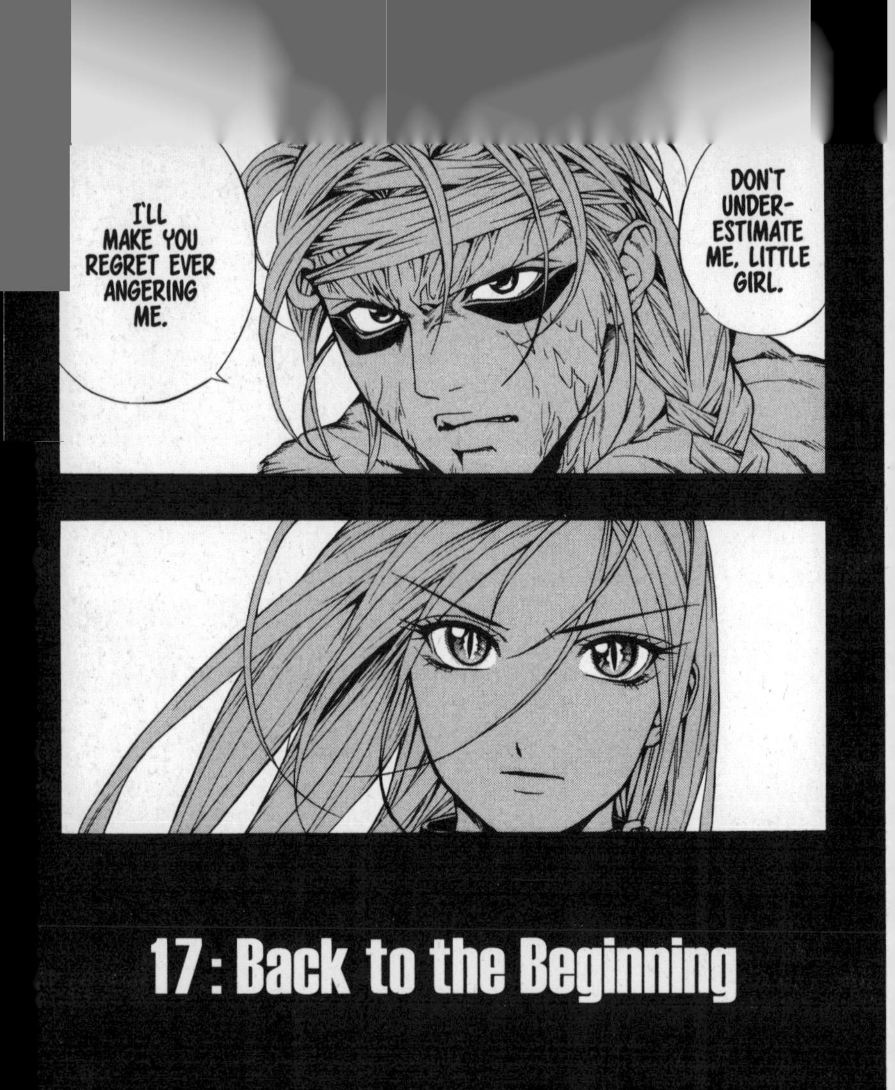
DON'T UNDER-ESTIMATE ME, LITTLE GIRL.
I'LL MAKE YOU REGRET EVER ANGERING ME.

17 : Back to the Beginning

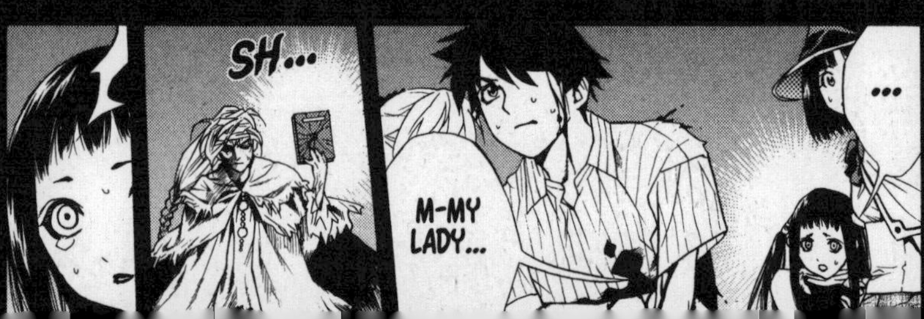
...
M-MY LADY...
SH...

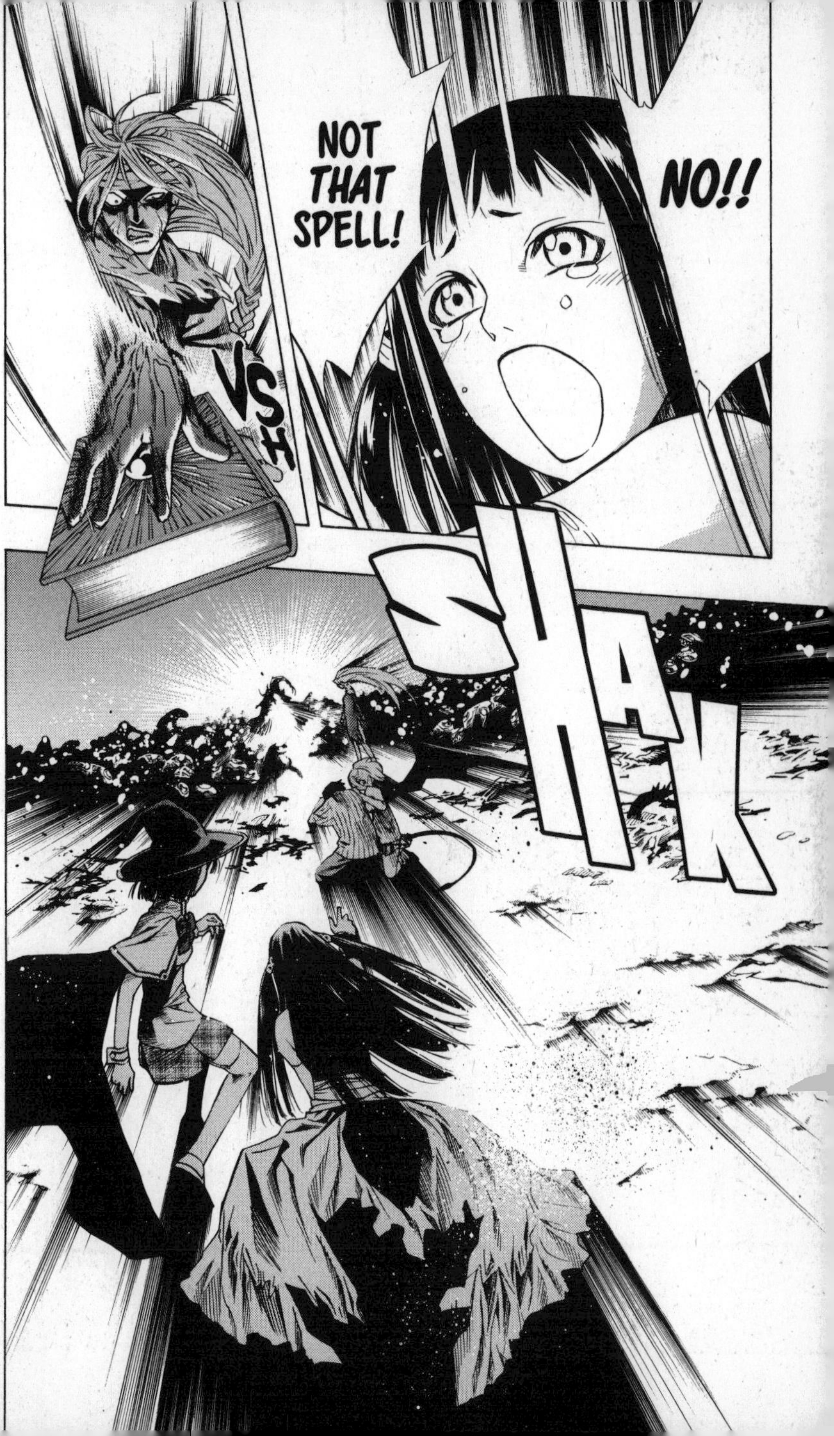
NO!!
NOT THAT SPELL!
VSH
SHAK

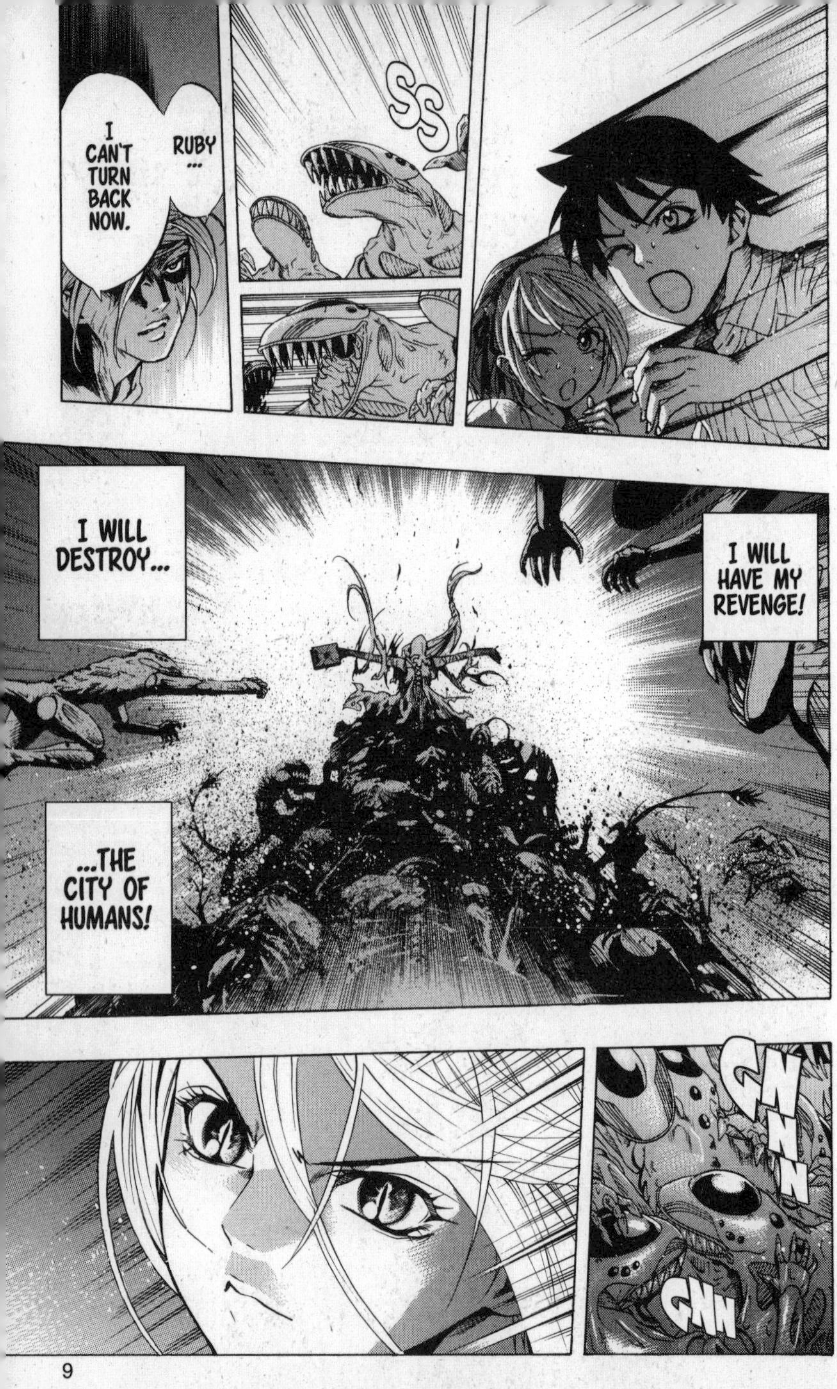
SS
RUBY ...
I CAN'T TURN BACK NOW.
I WILL HAVE MY REVENGE!
I WILL DESTROY...
...THE CITY OF HUMANS!
GNNN
GNN

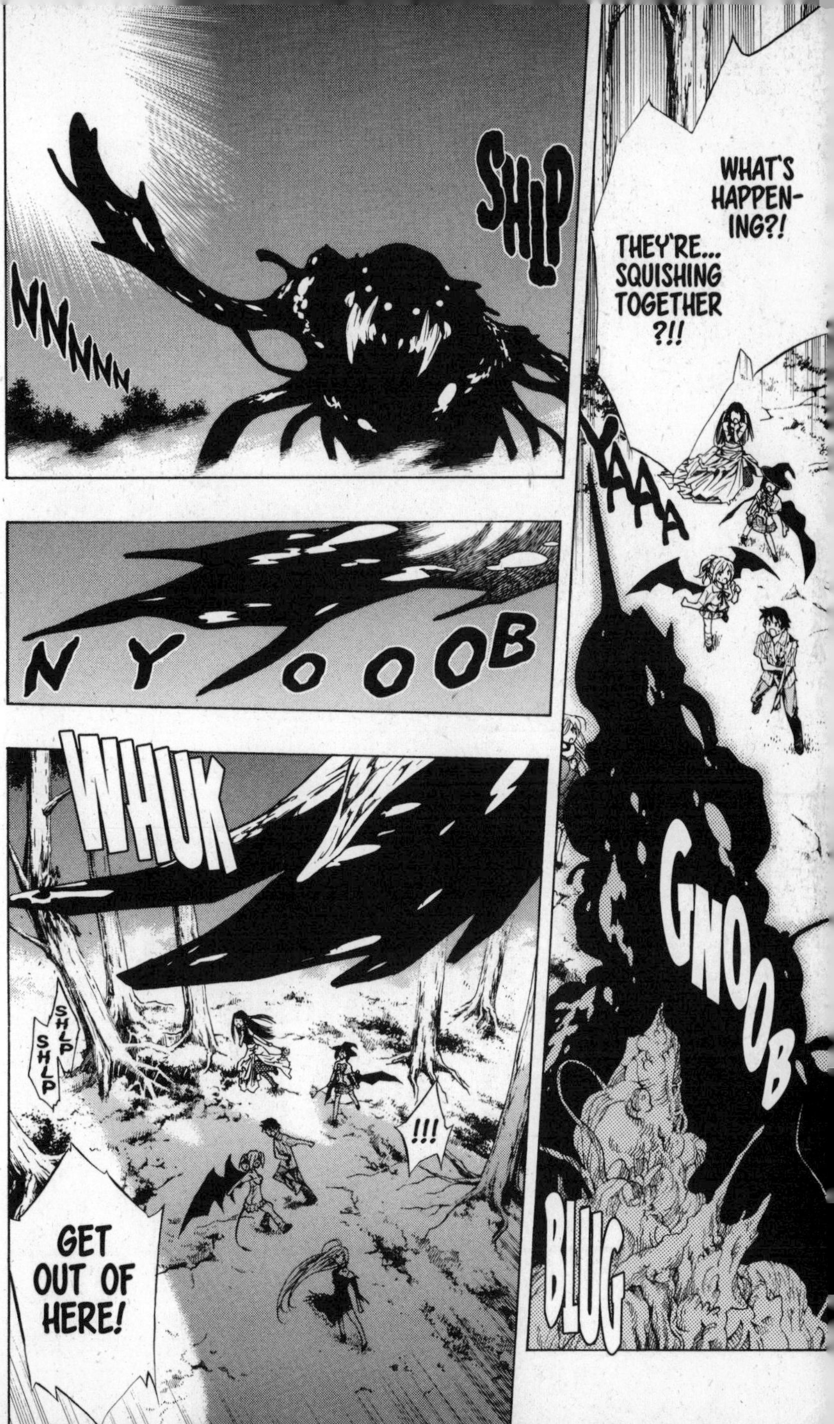
WHAT'S HAPPENING?!
THEY'RE... SQUISHING TOGETHER?!!
YAAAA
GNOOOB
BLUG
SHLP
NNNNNN
NYOOOB
WHUK
!!!
SHLP SHLP
GET OUT OF HERE!

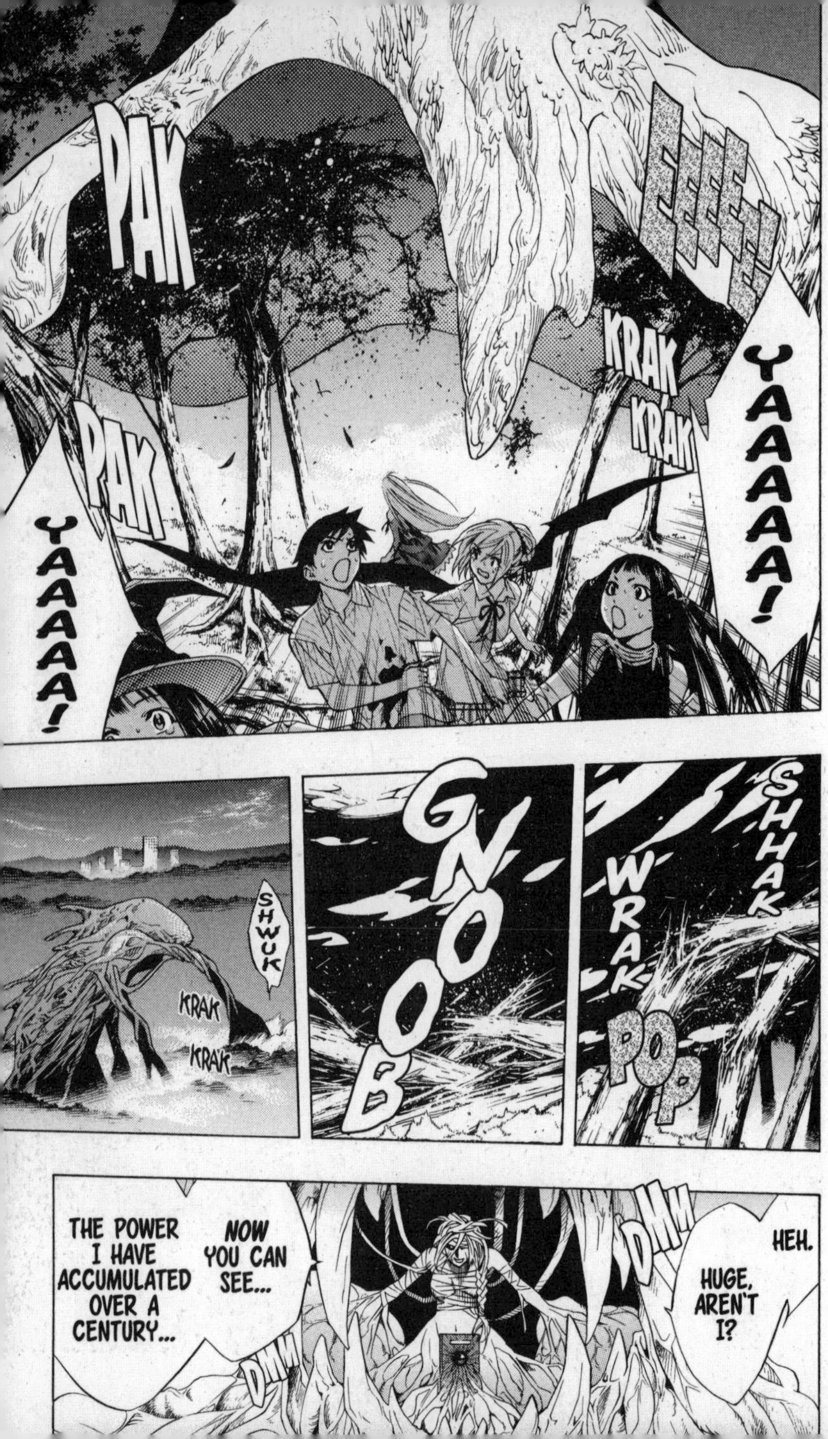
YAAAAAA!
KRAK
KRAK
PAK
PAK
YAAAAAA!
SHHAK
WRAK
POP
GNOOB
SHWUK
KRAK
KRAK
HEH.
HUGE, AREN'T I?
DMM
NOW YOU CAN SEE...
THE POWER I HAVE ACCUMULATED OVER A CENTURY...
DMM

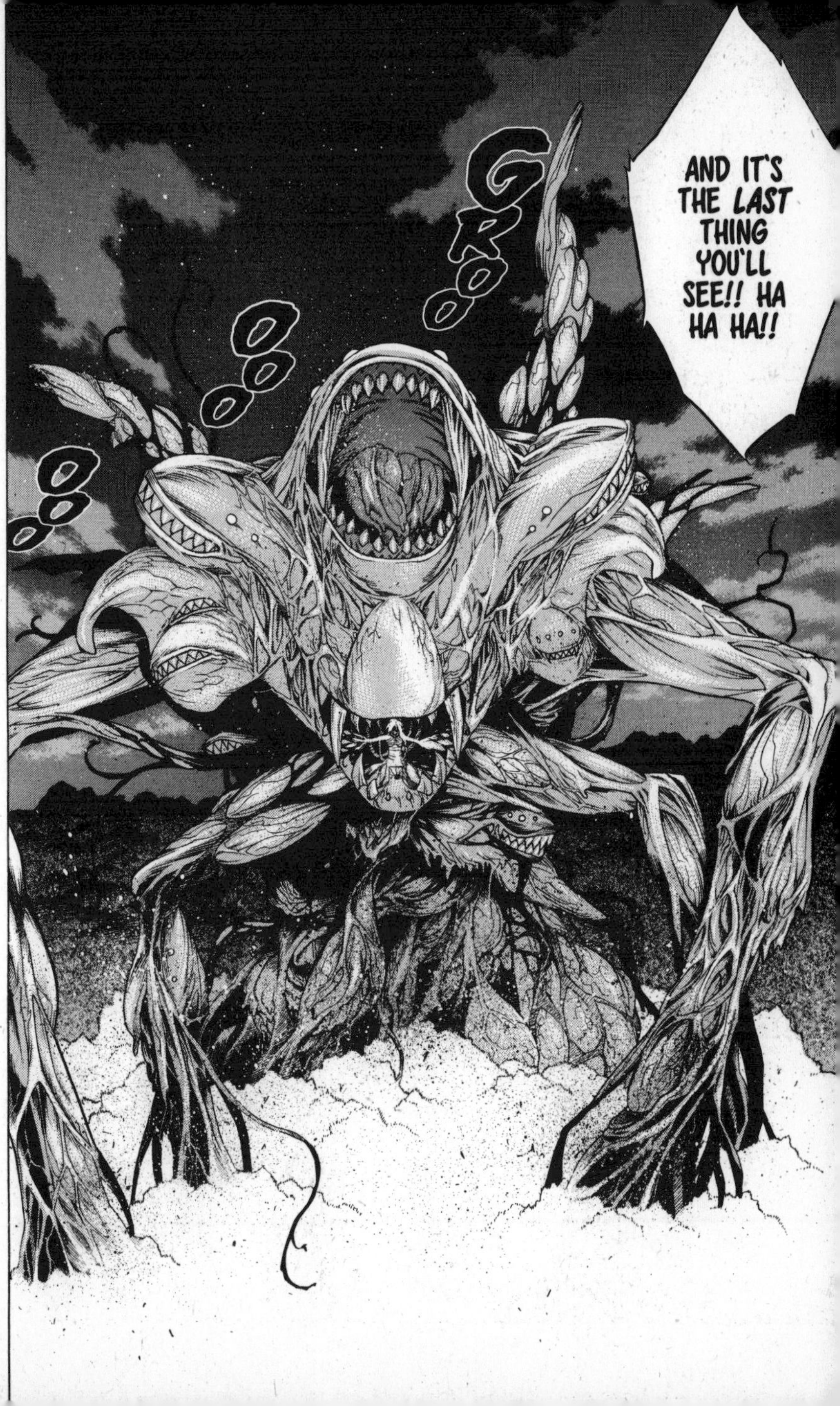
AND IT'S THE *LAST* THING YOU'LL SEE!! HA HA HA!!
GROOOOOOOO

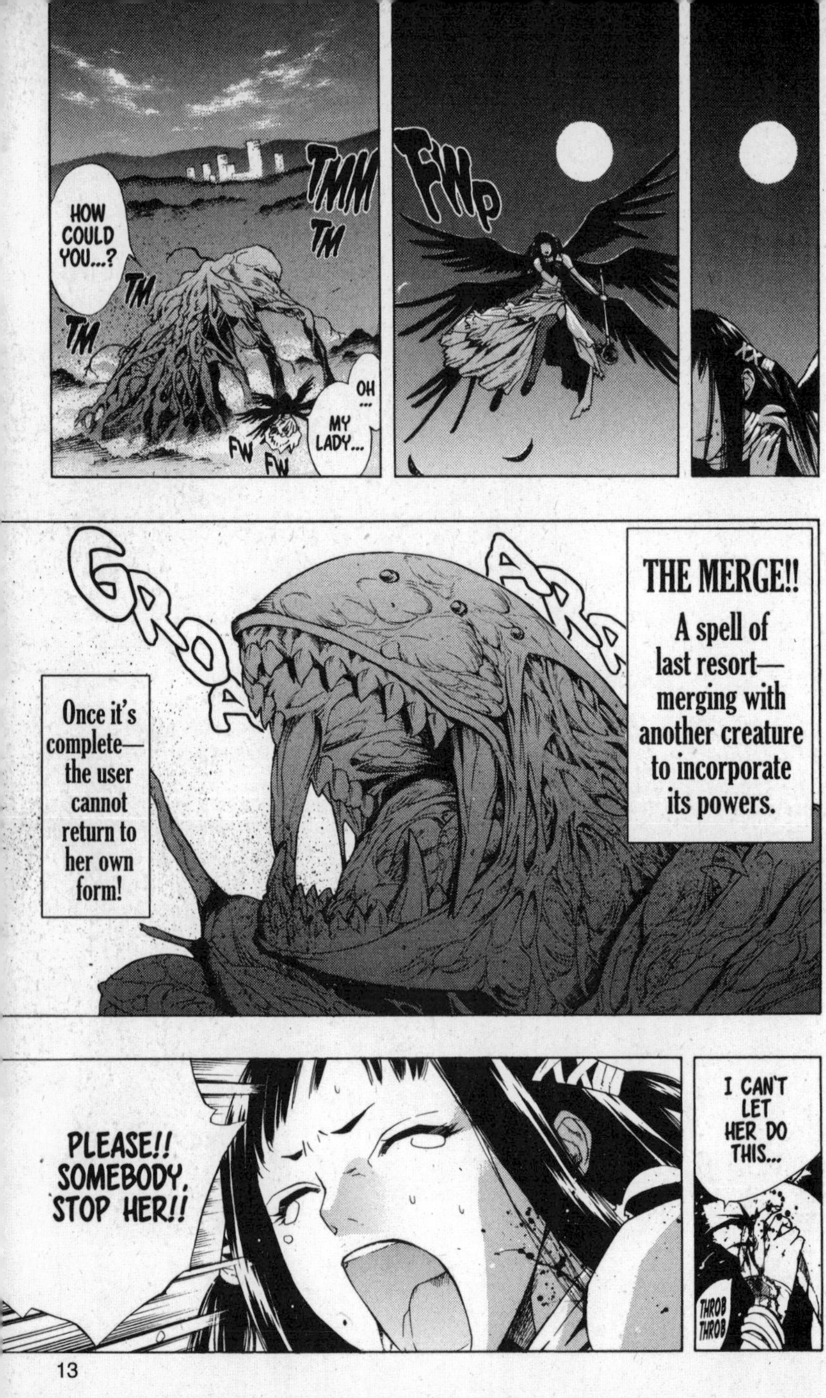
XXM
FWP
TMM TM
HOW COULD YOU...?
TM TM
OH... MY LADY...
FW FW
THE MERGE!! A spell of last resort—merging with another creature to incorporate its powers.
GROAARR
Once it's complete—the user cannot return to her own form!
I CAN'T LET HER DO THIS...
THROB THROB
XXIII
PLEASE!! SOMEBODY, STOP HER!!

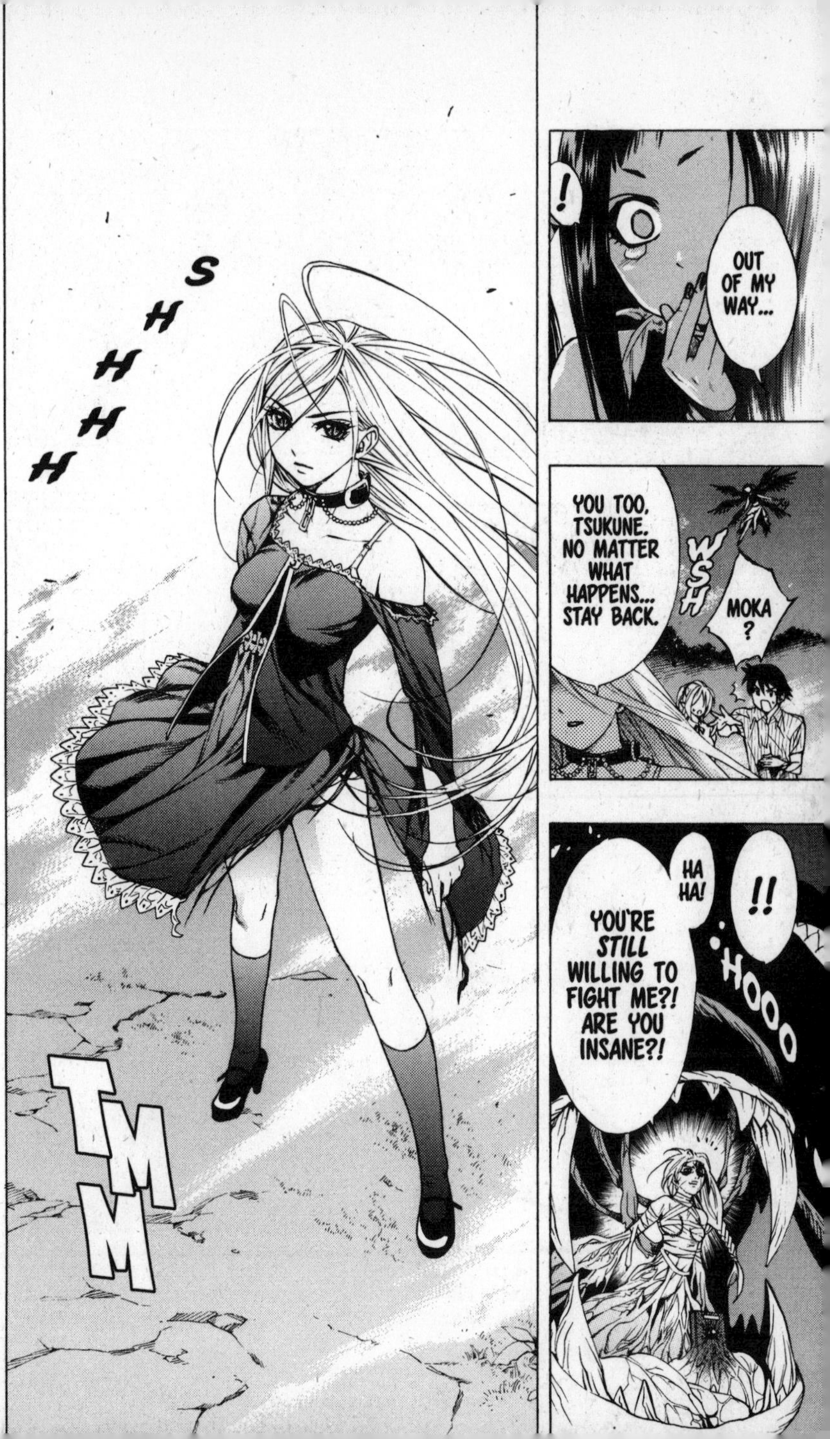
!
OUT OF MY WAY...
YOU TOO, TSUKUNE. NO MATTER WHAT HAPPENS... STAY BACK.
WSH
MOKA?
!!
HA HA!
YOU'RE *STILL* WILLING TO FIGHT ME?! ARE YOU INSANE?!
HOOO
SHHHHH
TMMM

READ THIS WAY

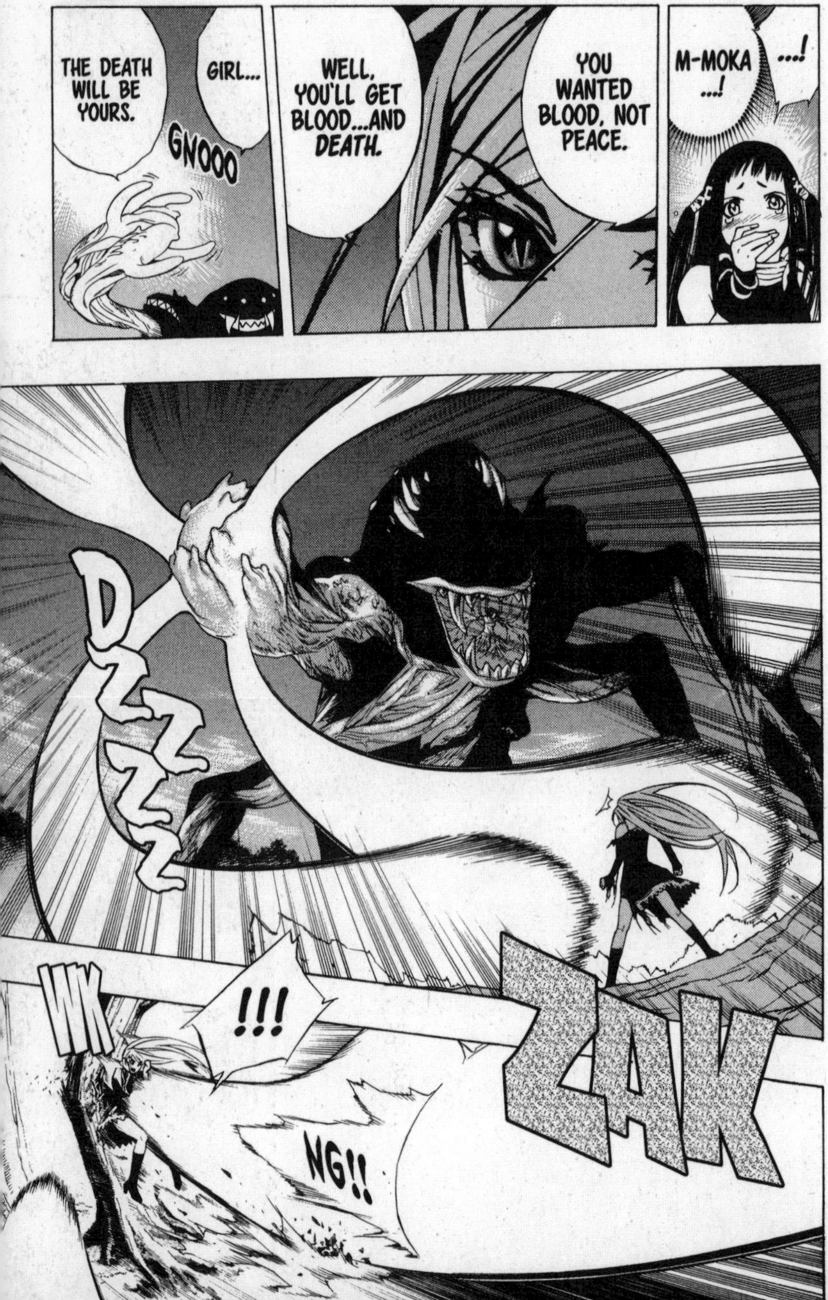
...!
M-MOKA ...!
YOU WANTED BLOOD, NOT PEACE.
WELL, YOU'LL GET BLOOD...AND DEATH.
GIRL...
THE DEATH WILL BE YOURS.
GNOOO
DZZZZ
ZAK
!!!
WK
NG!!

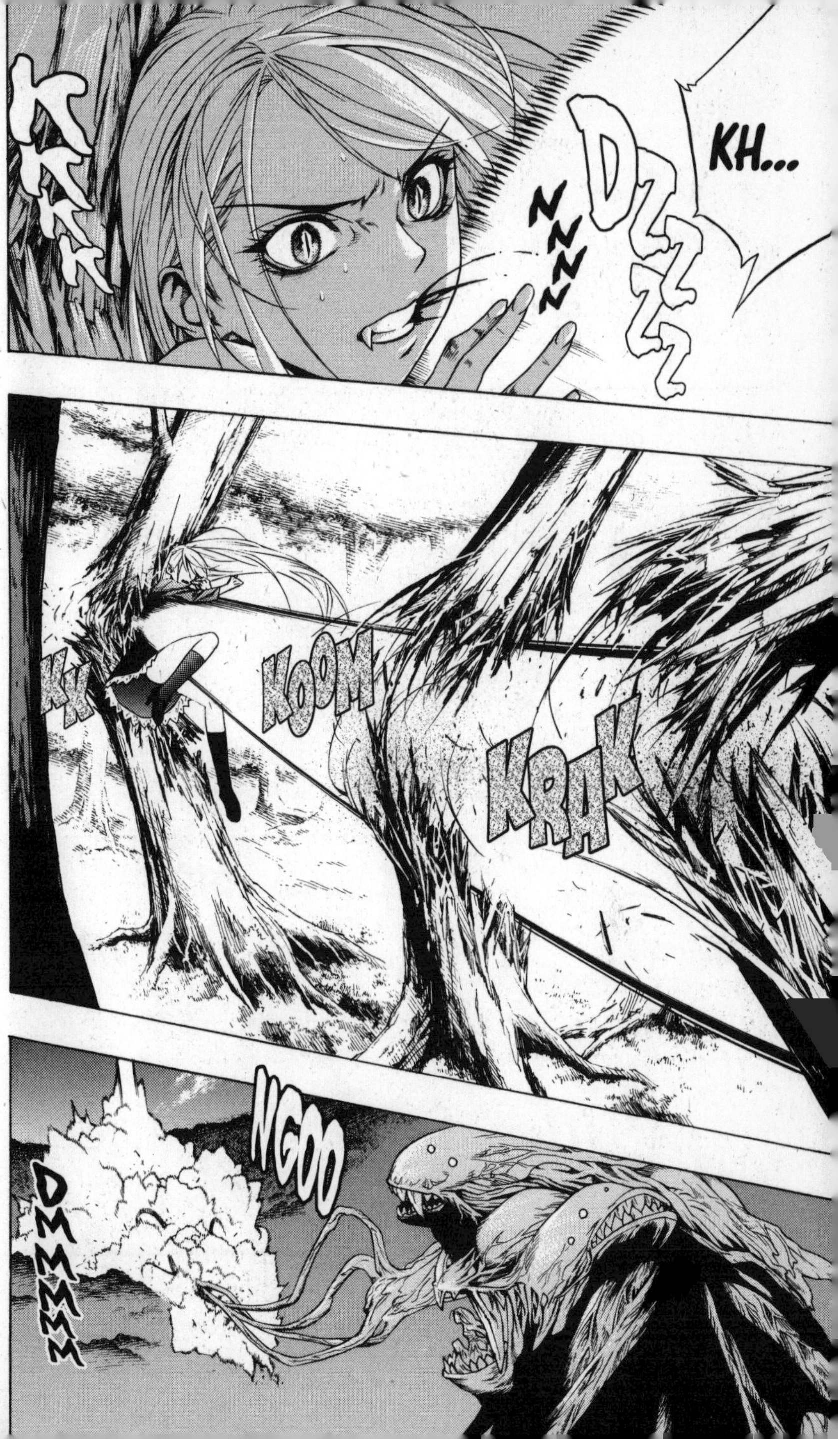
KH...
DZZZZ
NNNN
KKKKK
KRAK
KOOM
KK
NGOO
DMMMMM

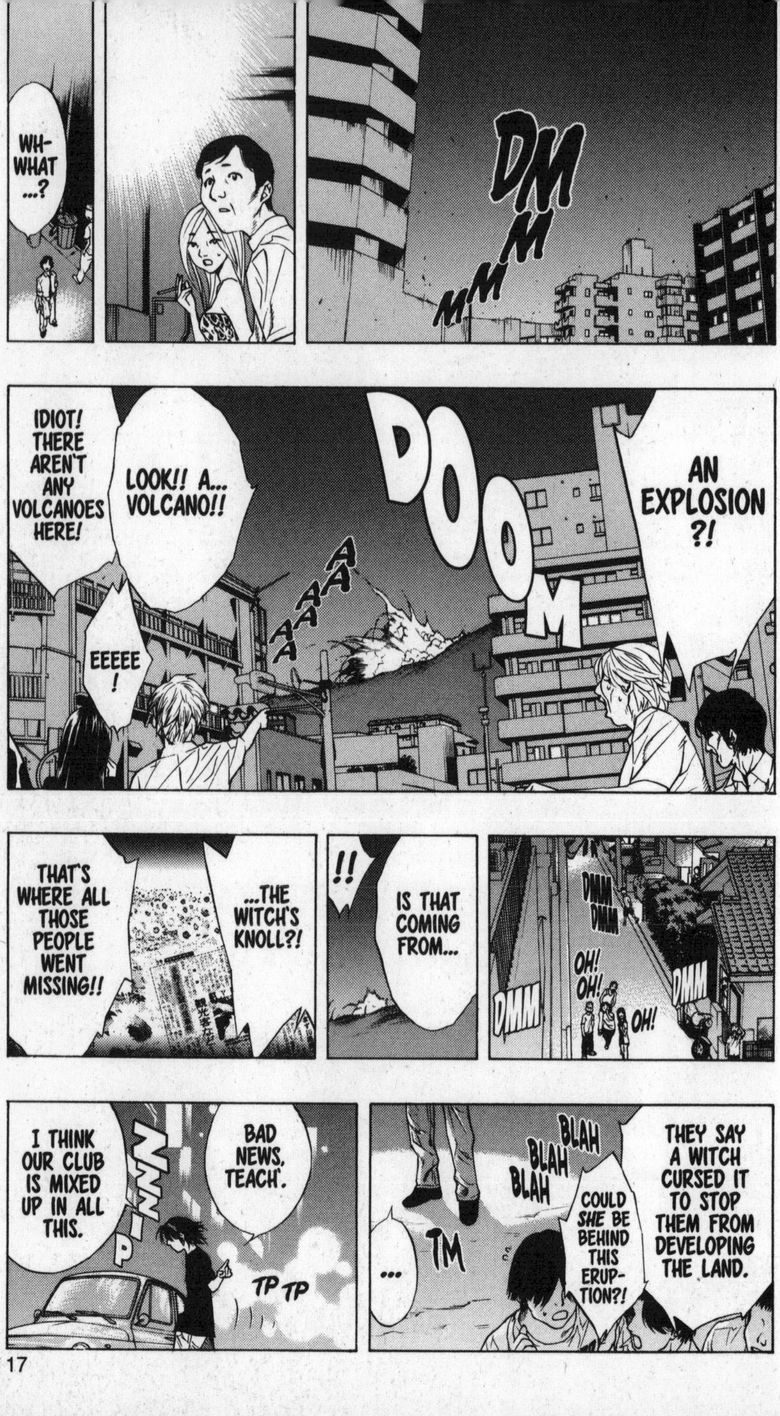
DMMMMM
WH-WHAT ...?
AN EXPLOSION ?!
DOOOM
AAAAAA
LOOK!! A... VOLCANO!!
IDIOT! THERE AREN'T ANY VOLCANOES HERE!
EEEEE !
DMM DMM
DMM
DMM
OH! OH!
OH!
!!
IS THAT COMING FROM...
...THE WITCH'S KNOLL?!
THAT'S WHERE ALL THOSE PEOPLE WENT MISSING!!
THEY SAY A WITCH CURSED IT TO STOP THEM FROM DEVELOPING THE LAND.
BLAH BLAH BLAH
COULD SHE BE BEHIND THIS ERUPTION?!
TM
...
BAD NEWS, TEACH'.
TP TP
I THINK OUR CLUB IS MIXED UP IN ALL THIS.

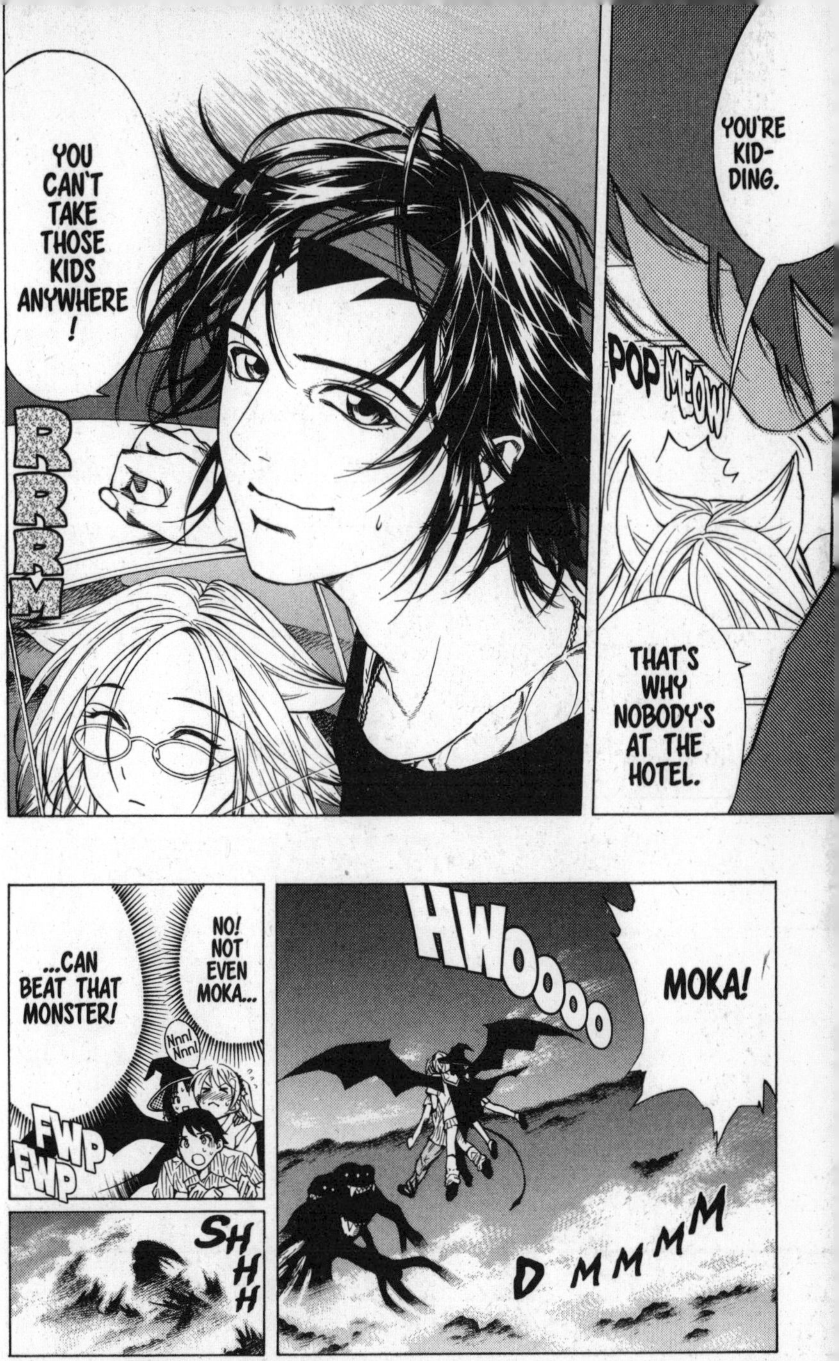
YOU'RE KID-DING.
POP
MEOW
THAT'S WHY NOBODY'S AT THE HOTEL.
YOU CAN'T TAKE THOSE KIDS ANYWHERE!
RRRM
MOKA!
HWOOOOO
DMMMM
NO! NOT EVEN MOKA...
...CAN BEAT THAT MONSTER!
Nnn! Nnn!
FWP FWP
SHHH

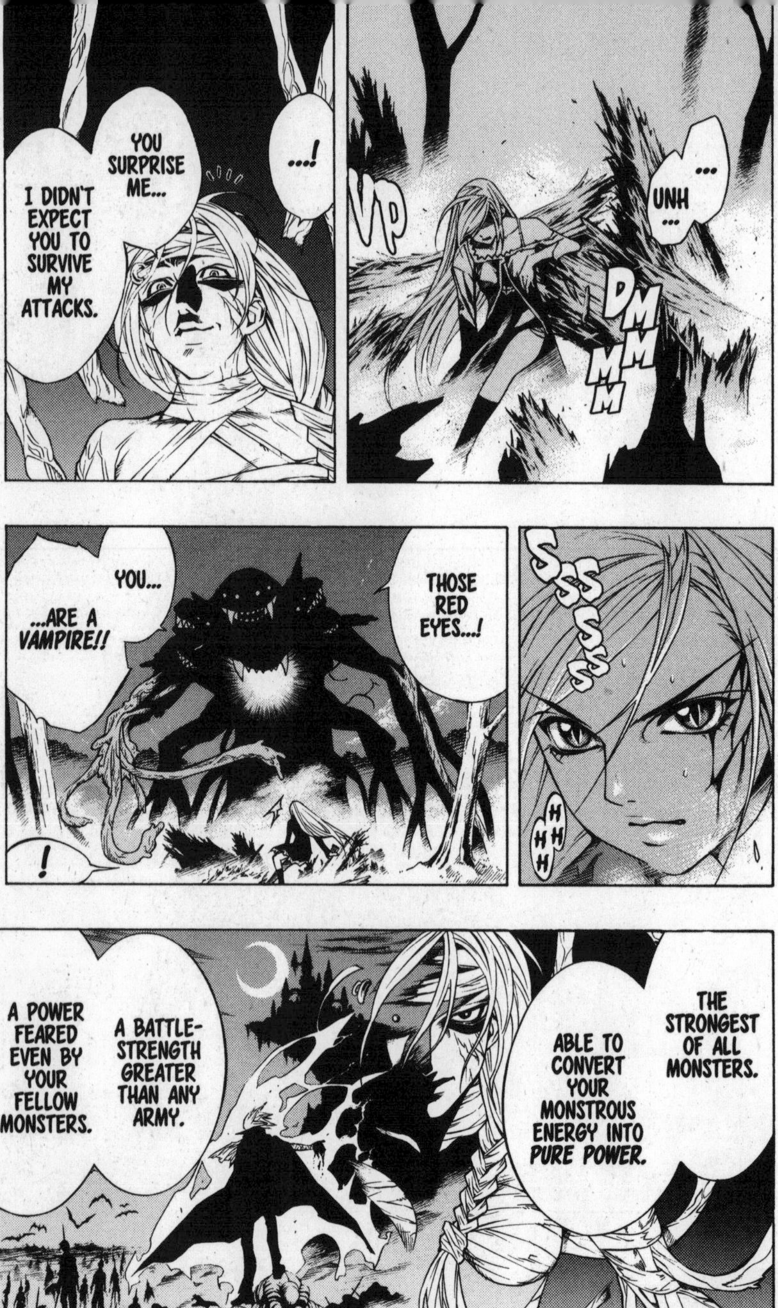
... UNH ...
VP
DMMMMM
...!
YOU SURPRISE ME...
I DIDN'T EXPECT YOU TO SURVIVE MY ATTACKS.
SSSSS
HHHHHH
THOSE RED EYES...!
YOU...
...ARE A VAMPIRE!!
!
THE STRONGEST OF ALL MONSTERS.
ABLE TO CONVERT YOUR MONSTROUS ENERGY INTO PURE POWER.
A BATTLE-STRENGTH GREATER THAN ANY ARMY.
A POWER FEARED EVEN BY YOUR FELLOW MONSTERS.

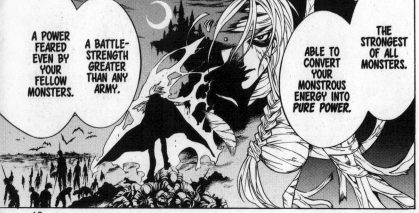

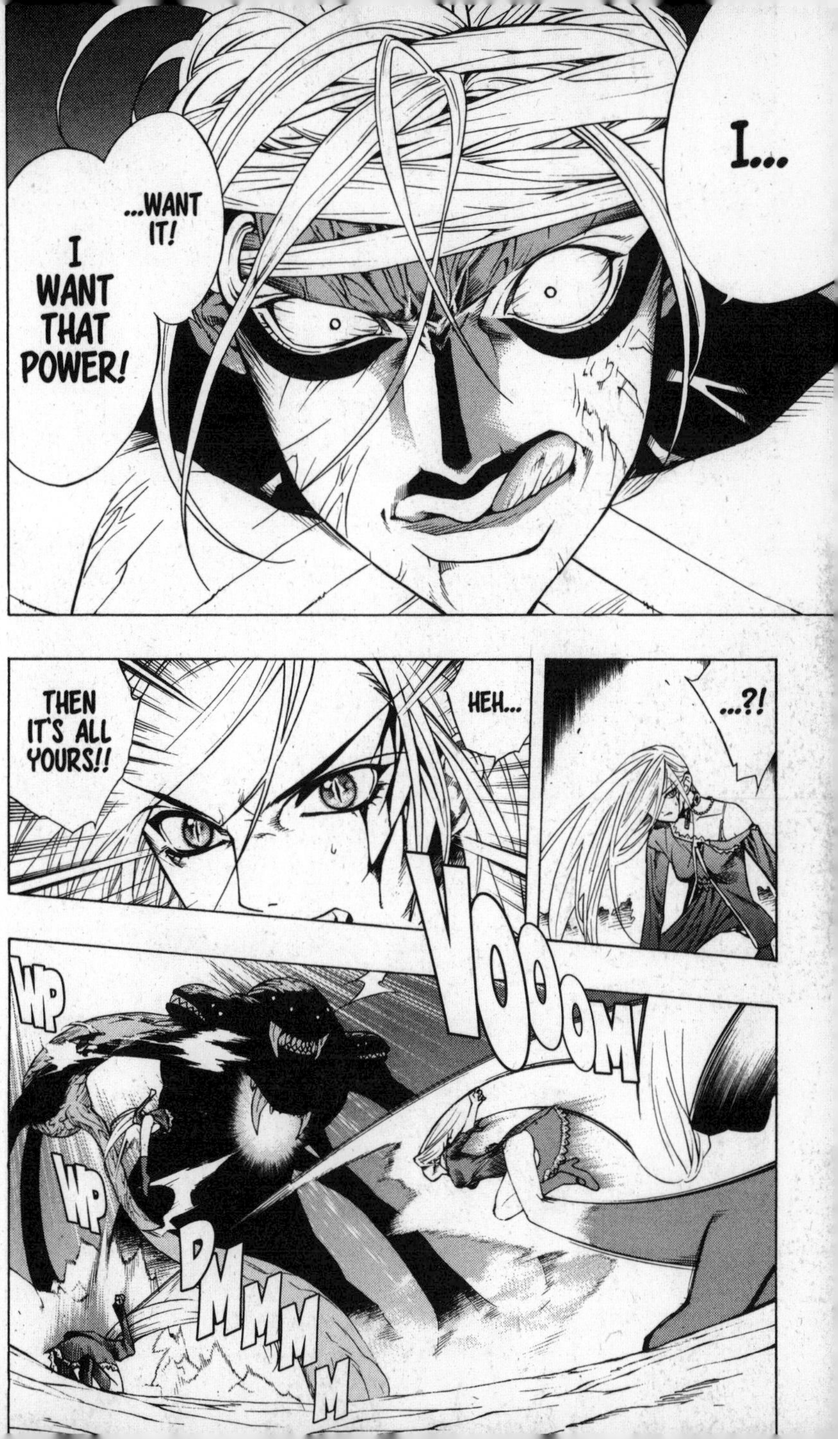
I...
...WANT IT!
I WANT THAT POWER!
...?!
HEH...
THEN IT'S ALL YOURS!!
VOOOM
WP
WP
DMMMMM

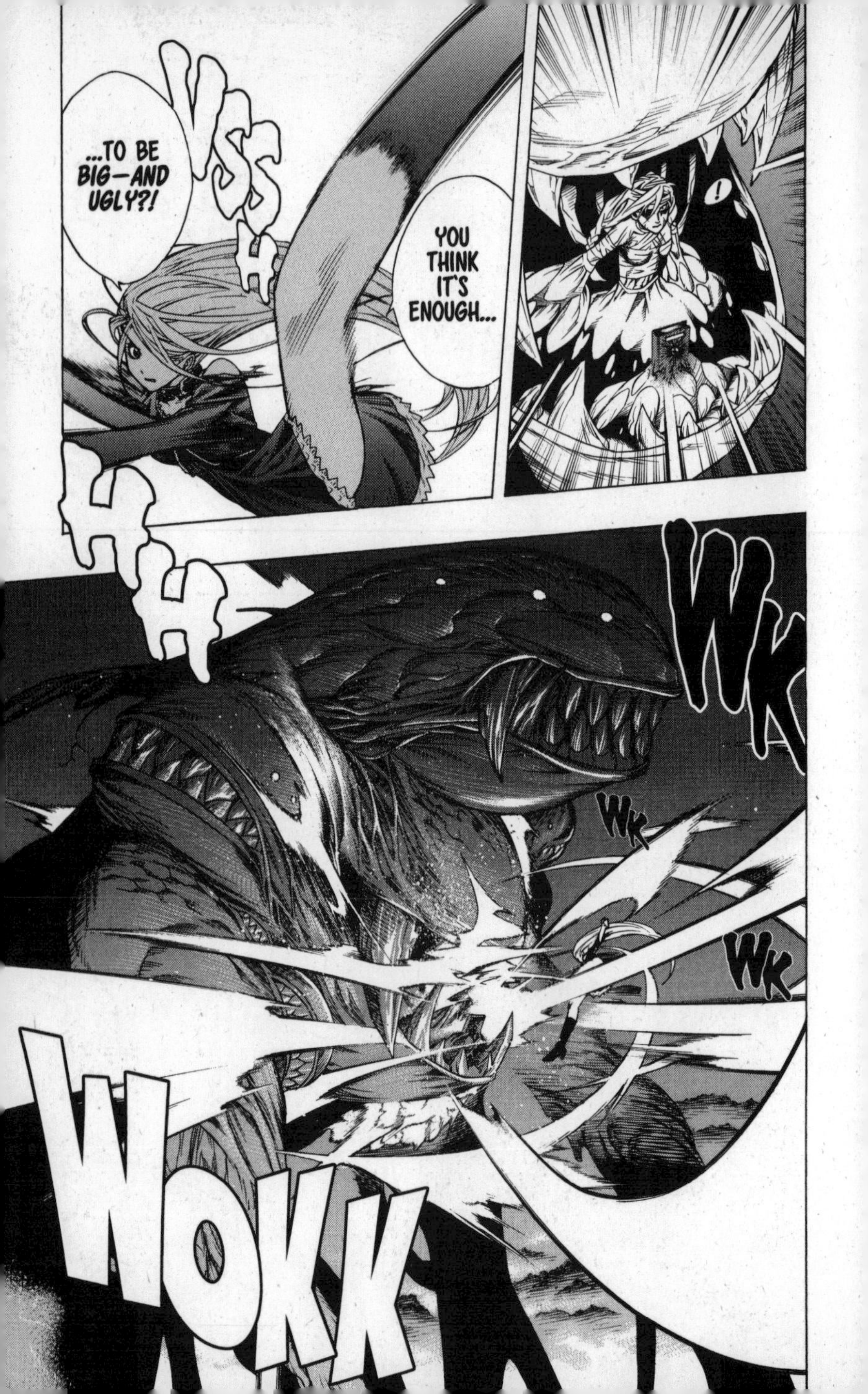
!
YOU THINK IT'S ENOUGH...
...TO BE BIG—AND UGLY?!
VSSHHH
WK
WK
WK
WOKK

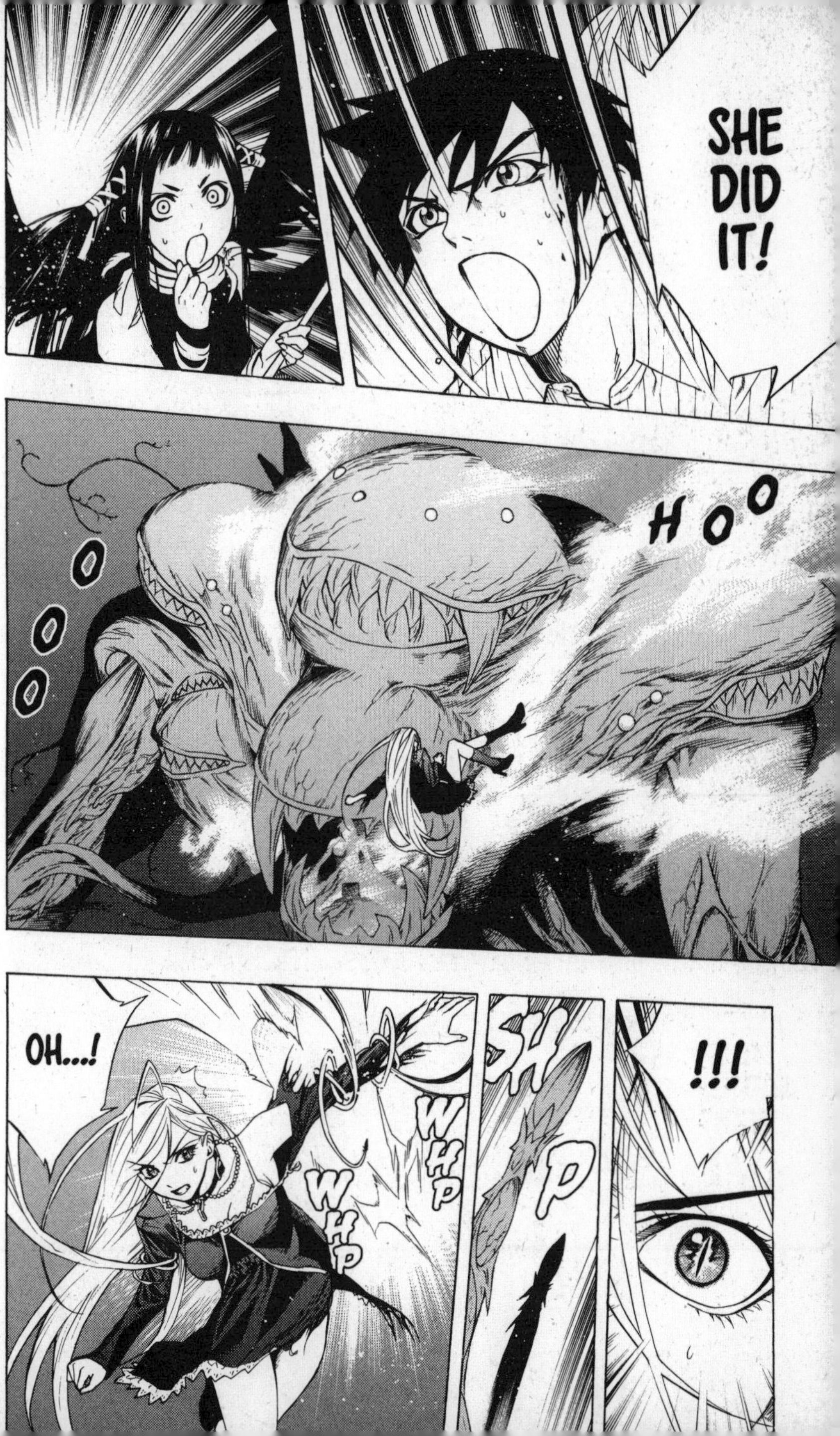
SHE DID IT!
HOO
OOOO
!!!
SHP
WHP
OH...!
WHP

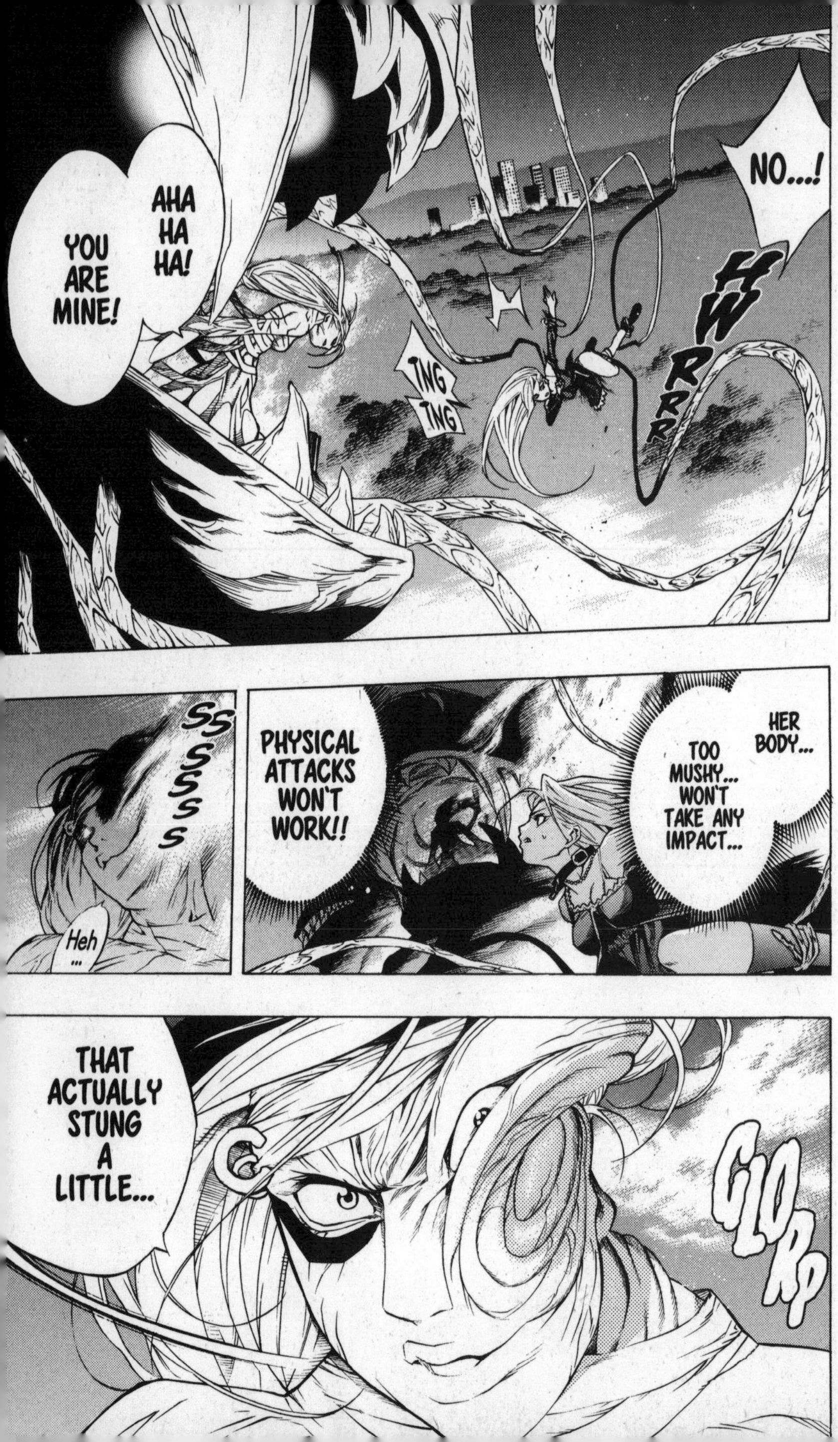
NO...!
HWRRR
TNG TNG
AHA HA HA!
YOU ARE MINE!
HER BODY...
TOO MUSHY... WON'T TAKE ANY IMPACT...
PHYSICAL ATTACKS WON'T WORK!!
SSSSSSS
Heh...
GLORP
THAT ACTUALLY STUNG A LITTLE...

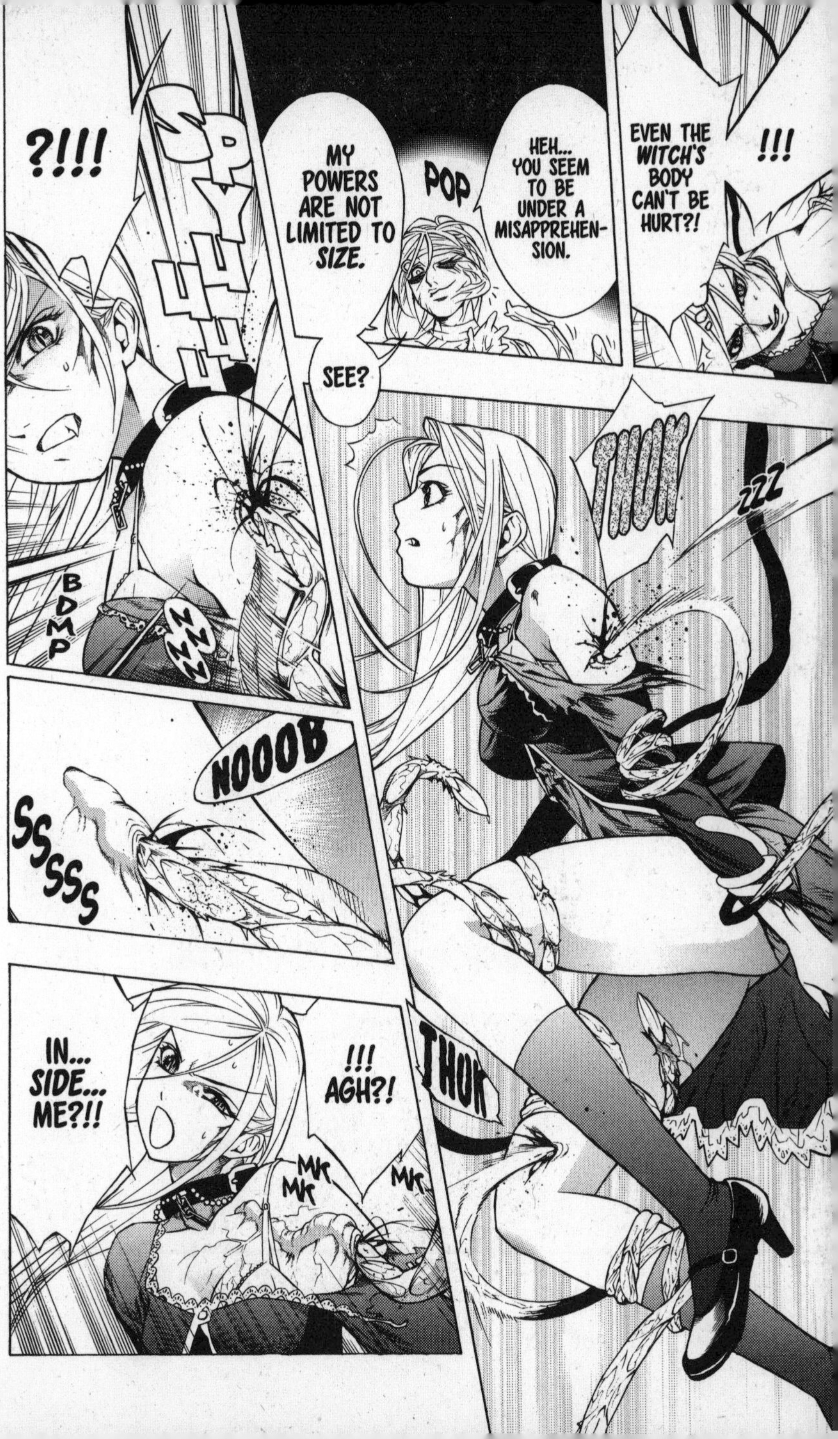
EVEN THE WITCH'S BODY CAN'T BE HURT?!
!!!
HEH... YOU SEEM TO BE UNDER A MISAPPREHENSION.
POP
MY POWERS ARE NOT LIMITED TO SIZE.
SEE?
SPYUUUU
?!!!
BDMP
NNNN
THUK
ZZZ
NOOOB
SSSSSS
THUK
!!! AGH?!
IN... SIDE... ME?!!
MK MK
MK

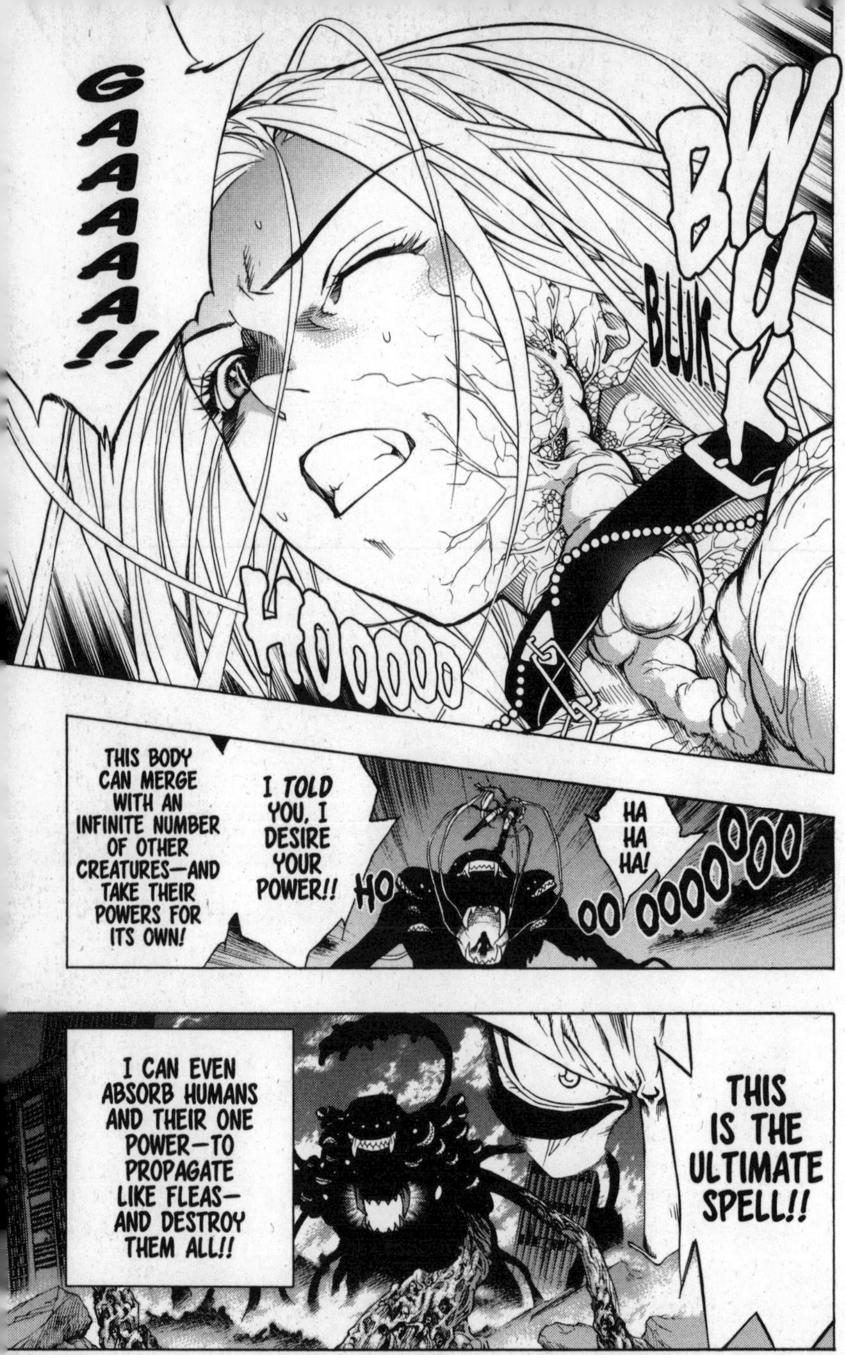
BWUK
BLUK
GAAAAAA!!
HOOOOO
HA HA HA!
OOOOOOOOOOO
HO
I TOLD YOU, I DESIRE YOUR POWER!!
THIS BODY CAN MERGE WITH AN INFINITE NUMBER OF OTHER CREATURES—AND TAKE THEIR POWERS FOR ITS OWN!
THIS IS THE ULTIMATE SPELL!!
I CAN EVEN ABSORB HUMANS AND THEIR ONE POWER—TO PROPAGATE LIKE FLEAS—AND DESTROY THEM ALL!!

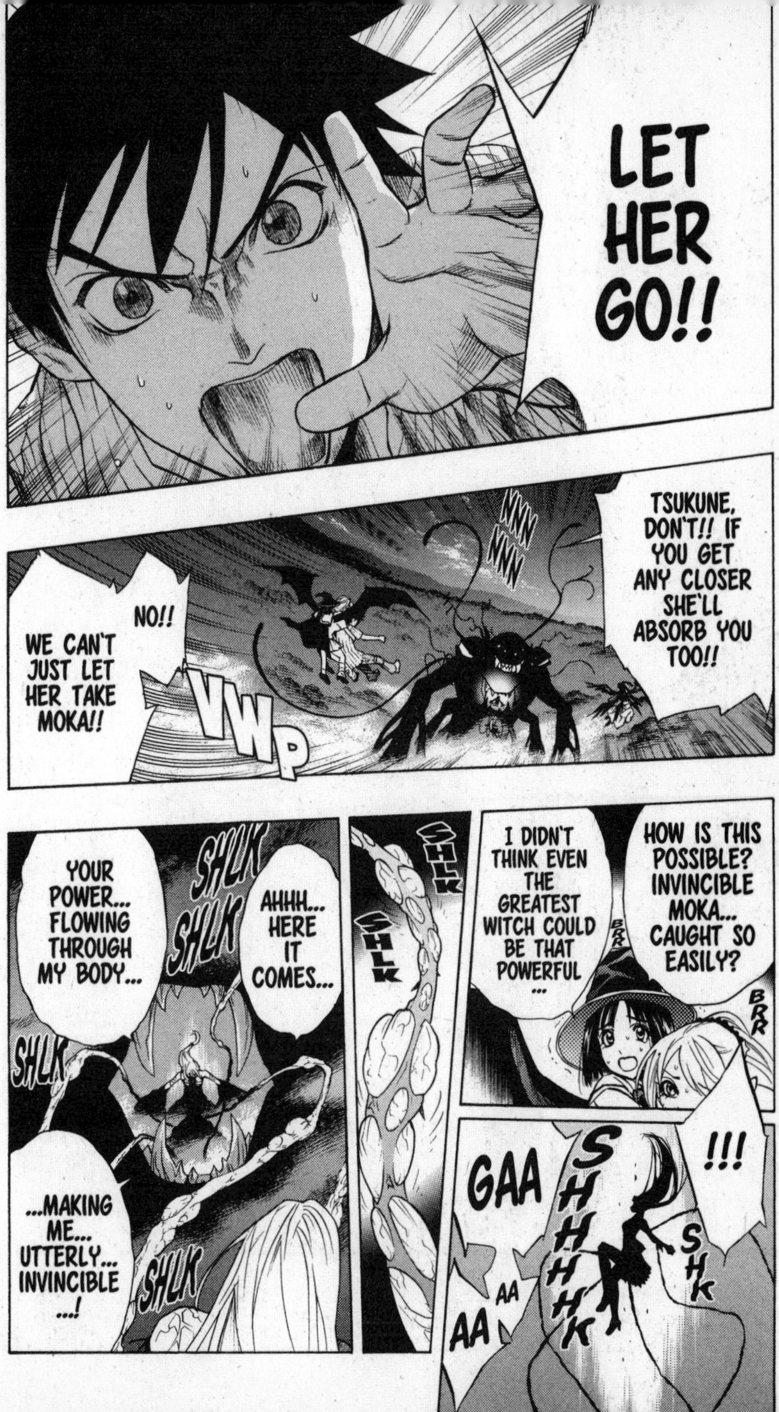
LET HER GO!!
TSUKUNE, DON'T!! IF YOU GET ANY CLOSER SHE'LL ABSORB YOU TOO!!
NNN NNN
NO!!
WE CAN'T JUST LET HER TAKE MOKA!!
VWP
HOW IS THIS POSSIBLE? INVINCIBLE MOKA... CAUGHT SO EASILY?
BRR
I DIDN'T THINK EVEN THE GREATEST WITCH COULD BE THAT POWERFUL ...
BRR
!!!
SHK
SHHHHHK
GAA
AA
AA
SHLK
SHLK
AHHH... HERE IT COMES...
SHLK
SHLK
YOUR POWER... FLOWING THROUGH MY BODY...
SHLK
...MAKING ME... UTTERLY... INVINCIBLE ...!
SHLK

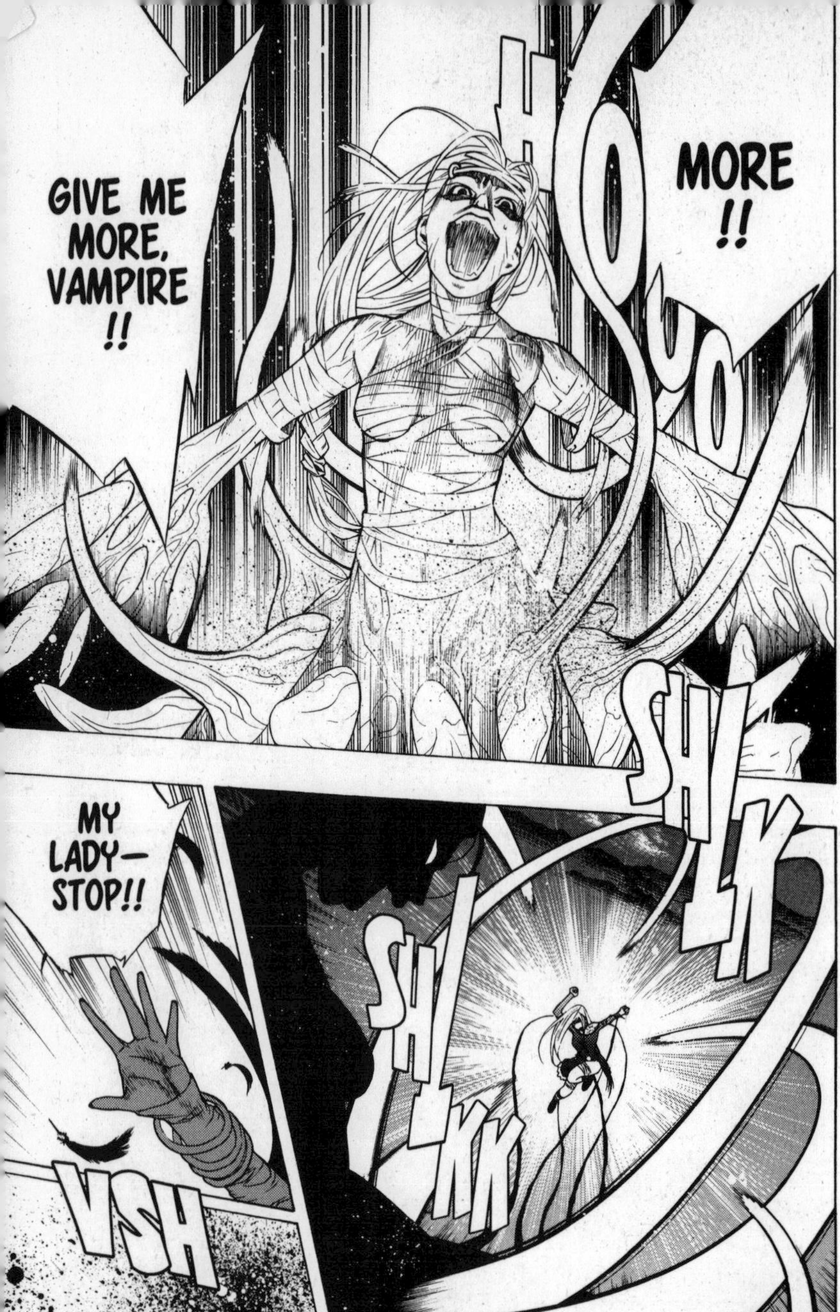
MORE!!
HOUO
GIVE ME MORE, VAMPIRE!!
SHLK
SHKK
MY LADY—STOP!!
VSH

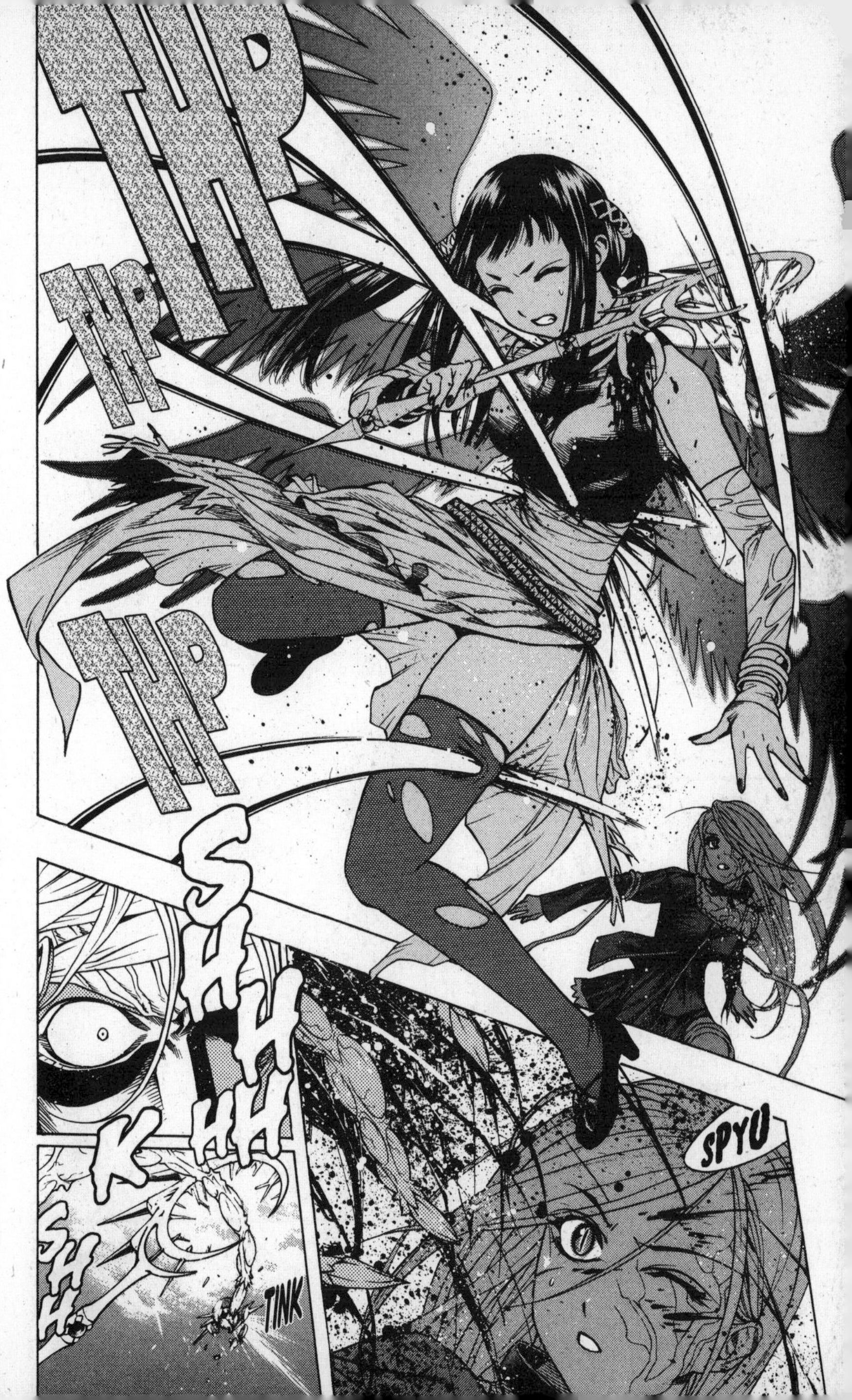
THP
THP
THP
THP
SHH
KHH
SPYU
SHH
TINK

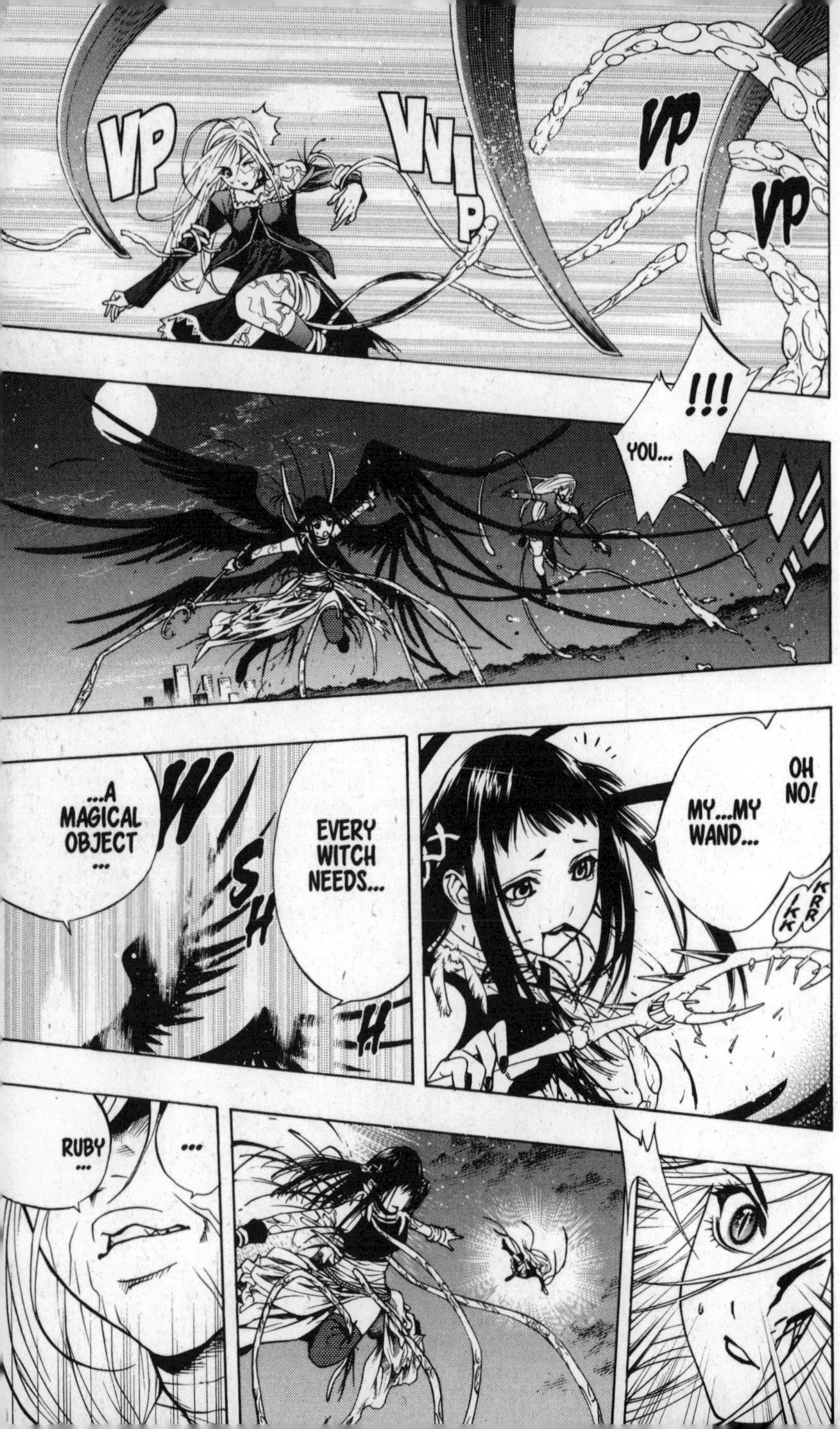
VP
VP
VVIP
VP
!!!
YOU...
OH NO!
MY...MY WAND...
KRR
IKK
EVERY WITCH NEEDS...
...A MAGICAL OBJECT ...
WISH
...
RUBY ...

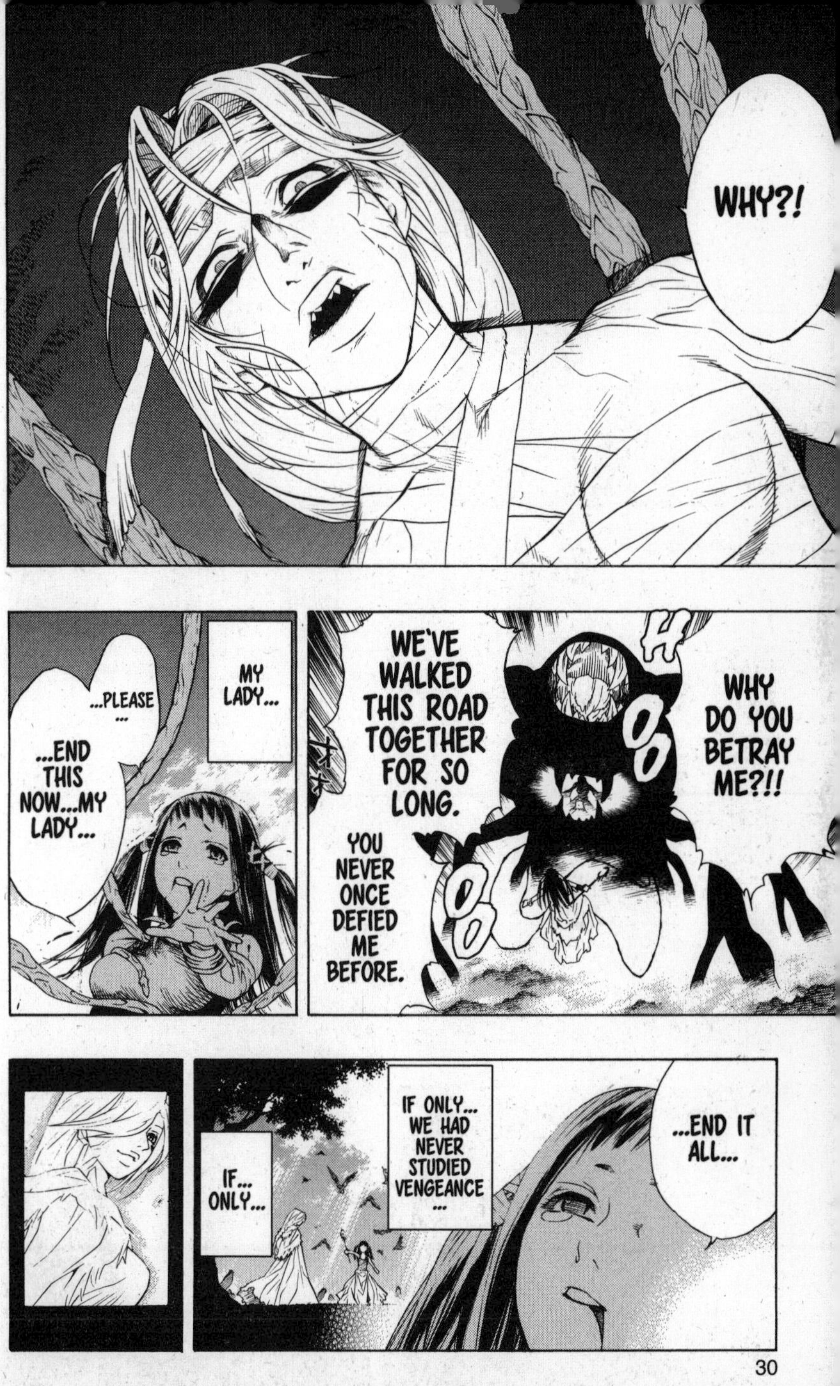
WHY?!
H
WHY DO YOU BETRAY ME?!!
WE'VE WALKED THIS ROAD TOGETHER FOR SO LONG.
YOU NEVER ONCE DEFIED ME BEFORE.
MY LADY...
...PLEASE...
...END THIS NOW...MY LADY...
...END IT ALL...
IF ONLY... WE HAD NEVER STUDIED VENGEANCE...
IF... ONLY...

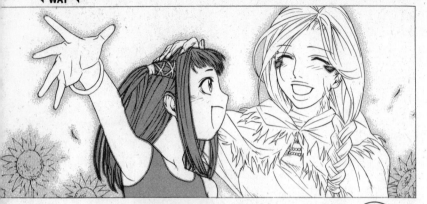

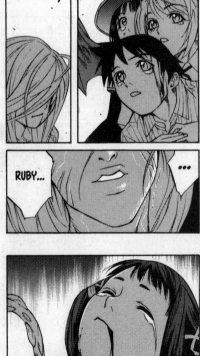

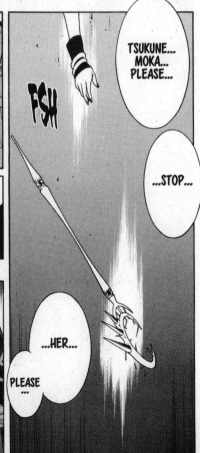

RUBY...

...

TSUKUNE...
MOKA...
PLEASE...

...STOP...

FSH

...HER...

PLEASE
...

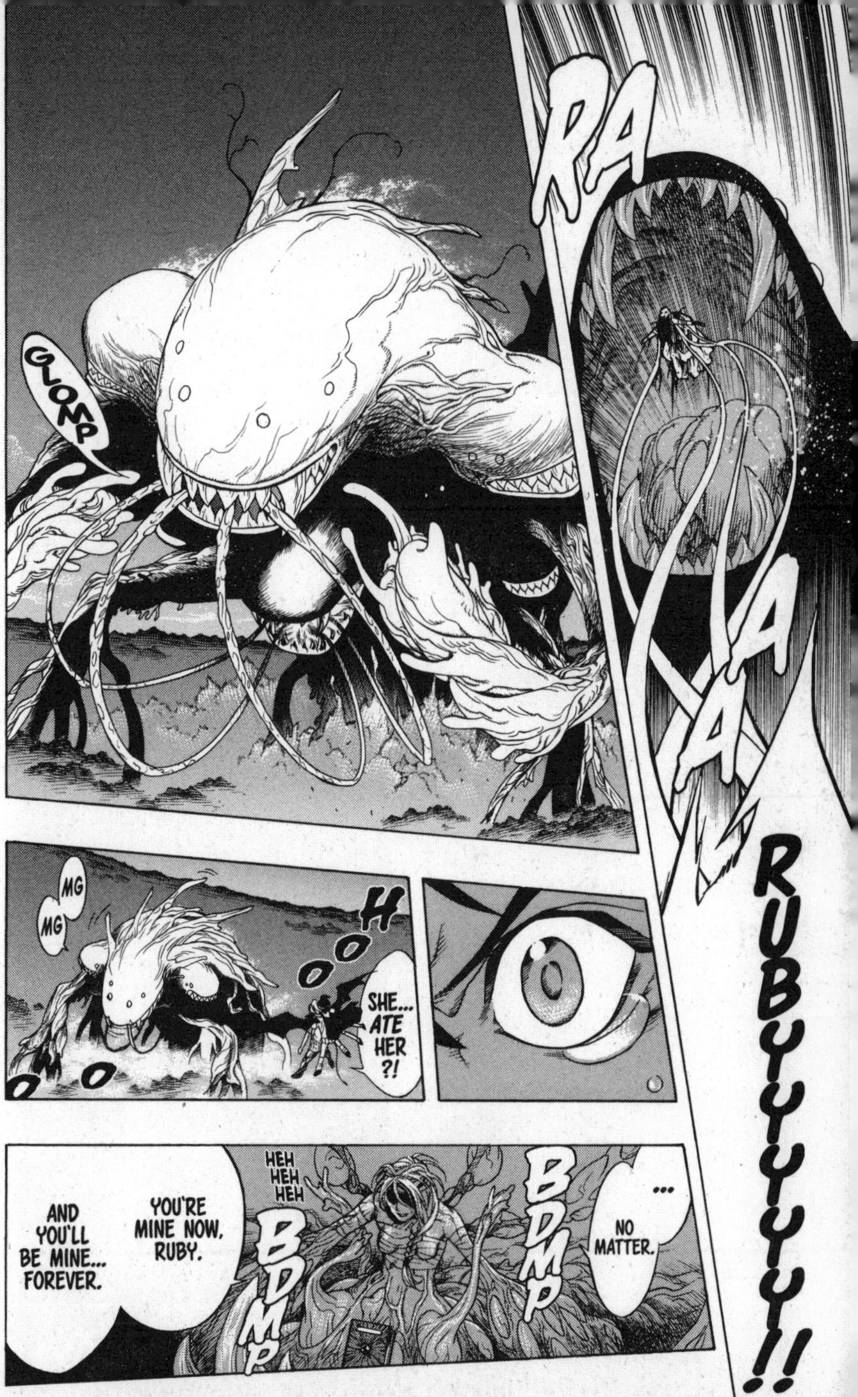
RAAAA
RUBYYYYYY!!
GLOMP
MG MG
HOOOOO
SHE... ATE HER?!
... NO MATTER.
BDMP
BDMP
HEH HEH HEH
YOU'RE MINE NOW, RUBY.
AND YOU'LL BE MINE... FOREVER.

READ THIS WAY

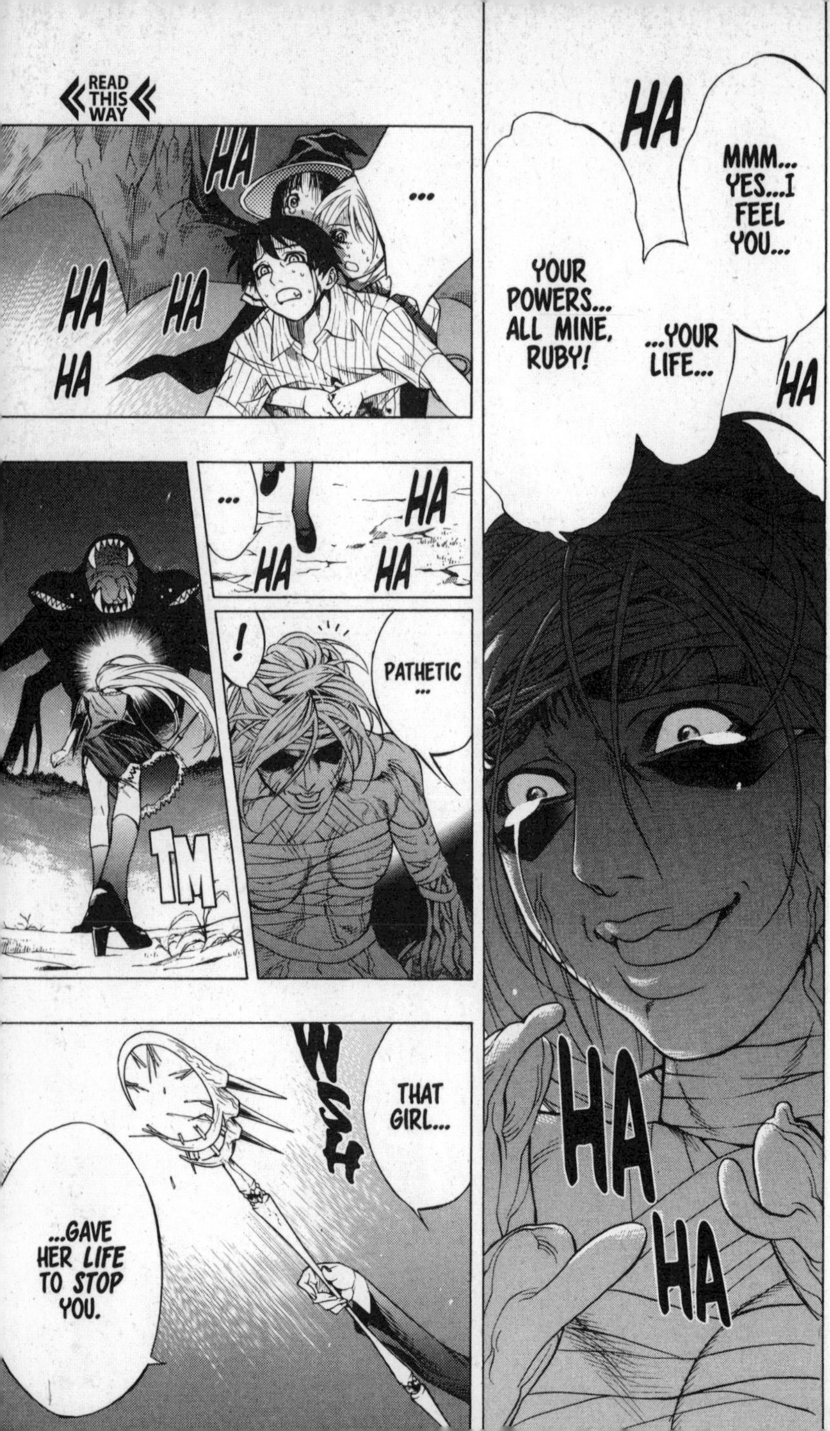
HA
MMM... YES...I FEEL YOU...
HA
...YOUR LIFE...
YOUR POWERS... ALL MINE, RUBY!
HA HA HA
...
HA
HA HA HA
HA HA HA
...
PATHETIC ...
!
TM
WSH
THAT GIRL...
...GAVE HER LIFE TO STOP YOU.

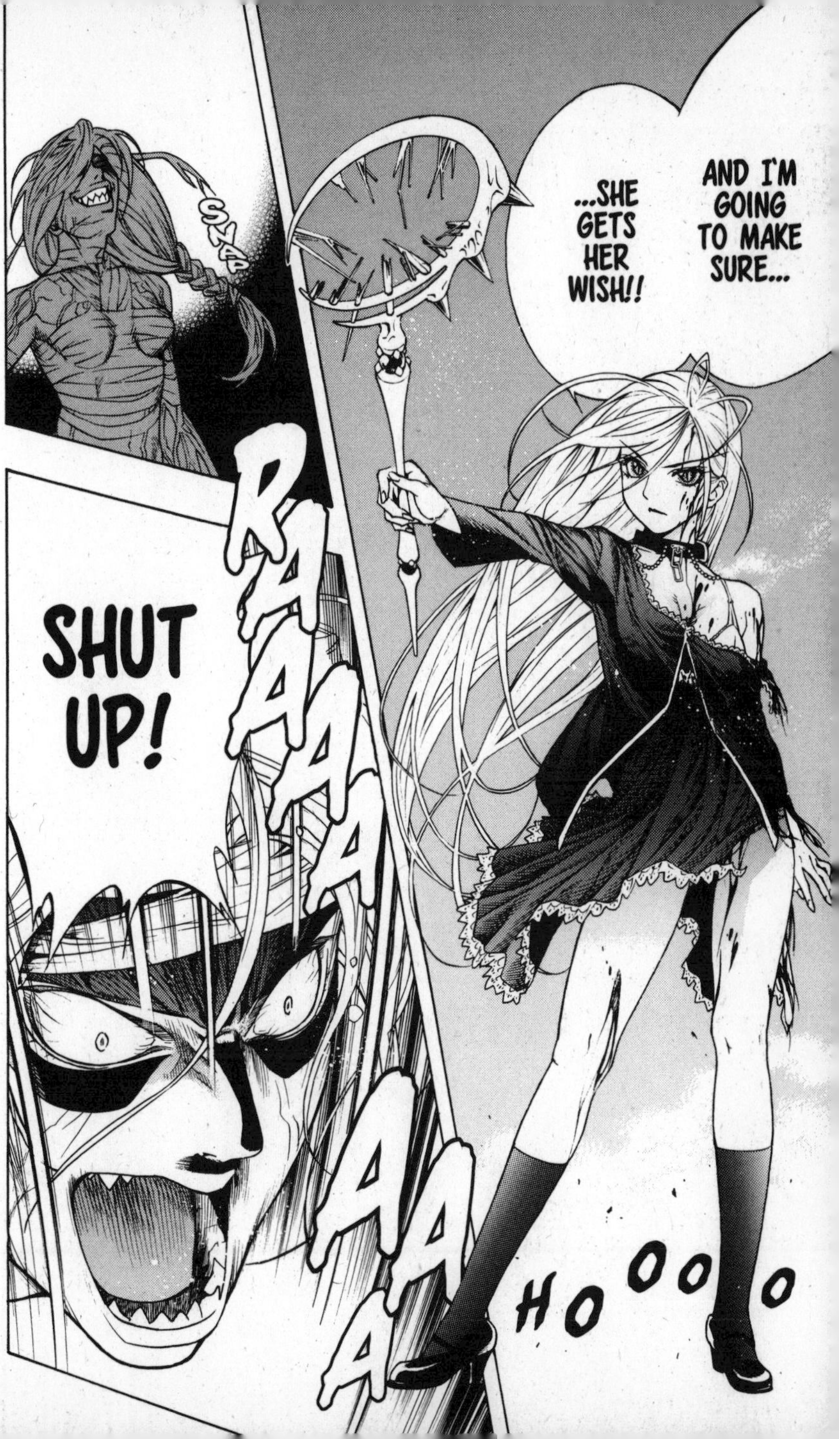
AND I'M GOING TO MAKE SURE...
...SHE GETS HER WISH!!
HOOOOO
SNAP
SHUT UP!
RAAAAAAAA

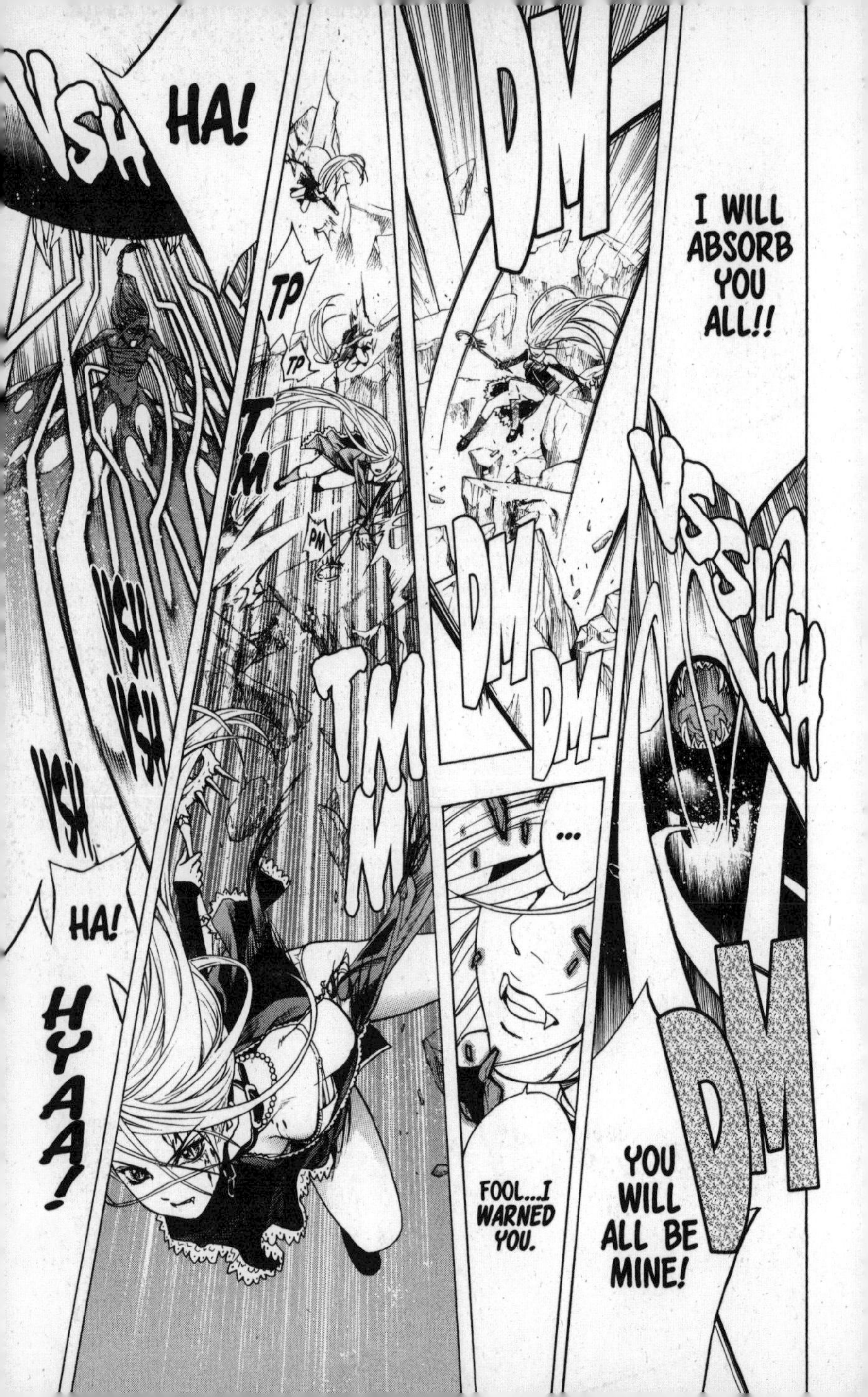
I WILL ABSORB YOU ALL!!
VSSH
YOU WILL ALL BE MINE!
DM
DM
DM
DM
DM
...
FOOL...I WARNED YOU.
TP
TP
TM
PM
TMM
VSH
HA!
VSH
VSH
VSH
HA!
HYAAA!

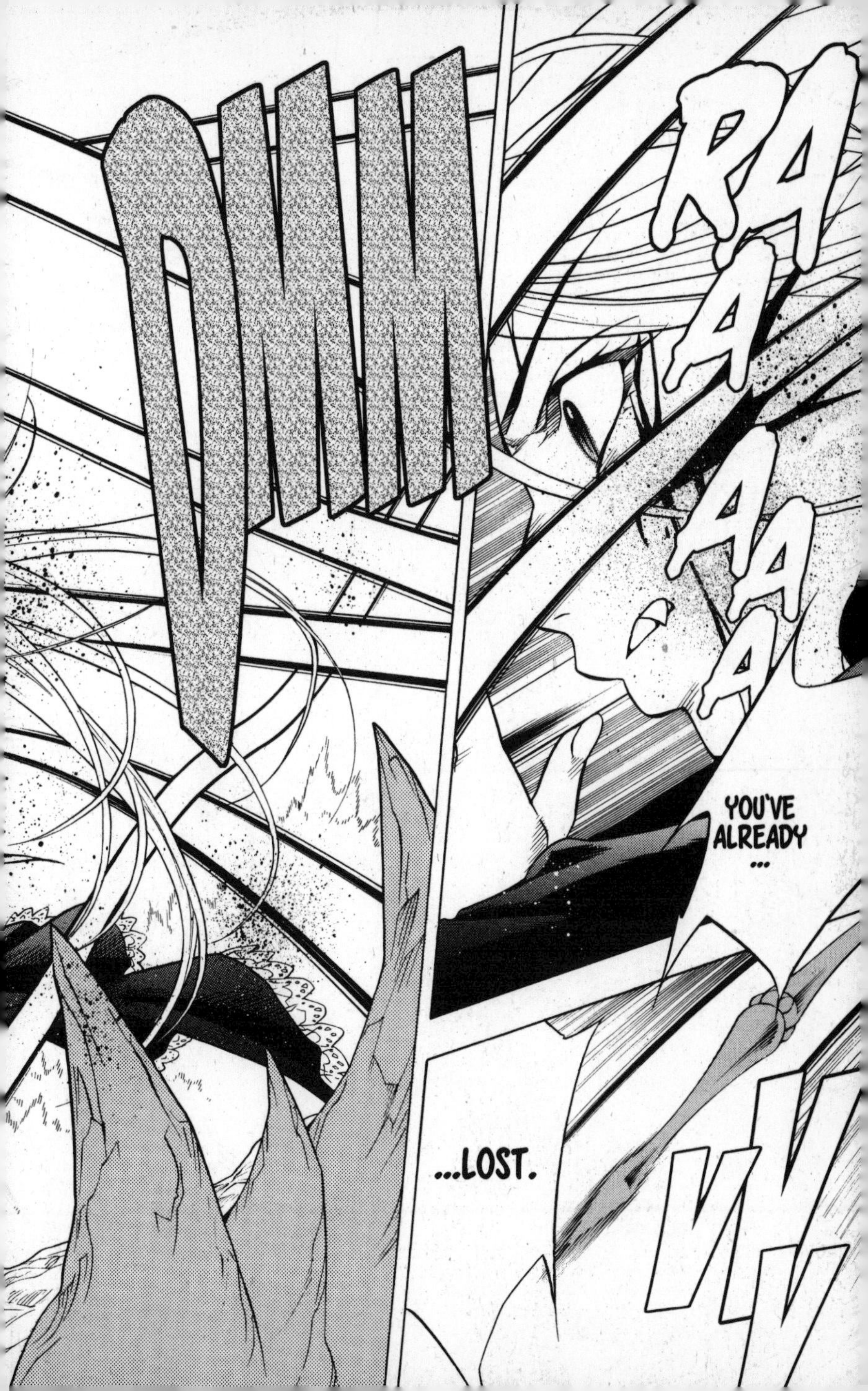
RAAAAA
YOU'VE ALREADY ...
...LOST.
DMM

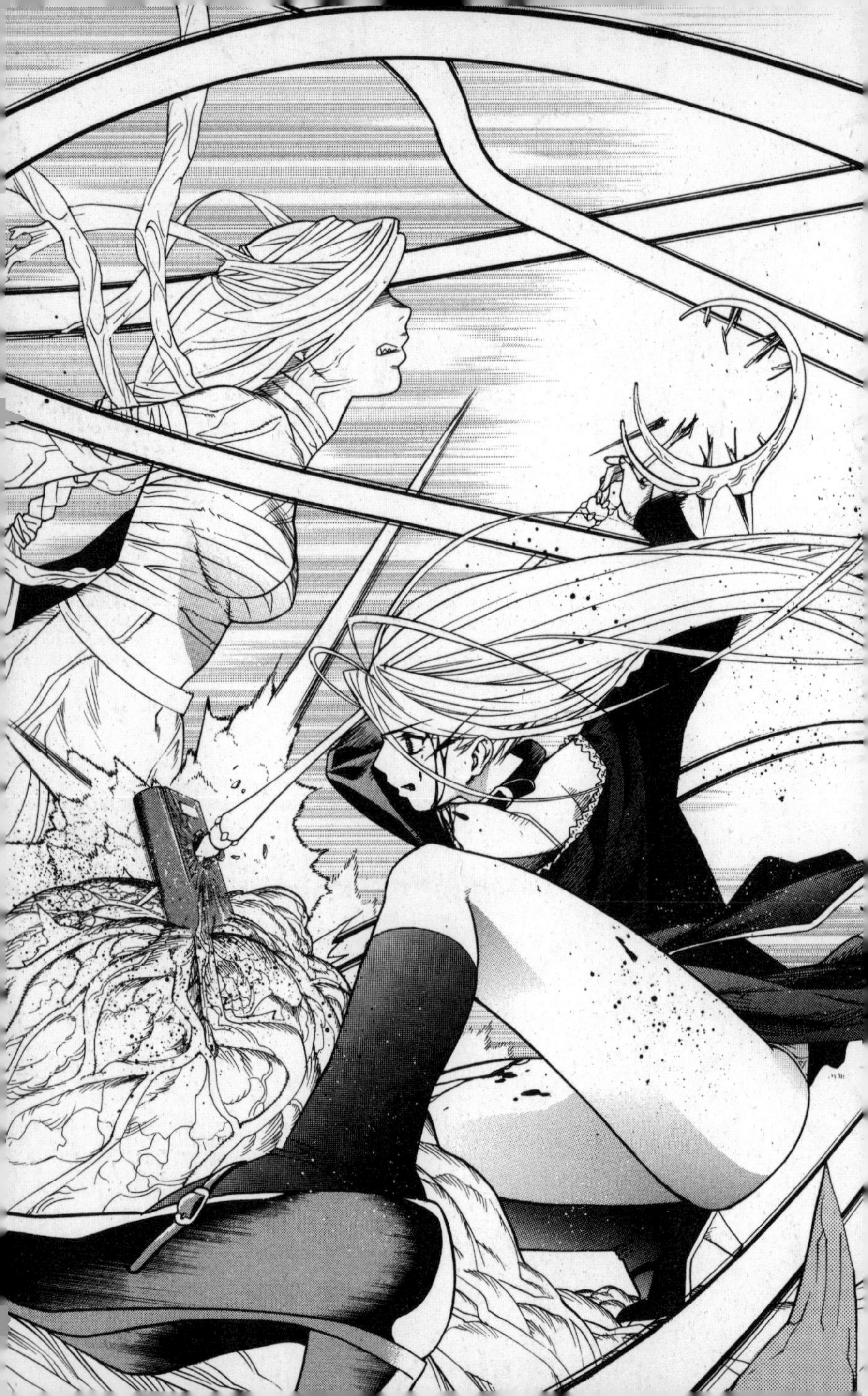

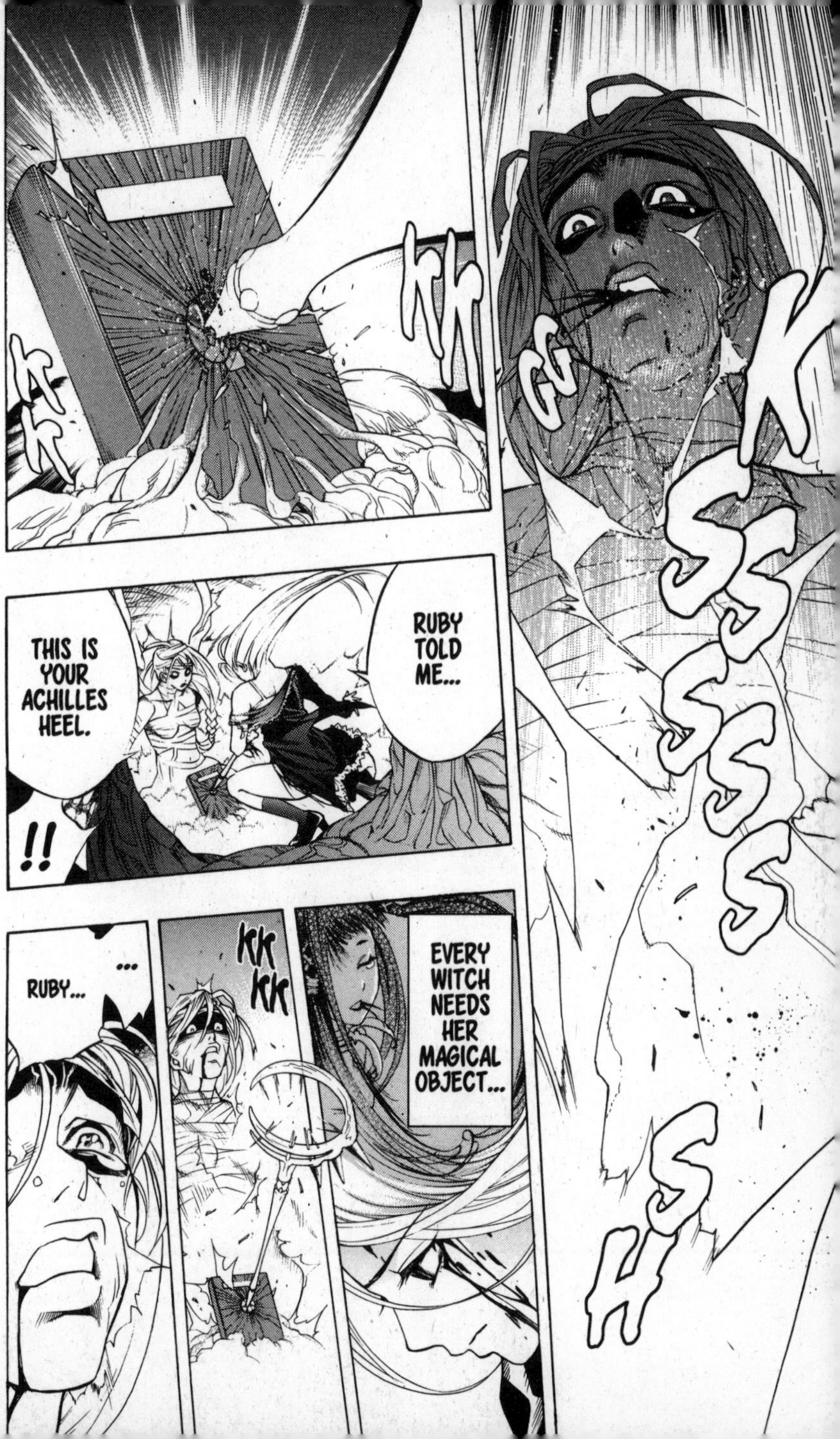

RUBY TOLD ME...
THIS IS YOUR ACHILLES HEEL.
!!
EVERY WITCH NEEDS HER MAGICAL OBJECT...
KK KK
...
RUBY...

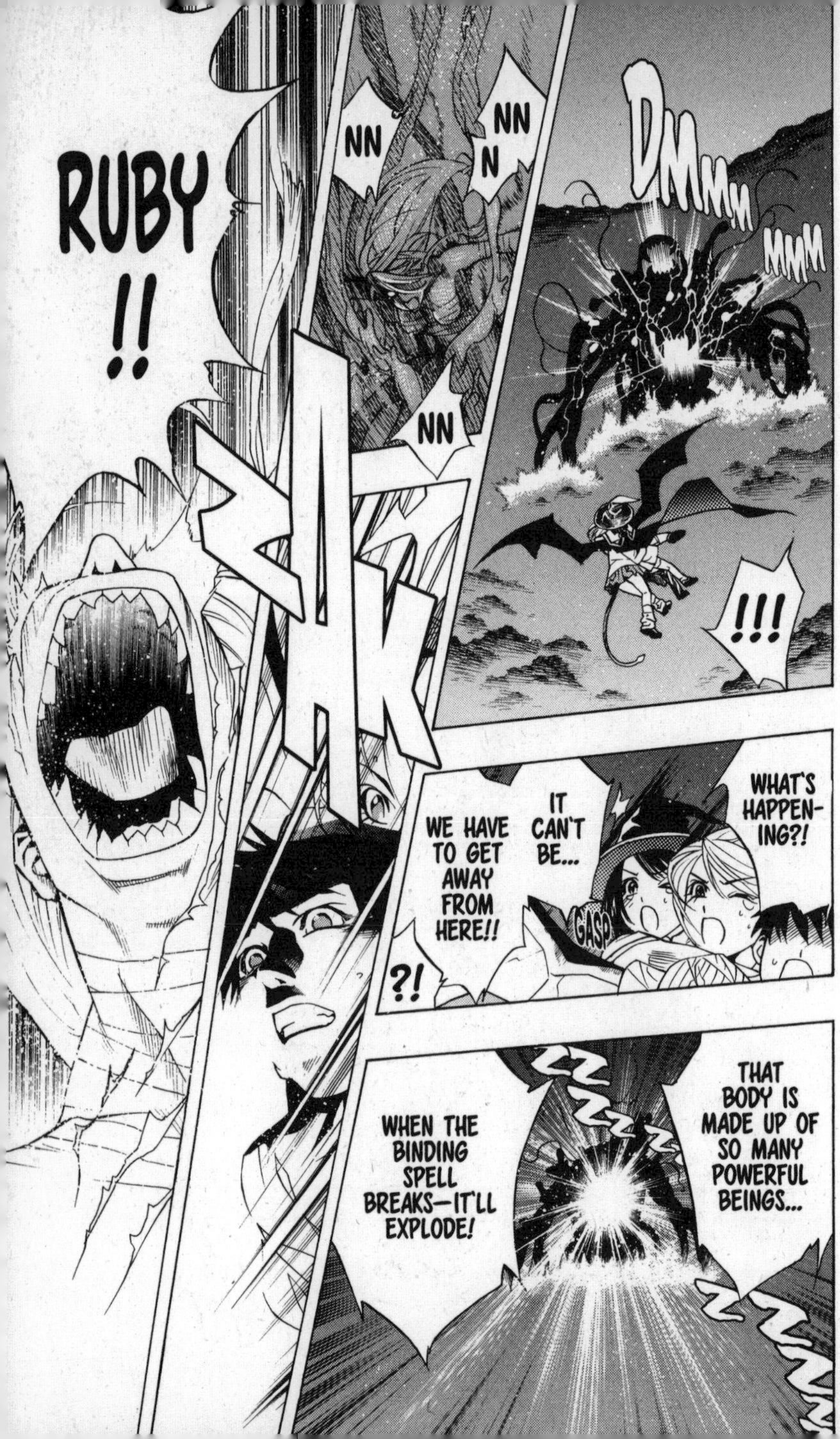
DMMMM
MMM
!!!
NN
NN
N
NN
ZAK
WHAT'S HAPPEN-ING?!
IT CAN'T BE...
GASP
WE HAVE TO GET AWAY FROM HERE!!
?!
THAT BODY IS MADE UP OF SO MANY POWERFUL BEINGS...
WHEN THE BINDING SPELL BREAKS—IT'LL EXPLODE!
RUBY!!

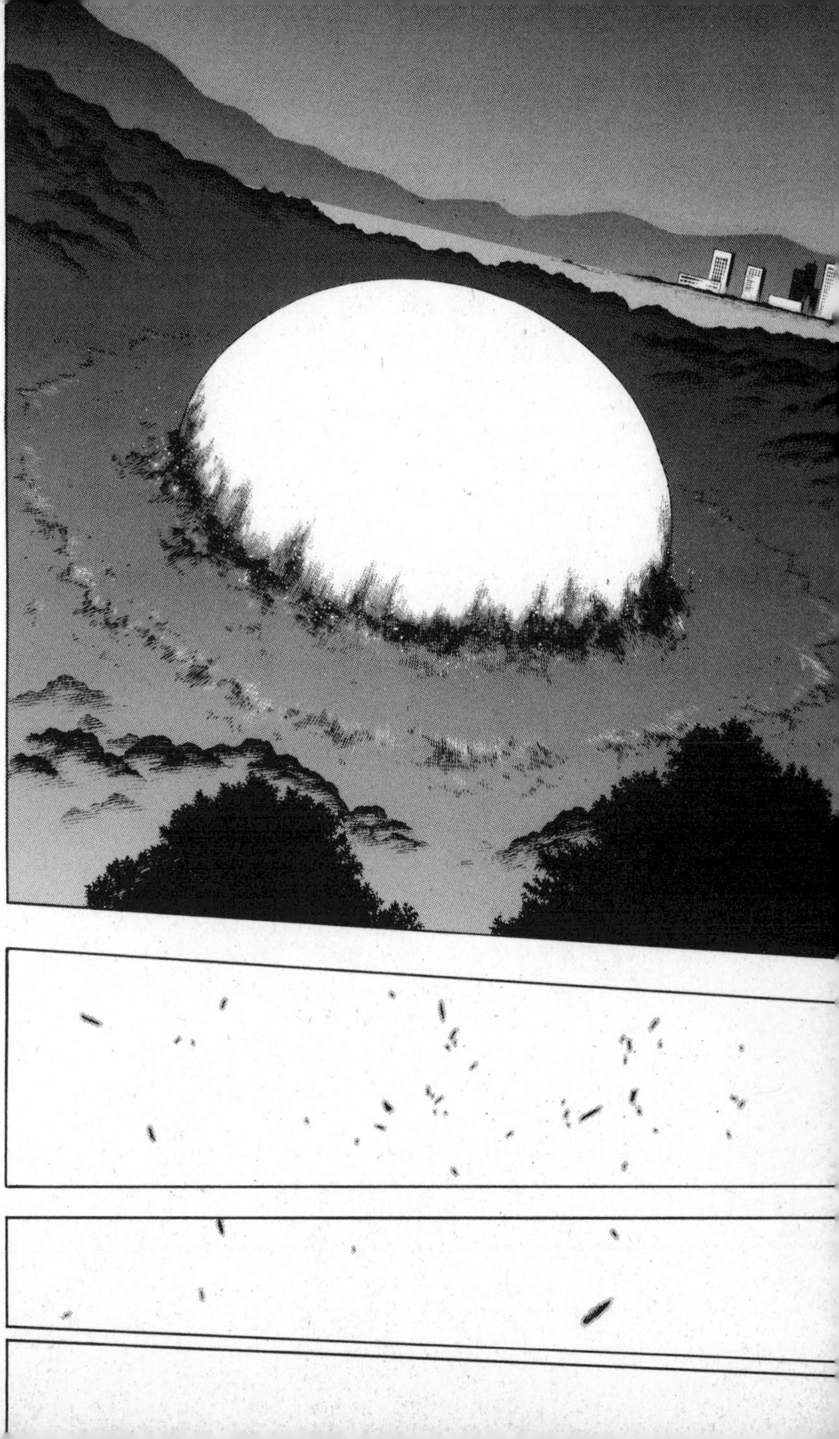

READ THIS WAY

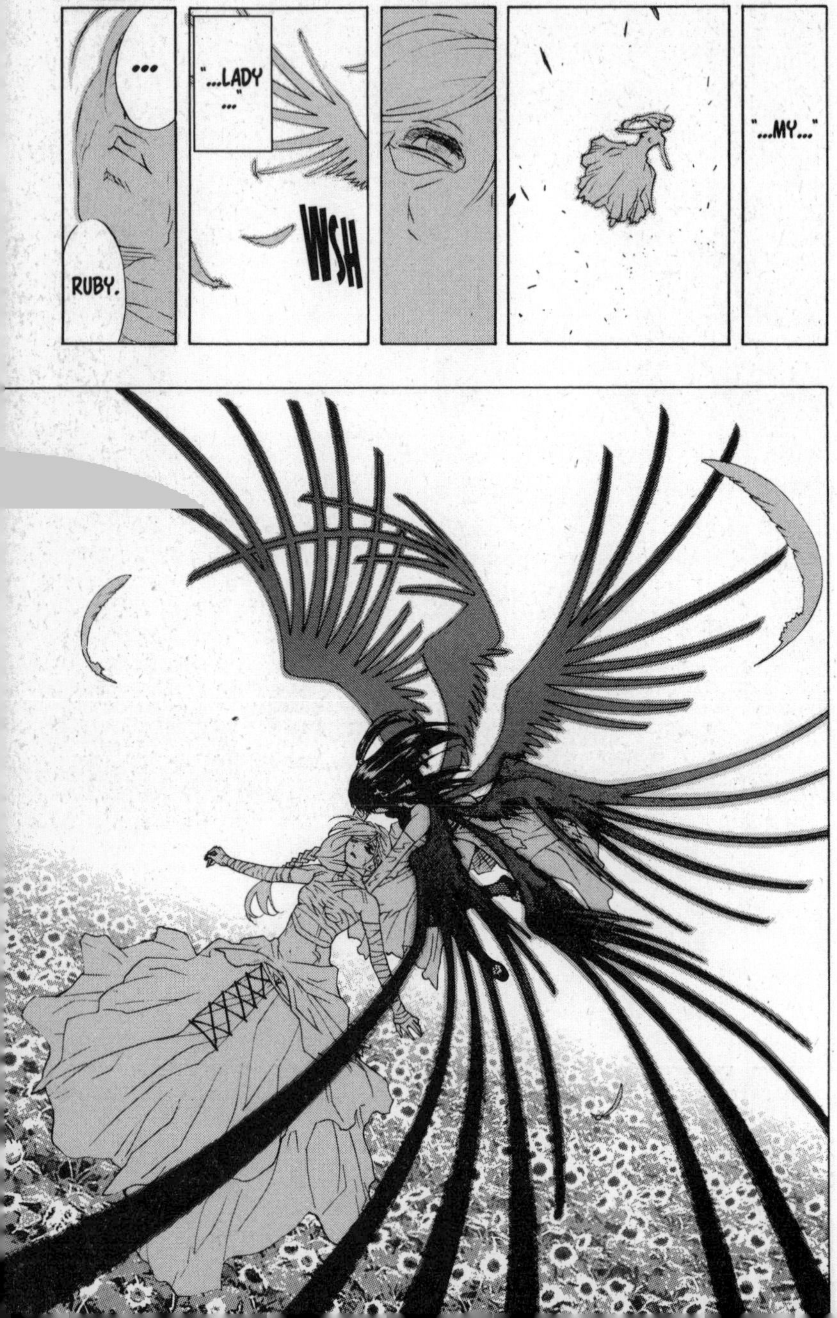
"...MY..."
"...LADY
..."
WSH
...
RUBY.

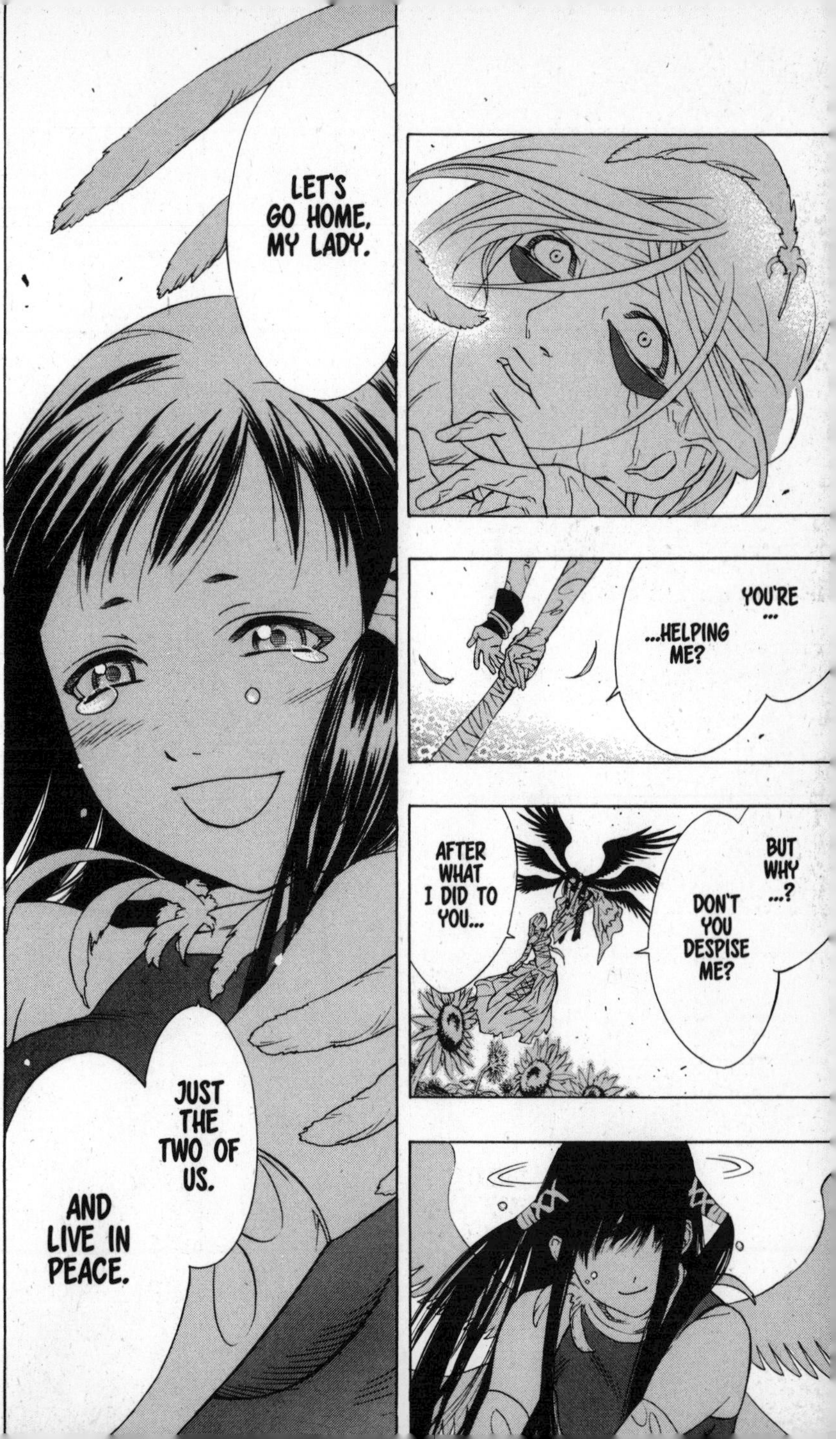
YOU'RE ...
...HELPING ME?
BUT WHY ...?
DON'T YOU DESPISE ME?
AFTER WHAT I DID TO YOU...
LET'S GO HOME, MY LADY.
JUST THE TWO OF US.
AND LIVE IN PEACE.

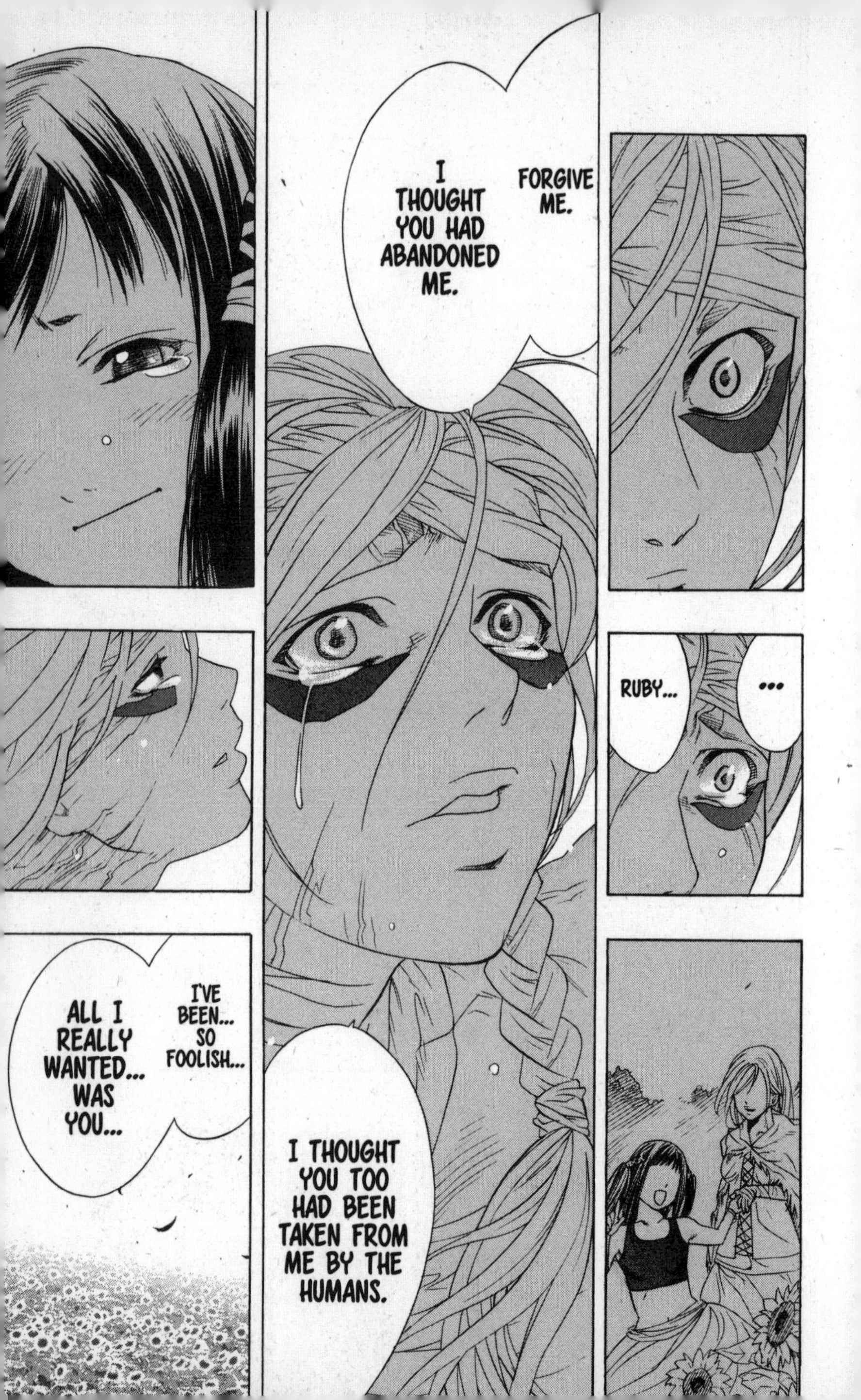
...
RUBY...
FORGIVE ME.
I THOUGHT YOU HAD ABANDONED ME.
I THOUGHT YOU TOO HAD BEEN TAKEN FROM ME BY THE HUMANS.
I'VE BEEN... SO FOOLISH...
ALL I REALLY WANTED... WAS YOU...

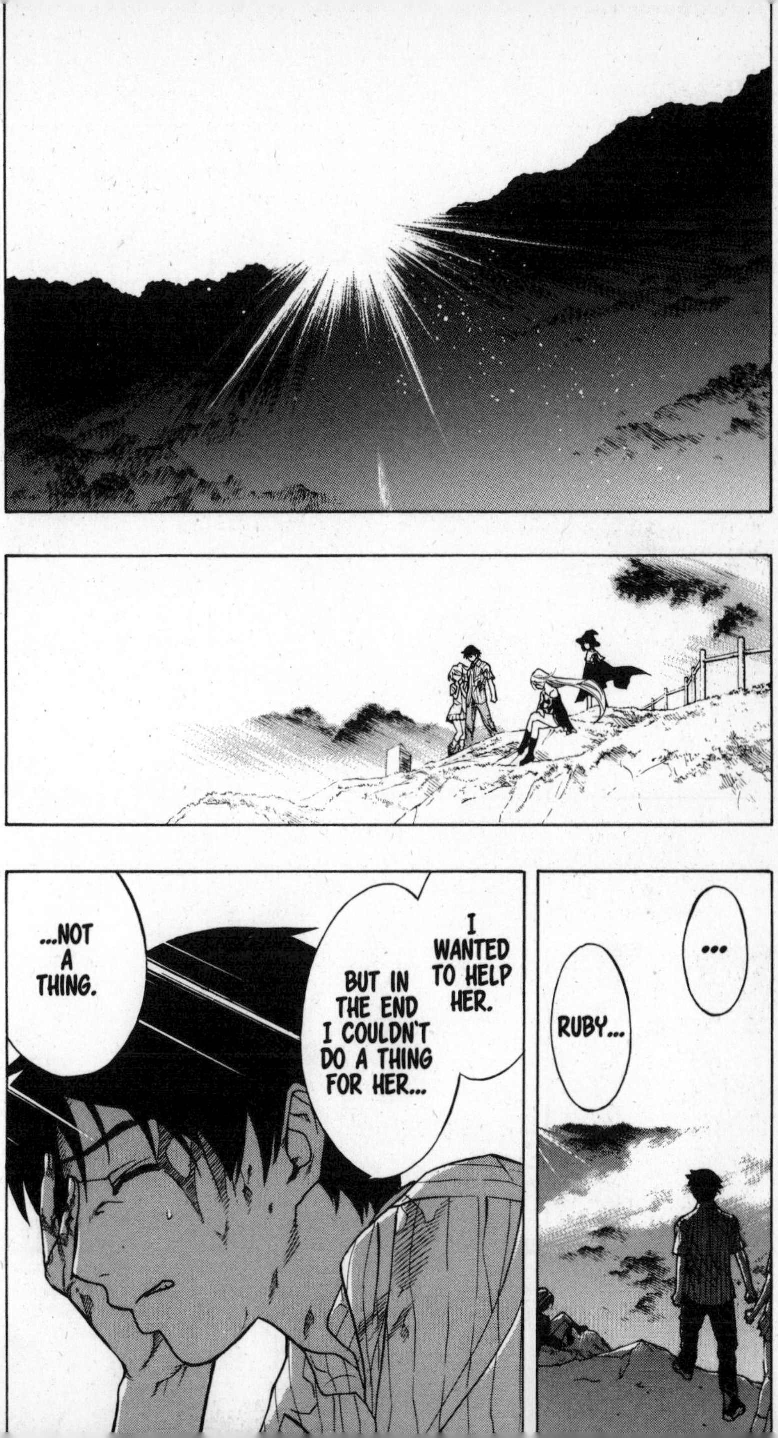
...
RUBY...
I WANTED TO HELP HER.
BUT IN THE END I COULDN'T DO A THING FOR HER...
...NOT A THING.

READ THIS WAY

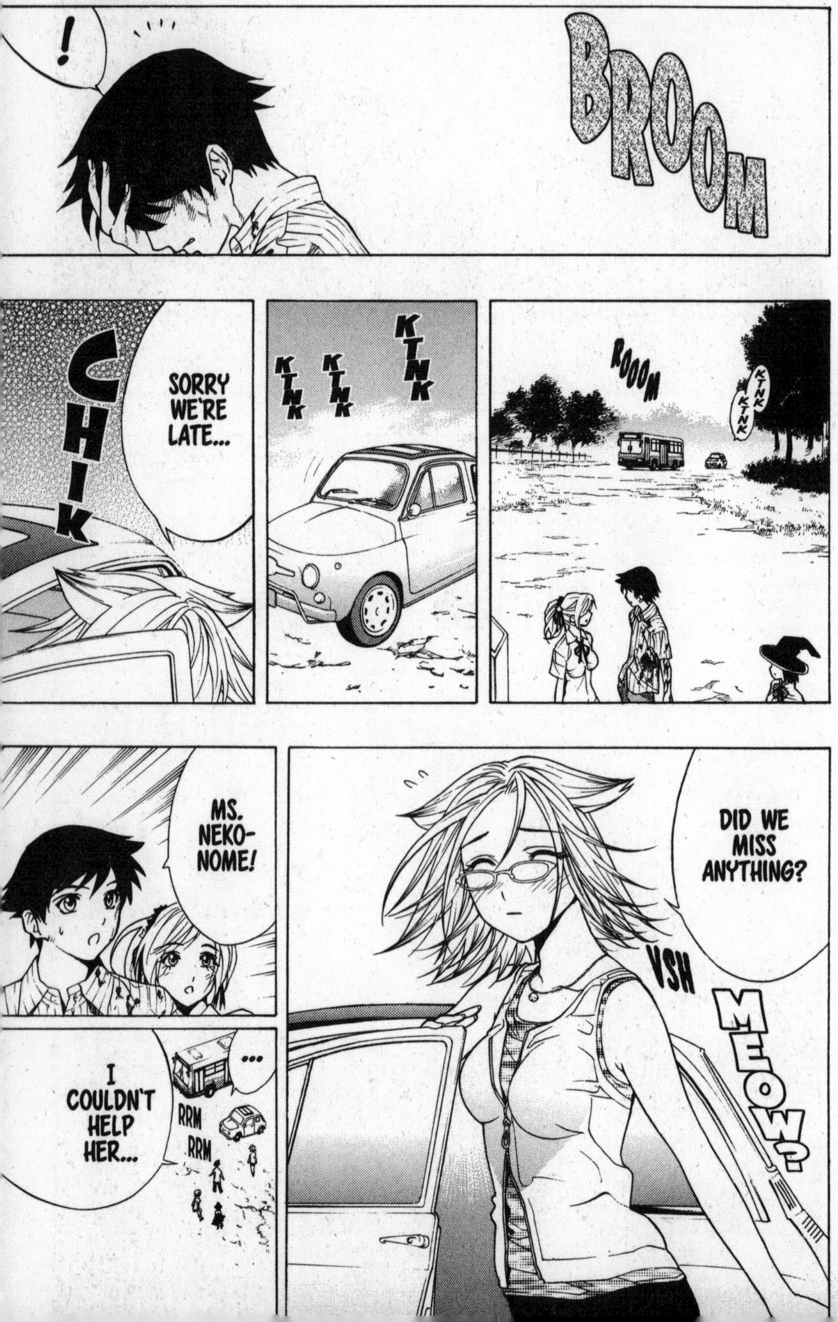
BROOOM
!
ROOOM
KTNK KTNK
KTNK KTNK KTNK
SORRY WE'RE LATE...
CHIK
DID WE MISS ANYTHING?
VSH
MEOW?
MS. NEKO-NOME!
...
RRM RRM
I COULDN'T HELP HER...

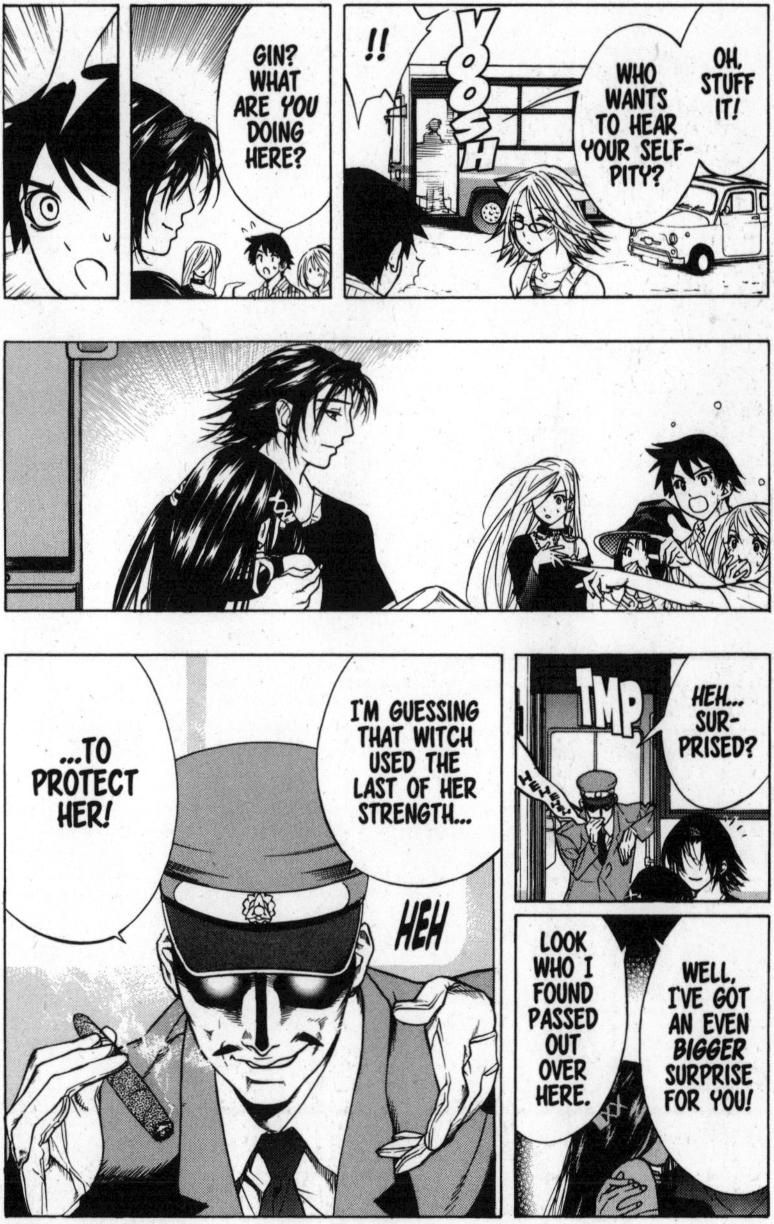
OH, STUFF IT!
WHO WANTS TO HEAR YOUR SELF-PITY?
YOSH
!!
GIN? WHAT ARE YOU DOING HERE?
TMP
HEH... SUR-PRISED?
WELL, I'VE GOT AN EVEN BIGGER SURPRISE FOR YOU!
LOOK WHO I FOUND PASSED OUT OVER HERE.
I'M GUESSING THAT WITCH USED THE LAST OF HER STRENGTH...
HEH
...TO PROTECT HER!

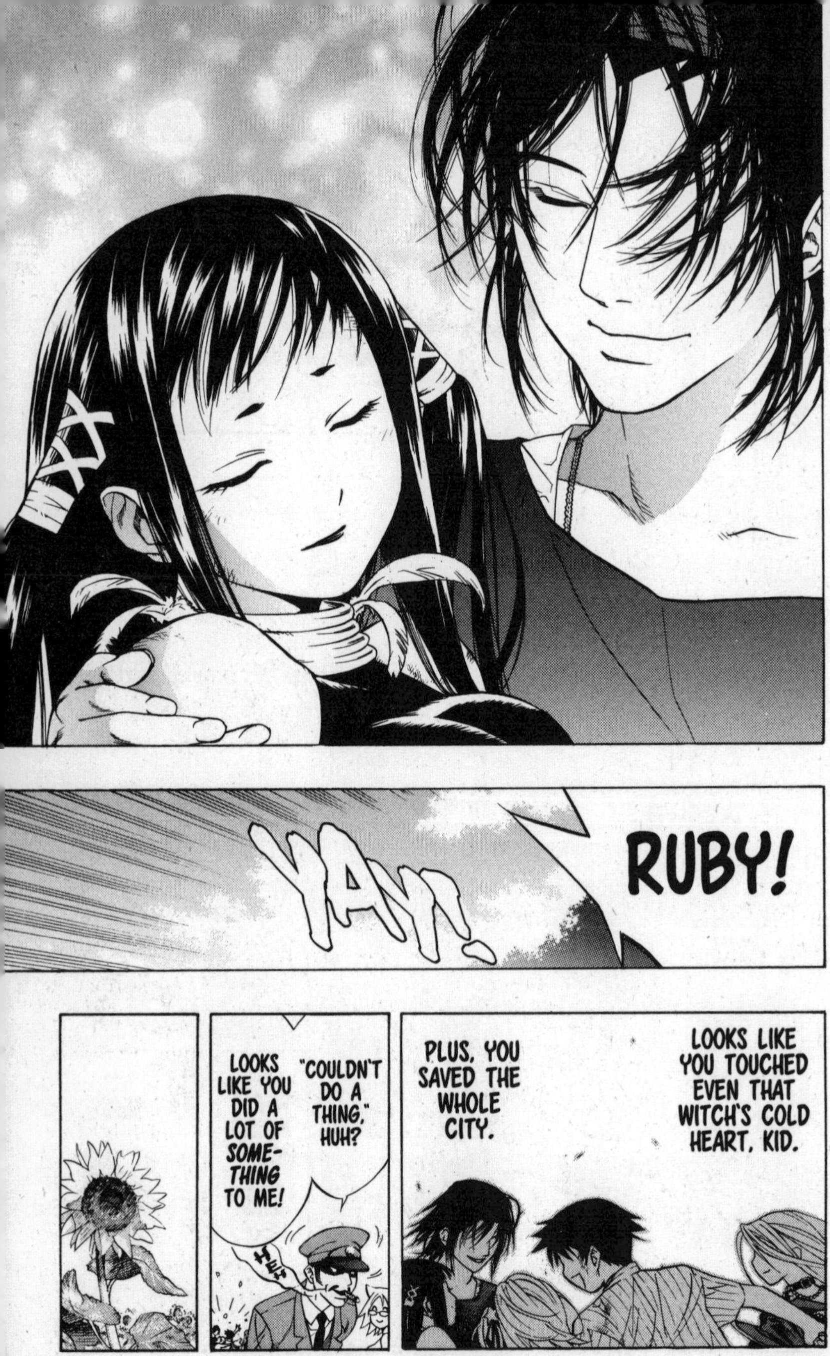
RUBY!
YAY!
LOOKS LIKE YOU TOUCHED EVEN THAT WITCH'S COLD HEART, KID.
PLUS, YOU SAVED THE WHOLE CITY.
"COULDN'T DO A THING," HUH?
LOOKS LIKE YOU DID A LOT OF *SOME-THING* TO ME!
HEH

ROSARIO+VAMPIRE

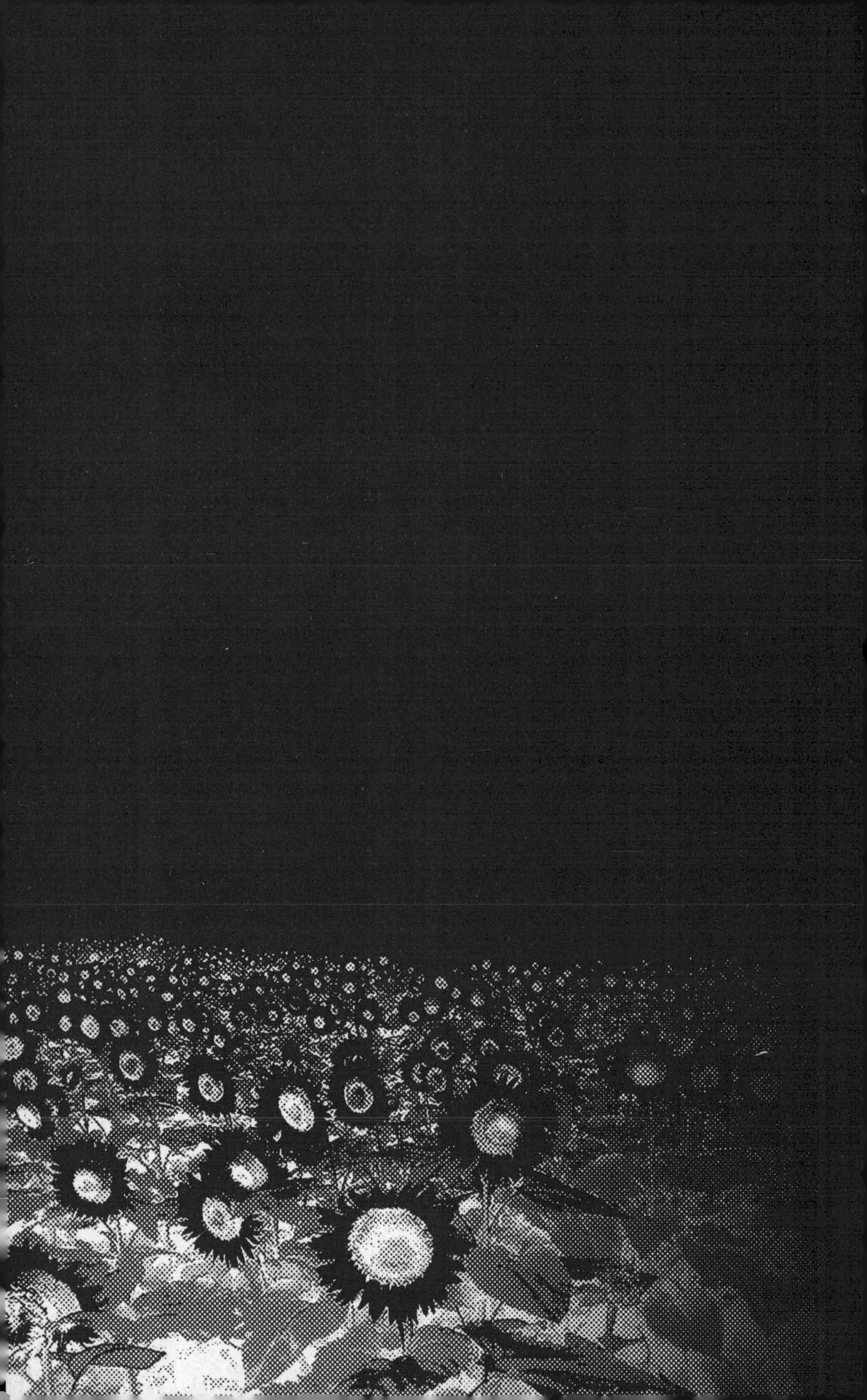

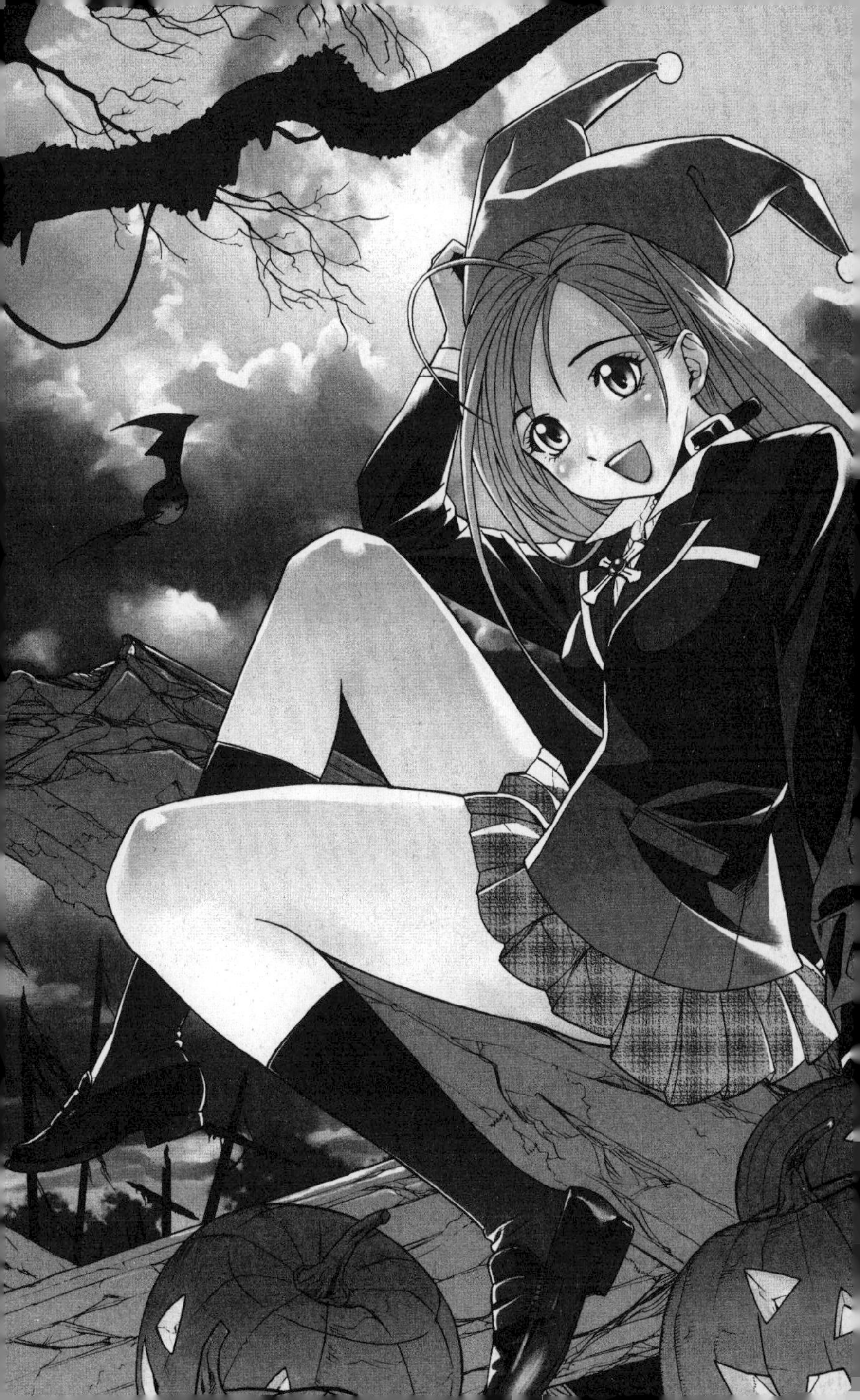

18: A New Semester

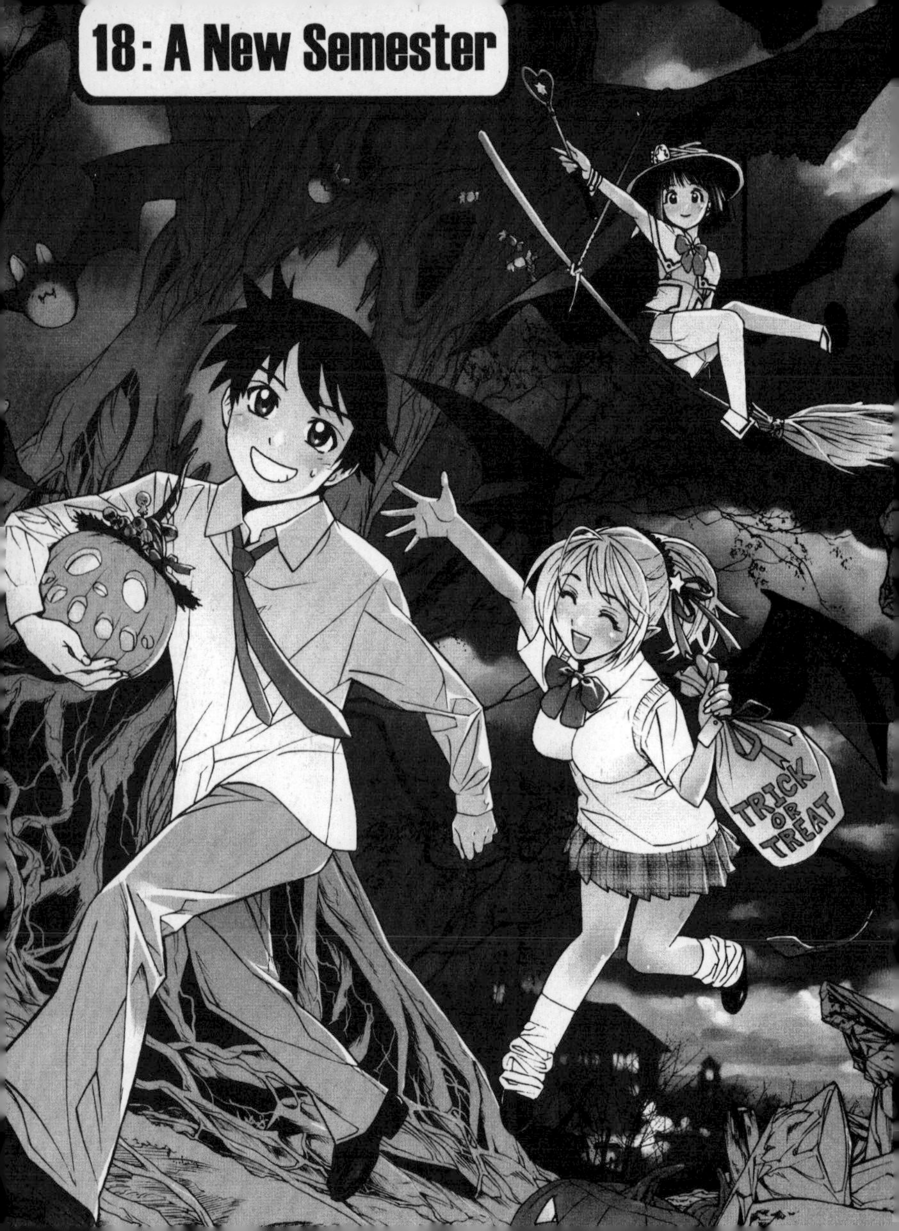
TRICK OR TREAT

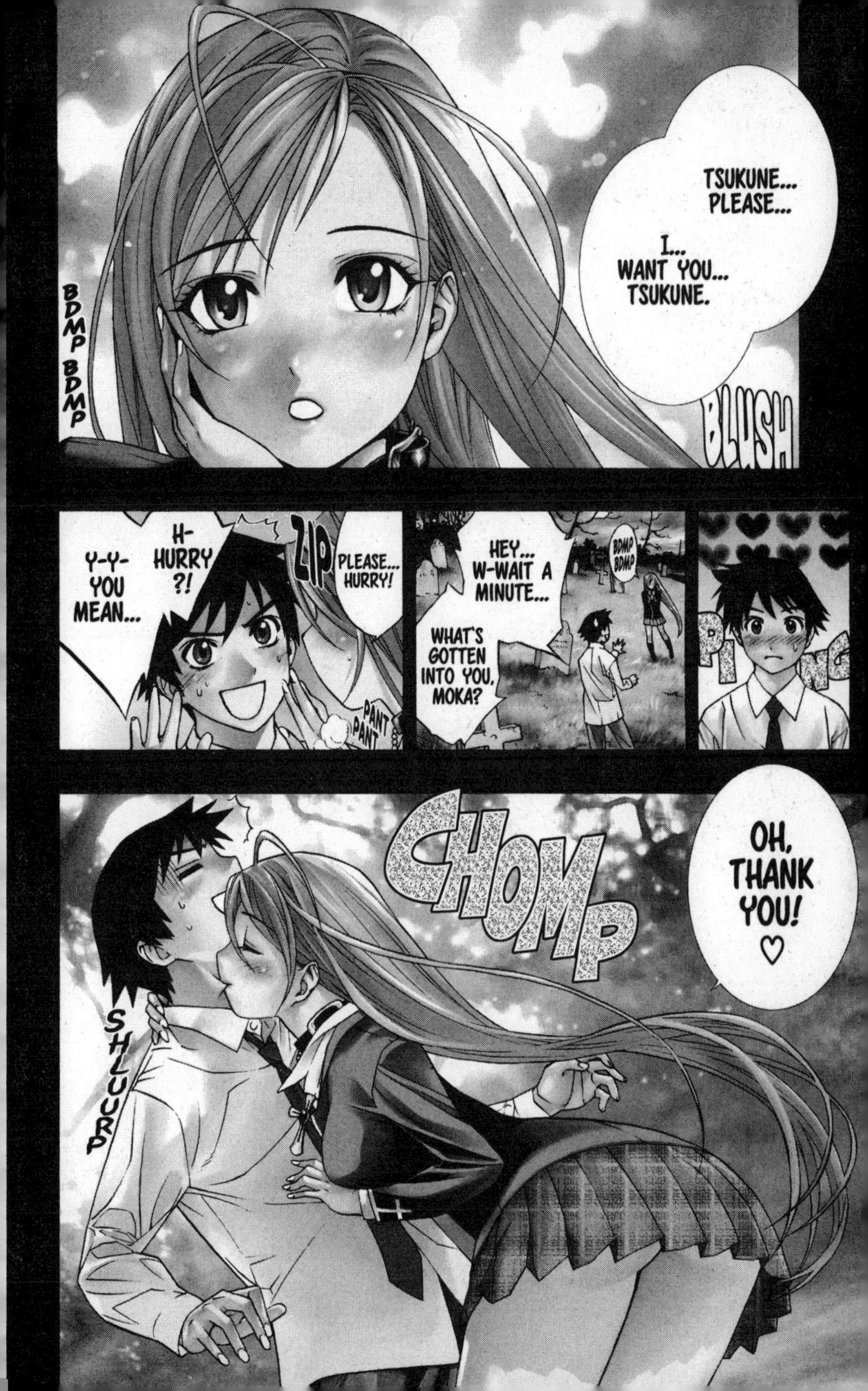
TSUKUNE... PLEASE...
I... WANT YOU... TSUKUNE.
BLUSH
BDMP BDMP BDMP
PI-TING
HEY... W-WAIT A MINUTE...
WHAT'S GOTTEN INTO YOU, MOKA?
BDMP BDMP
PLEASE... HURRY!
ZIP
H-HURRY ?!
Y-Y-YOU MEAN...
PANT PANT
OH, THANK YOU! ♡
CHOMP
SHLUURP

READ THIS WAY

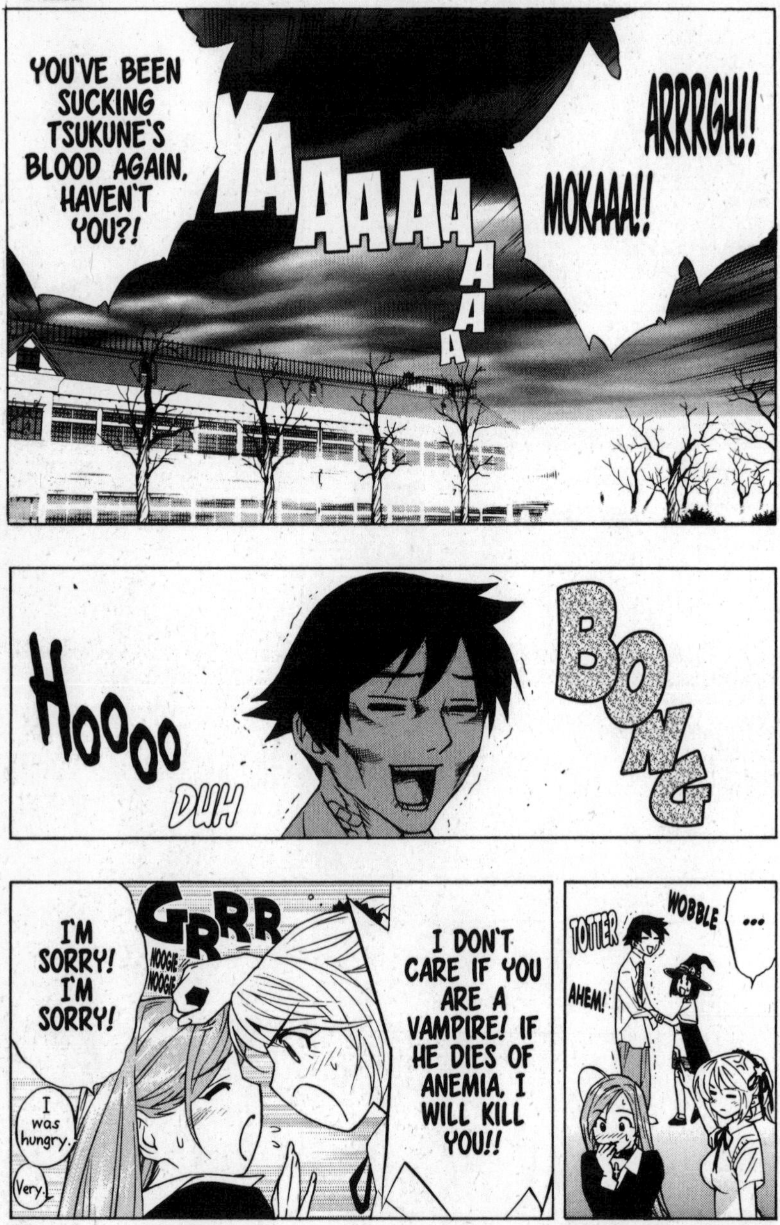

ARRRGH!!
MOKAAA!!
YAAAAAAAA
YOU'VE BEEN SUCKING TSUKUNE'S BLOOD AGAIN, HAVEN'T YOU?!
BONG
HOOOO
DUH
WOBBLE
...
TOTTER
AHEM!
I DON'T CARE IF YOU ARE A VAMPIRE! IF HE DIES OF ANEMIA, I WILL KILL YOU!!
GRRR
NOOGIE NOOGIE
I'M SORRY! I'M SORRY!
I was hungry.
Very.

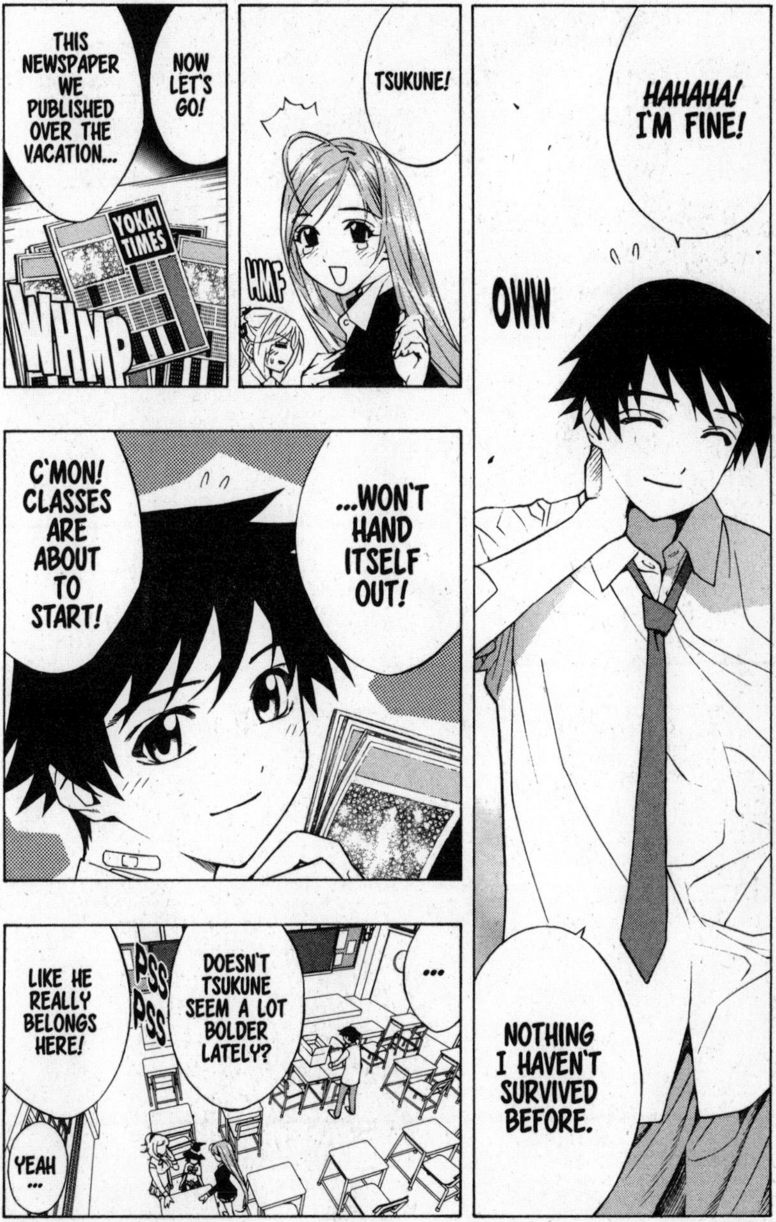
HAHAHA! I'M FINE!
OWW
NOTHING I HAVEN'T SURVIVED BEFORE.
TSUKUNE!
HMF
NOW LET'S GO!
THIS NEWSPAPER WE PUBLISHED OVER THE VACATION...
YOKAI TIMES
WHMP
...WON'T HAND ITSELF OUT!
C'MON! CLASSES ARE ABOUT TO START!
...
DOESN'T TSUKUNE SEEM A LOT BOLDER LATELY?
PSS PSS
LIKE HE REALLY BELONGS HERE!
YEAH ...

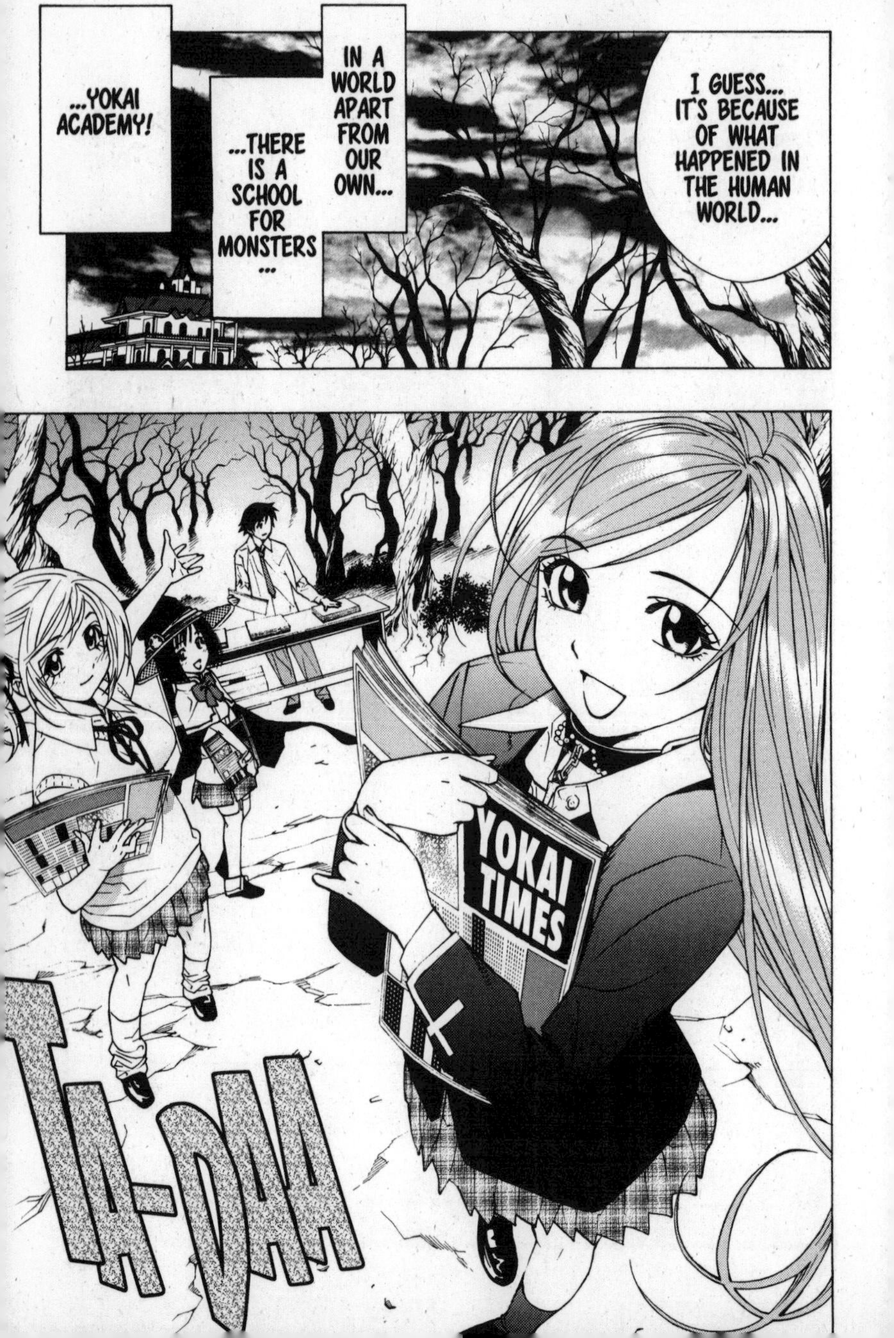
I GUESS... IT'S BECAUSE OF WHAT HAPPENED IN THE HUMAN WORLD...
IN A WORLD APART FROM OUR OWN...
...THERE IS A SCHOOL FOR MONSTERS...
...YOKAI ACADEMY!
YOKAI TIMES
TA-DAA

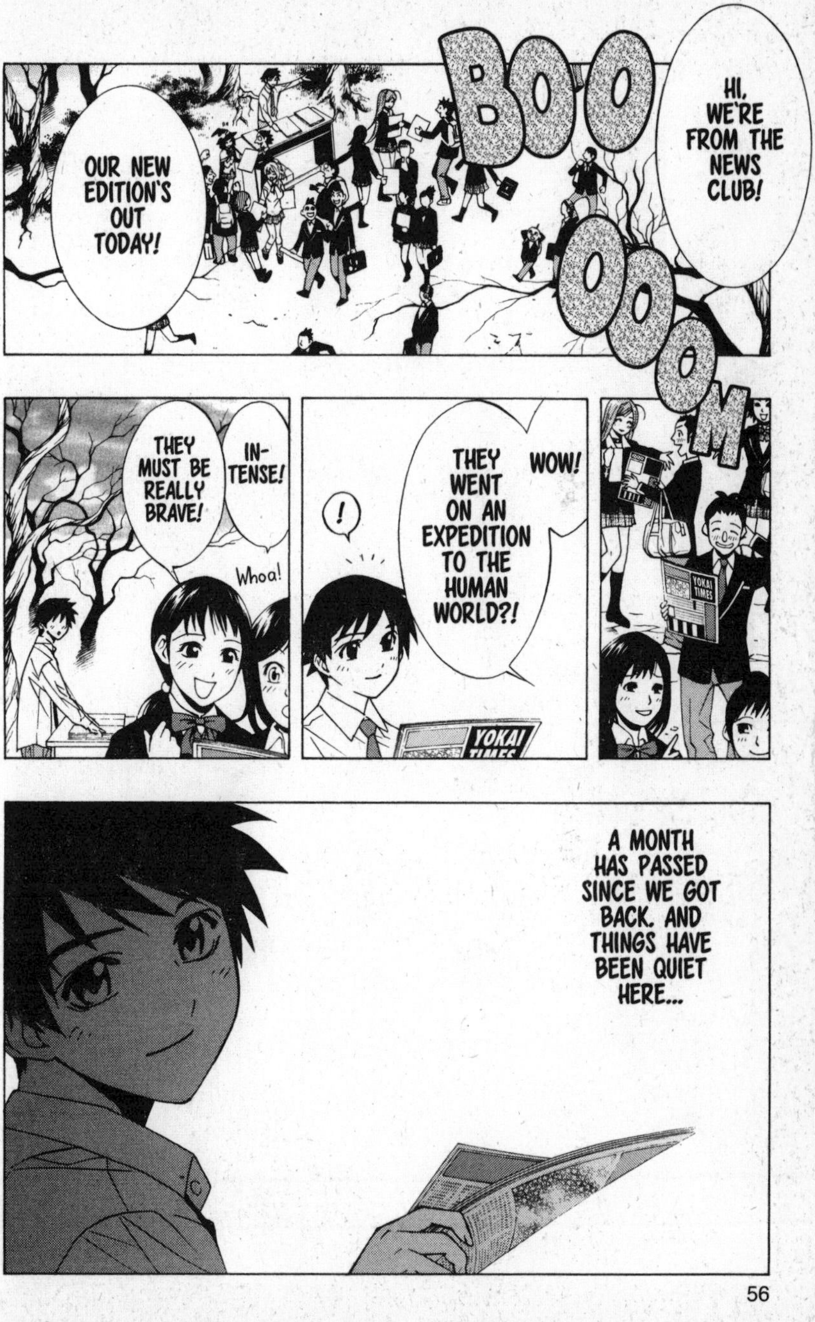
HI, WE'RE FROM THE NEWS CLUB!
BOOOOOOOM
OUR NEW EDITION'S OUT TODAY!
YOKAI TIMES
WOW!
THEY WENT ON AN EXPEDITION TO THE HUMAN WORLD?!
!
YOKAI TIMES
IN-TENSE!
THEY MUST BE REALLY BRAVE!
Whoa!
A MONTH HAS PASSED SINCE WE GOT BACK. AND THINGS HAVE BEEN QUIET HERE...

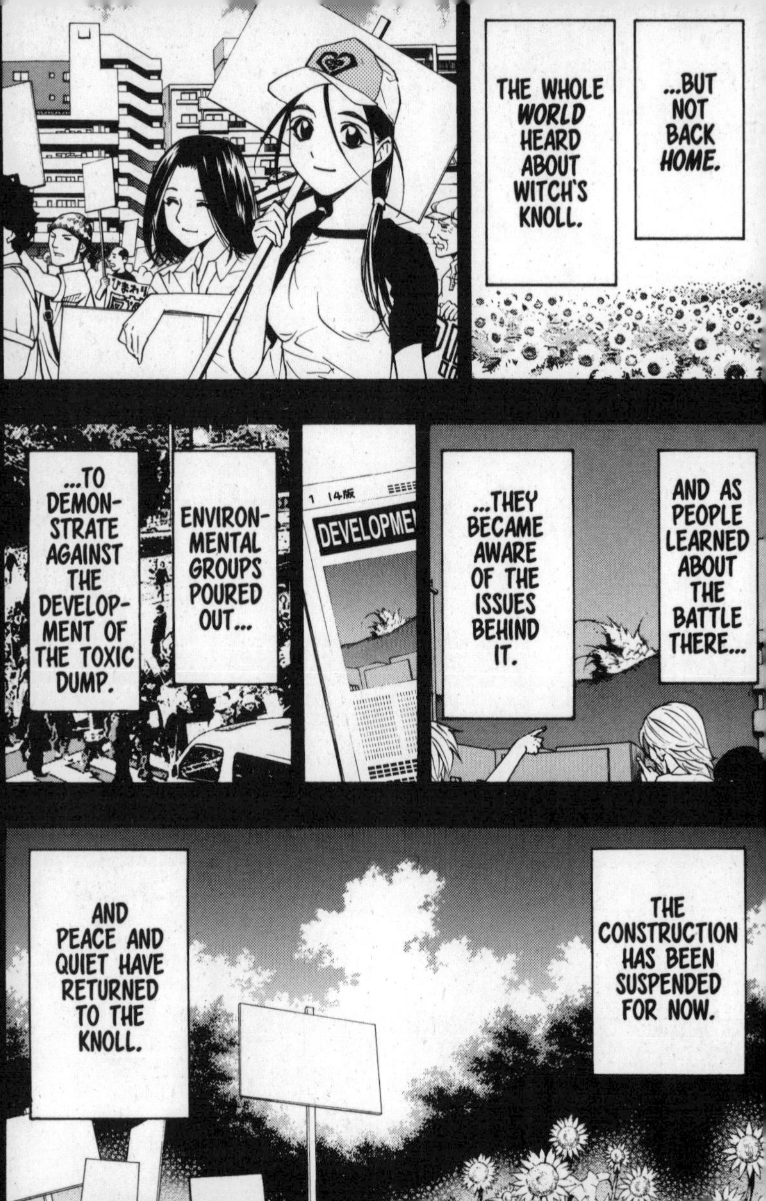
ひまわり
THE WHOLE WORLD HEARD ABOUT WITCH'S KNOLL.
...BUT NOT BACK HOME.
AND AS PEOPLE LEARNED ABOUT THE BATTLE THERE...
...THEY BECAME AWARE OF THE ISSUES BEHIND IT.
1 14版
DEVELOPMEN
ENVIRON-MENTAL GROUPS POURED OUT...
...TO DEMON-STRATE AGAINST THE DEVELOP-MENT OF THE TOXIC DUMP.
THE CONSTRUCTION HAS BEEN SUSPENDED FOR NOW.
AND PEACE AND QUIET HAVE RETURNED TO THE KNOLL.

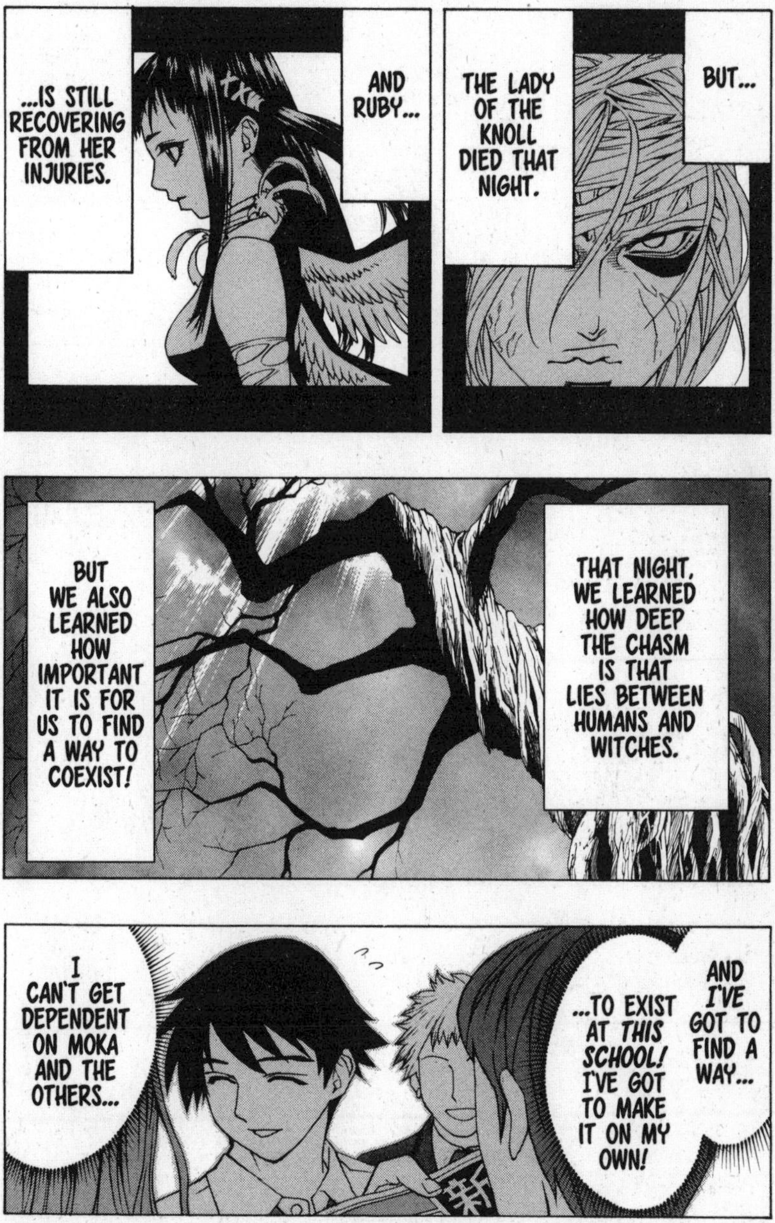
BUT...
THE LADY OF THE KNOLL DIED THAT NIGHT.
AND RUBY...
...IS STILL RECOVERING FROM HER INJURIES.
THAT NIGHT, WE LEARNED HOW DEEP THE CHASM IS THAT LIES BETWEEN HUMANS AND WITCHES.
BUT WE ALSO LEARNED HOW IMPORTANT IT IS FOR US TO FIND A WAY TO COEXIST!
AND *I'VE* GOT TO FIND A WAY...
...TO EXIST AT *THIS SCHOOL!* I'VE GOT TO MAKE IT ON MY OWN!
I CAN'T GET DEPENDENT ON MOKA AND THE OTHERS...

READ THIS WAY

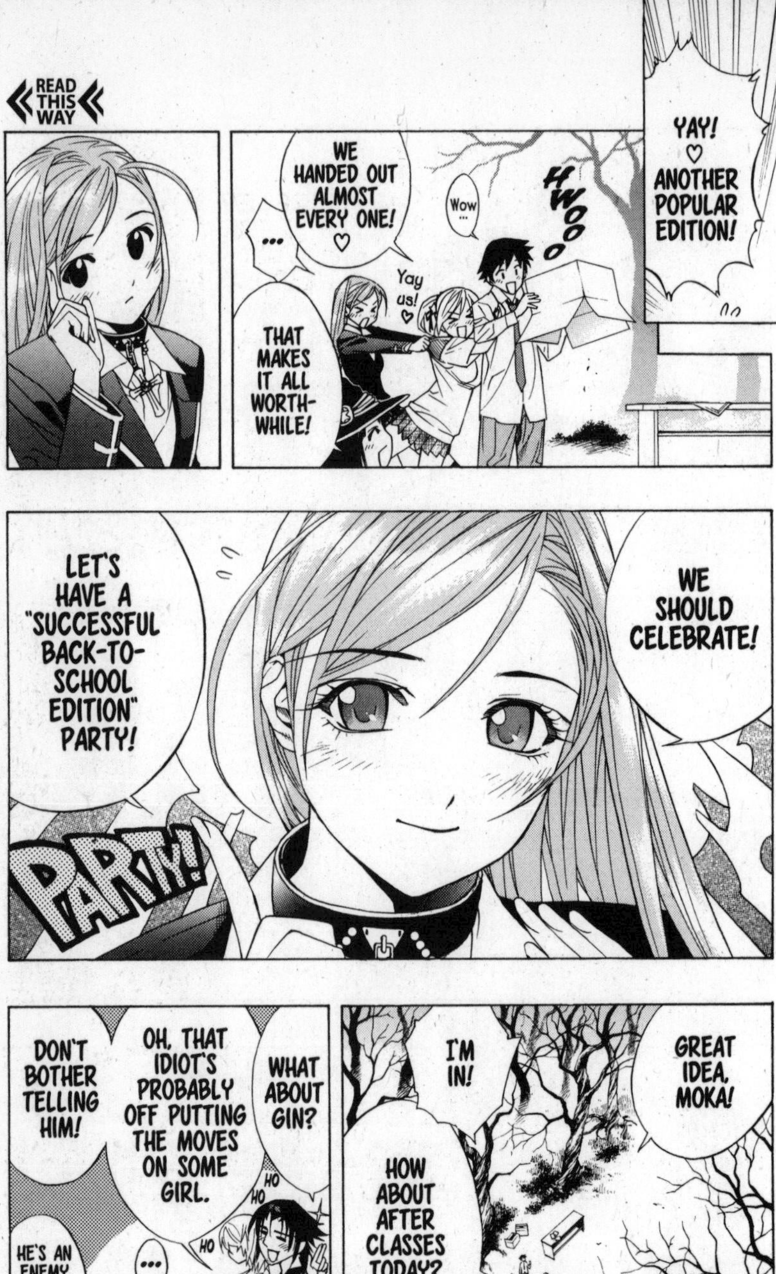

YAY! ♡ ANOTHER POPULAR EDITION!
HWOOO
Wow...
WE HANDED OUT ALMOST EVERY ONE! ♡
Yay us! ♡
...
THAT MAKES IT ALL WORTH-WHILE!
WE SHOULD CELEBRATE!
LET'S HAVE A "SUCCESSFUL BACK-TO-SCHOOL EDITION" PARTY!
PARTY!
GREAT IDEA, MOKA!
I'M IN!
HOW ABOUT AFTER CLASSES TODAY? ♡
WHAT ABOUT GIN?
OH, THAT IDIOT'S PROBABLY OFF PUTTING THE MOVES ON SOME GIRL.
DON'T BOTHER TELLING HIM!
HO HO HO
...
HE'S AN ENEMY OF WOMAN-KIND!
GRRR

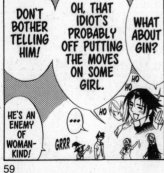

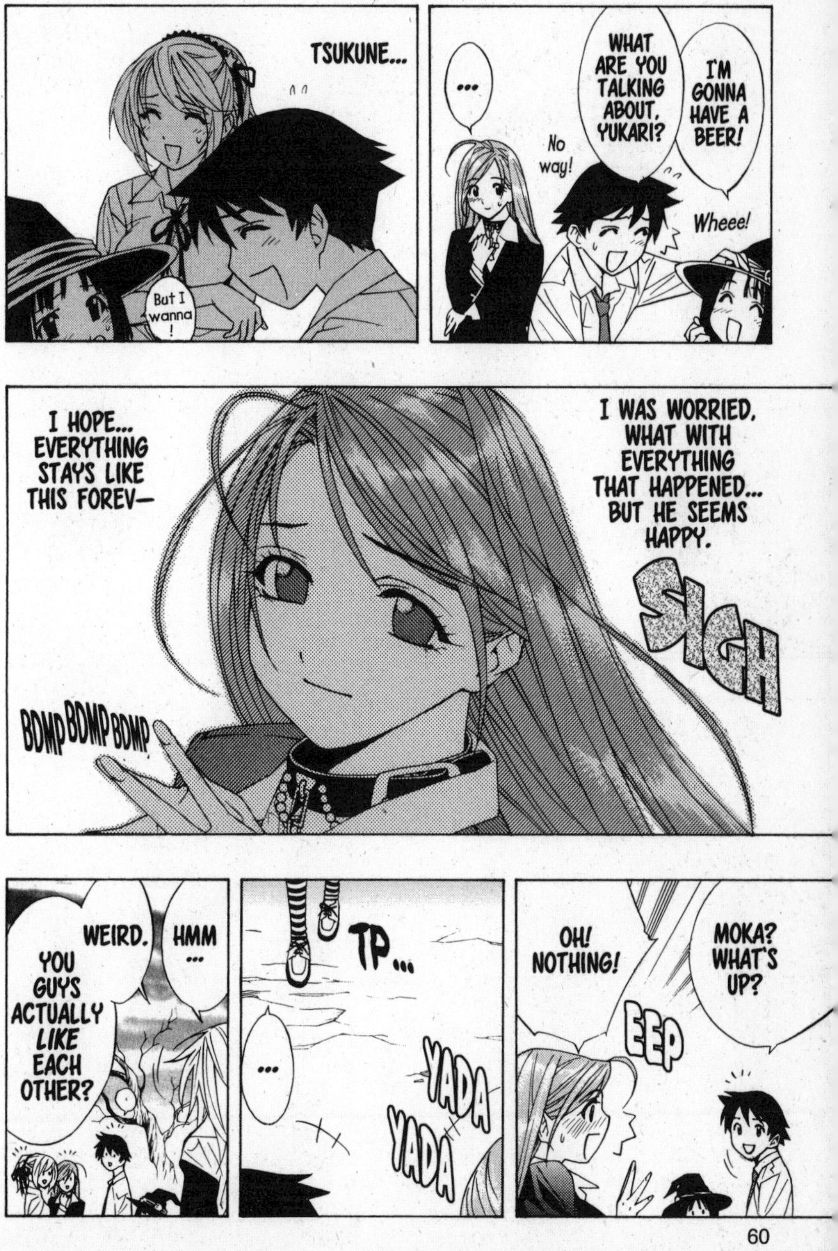
I'M GONNA HAVE A BEER!
WHAT ARE YOU TALKING ABOUT, YUKARI?
...
Wheee!
No way!
TSUKUNE...
But I wanna!
I WAS WORRIED. WHAT WITH EVERYTHING THAT HAPPENED... BUT HE SEEMS HAPPY.
SIGH
I HOPE... EVERYTHING STAYS LIKE THIS FOREV—
BDMP BDMP BDMP
MOKA? WHAT'S UP?
OH! NOTHING!
EEP
TP...
YADA YADA
...
HMM ...
WEIRD. YOU GUYS ACTUALLY LIKE EACH OTHER?

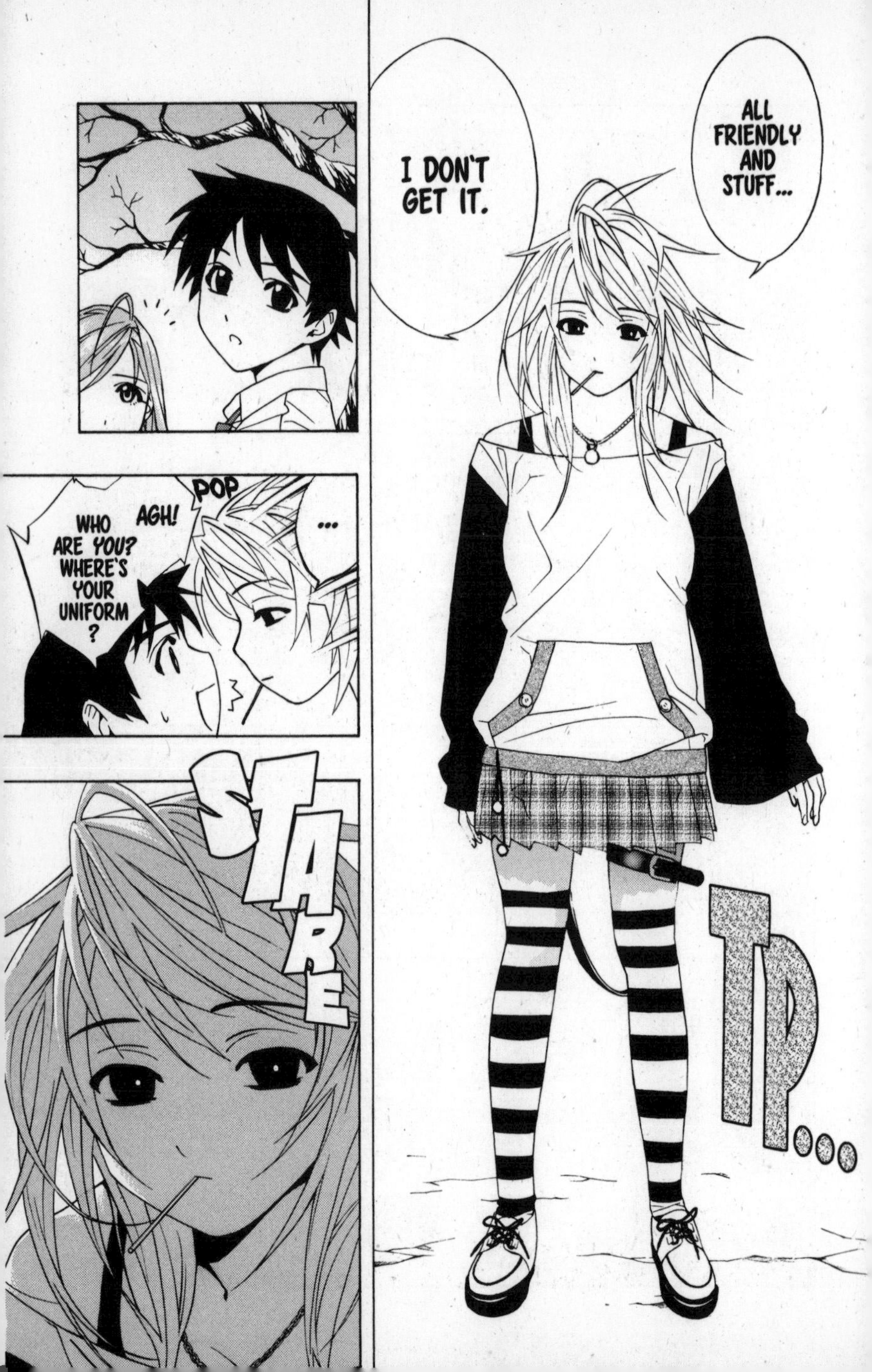
ALL FRIENDLY AND STUFF...
I DON'T GET IT.
TP...
POP
...
AGH!
WHO ARE YOU? WHERE'S YOUR UNIFORM?
STARE

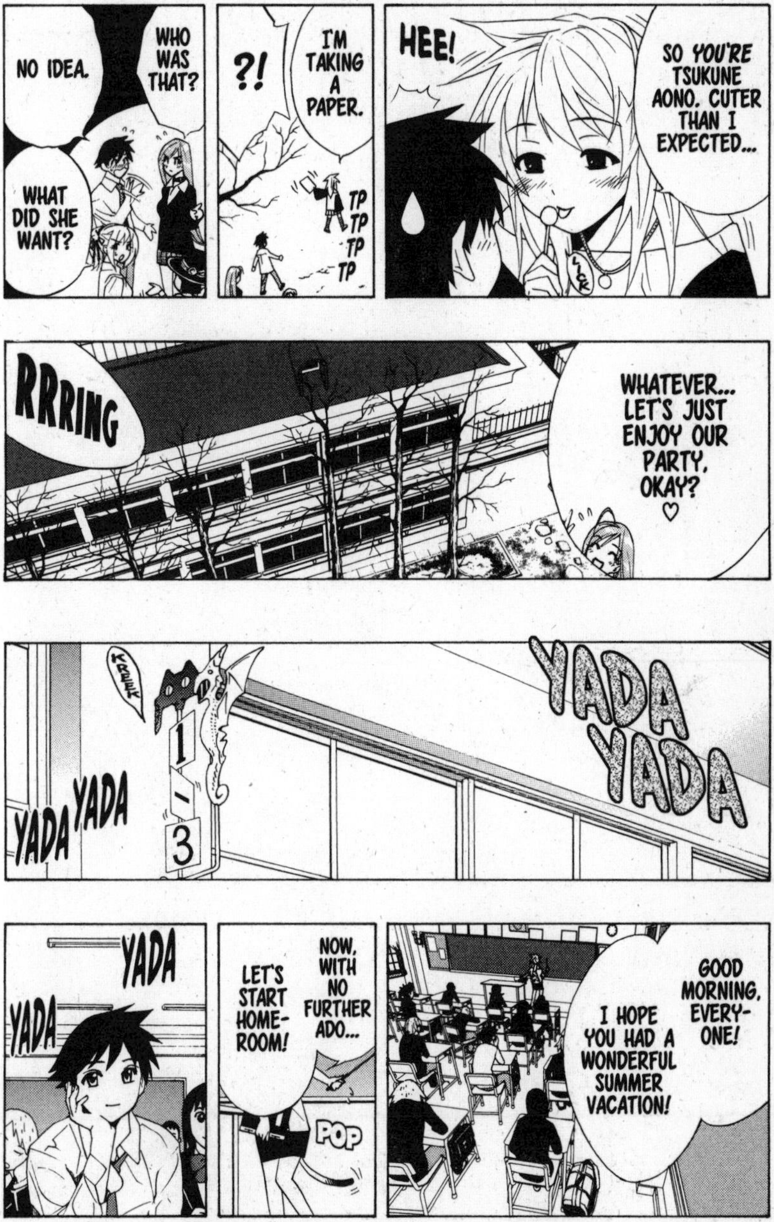
SO YOU'RE TSUKUNE AONO. CUTER THAN I EXPECTED...
HEE!
LICK
I'M TAKING A PAPER.
?!
TP TP TP TP
WHO WAS THAT?
NO IDEA.
WHAT DID SHE WANT?
WHATEVER... LET'S JUST ENJOY OUR PARTY, OKAY? ♡
RRRING
YADA YADA
KREEK
1-3
YADA YADA
GOOD MORNING, EVERYONE!
I HOPE YOU HAD A WONDERFUL SUMMER VACATION!
NOW, WITH NO FURTHER ADO...
LET'S START HOME-ROOM!
POP
YADA
YADA

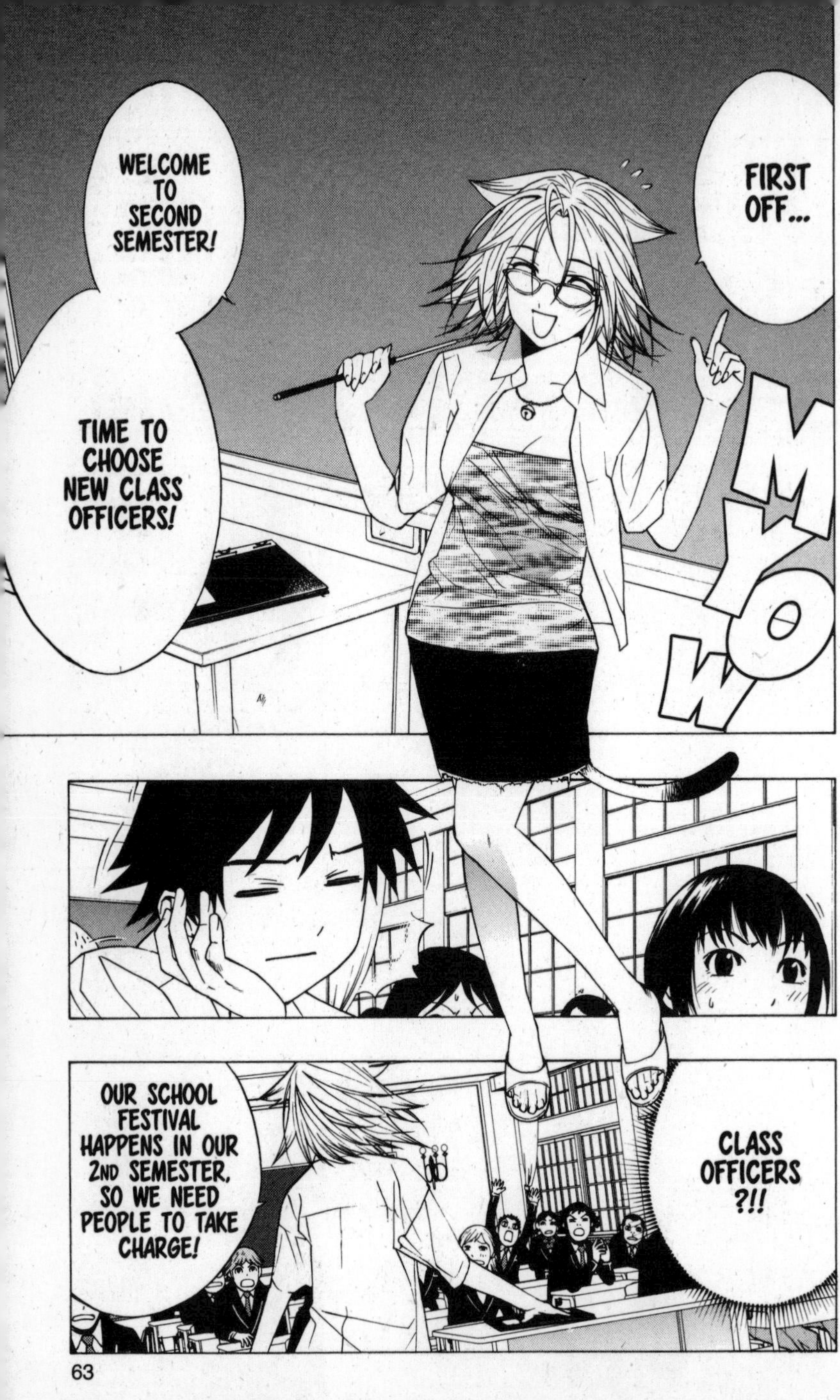
FIRST OFF...
MYOWW
WELCOME TO SECOND SEMESTER!
TIME TO CHOOSE NEW CLASS OFFICERS!
CLASS OFFICERS ?!!
OUR SCHOOL FESTIVAL HAPPENS IN OUR 2ND SEMESTER, SO WE NEED PEOPLE TO TAKE CHARGE!

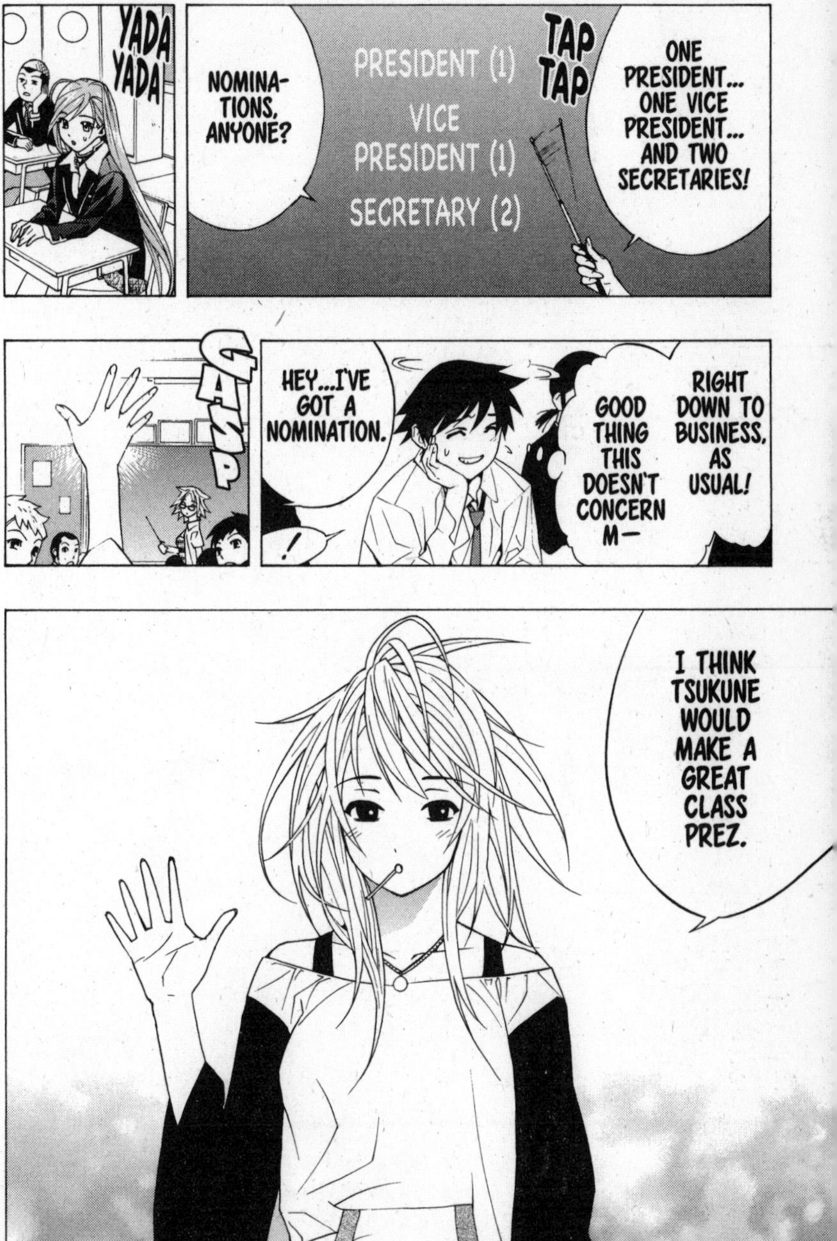
ONE PRESIDENT... ONE VICE PRESIDENT... AND TWO SECRETARIES!
TAP TAP
PRESIDENT (1)
VICE PRESIDENT (1)
SECRETARY (2)
NOMINATIONS, ANYONE?
YADA YADA
RIGHT DOWN TO BUSINESS, AS USUAL!
GOOD THING THIS DOESN'T CONCERN M—
HEY...I'VE GOT A NOMINATION.
!
GASP
I THINK TSUKUNE WOULD MAKE A GREAT CLASS PREZ.

READ THIS WAY

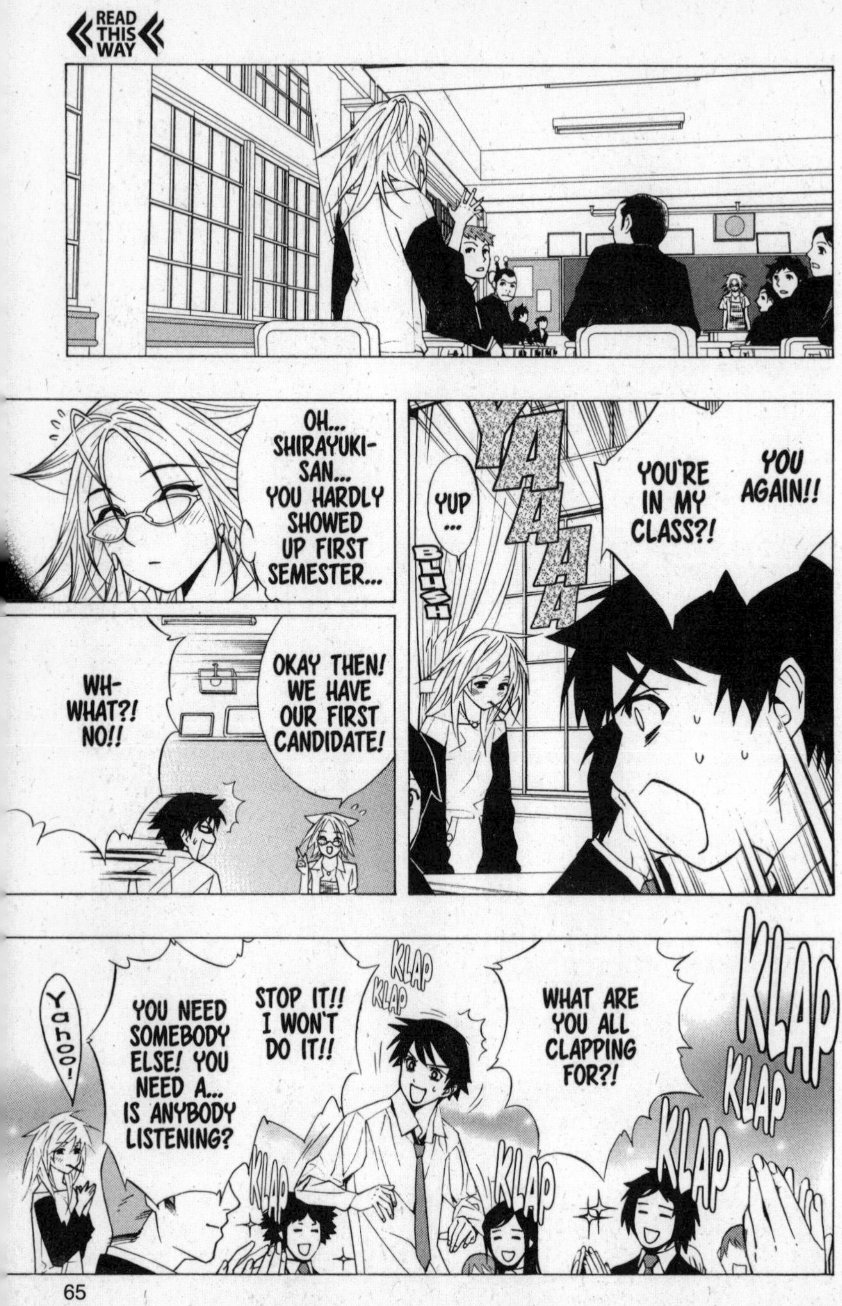
YOU AGAIN!!
YOU'RE IN MY CLASS?!
YAAAAA
YUP...
BLUSH
OH... SHIRAYUKI-SAN... YOU HARDLY SHOWED UP FIRST SEMESTER...
OKAY THEN! WE HAVE OUR FIRST CANDIDATE!
WH-WHAT?! NO!!
KLAP
KLAP
KLAP
WHAT ARE YOU ALL CLAPPING FOR?!
KLAP
KLAP
KLAP KLAP
STOP IT!! I WON'T DO IT!!
YOU NEED SOMEBODY ELSE! YOU NEED A... IS ANYBODY LISTENING?
KLAP
Yahoo!

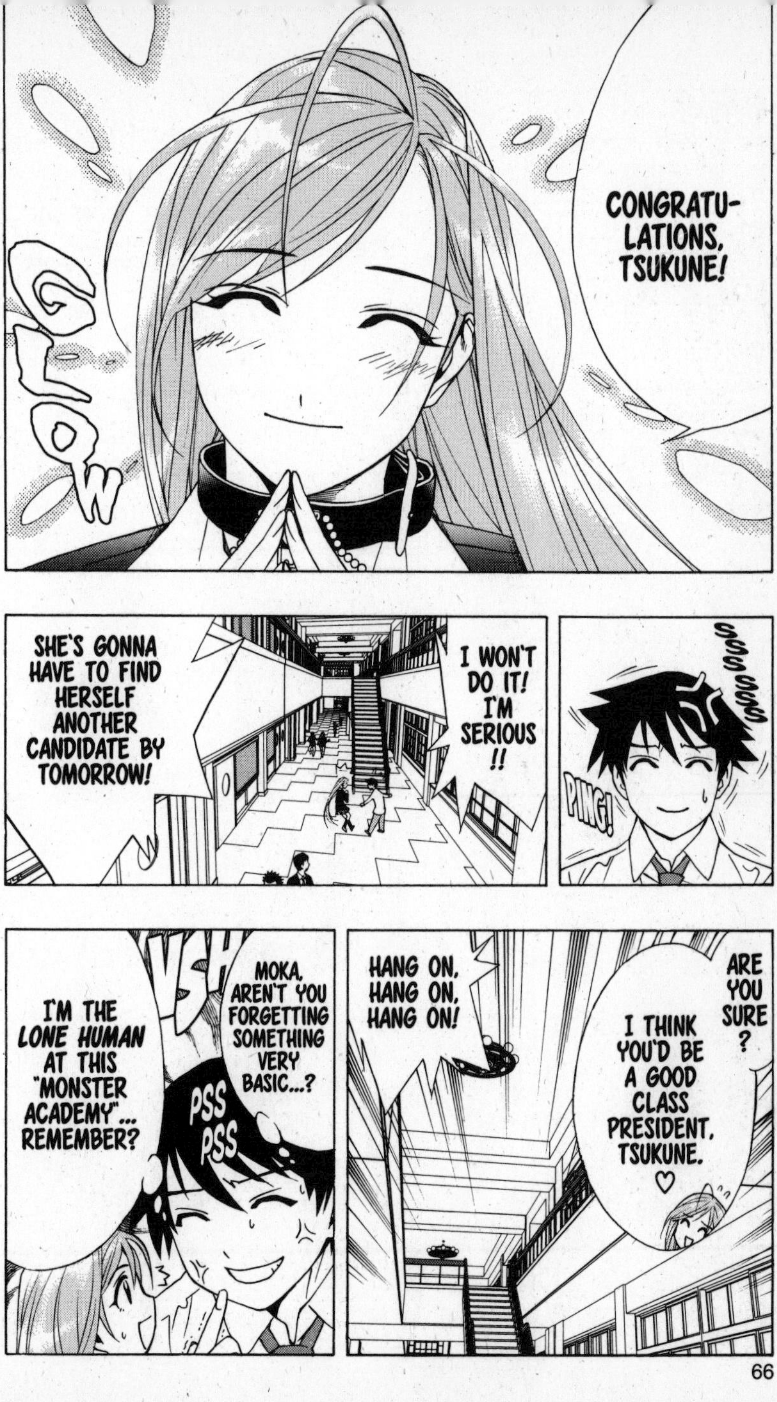
CONGRATU-LATIONS, TSUKUNE!
GLOW
SSSSSS
PING!
I WON'T DO IT! I'M SERIOUS!!
SHE'S GONNA HAVE TO FIND HERSELF ANOTHER CANDIDATE BY TOMORROW!
ARE YOU SURE?
I THINK YOU'D BE A GOOD CLASS PRESIDENT, TSUKUNE. ♡
HANG ON, HANG ON, HANG ON!
MOKA, AREN'T YOU FORGETTING SOMETHING VERY BASIC...?
I'M THE *LONE HUMAN* AT THIS "MONSTER ACADEMY"... REMEMBER?
PSS PSS

READ THIS WAY

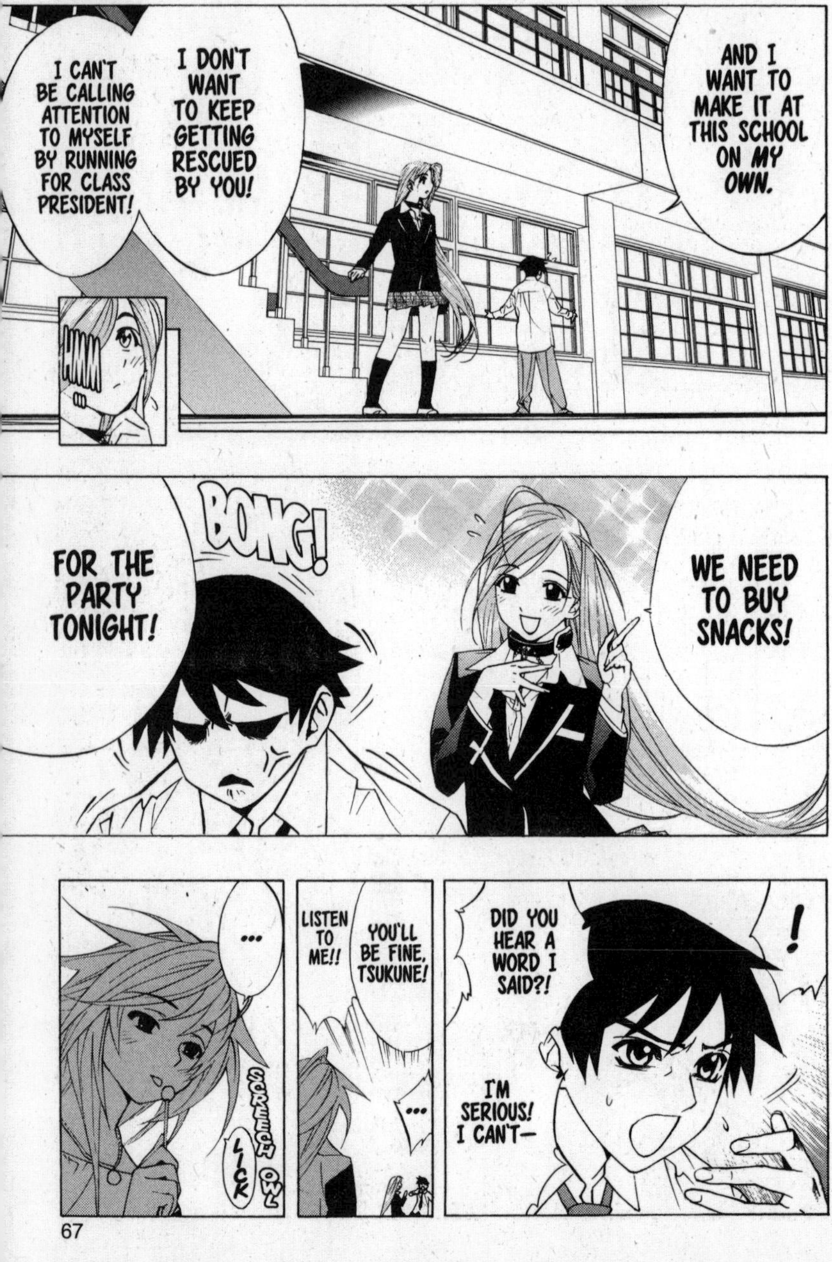
AND I WANT TO MAKE IT AT THIS SCHOOL ON *MY OWN*.
I DON'T WANT TO KEEP GETTING RESCUED BY YOU!
I CAN'T BE CALLING ATTENTION TO MYSELF BY RUNNING FOR CLASS PRESIDENT!
HMM
WE NEED TO BUY SNACKS!
BONG!
FOR THE PARTY TONIGHT!
!
DID YOU HEAR A WORD I SAID?!
I'M SERIOUS! I CAN'T—
YOU'LL BE FINE, TSUKUNE!
LISTEN TO ME!!
...
...
SCREECH OWL
LICK

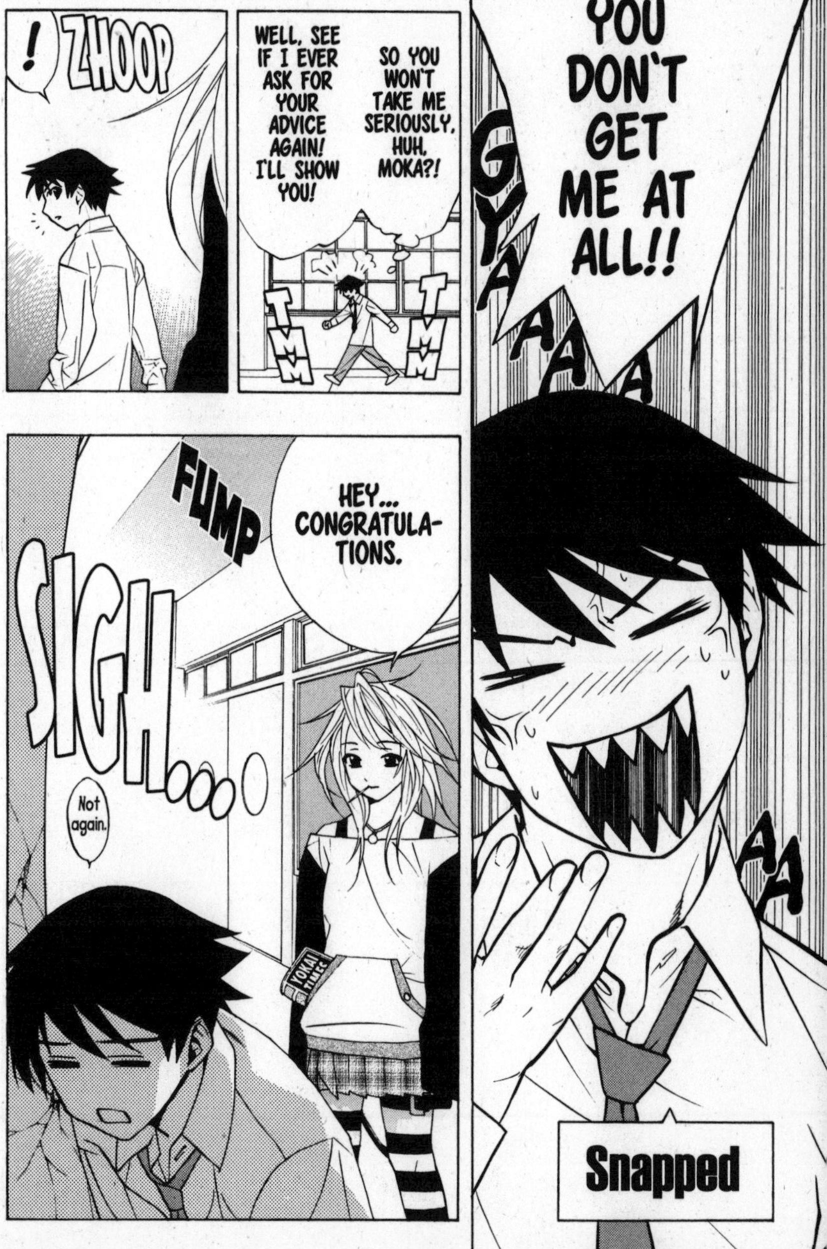
YOU DON'T GET ME AT ALL!!
GYAAAAA
AAA
Snapped
SO YOU WON'T TAKE ME SERIOUSLY, HUH, MOKA?!
WELL, SEE IF I EVER ASK FOR YOUR ADVICE AGAIN! I'LL SHOW YOU!
TMM
TMM
ZHOOP
!
HEY... CONGRATULA-TIONS.
FUMP
SIGH...
Not again.

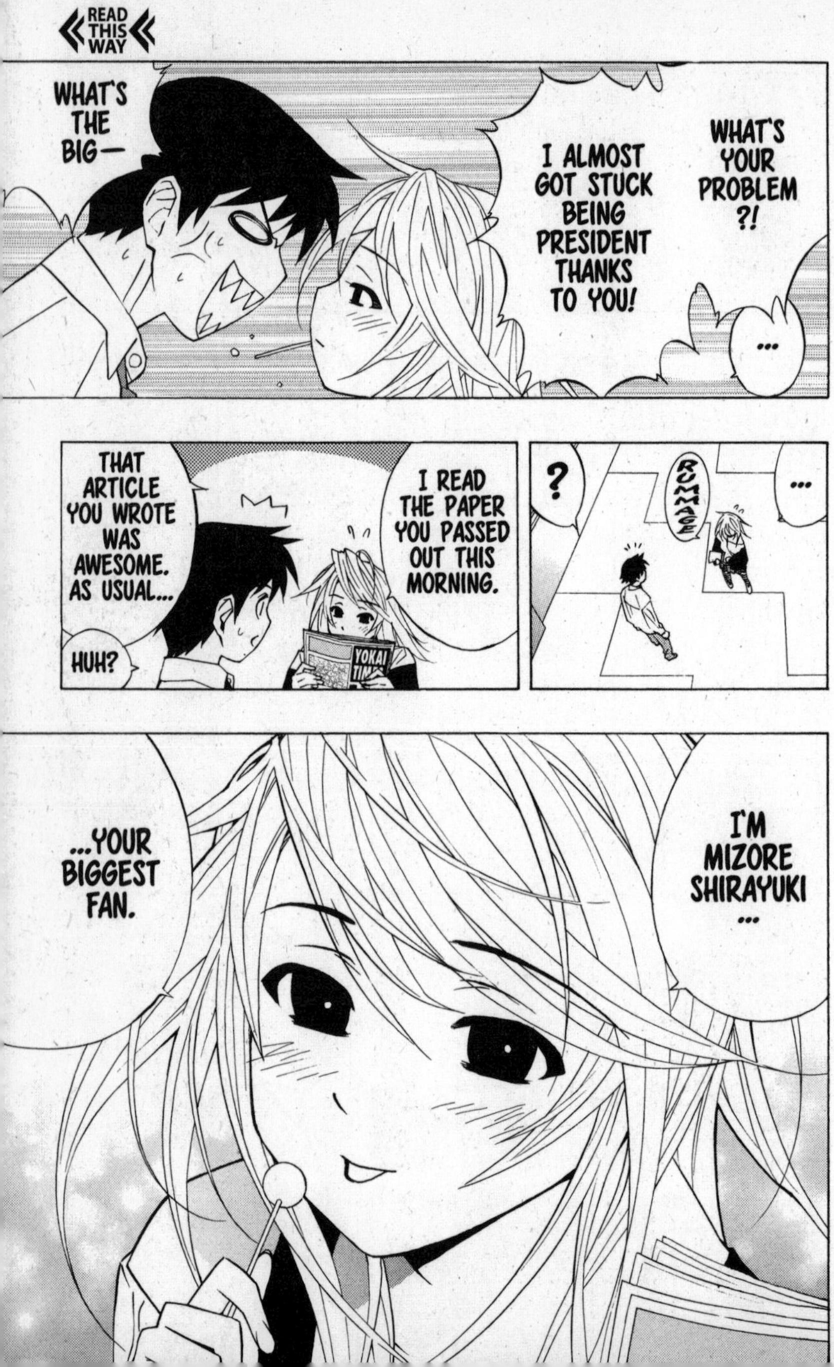
READ THIS WAY
WHAT'S YOUR PROBLEM?!
I ALMOST GOT STUCK BEING PRESIDENT THANKS TO YOU!
...
WHAT'S THE BIG—
...
RUMMAGE
?
I READ THE PAPER YOU PASSED OUT THIS MORNING.
THAT ARTICLE YOU WROTE WAS AWESOME. AS USUAL...
HUH?
YOKAI TIMES
I'M MIZORE SHIRAYUKI...
...YOUR BIGGEST FAN.

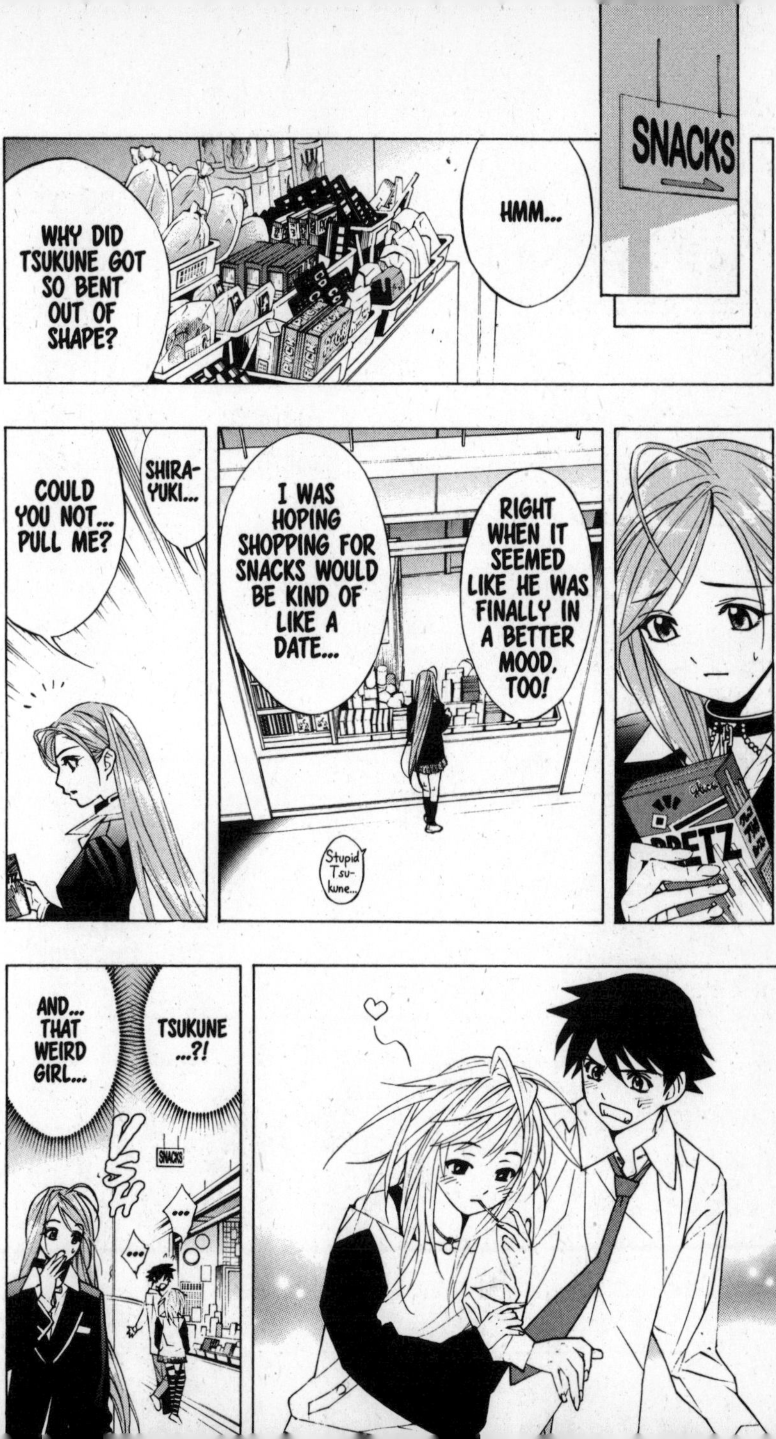
SNACKS
HMM...
WHY DID TSUKUNE GOT SO BENT OUT OF SHAPE?
PRETZ
RIGHT WHEN IT SEEMED LIKE HE WAS FINALLY IN A BETTER MOOD, TOO!
I WAS HOPING SHOPPING FOR SNACKS WOULD BE KIND OF LIKE A DATE...
Stupid Tsu-kune...
SHIRA-YUKI...
COULD YOU NOT... PULL ME?
TSUKUNE ...?!
AND... THAT WEIRD GIRL...
SNACKS
...
...

READ THIS WAY

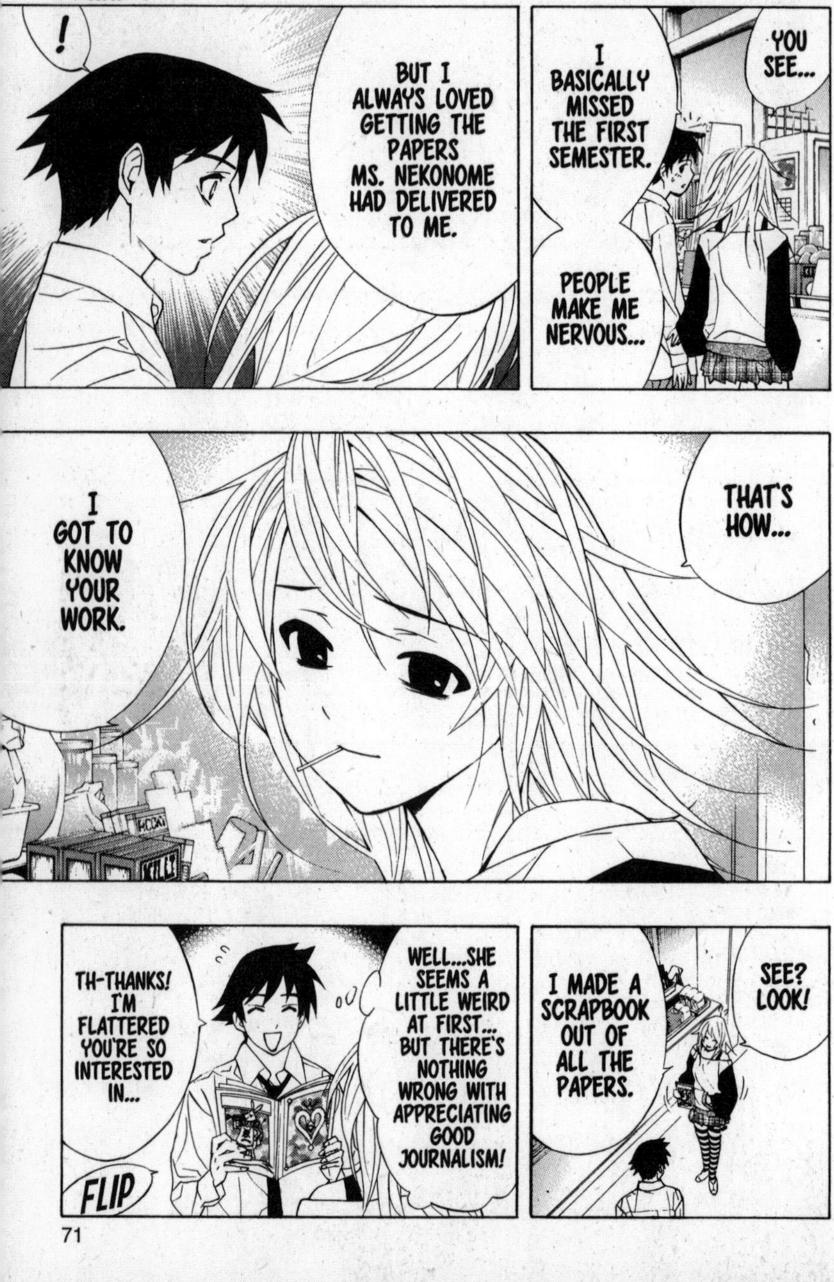

YOU SEE...
I BASICALLY MISSED THE FIRST SEMESTER.
PEOPLE MAKE ME NERVOUS...
BUT I ALWAYS LOVED GETTING THE PAPERS MS. NEKONOME HAD DELIVERED TO ME.
!
THAT'S HOW...
I GOT TO KNOW YOUR WORK.
SEE? LOOK!
I MADE A SCRAPBOOK OUT OF ALL THE PAPERS.
WELL...SHE SEEMS A LITTLE WEIRD AT FIRST... BUT THERE'S NOTHING WRONG WITH APPRECIATING GOOD JOURNALISM!
TH-THANKS! I'M FLATTERED YOU'RE SO INTERESTED IN...
FLIP

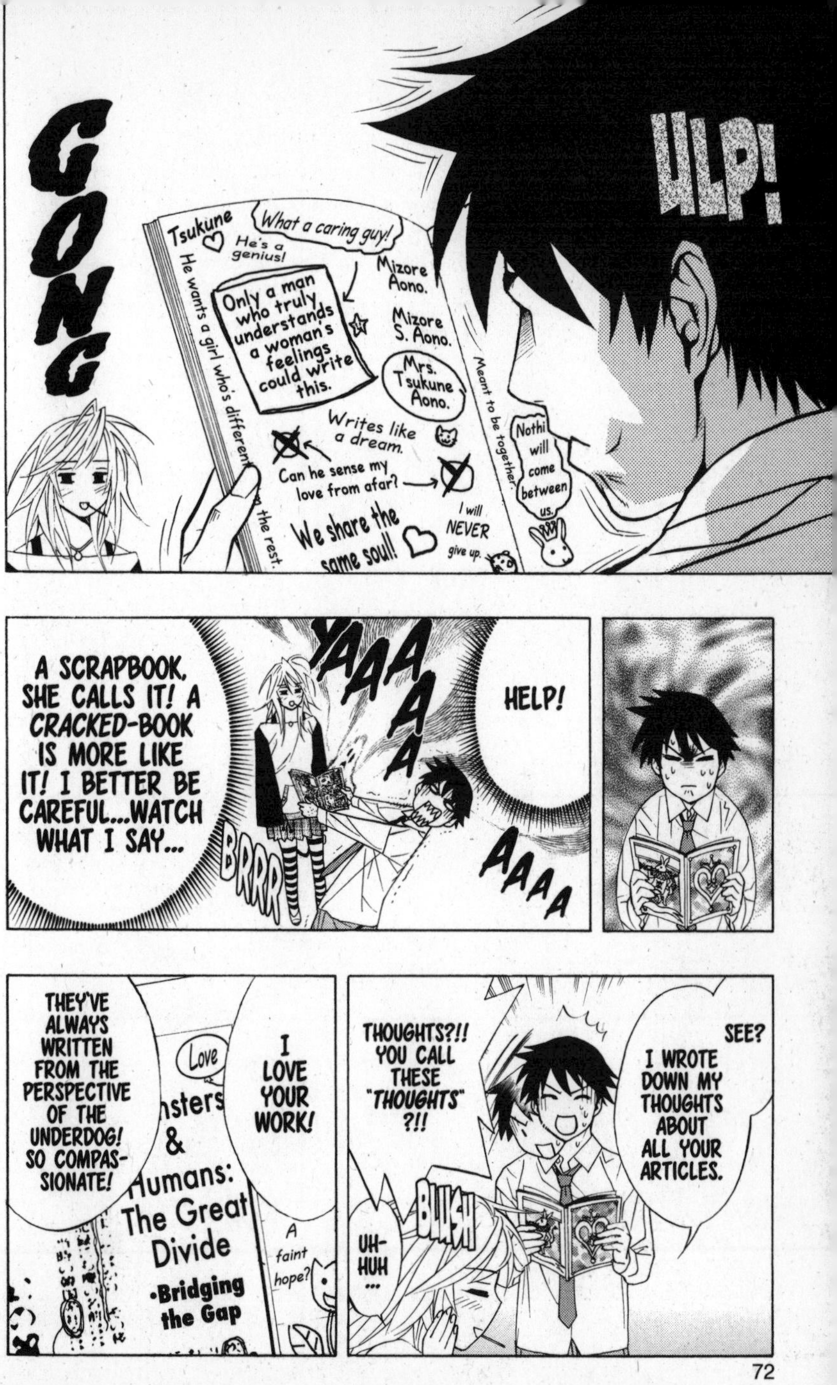

HULP!
GONG
What a caring guy!
Tsukune ♥
He's a genius!
Mizore Aono.
Mizore S. Aono.
Only a man who truly understands a woman's feelings could write this.
Mrs. Tsukune Aono.
Meant to be together.
He wants a girl who's differen
the rest.
Writes like a dream.
Can he sense my love from afar?
Nothi will come between us.
I will NEVER give up.
We share the same soul!
HELP!
YAAAAAA
A SCRAPBOOK, SHE CALLS IT! A CRACKED-BOOK IS MORE LIKE IT! I BETTER BE CAREFUL...WATCH WHAT I SAY...
BRRRR
AAAA
SEE? I WROTE DOWN MY THOUGHTS ABOUT ALL YOUR ARTICLES.
THOUGHTS?!! YOU CALL THESE "THOUGHTS"?!!
BLUSH
UH-HUH...
I LOVE YOUR WORK!
THEY'VE ALWAYS WRITTEN FROM THE PERSPECTIVE OF THE UNDERDOG! SO COMPASSIONATE!
Love
nsters & Humans: The Great Divide
•Bridging the Gap
A faint hope?

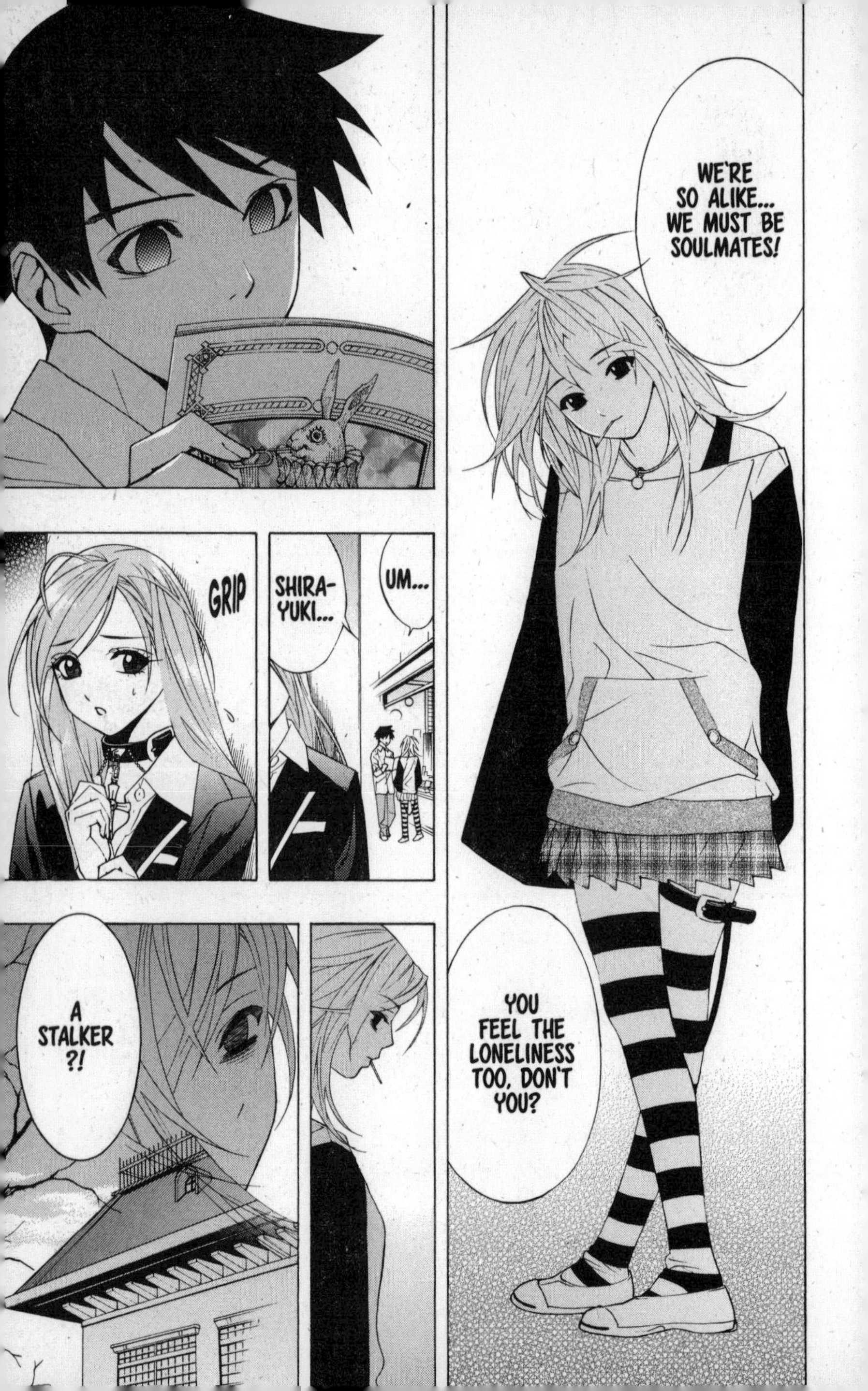
WE'RE SO ALIKE... WE MUST BE SOULMATES!
YOU FEEL THE LONELINESS TOO, DON'T YOU?
UM...
SHIRA-YUKI...
GRIP
A STALKER ?!

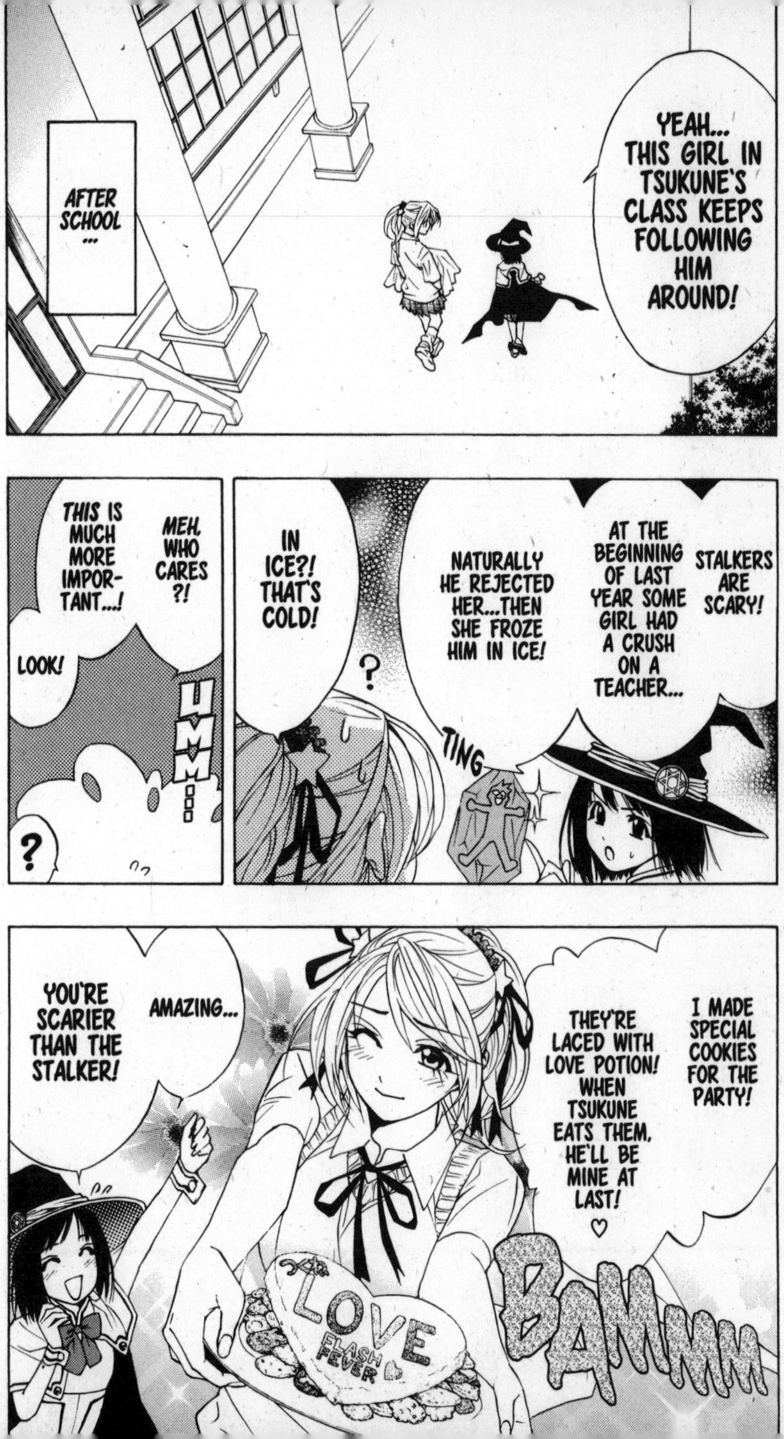

YEAH... THIS GIRL IN TSUKUNE'S CLASS KEEPS FOLLOWING HIM AROUND!
AFTER SCHOOL...
STALKERS ARE SCARY!
AT THE BEGINNING OF LAST YEAR SOME GIRL HAD A CRUSH ON A TEACHER...
NATURALLY HE REJECTED HER...THEN SHE FROZE HIM IN ICE!
TING
IN ICE?! THAT'S COLD!
?
MEH, WHO CARES?!
THIS IS MUCH MORE IMPOR-TANT...!
UMMM...
LOOK!
?
I MADE SPECIAL COOKIES FOR THE PARTY!
THEY'RE LACED WITH LOVE POTION! WHEN TSUKUNE EATS THEM, HE'LL BE MINE AT LAST! ♡
BAMMM
LOVE FLASH FEVER ♡
AMAZING...
YOU'RE SCARIER THAN THE STALKER!

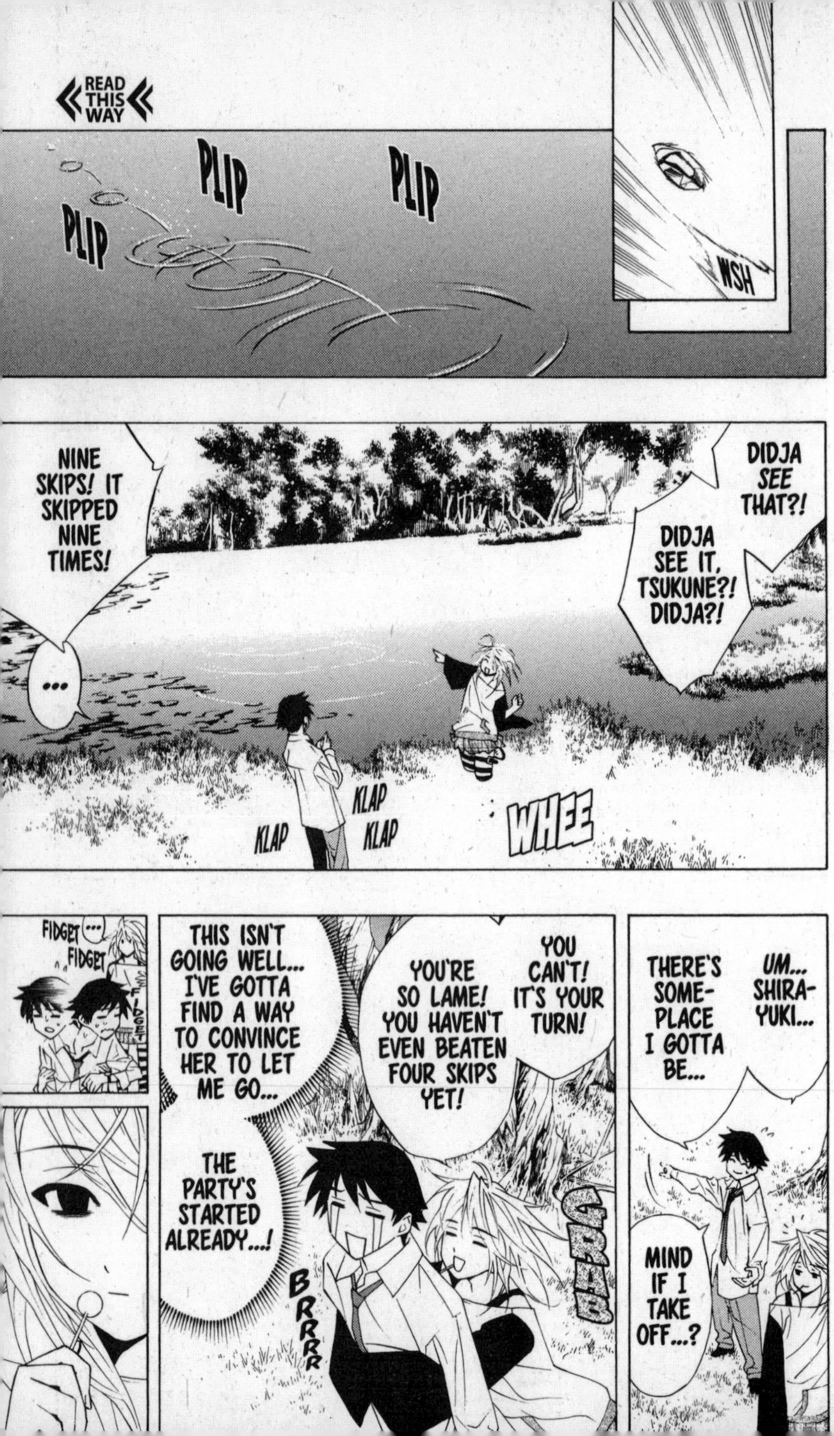
READ THIS WAY
WSH
PLIP
PLIP
PLIP
DIDJA SEE THAT?!
DIDJA SEE IT, TSUKUNE?! DIDJA?!
WHEE
KLAP
KLAP
KLAP
NINE SKIPS! IT SKIPPED NINE TIMES!
...
UM... SHIRAYUKI...
THERE'S SOMEPLACE I GOTTA BE...
MIND IF I TAKE OFF...?
YOU CAN'T! IT'S YOUR TURN!
YOU'RE SO LAME! YOU HAVEN'T EVEN BEATEN FOUR SKIPS YET!
THIS ISN'T GOING WELL... I'VE GOTTA FIND A WAY TO CONVINCE HER TO LET ME GO...
THE PARTY'S STARTED ALREADY...!
GRAB
BRRRR
...
FIDGET
FIDGET
FIDGET

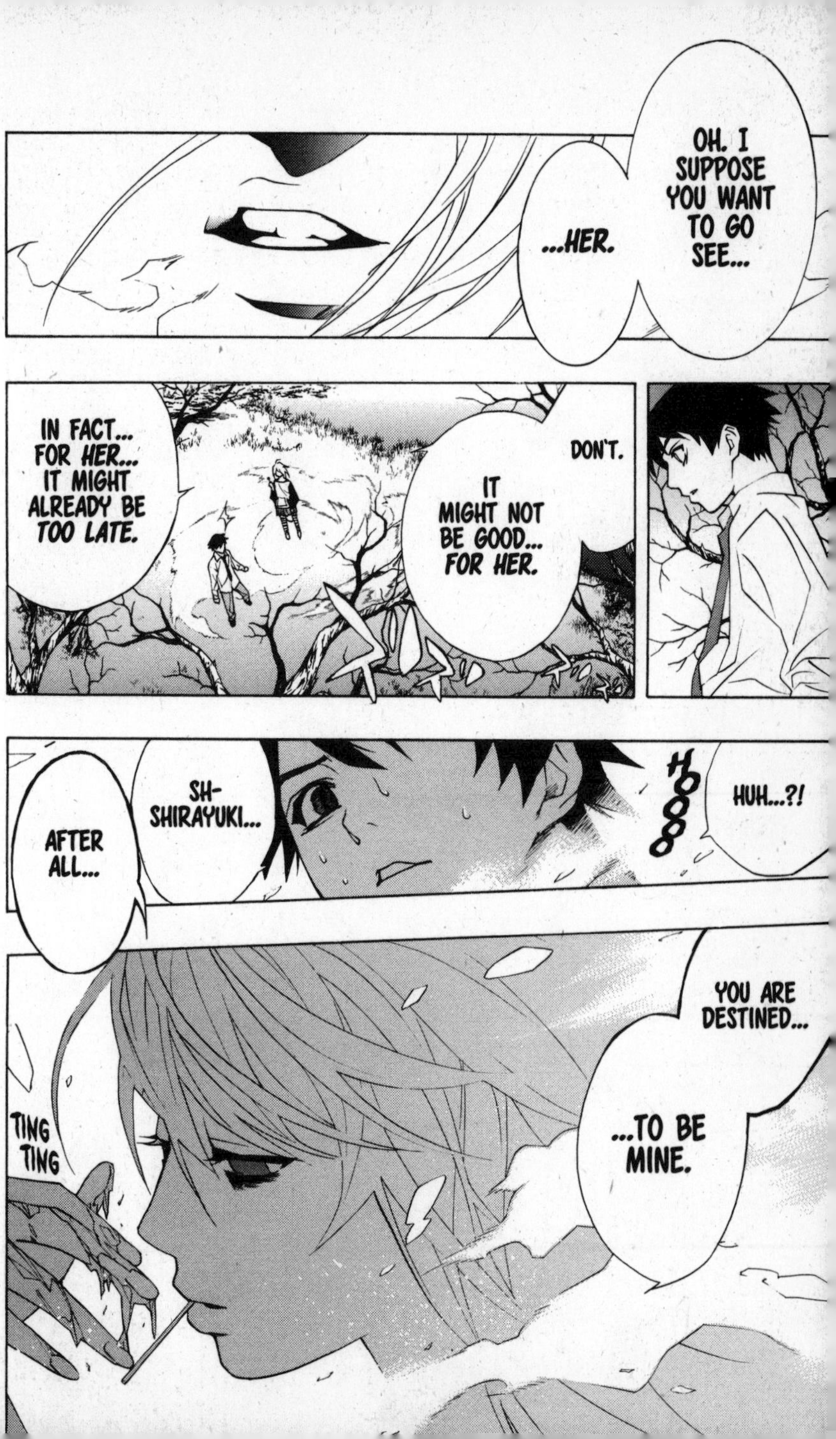
OH. I SUPPOSE YOU WANT TO GO SEE...
...HER.
HUH...?!
HOOOO
SH-SHIRAYUKI...
DON'T.
IT MIGHT NOT BE GOOD... FOR HER.
IN FACT... FOR HER... IT MIGHT ALREADY BE TOO LATE.
AFTER ALL...
YOU ARE DESTINED...
...TO BE MINE.
TING TING

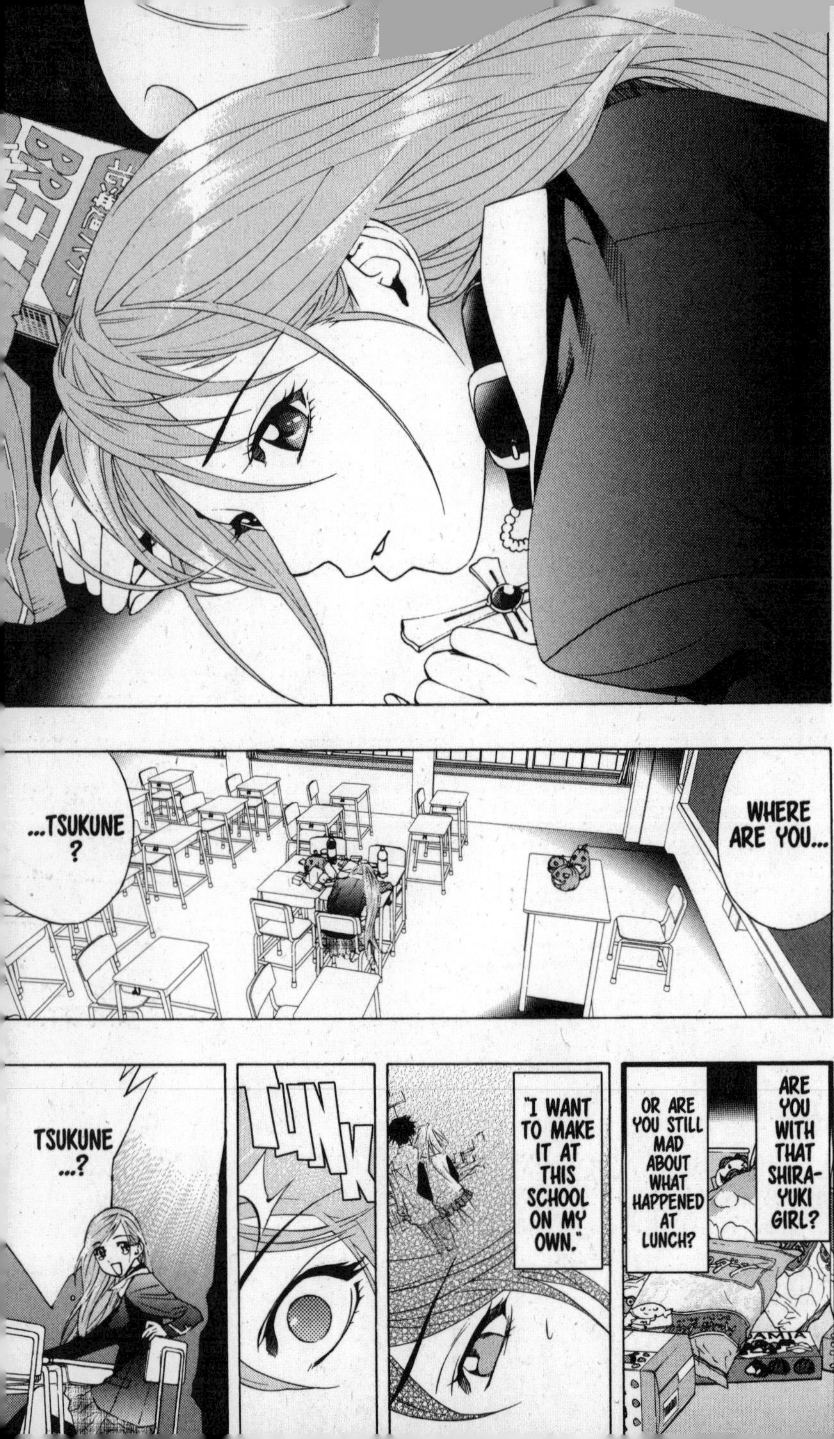
WHERE ARE YOU...
...TSUKUNE ?
ARE YOU WITH THAT SHIRAYUKI GIRL?
OR ARE YOU STILL MAD ABOUT WHAT HAPPENED AT LUNCH?
"I WANT TO MAKE IT AT THIS SCHOOL ON MY OWN."
TUNK
TSUKUNE ...?

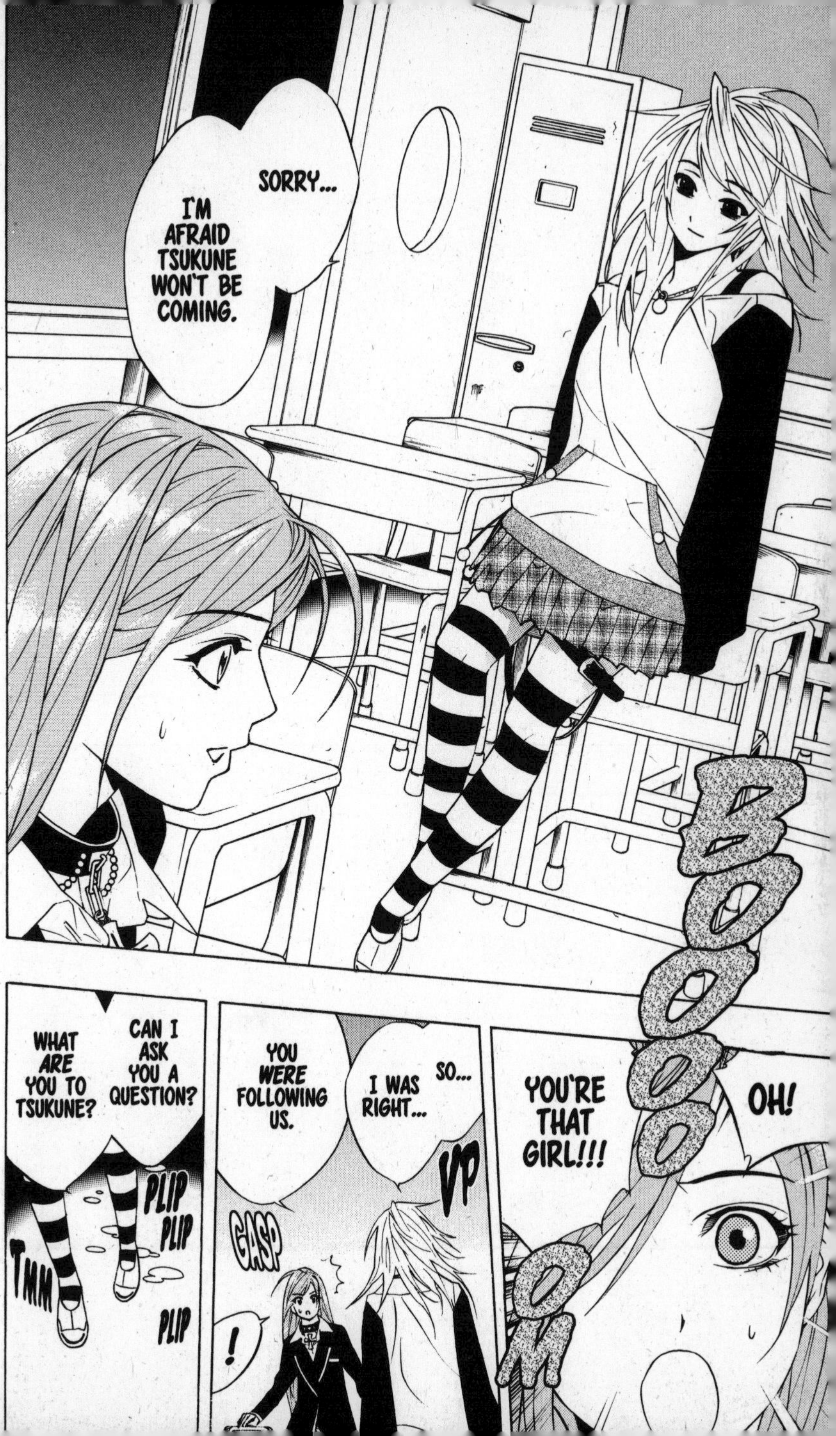
SORRY...
I'M AFRAID TSUKUNE WON'T BE COMING.
BOOOOOM
OH!
YOU'RE THAT GIRL!!!
SO...
I WAS RIGHT...
YOU WERE FOLLOWING US.
VP
GASP
!
CAN I ASK YOU A QUESTION?
WHAT ARE YOU TO TSUKUNE?
PLIP
PLIP
TMM
PLIP

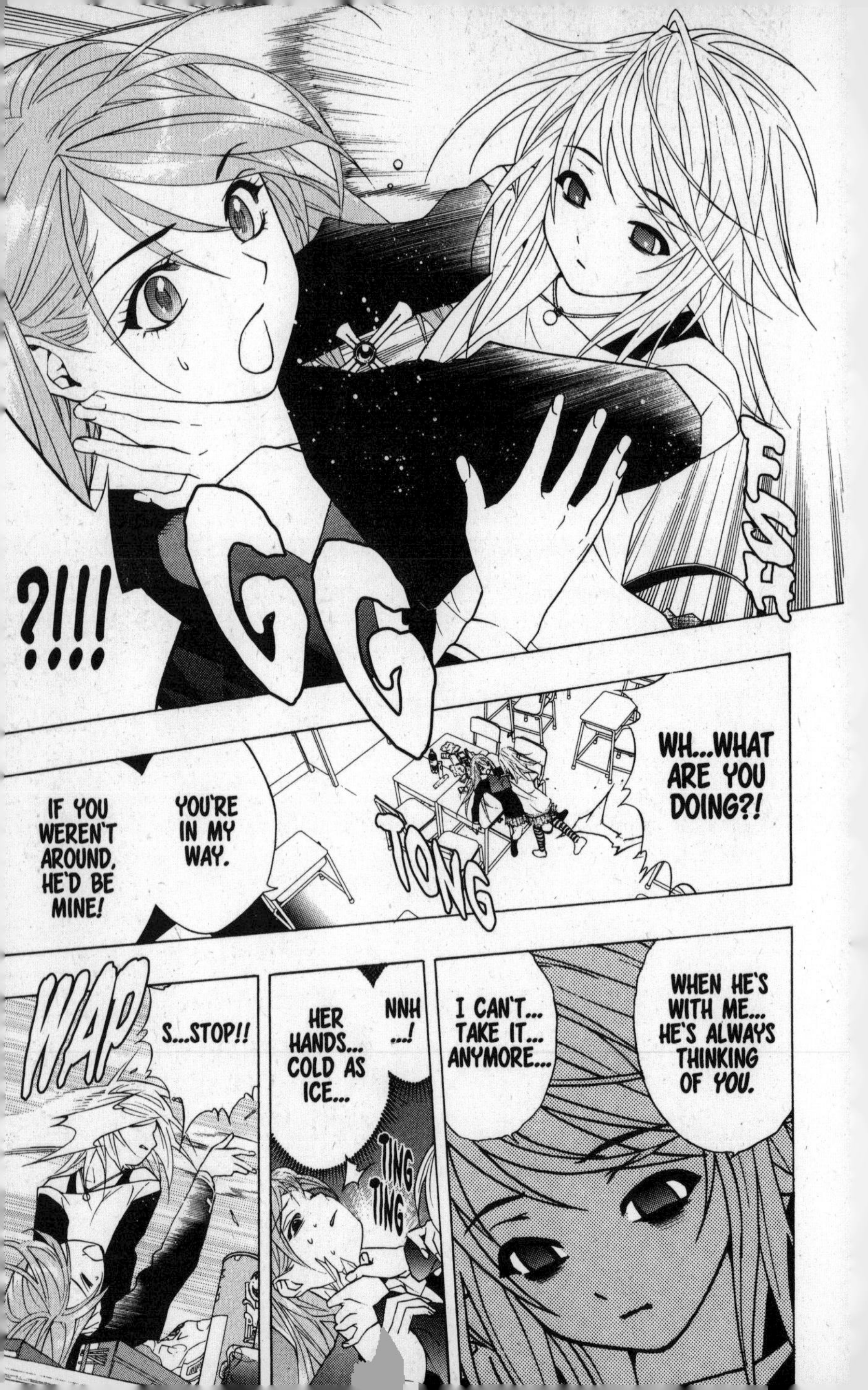

FSH
?!!!
GG
WH...WHAT ARE YOU DOING?!
TONG
YOU'RE IN MY WAY.
IF YOU WEREN'T AROUND, HE'D BE MINE!
WHEN HE'S WITH ME... HE'S ALWAYS THINKING OF YOU.
I CAN'T... TAKE IT... ANYMORE...
NNH ...!
HER HANDS... COLD AS ICE...
TING TING
S...STOP!!
WAP

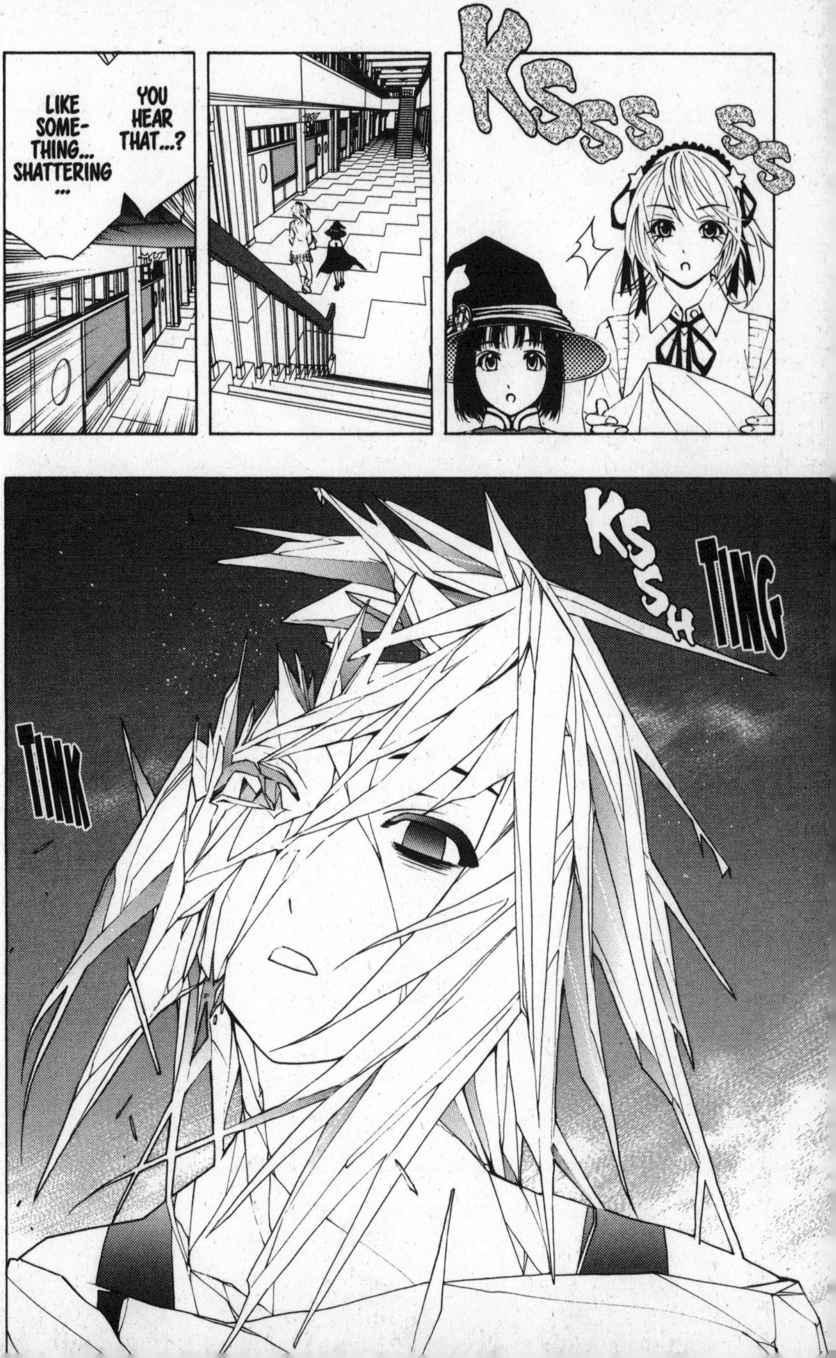
KSSSS SSS
YOU HEAR THAT...?
LIKE SOME-THING... SHATTERING...
KSSSH
TING
TINK

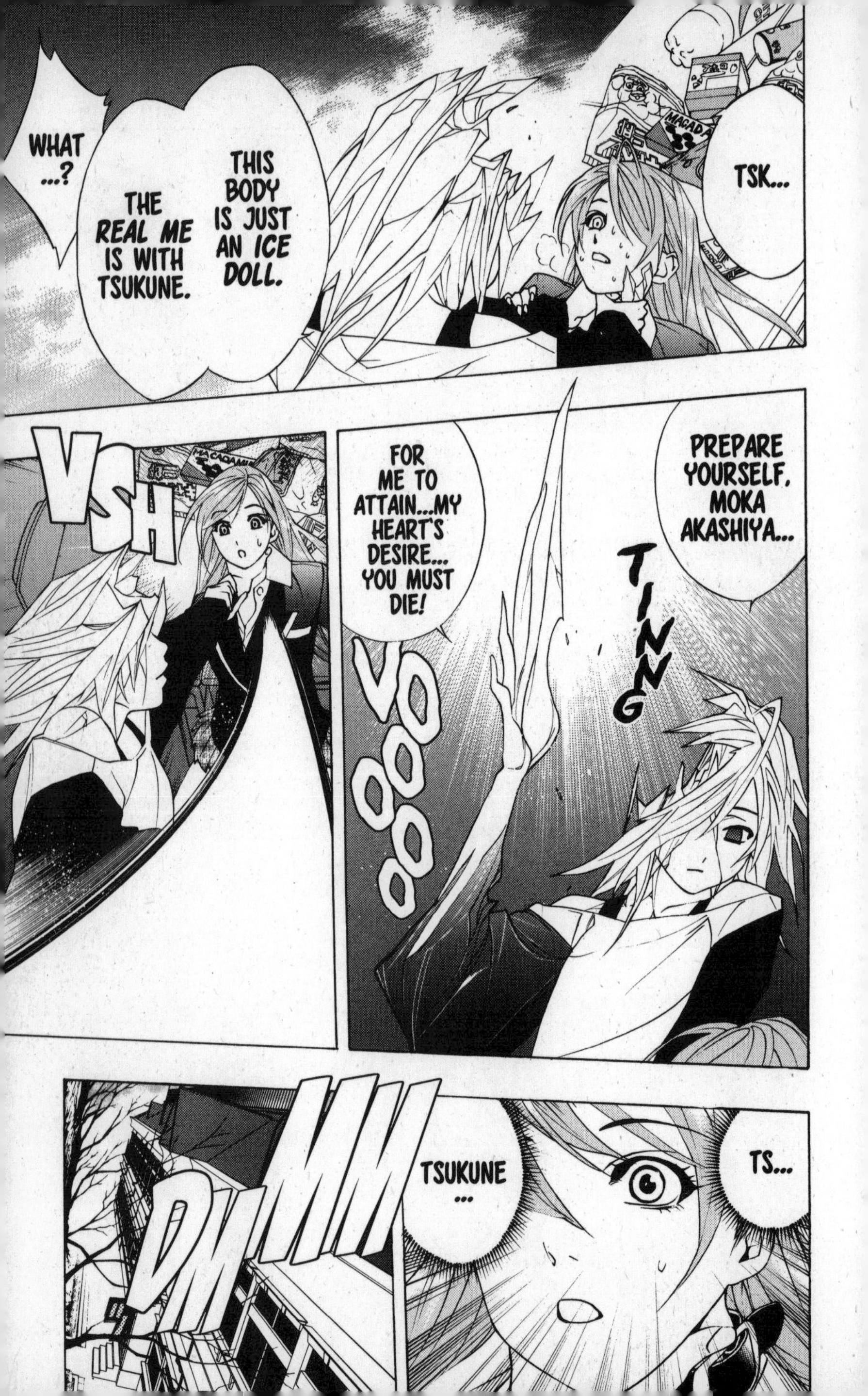
TSK...
THIS BODY IS JUST AN ICE DOLL.
THE REAL ME IS WITH TSUKUNE.
WHAT ...?
PREPARE YOURSELF, MOKA AKASHIYA...
TINNG
FOR ME TO ATTAIN...MY HEART'S DESIRE... YOU MUST DIE!
VOOOOO
VSH
TS...
TSUKUNE ...
DMMM

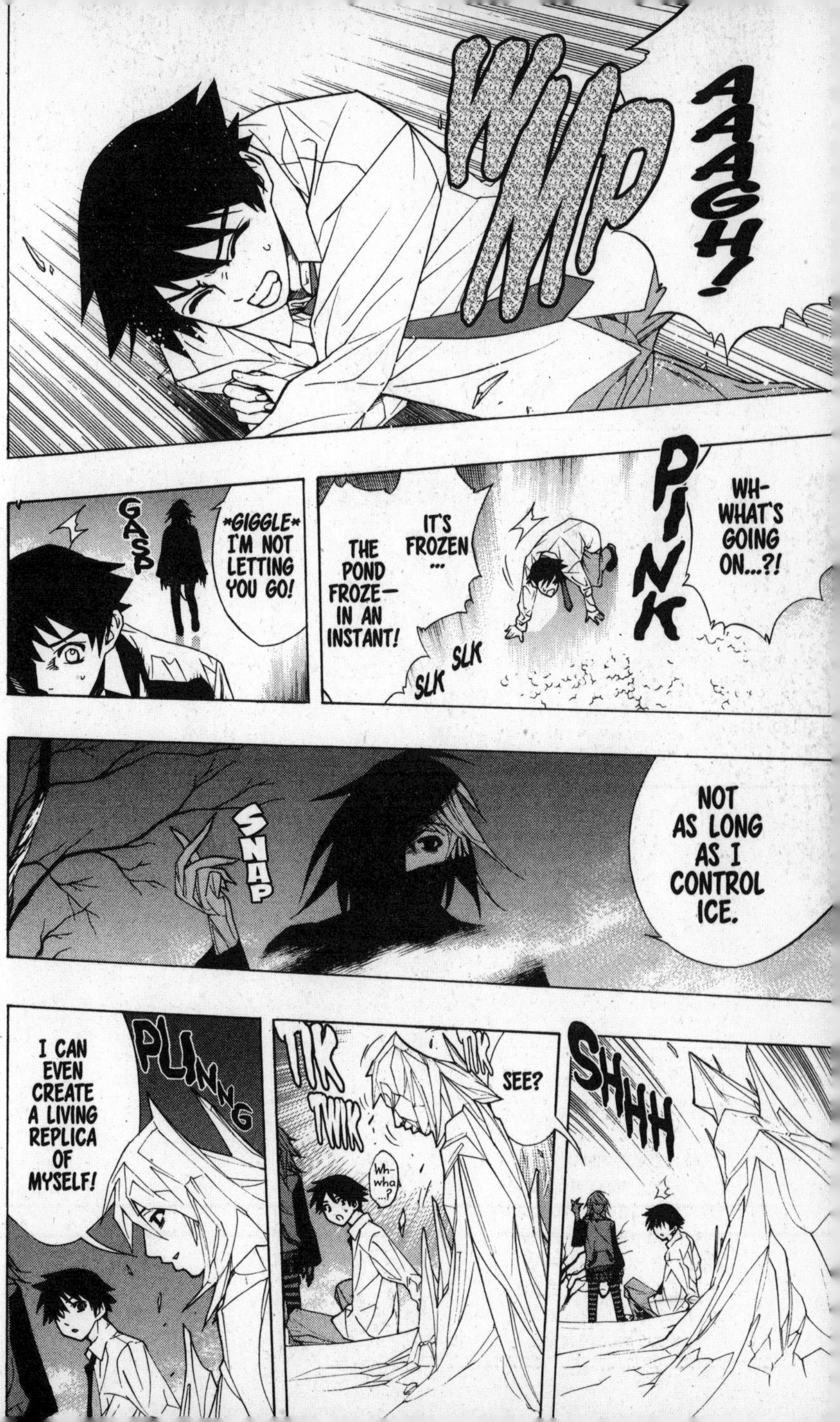
WMP
AAAAGH!
WH-WHAT'S GOING ON...?!
PINK
IT'S FROZEN...
THE POND FROZE— IN AN INSTANT!
SLK SLK
GIGGLE I'M NOT LETTING YOU GO!
GASP
NOT AS LONG AS I CONTROL ICE.
SNAP
SHHH
TIK
SEE?
TIK TWIK
Wh-wha...?
PLINNG
I CAN EVEN CREATE A LIVING REPLICA OF MYSELF!

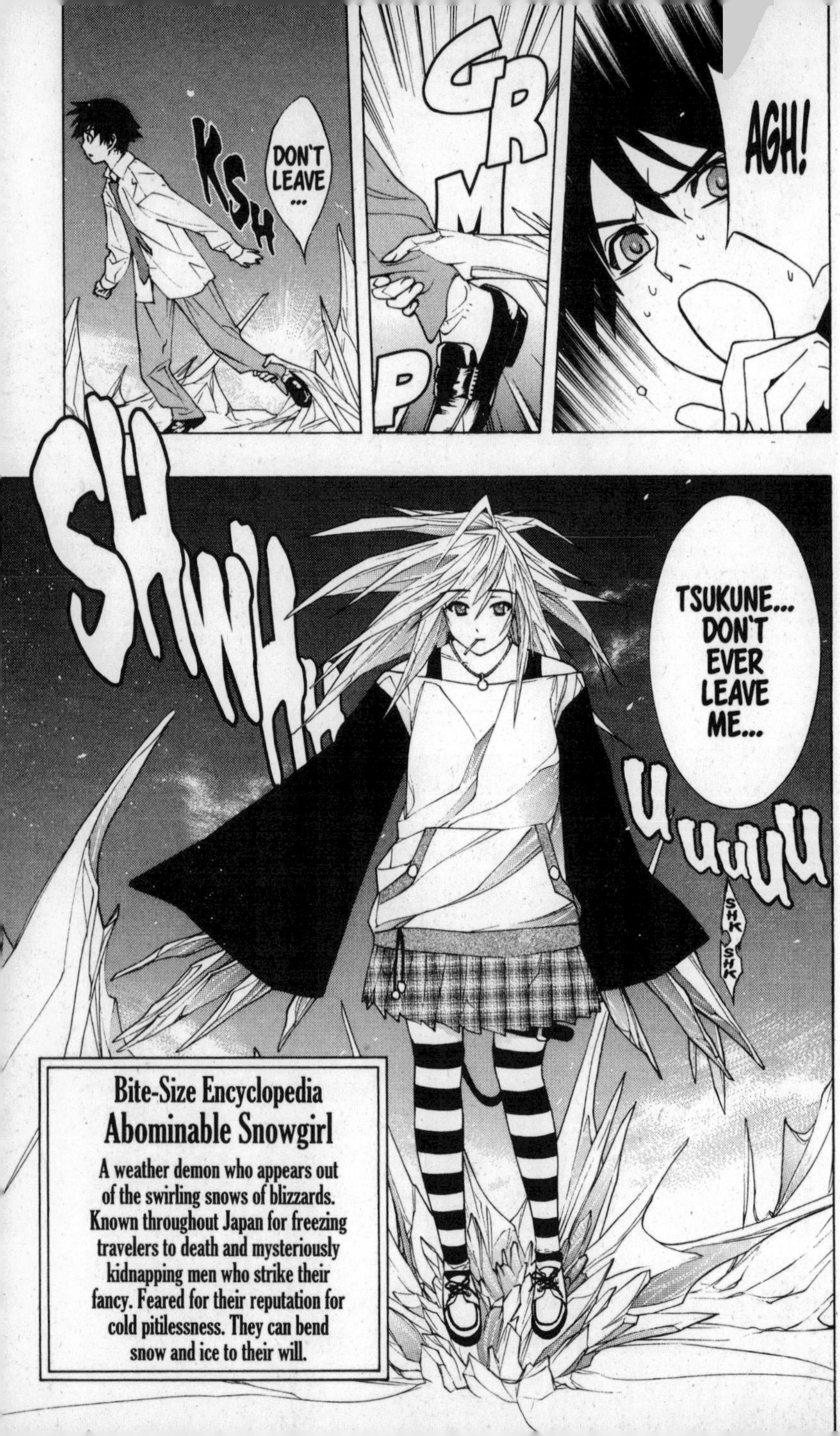
AGH!
GRMP
DON'T LEAVE ...
KSH
TSUKUNE... DON'T EVER LEAVE ME...
UuuuU
SHK SHK
SHWH
Bite-Size Encyclopedia
Abominable Snowgirl
A weather demon who appears out of the swirling snows of blizzards. Known throughout Japan for freezing travelers to death and mysteriously kidnapping men who strike their fancy. Feared for their reputation for cold pitilessness. They can bend snow and ice to their will.

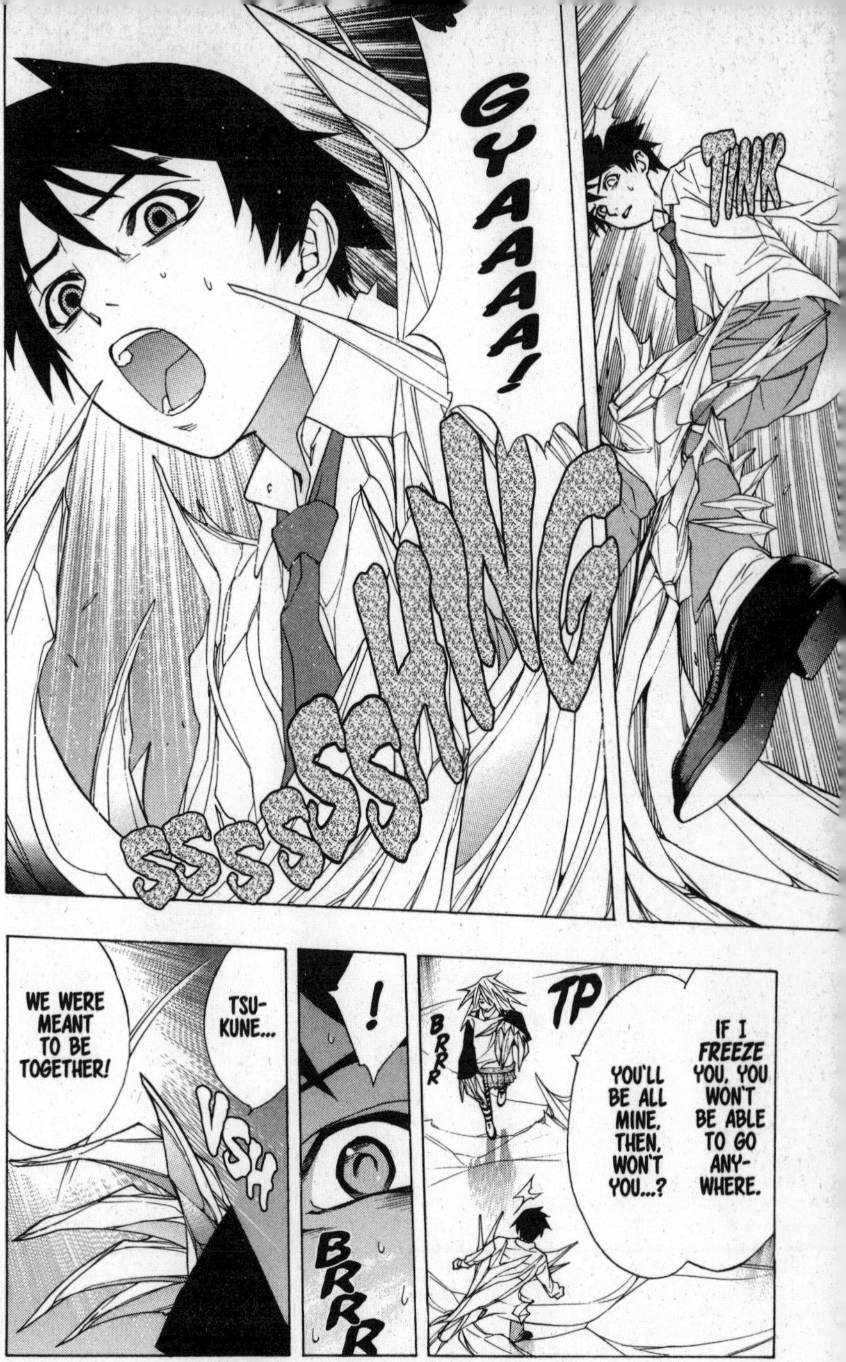
TINK
GYAAAAA!
SSSSSSHING
TP
BRRR
IF I FREEZE YOU, YOU WON'T BE ABLE TO GO ANY-WHERE.
YOU'LL BE ALL MINE, THEN, WON'T YOU...?
!
BRRRR
TSU-KUNE...
WE WERE MEANT TO BE TOGETHER!
VSH

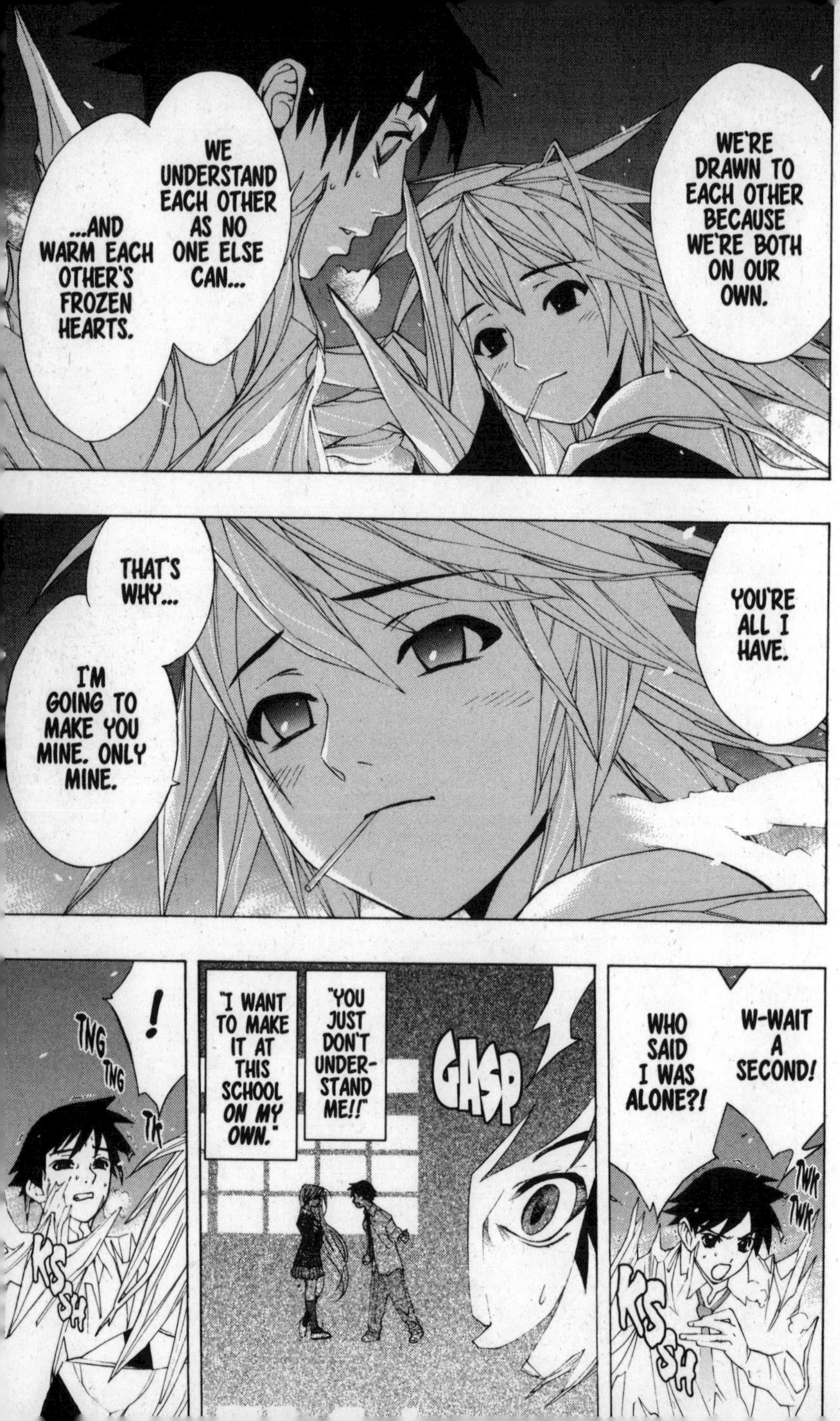

WE'RE DRAWN TO EACH OTHER BECAUSE WE'RE BOTH ON OUR OWN.
WE UNDERSTAND EACH OTHER AS NO ONE ELSE CAN...
...AND WARM EACH OTHER'S FROZEN HEARTS.
YOU'RE ALL I HAVE.
THAT'S WHY...
I'M GOING TO MAKE YOU MINE. ONLY MINE.
W-WAIT A SECOND!
WHO SAID I WAS ALONE?!
TWK TWK
KSSH
GASP
"YOU JUST DON'T UNDERSTAND ME!!"
"I WANT TO MAKE IT AT THIS SCHOOL ON MY OWN."
!
TNG TNG
TK
KSSH

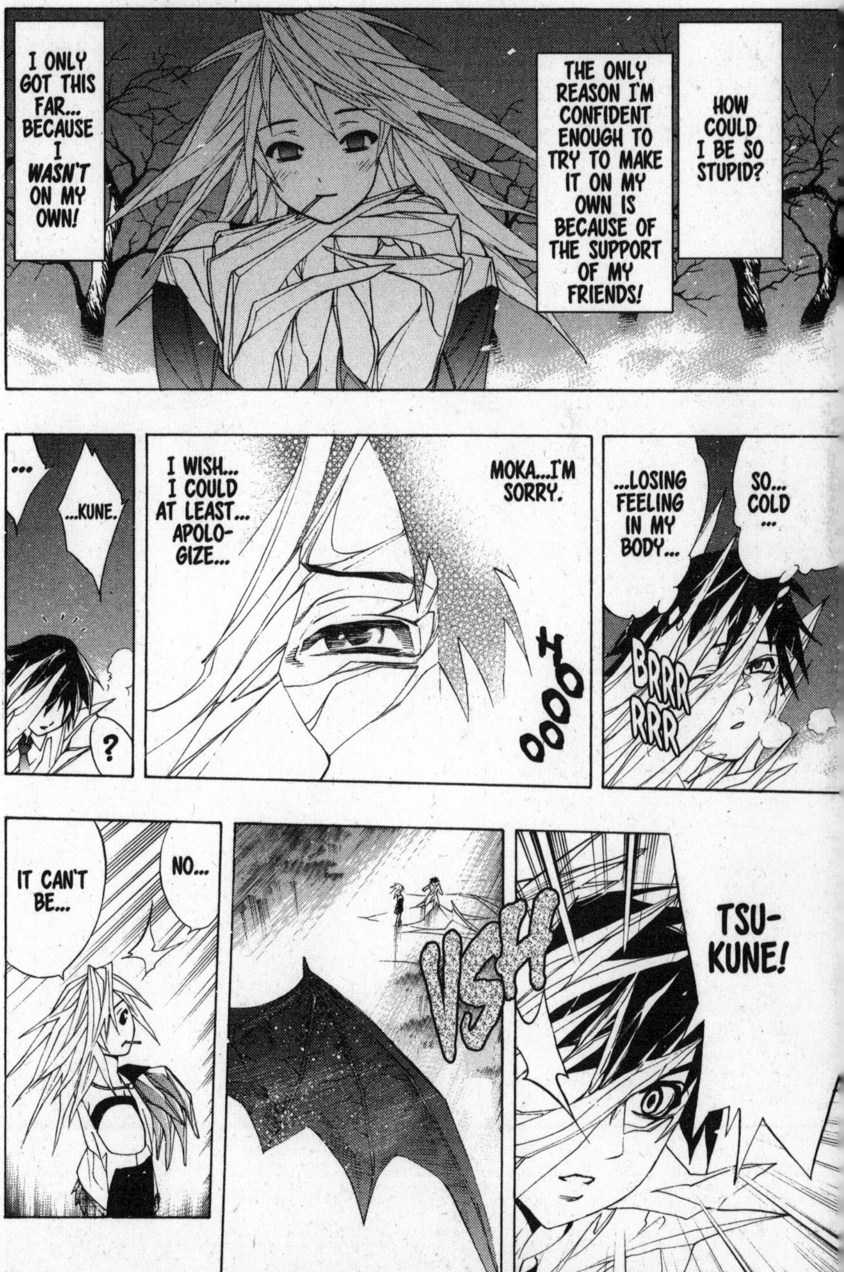
HOW COULD I BE SO STUPID?
THE ONLY REASON I'M CONFIDENT ENOUGH TO TRY TO MAKE IT ON MY OWN IS BECAUSE OF THE SUPPORT OF MY FRIENDS!
I ONLY GOT THIS FAR... BECAUSE I *WASN'T* ON MY OWN!
SO... COLD ...
...LOSING FEELING IN MY BODY...
BRRRRRR
MOKA...I'M SORRY.
I WISH... I COULD AT LEAST... APOLOGIZE...
HOOOO
...
...KUNE.
?
TSU-KUNE!
VSH
NO...
IT CAN'T BE...

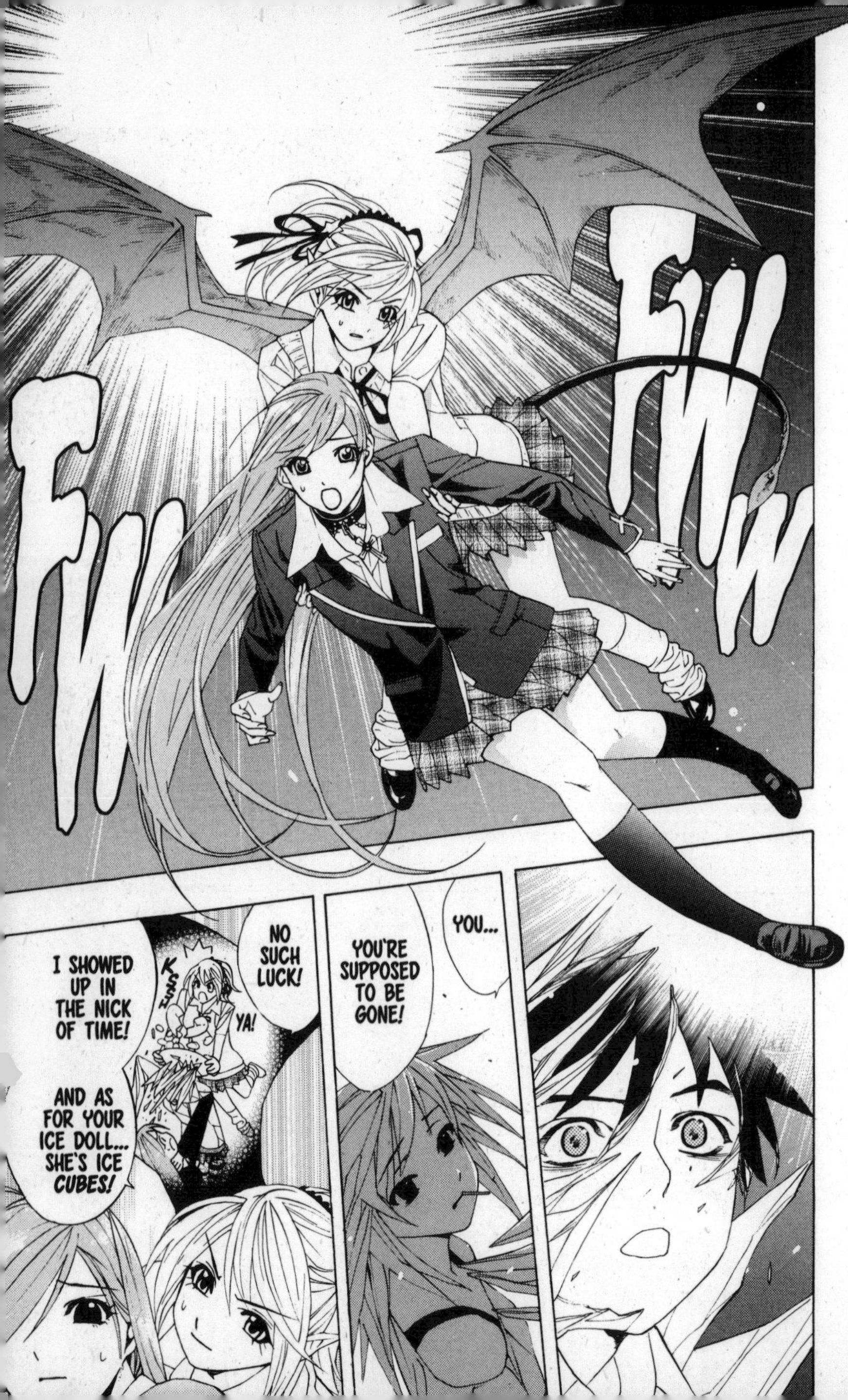
FW
FW
FW
YOU...
YOU'RE SUPPOSED TO BE GONE!
NO SUCH LUCK!
I SHOWED UP IN THE NICK OF TIME!
YA!
AND AS FOR YOUR ICE DOLL... SHE'S ICE *CUBES!*

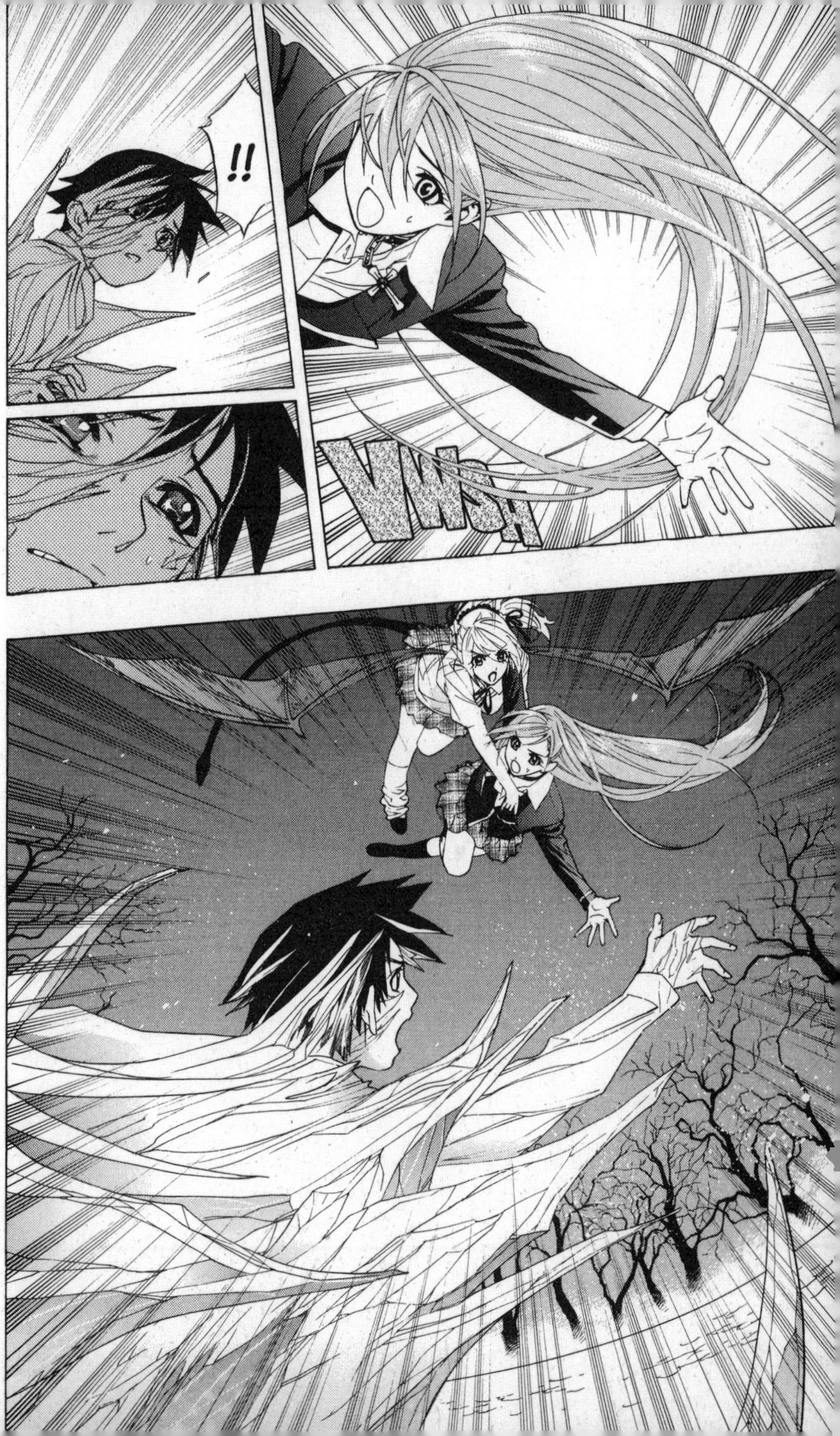
!!
VWSH

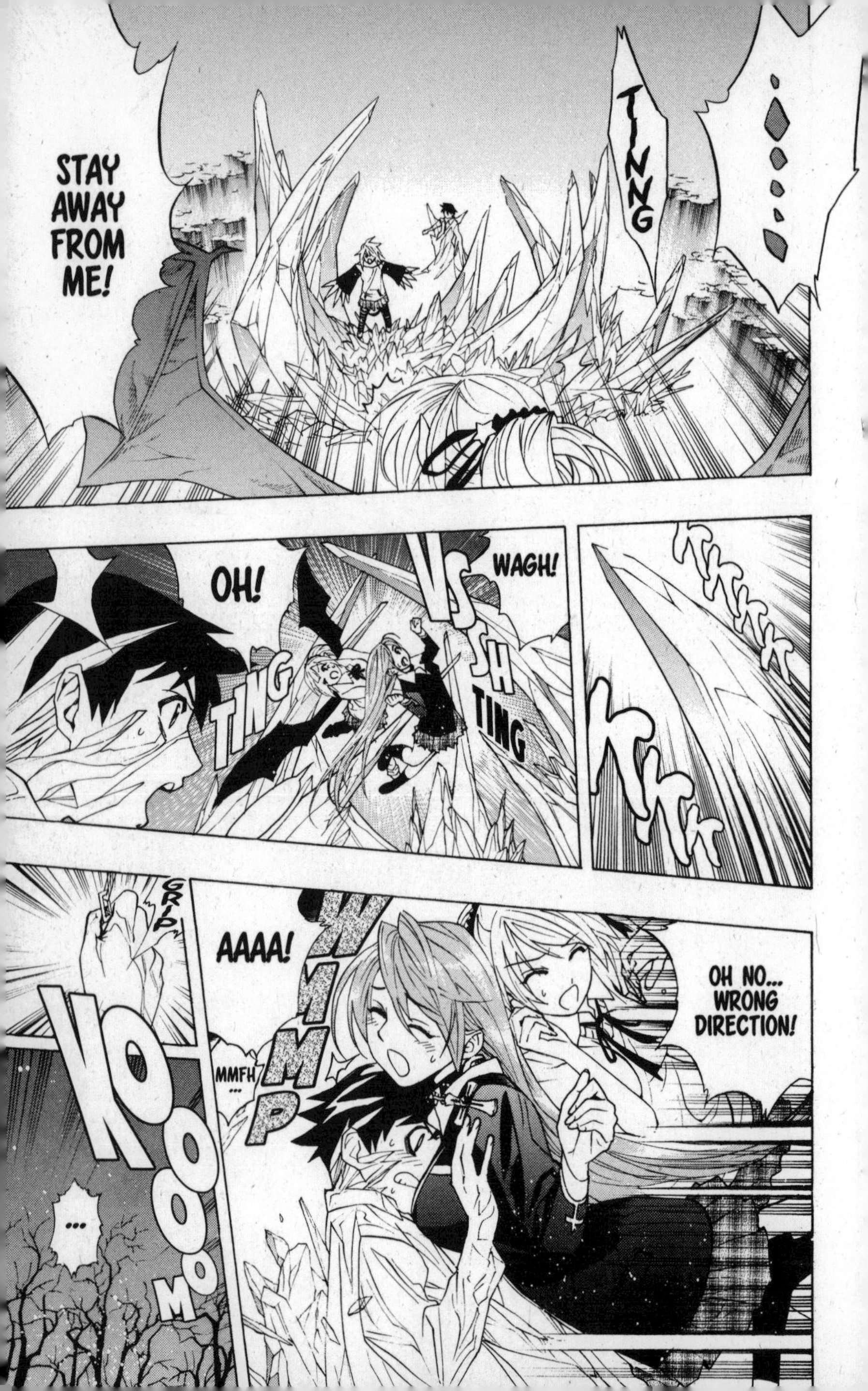

...
TINNG
STAY AWAY FROM ME!
KKKKK
KKKK
WAGH!
VSSH
TING
OH!
TING
OH NO... WRONG DIRECTION!
AAAA!
WMMP
MMFH...
GRIP
VOOOOOM
...

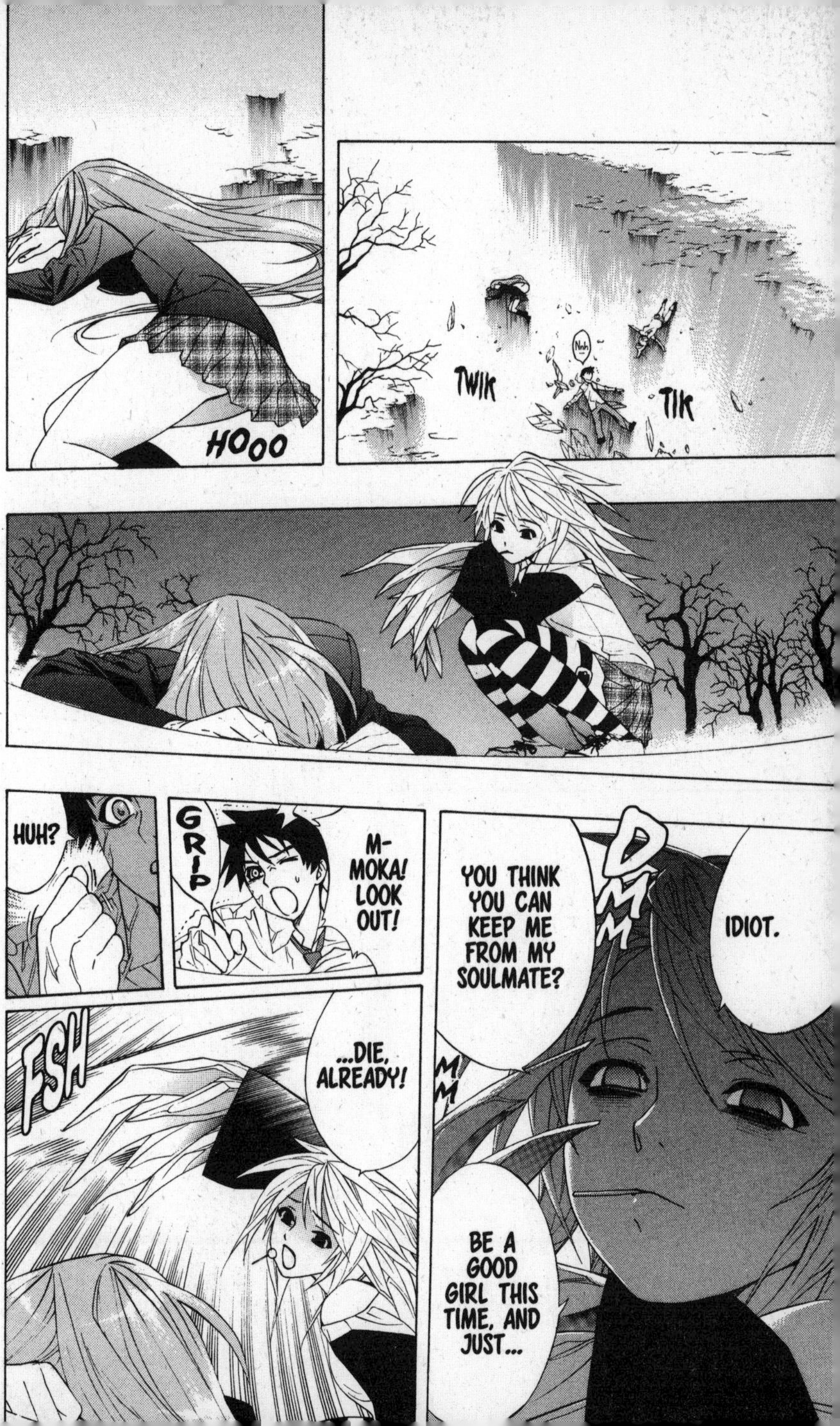
Nnh...
TWIK
TIK
HOOO
IDIOT.
YOU THINK YOU CAN KEEP ME FROM MY SOULMATE?
DMMMM
BE A GOOD GIRL THIS TIME, AND JUST...
M-MOKA! LOOK OUT!
GRIP
HUH?
...DIE, ALREADY!
FSH

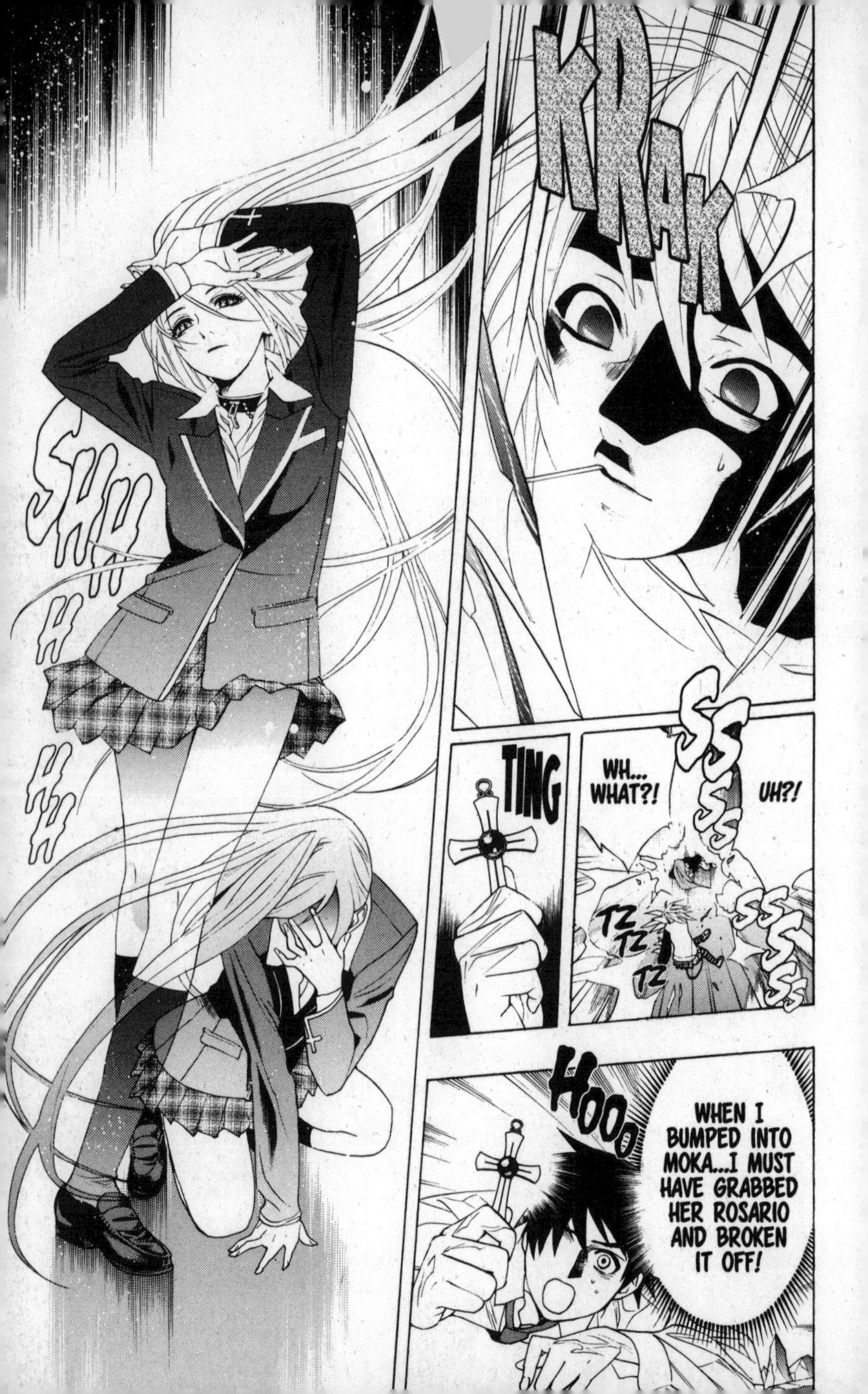
KRAK
SSSS
UH?!
WH... WHAT?!
SSSSS
TZ TZ TZ
TING
WHEN I BUMPED INTO MOKA...I MUST HAVE GRABBED HER ROSARIO AND BROKEN IT OFF!
HOOO
SHHHH
HHH

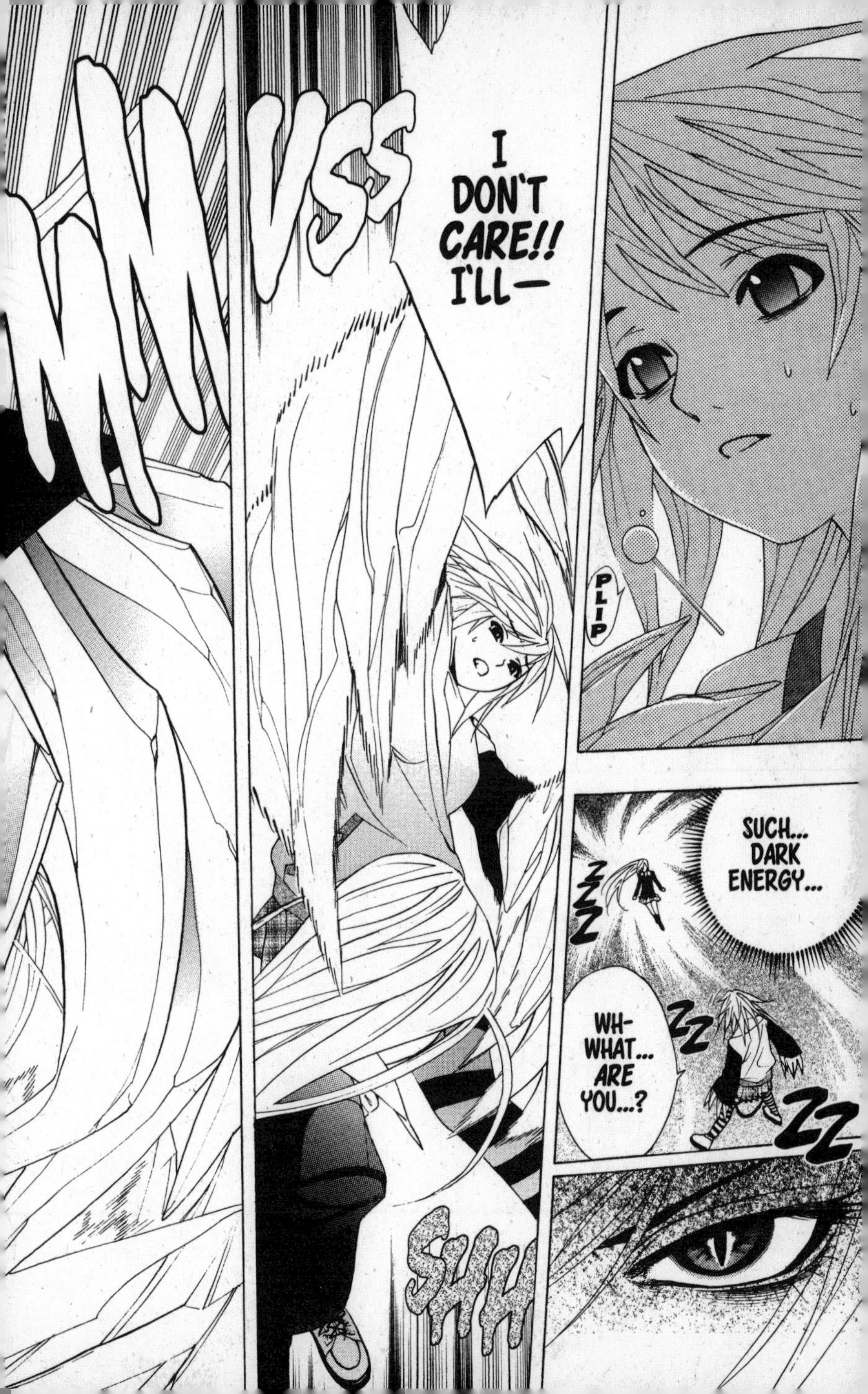
PLIP
SUCH... DARK ENERGY...
ZZZ
WH- WHAT... ARE YOU...?
ZZ
ZZ
I DON'T CARE!! I'LL—
VSS
SHH
WMM

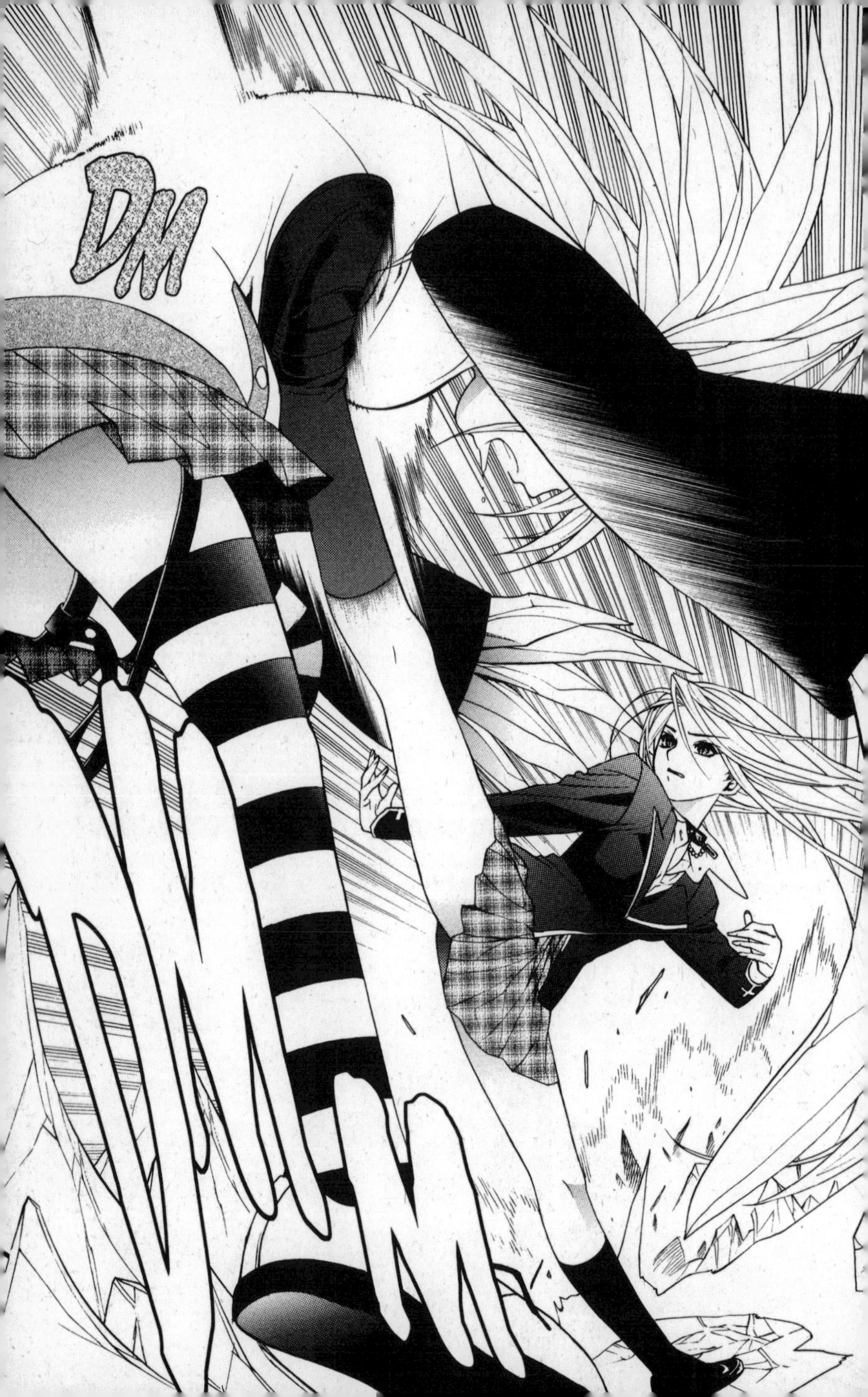
DM
DMM

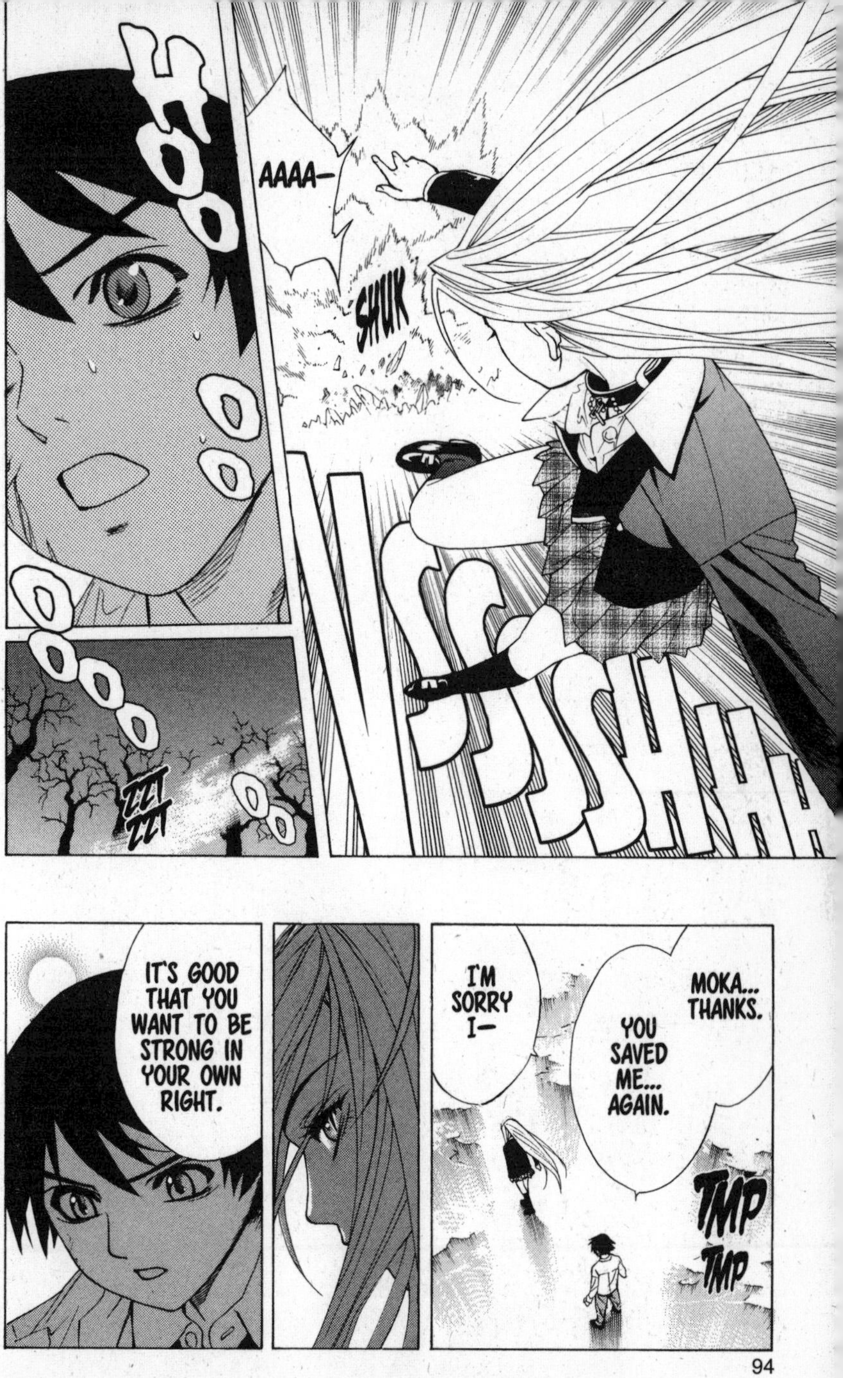
AAAA—
SHUK
VSSSHHH
HOOOOOOOOOOOOOO
ZZZ
ZZZ
MOKA... THANKS.
YOU SAVED ME... AGAIN.
I'M SORRY I—
TMP
TMP
IT'S GOOD THAT YOU WANT TO BE STRONG IN YOUR OWN RIGHT.

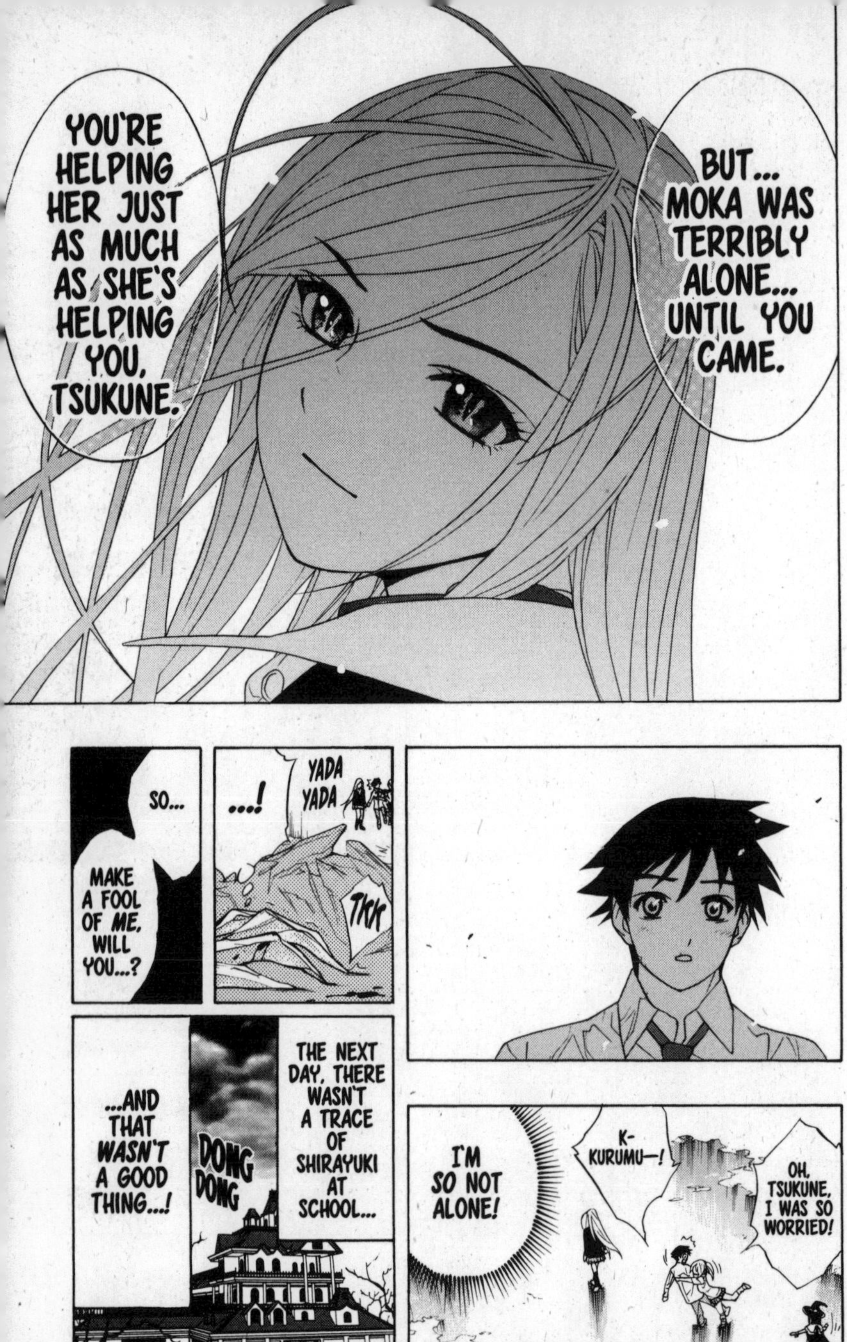
BUT... MOKA WAS TERRIBLY ALONE... UNTIL YOU CAME.
YOU'RE HELPING HER JUST AS MUCH AS SHE'S HELPING YOU, TSUKUNE.
YADA YADA
...!
TKK
SO...
MAKE A FOOL OF ME, WILL YOU...?
OH, TSUKUNE, I WAS SO WORRIED!
K-KURUMU—!
I'M SO NOT ALONE!
THE NEXT DAY, THERE WASN'T A TRACE OF SHIRAYUKI AT SCHOOL...
DONG DONG
...AND THAT WASN'T A GOOD THING...!

ROSARIO+VAMPIRE

19: Girl of the Thaw

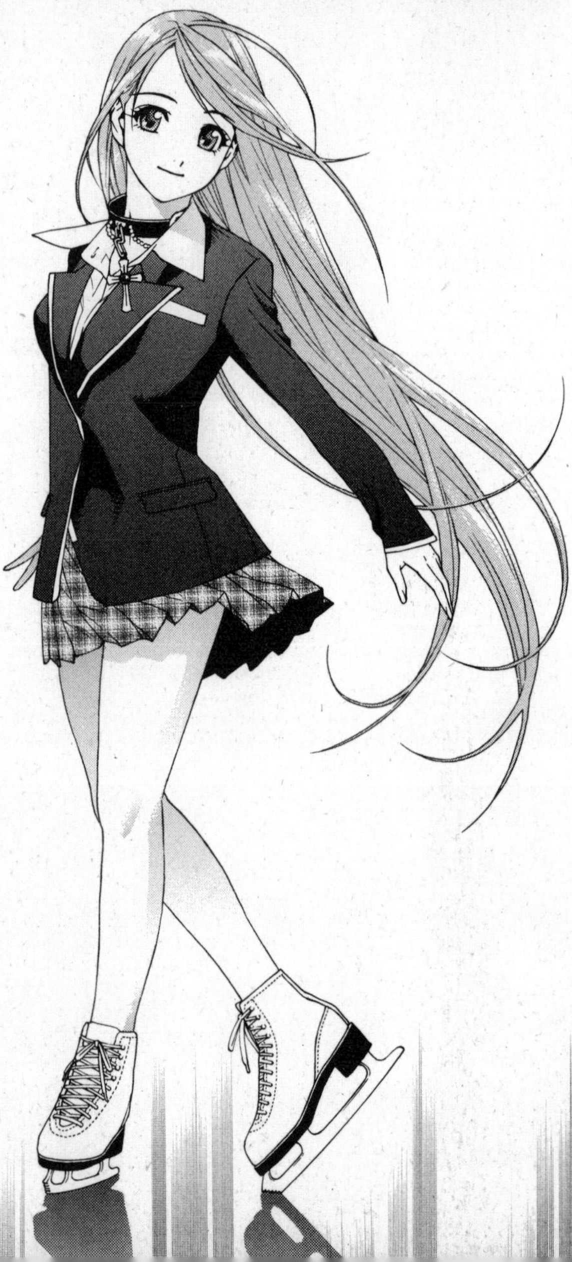

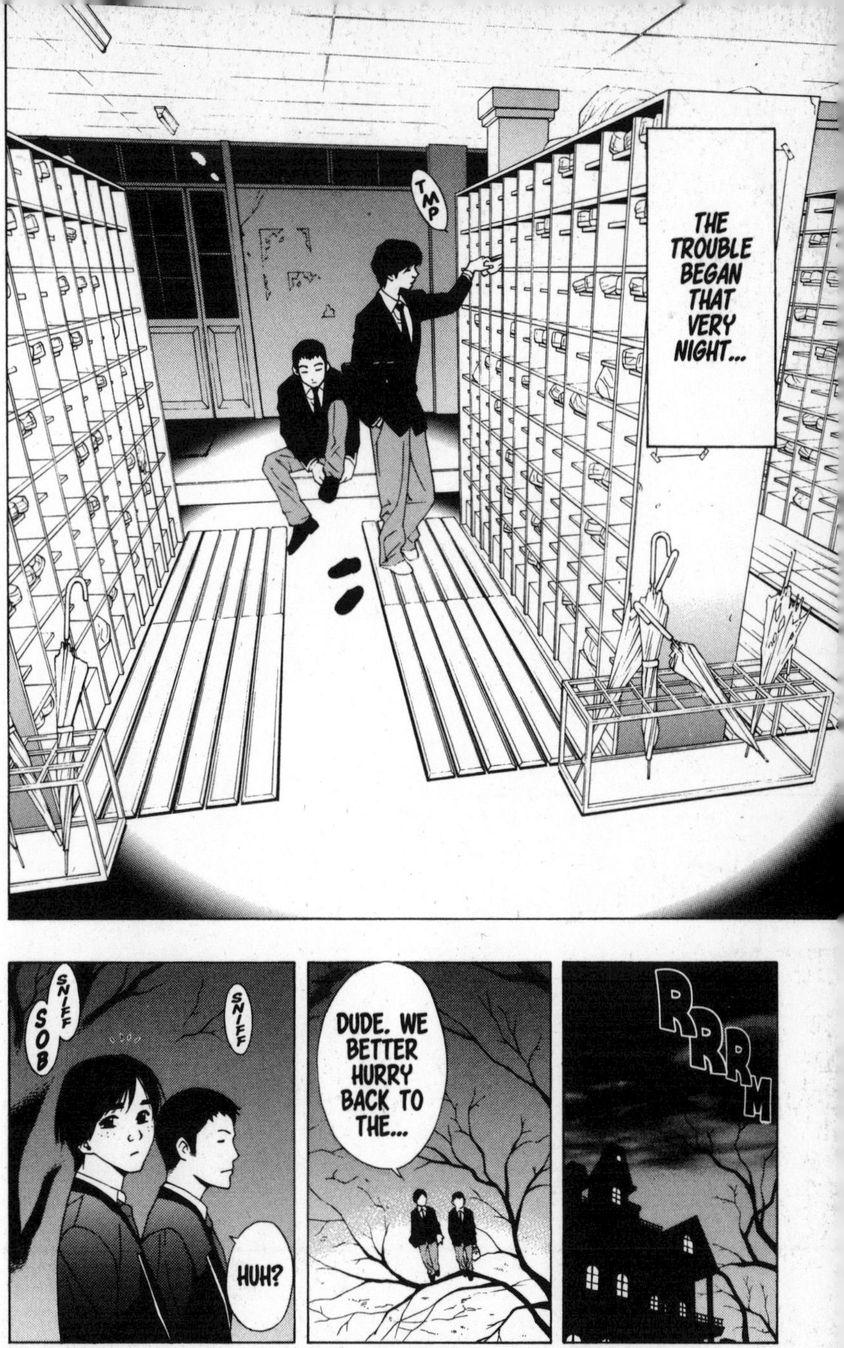
THE TROUBLE BEGAN THAT VERY NIGHT...
TMP
RRRM
DUDE. WE BETTER HURRY BACK TO THE...
SNIFF
SNIFF SOB
HUH?

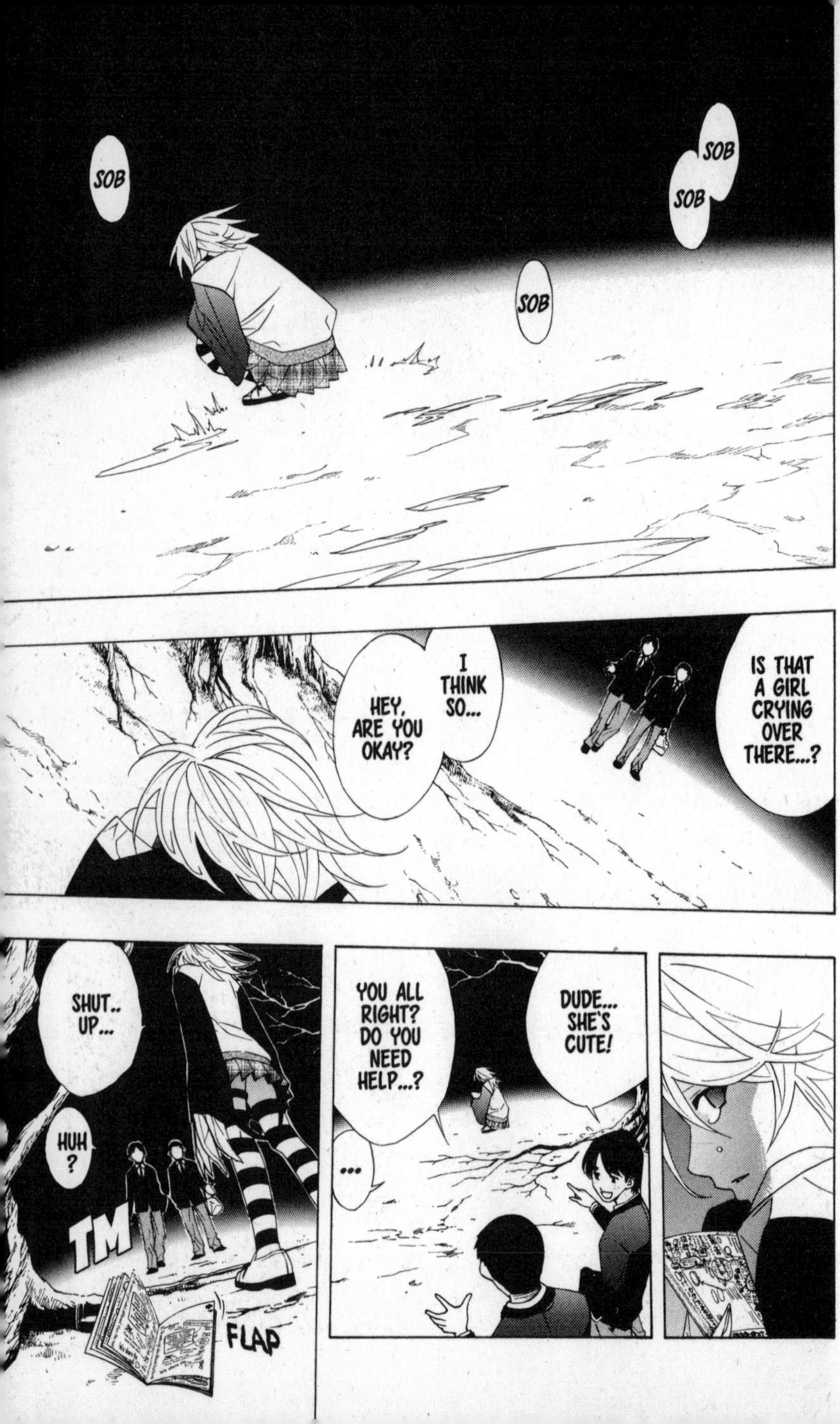
SOB
SOB
SOB
SOB
IS THAT A GIRL CRYING OVER THERE...?
I THINK SO...
HEY, ARE YOU OKAY?
DUDE... SHE'S CUTE!
YOU ALL RIGHT? DO YOU NEED HELP...?
...
SHUT.. UP...
HUH ?
TM
FLAP

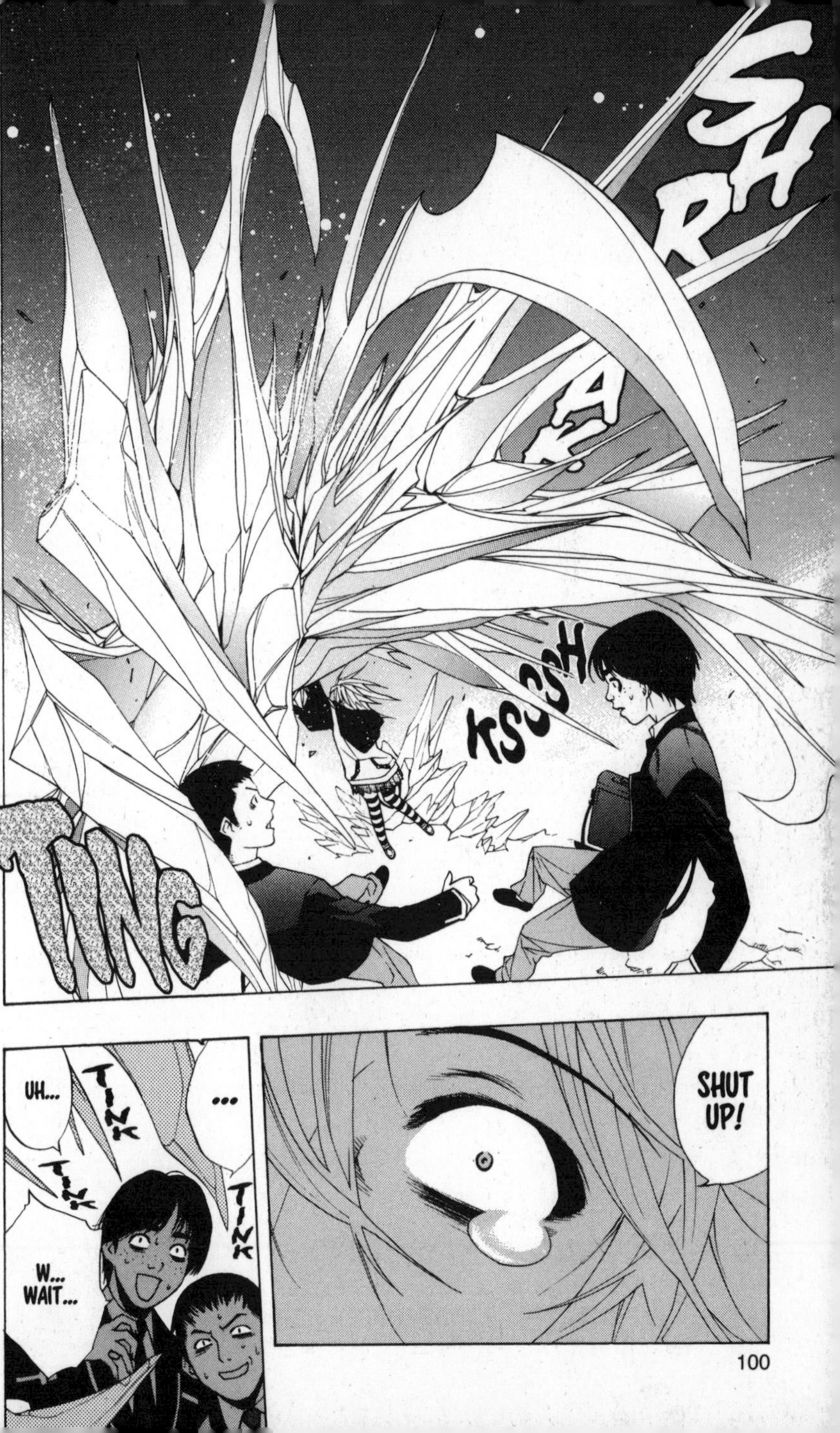
SHRAK!
KSSSH
TING
SHUT UP!
...
TINK
UH...
TINK
TINK
W... WAIT...

READ THIS WAY

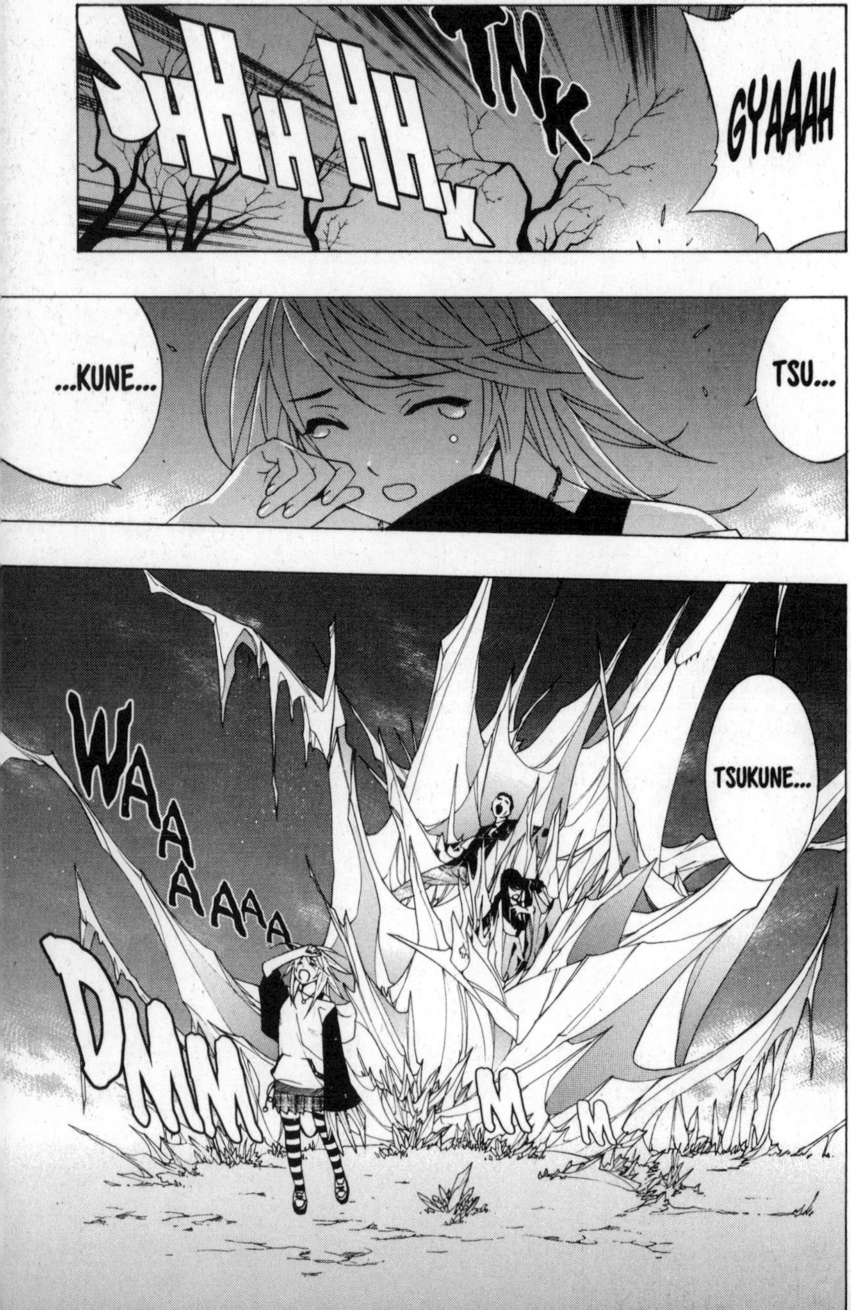
GYAAAH
TNK
SHHHHHK
TSU...
...KUNE...
TSUKUNE...
WAAAAAA
DMMMMM

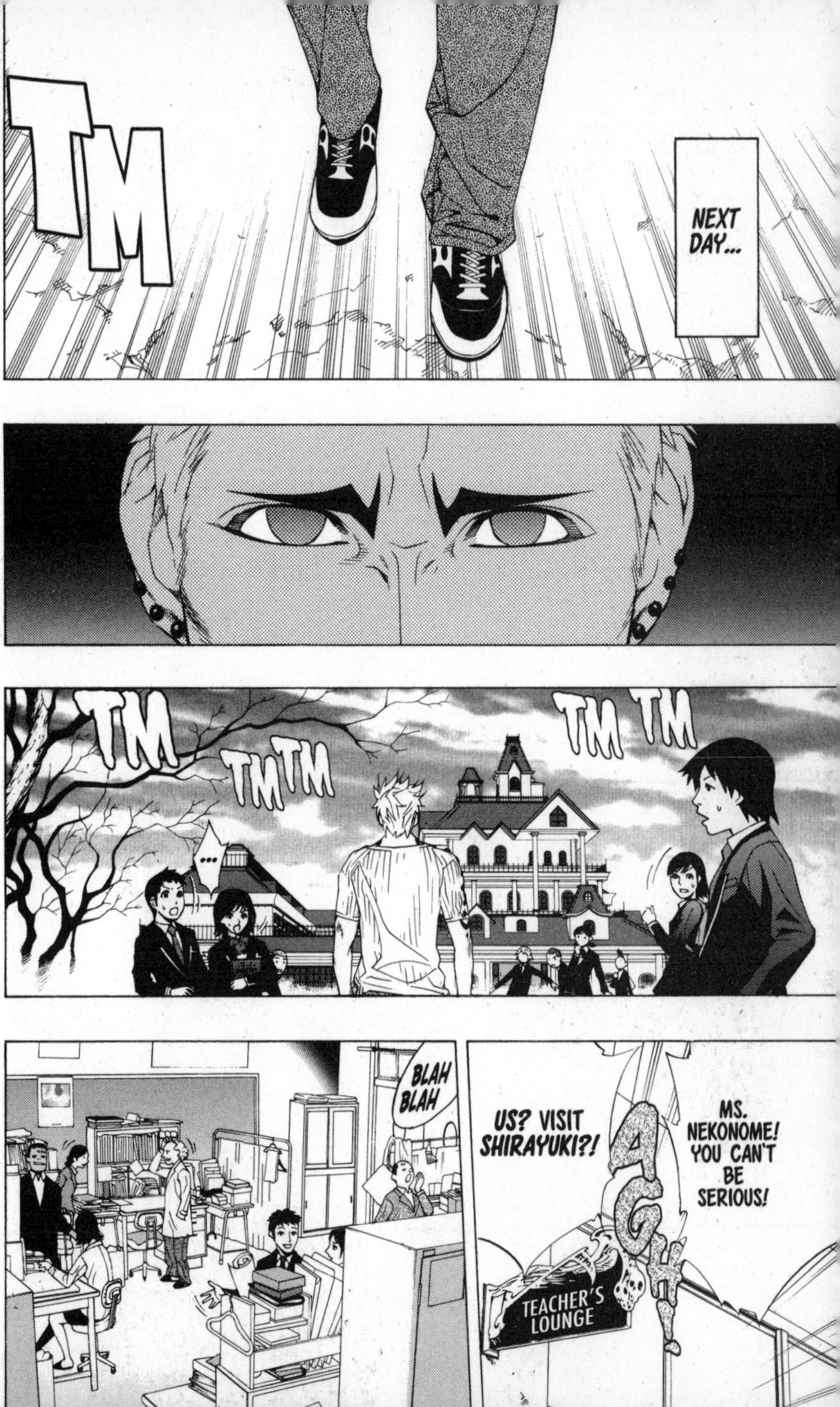
NEXT DAY...
TM
TM TM
TMTM
TM
...
MS. NEKONOME! YOU CAN'T BE SERIOUS!
US? VISIT SHIRAYUKI?!
AGH
TEACHER'S LOUNGE
BLAH BLAH

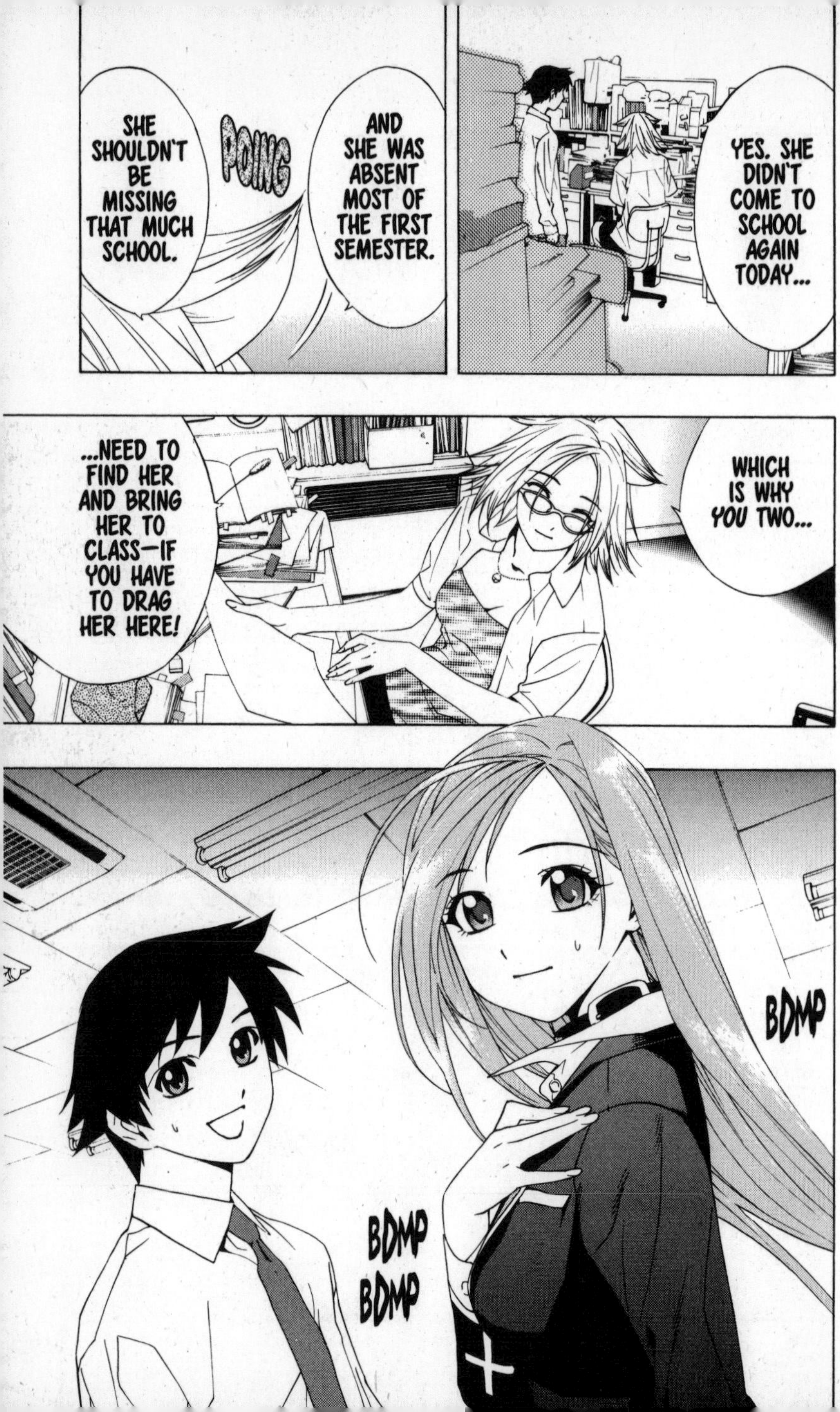
YES. SHE DIDN'T COME TO SCHOOL AGAIN TODAY...
AND SHE WAS ABSENT MOST OF THE FIRST SEMESTER.
POING
SHE SHOULDN'T BE MISSING THAT MUCH SCHOOL.
WHICH IS WHY YOU TWO...
...NEED TO FIND HER AND BRING HER TO CLASS—IF YOU HAVE TO DRAG HER HERE!
BDMP
BDMP
BDMP
BDMP

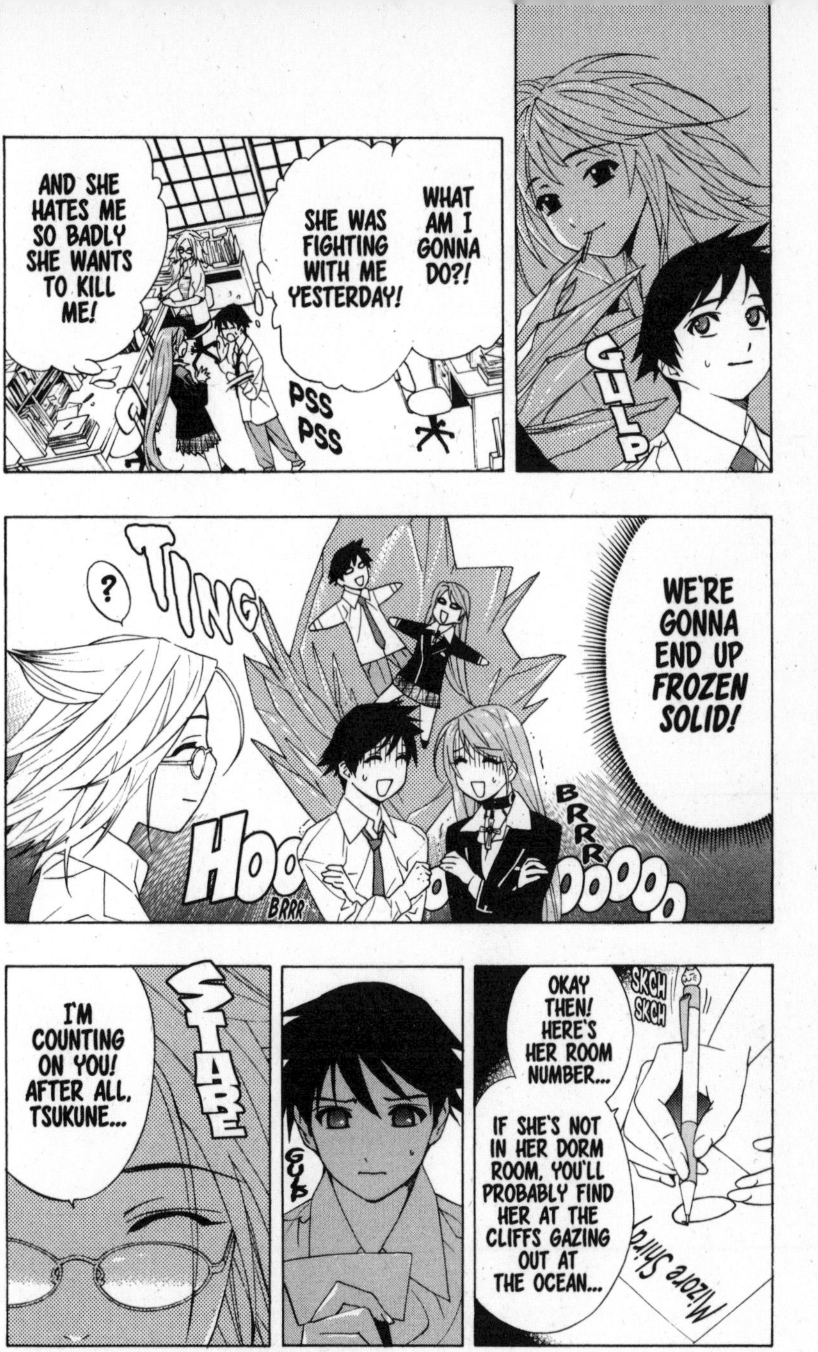
GULP
WHAT AM I GONNA DO?!
SHE WAS FIGHTING WITH ME YESTERDAY!
AND SHE HATES ME SO BADLY SHE WANTS TO KILL ME!
PSS PSS
WE'RE GONNA END UP FROZEN SOLID!
TING
?
BRRR
HOOOOOOOOO
BRRR
SKCH SKCH
OKAY THEN! HERE'S HER ROOM NUMBER...
IF SHE'S NOT IN HER DORM ROOM, YOU'LL PROBABLY FIND HER AT THE CLIFFS GAZING OUT AT THE OCEAN...
GULP
STARE
I'M COUNTING ON YOU! AFTER ALL, TSUKUNE...

READ THIS WAY

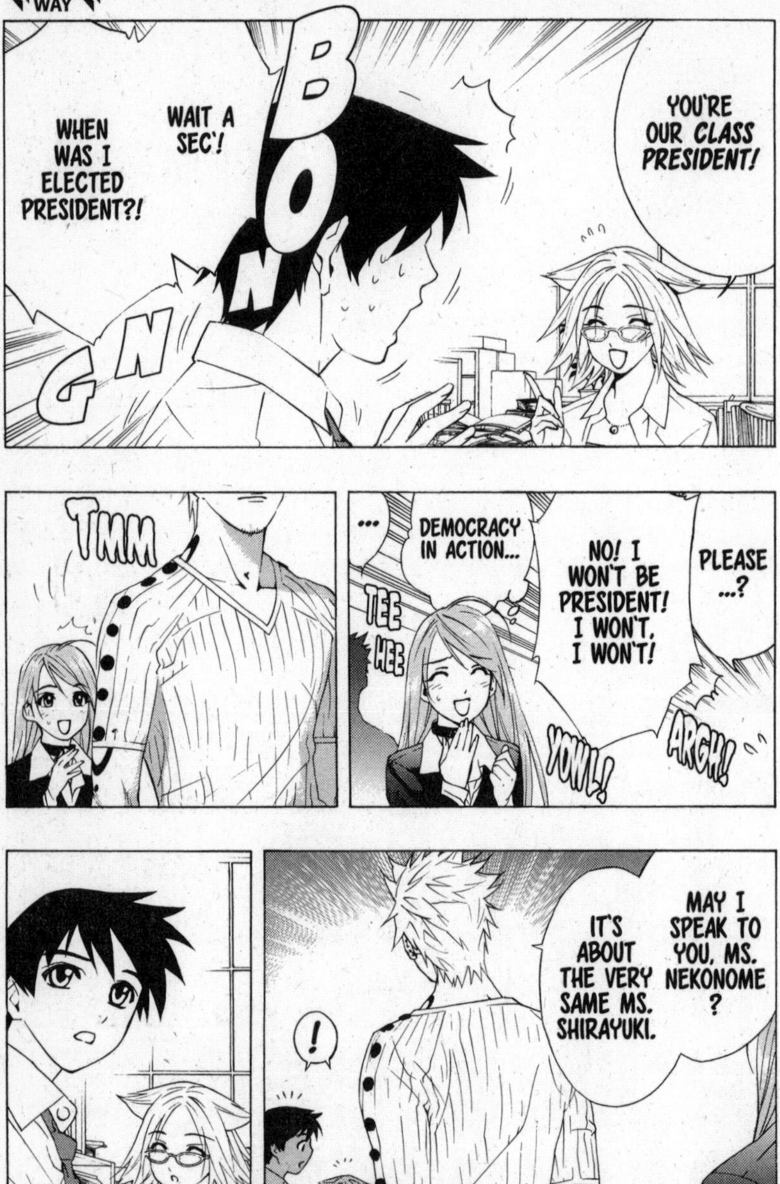

YOU'RE OUR CLASS PRESIDENT!
BONNG
WAIT A SEC'!
WHEN WAS I ELECTED PRESIDENT?!
PLEASE ...?
NO! I WON'T BE PRESIDENT! I WON'T, I WON'T!
ARGH!!
YOWL!
DEMOCRACY IN ACTION...
...
TEE HEE
TMM
MAY I SPEAK TO YOU, MS. NEKONOME?
IT'S ABOUT THE VERY SAME MS. SHIRAYUKI.
!

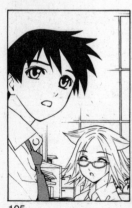

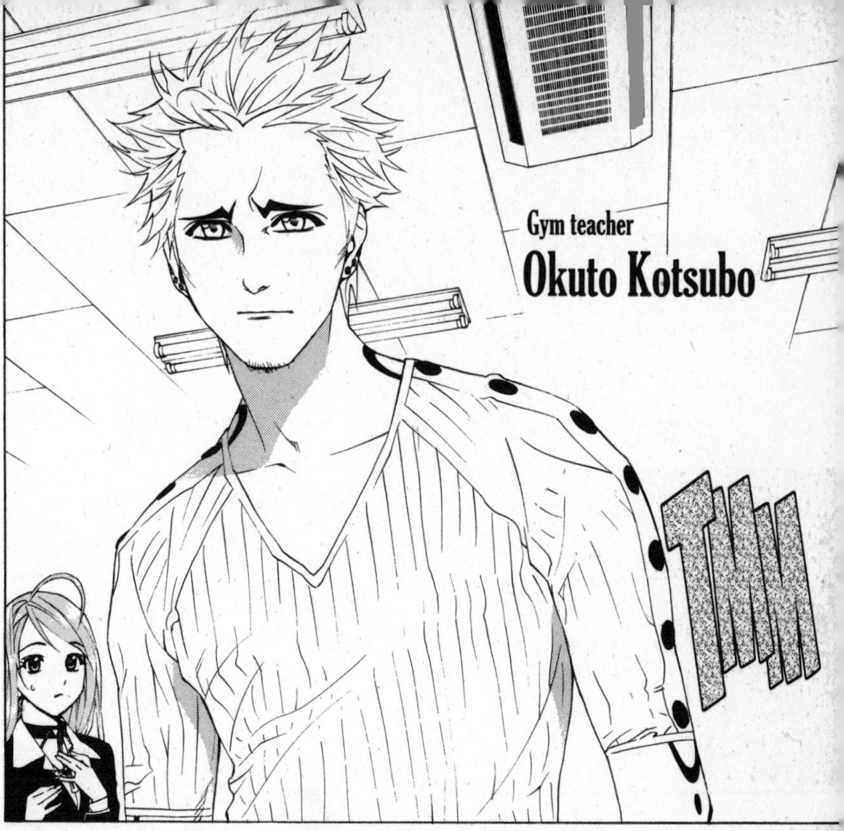
Gym teacher
Okuto Kotsubo
TMM

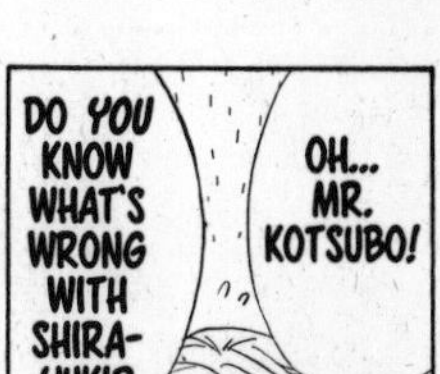
OH... MR. KOTSUBO!
DO YOU KNOW WHAT'S WRONG WITH SHIRAYUKI?

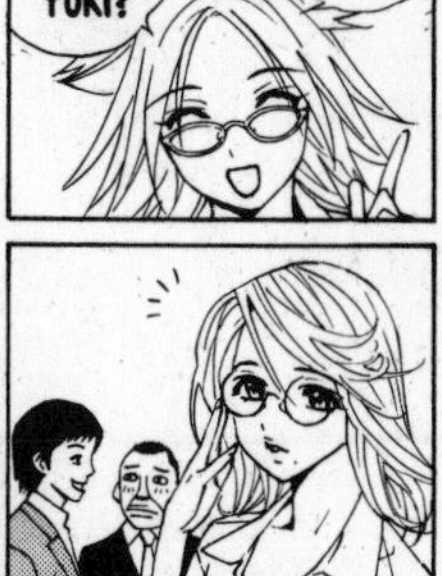

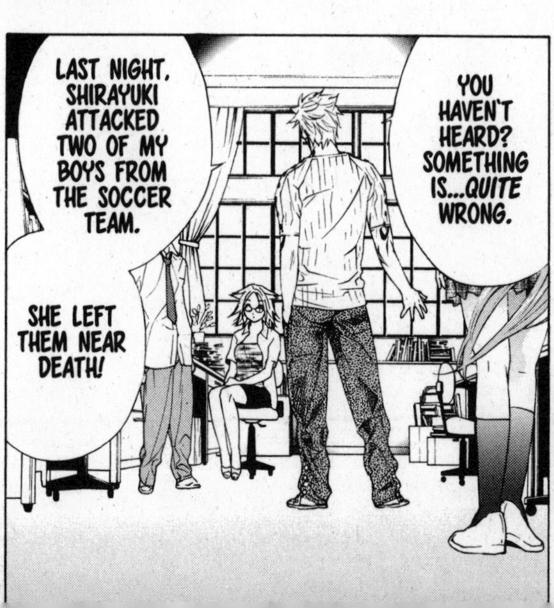
YOU HAVEN'T HEARD? SOMETHING IS...QUITE WRONG.
LAST NIGHT, SHIRAYUKI ATTACKED TWO OF MY BOYS FROM THE SOCCER TEAM.
SHE LEFT THEM NEAR DEATH!

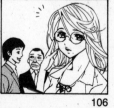

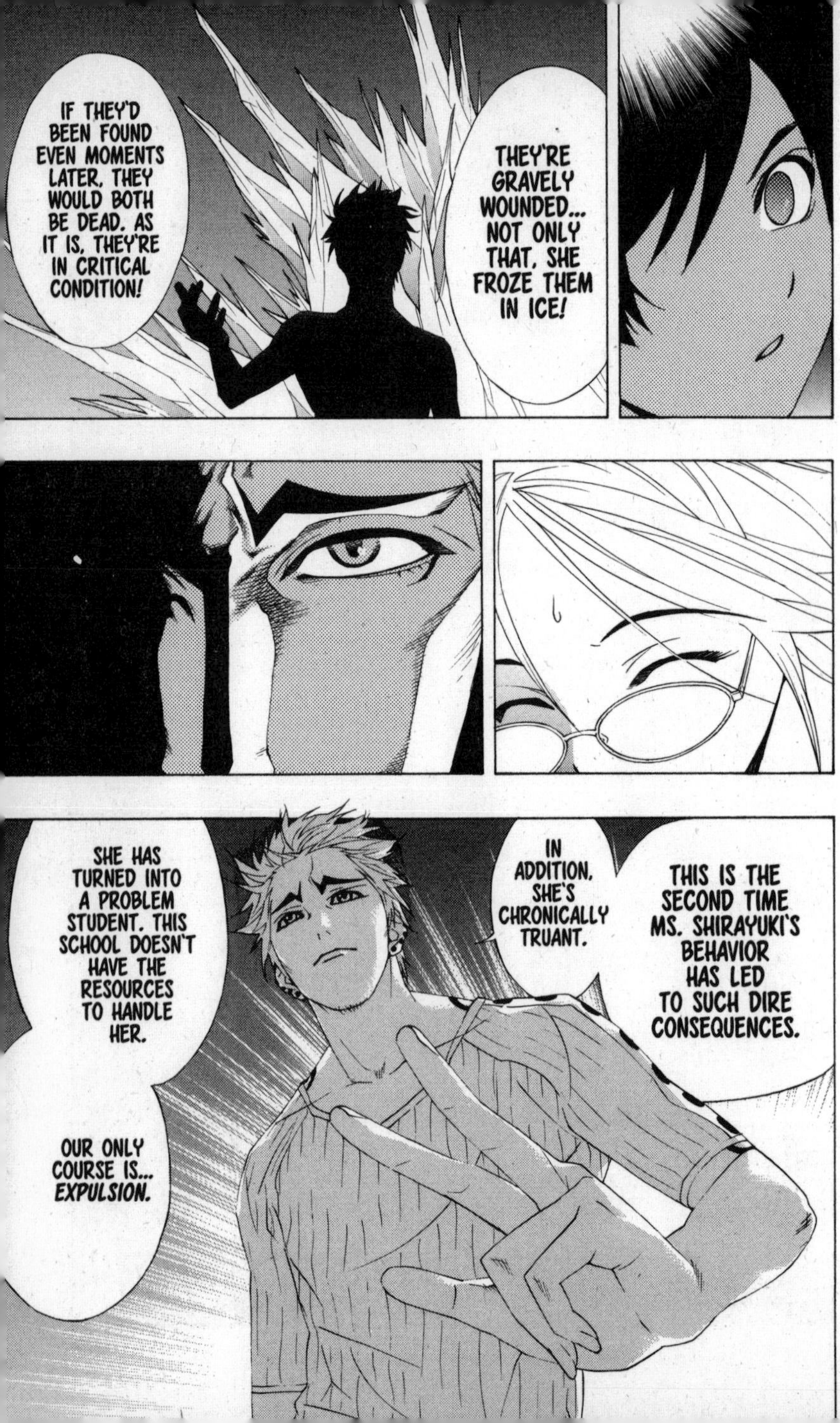
THEY'RE GRAVELY WOUNDED... NOT ONLY THAT, SHE FROZE THEM IN ICE!
IF THEY'D BEEN FOUND EVEN MOMENTS LATER, THEY WOULD BOTH BE DEAD. AS IT IS, THEY'RE IN CRITICAL CONDITION!
THIS IS THE SECOND TIME MS. SHIRAYUKI'S BEHAVIOR HAS LED TO SUCH DIRE CONSEQUENCES.
IN ADDITION, SHE'S CHRONICALLY TRUANT.
SHE HAS TURNED INTO A PROBLEM STUDENT. THIS SCHOOL DOESN'T HAVE THE RESOURCES TO HANDLE HER.
OUR ONLY COURSE IS... *EXPULSION.*

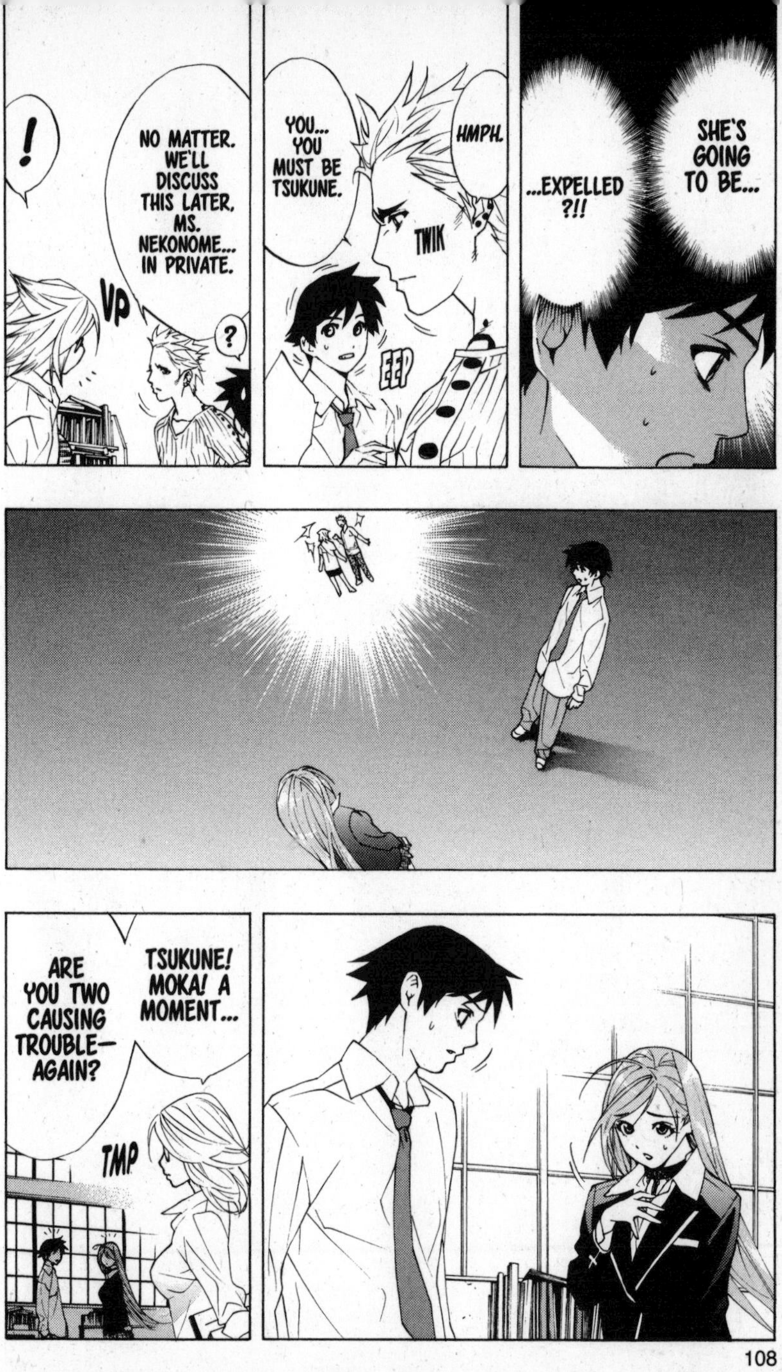
SHE'S GOING TO BE...
...EXPELLED ?!!
HMPH.
TWIK
YOU... YOU MUST BE TSUKUNE.
EEP
NO MATTER. WE'LL DISCUSS THIS LATER, MS. NEKONOME... IN PRIVATE.
!
VP
?
TSUKUNE! MOKA! A MOMENT...
ARE YOU TWO CAUSING TROUBLE—AGAIN?
TMP

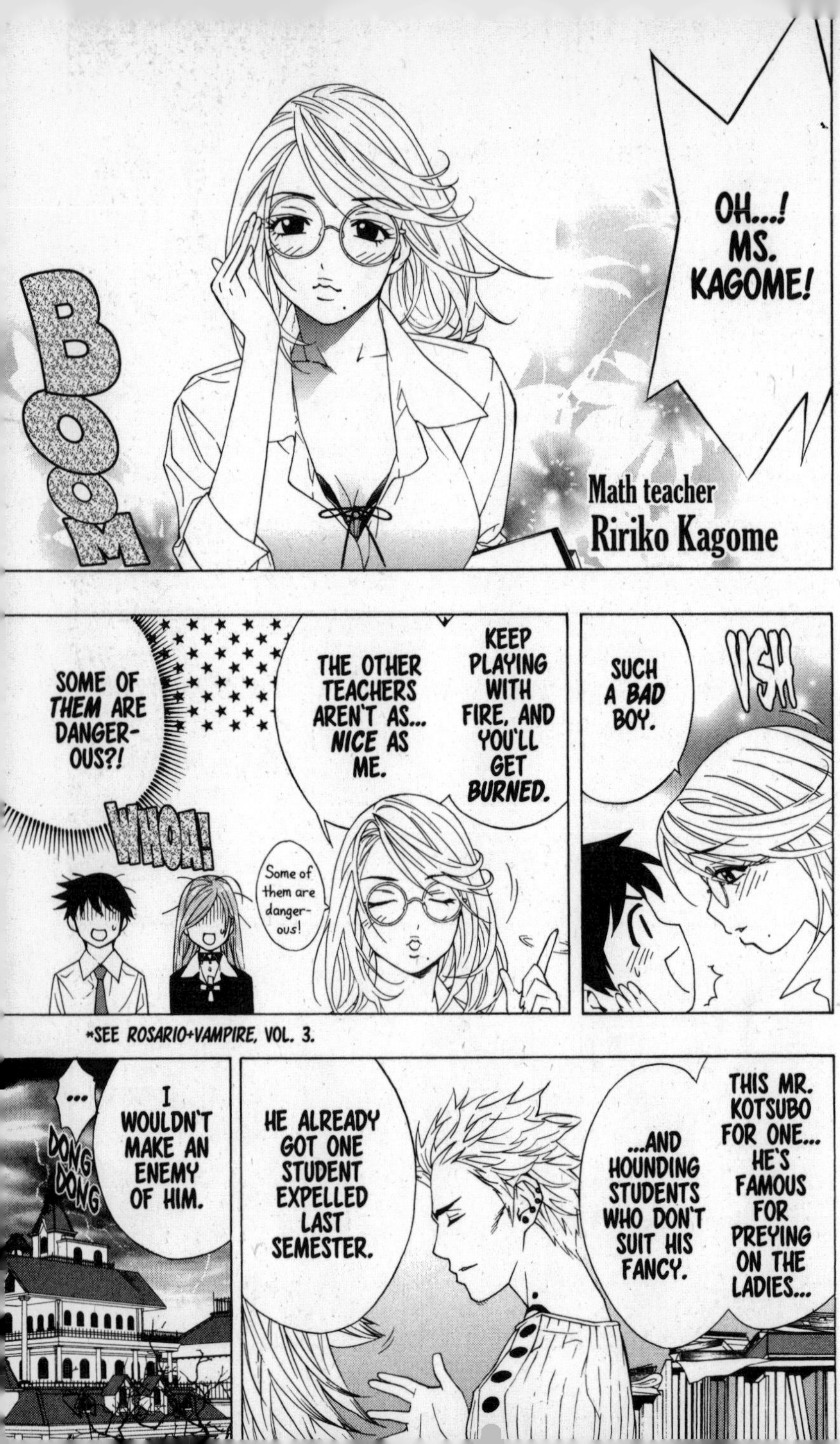
OH...! MS. KAGOME!
Math teacher Ririko Kagome
BOOM
SUCH A *BAD* BOY.
VSH
KEEP PLAYING WITH FIRE, AND YOU'LL GET *BURNED*.
THE OTHER TEACHERS AREN'T AS... *NICE* AS ME.
Some of them are danger-ous!
SOME OF *THEM* ARE DANGER-OUS?!
WHOA!
*SEE *ROSARIO+VAMPIRE*, VOL. 3.
THIS MR. KOTSUBO FOR ONE... HE'S FAMOUS FOR PREYING ON THE LADIES...
...AND HOUNDING STUDENTS WHO DON'T SUIT HIS FANCY.
HE ALREADY GOT ONE STUDENT EXPELLED LAST SEMESTER.
I WOULDN'T MAKE AN ENEMY OF HIM.
...
DONG DONG

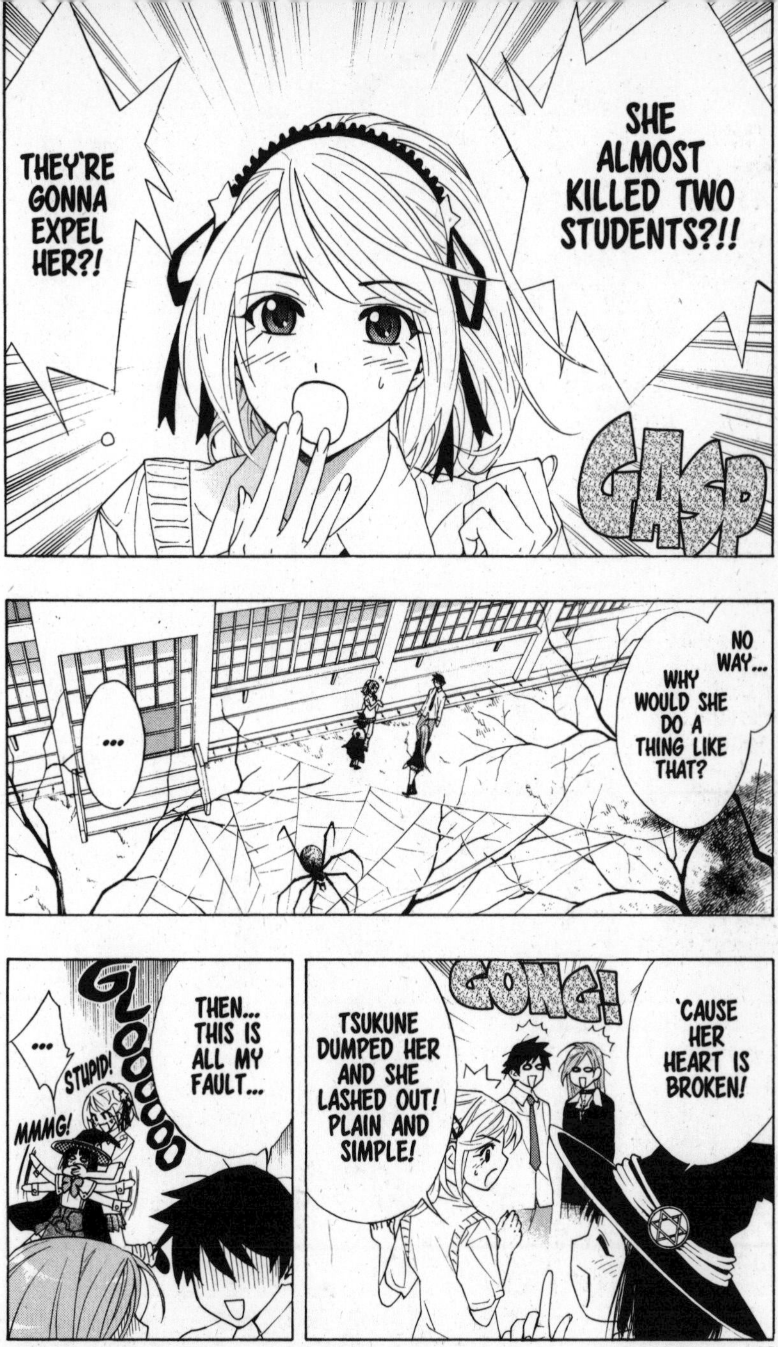
SHE ALMOST KILLED TWO STUDENTS?!!
THEY'RE GONNA EXPEL HER?!
GASP
NO WAY... WHY WOULD SHE DO A THING LIKE THAT?
...
'CAUSE HER HEART IS BROKEN!
GONG!
TSUKUNE DUMPED HER AND SHE LASHED OUT! PLAIN AND SIMPLE!
THEN... THIS IS ALL MY FAULT...
GLOOOOOOO
STUPID!
MMMG!
...

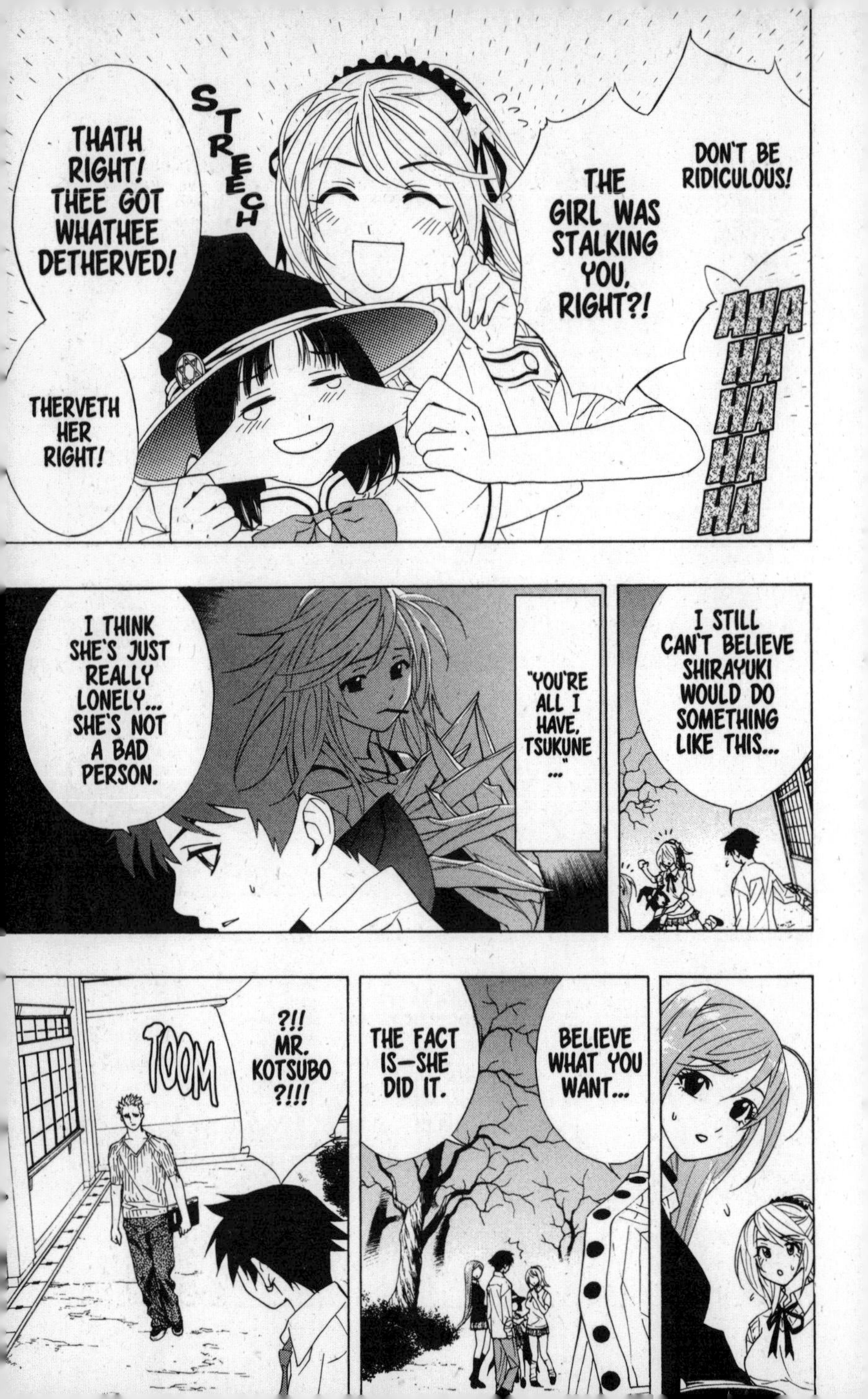
DON'T BE RIDICULOUS!
AHA HA HA HA HA HA
THE GIRL WAS STALKING YOU, RIGHT?!
STRECH
THATH RIGHT! THEE GOT WHATHEE DETHERVED!
THERVETH HER RIGHT!
I STILL CAN'T BELIEVE SHIRAYUKI WOULD DO SOMETHING LIKE THIS...
"YOU'RE ALL I HAVE, TSUKUNE"...
I THINK SHE'S JUST REALLY LONELY... SHE'S NOT A BAD PERSON.
BELIEVE WHAT YOU WANT...
THE FACT IS—SHE DID IT.
?!! MR. KOTSUBO ?!!!
TOOM

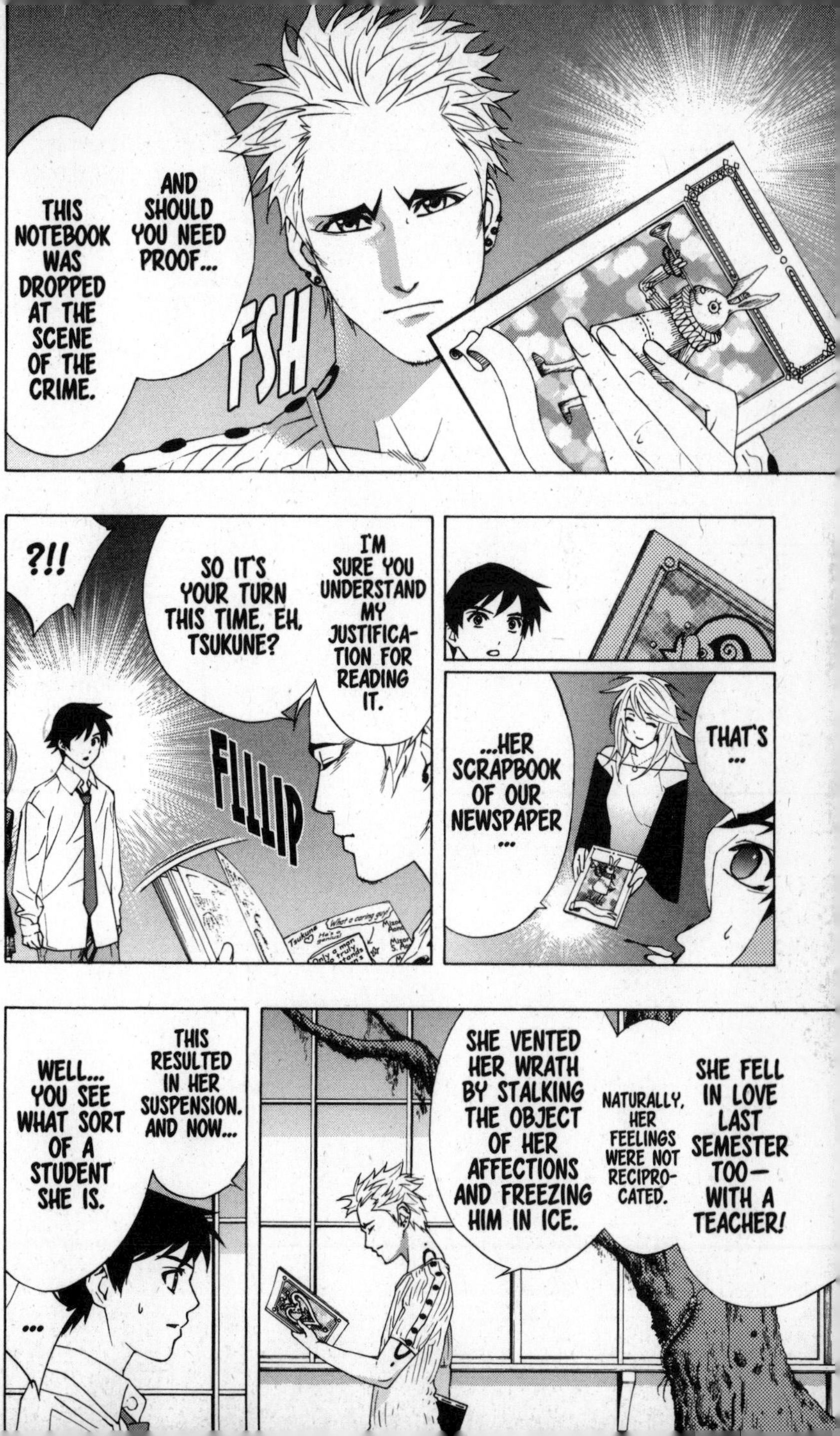
AND SHOULD YOU NEED PROOF...
THIS NOTEBOOK WAS DROPPED AT THE SCENE OF THE CRIME.
FSH
THAT'S...
...HER SCRAPBOOK OF OUR NEWSPAPER...
I'M SURE YOU UNDERSTAND MY JUSTIFICATION FOR READING IT.
SO IT'S YOUR TURN THIS TIME, EH, TSUKUNE?
?!!
FLLLIP
Tsukune
What a caring guy!
He's a genius!
SHE FELL IN LOVE LAST SEMESTER TOO—WITH A TEACHER!
NATURALLY, HER FEELINGS WERE NOT RECIPROCATED.
SHE VENTED HER WRATH BY STALKING THE OBJECT OF HER AFFECTIONS AND FREEZING HIM IN ICE.
THIS RESULTED IN HER SUSPENSION. AND NOW...
WELL... YOU SEE WHAT SORT OF A STUDENT SHE IS.
...

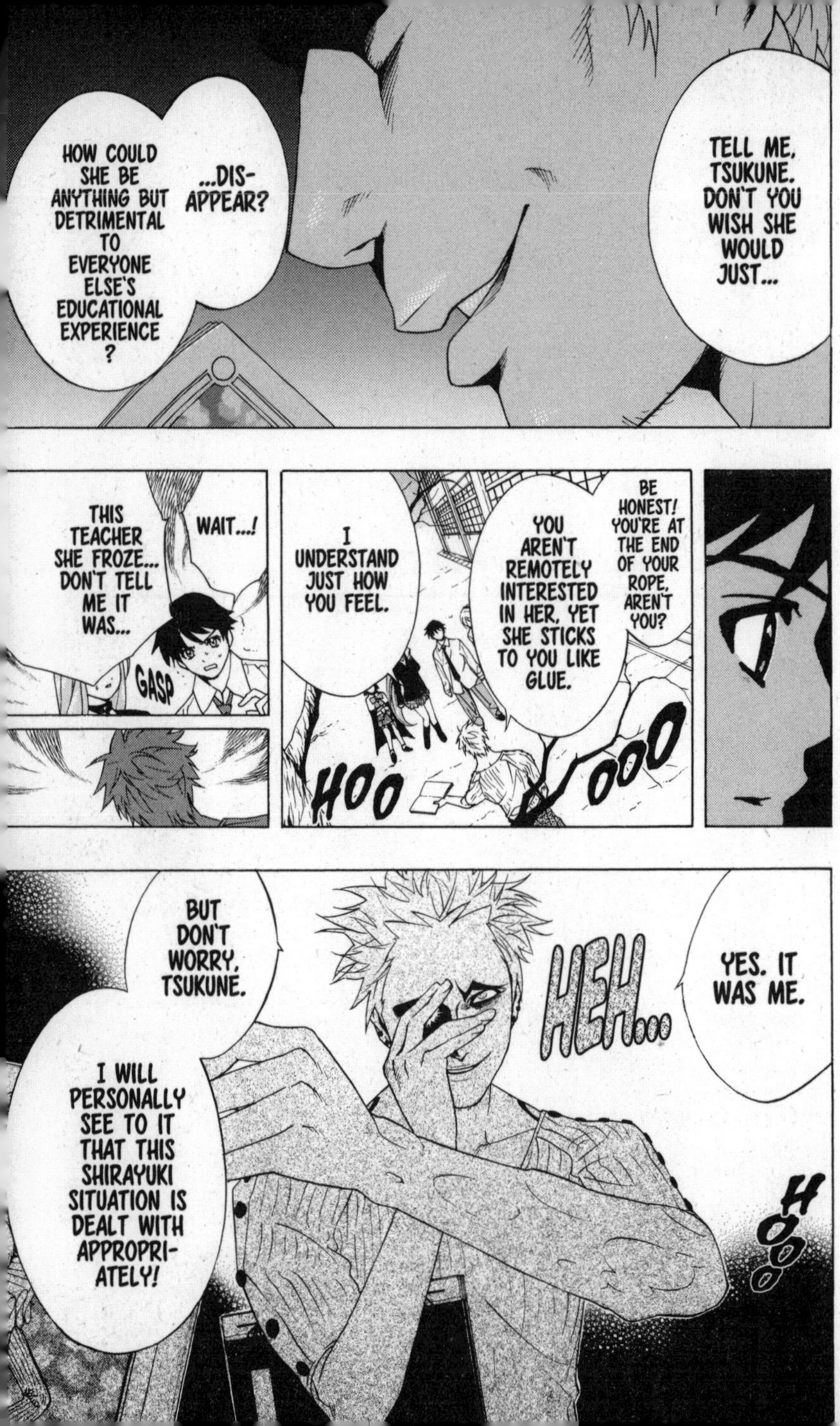
TELL ME, TSUKUNE. DON'T YOU WISH SHE WOULD JUST...
...DIS-APPEAR?
HOW COULD SHE BE ANYTHING BUT DETRIMENTAL TO EVERYONE ELSE'S EDUCATIONAL EXPERIENCE?
BE HONEST! YOU'RE AT THE END OF YOUR ROPE, AREN'T YOU?
YOU AREN'T REMOTELY INTERESTED IN HER, YET SHE STICKS TO YOU LIKE GLUE.
I UNDERSTAND JUST HOW YOU FEEL.
HOO OOO
WAIT...!
THIS TEACHER SHE FROZE... DON'T TELL ME IT WAS...
GASP
YES. IT WAS ME.
HOOOO
HEH...
BUT DON'T WORRY, TSUKUNE.
I WILL PERSONALLY SEE TO IT THAT THIS SHIRAYUKI SITUATION IS DEALT WITH APPROPRIATELY!

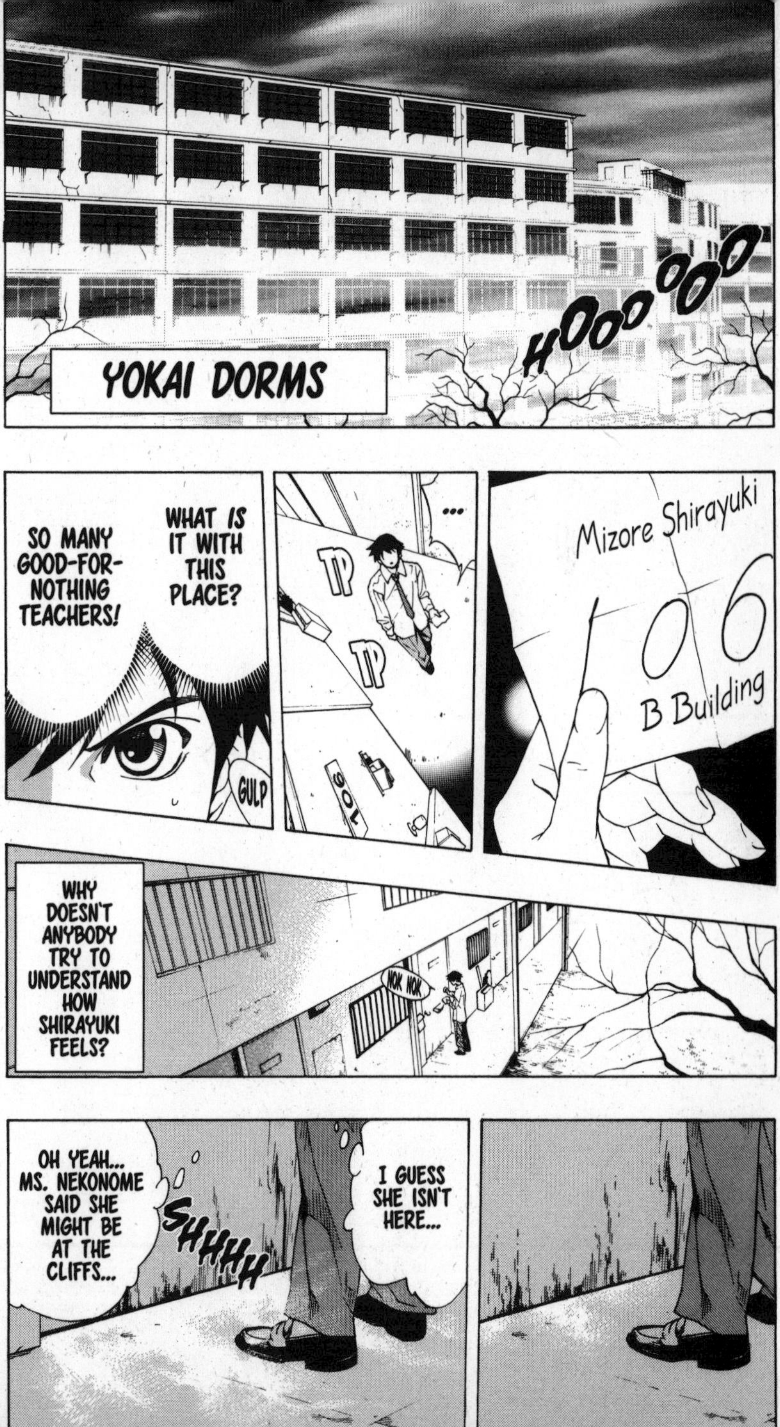
YOKAI DORMS
HOOOOOOO
Mizore Shirayuki
106
B Building
...
TP
TP
106
WHAT IS IT WITH THIS PLACE?
SO MANY GOOD-FOR-NOTHING TEACHERS!
GULP
WHY DOESN'T ANYBODY TRY TO UNDERSTAND HOW SHIRAYUKI FEELS?
NOK NOK
I GUESS SHE ISN'T HERE...
SHHHH
OH YEAH... MS. NEKONOME SAID SHE MIGHT BE AT THE CLIFFS...

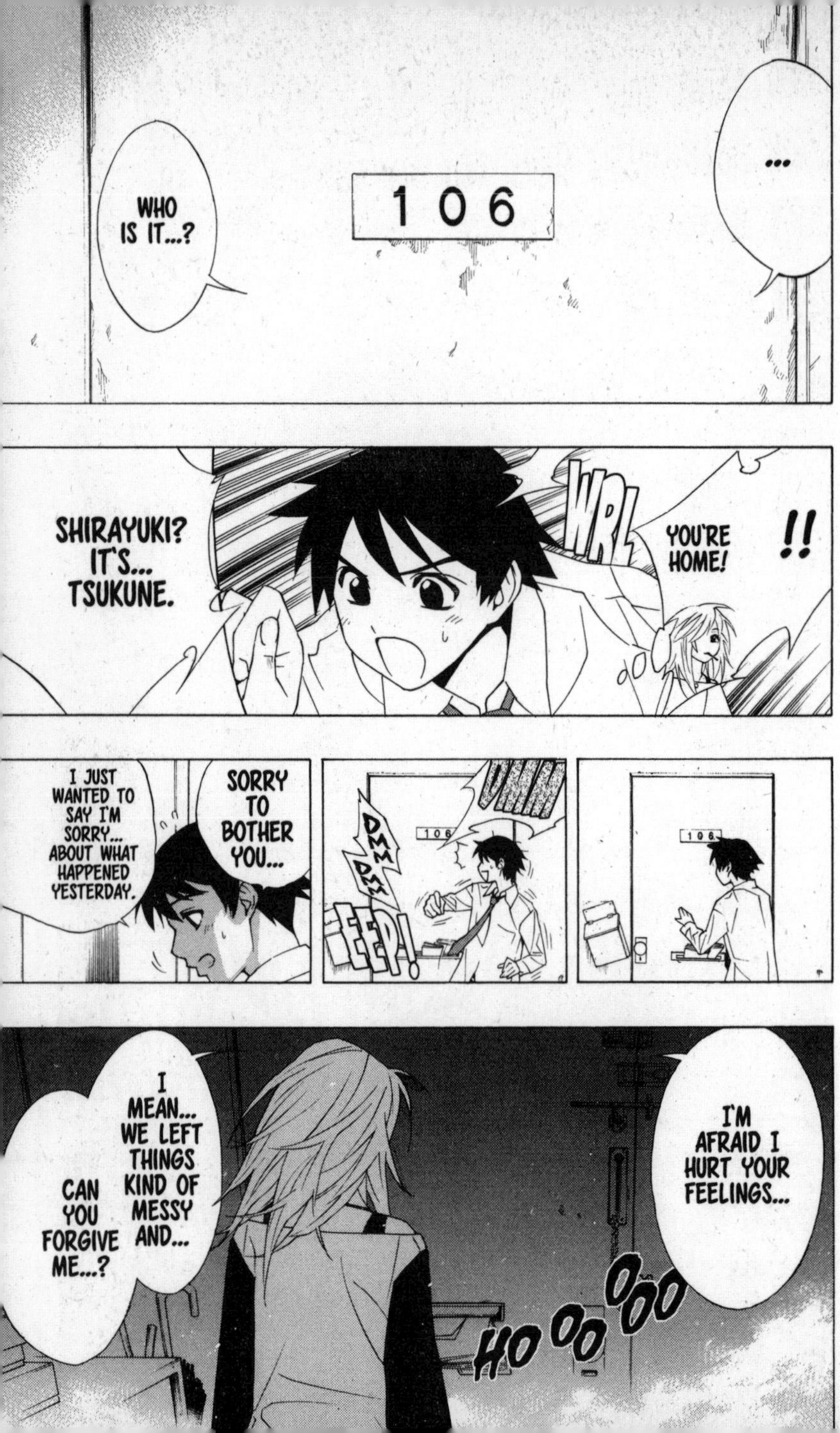
...
106
WHO IS IT...?
!!
YOU'RE HOME!
WRL
SHIRAYUKI? IT'S... TSUKUNE.
106
DMM
DMM
EEEP!
106
SORRY TO BOTHER YOU...
I JUST WANTED TO SAY I'M SORRY... ABOUT WHAT HAPPENED YESTERDAY.
I'M AFRAID I HURT YOUR FEELINGS...
HOOOOOOO
I MEAN... WE LEFT THINGS KIND OF MESSY AND...
CAN YOU FORGIVE ME...?

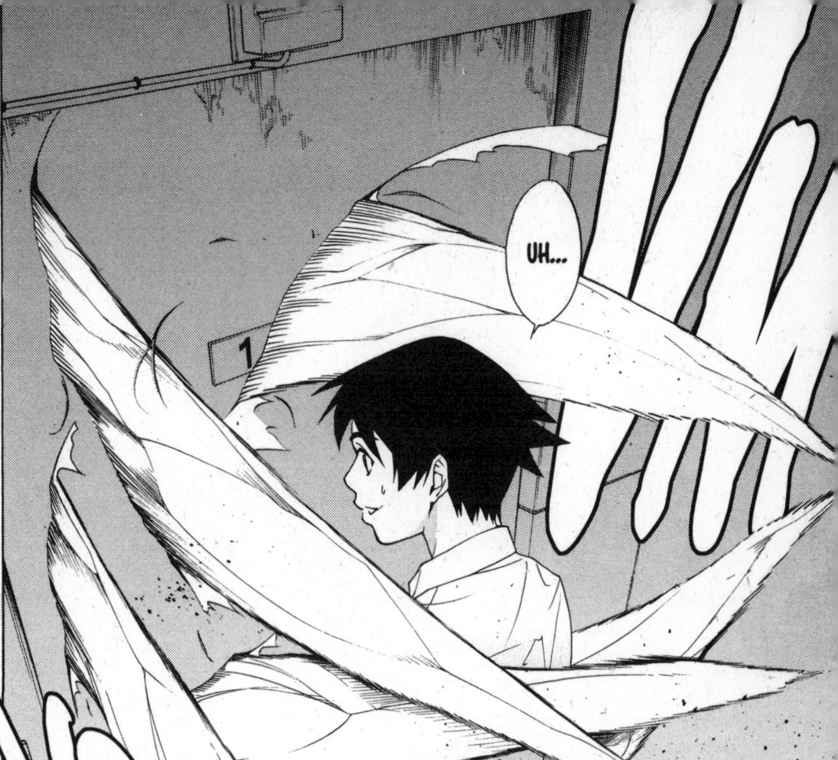
UH...
VSSSSSH
YAAAAA!!!
BO OO OM

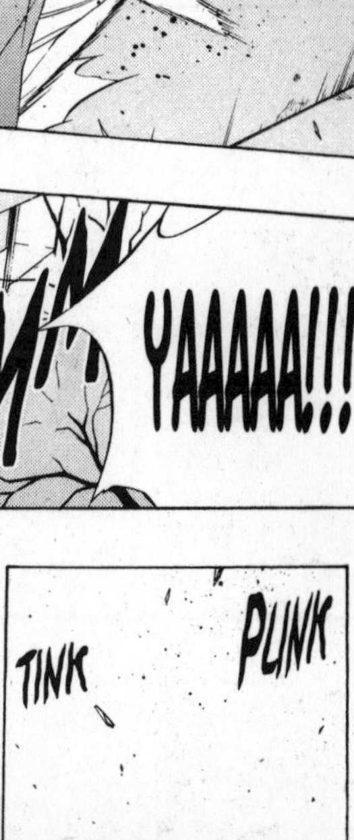
PUNK
TINK

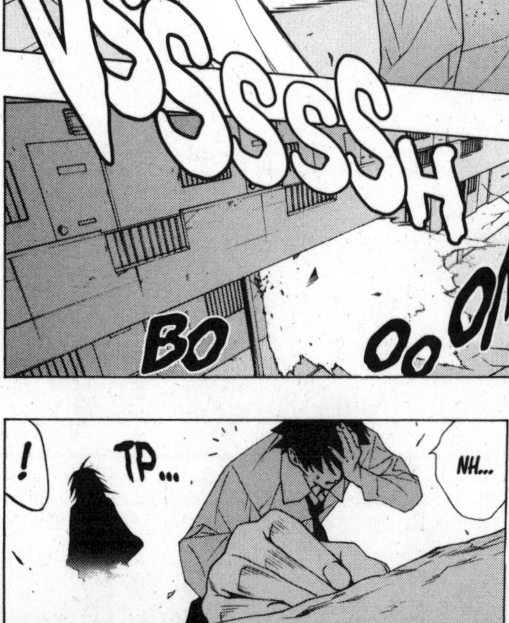
NH...
TP...
!

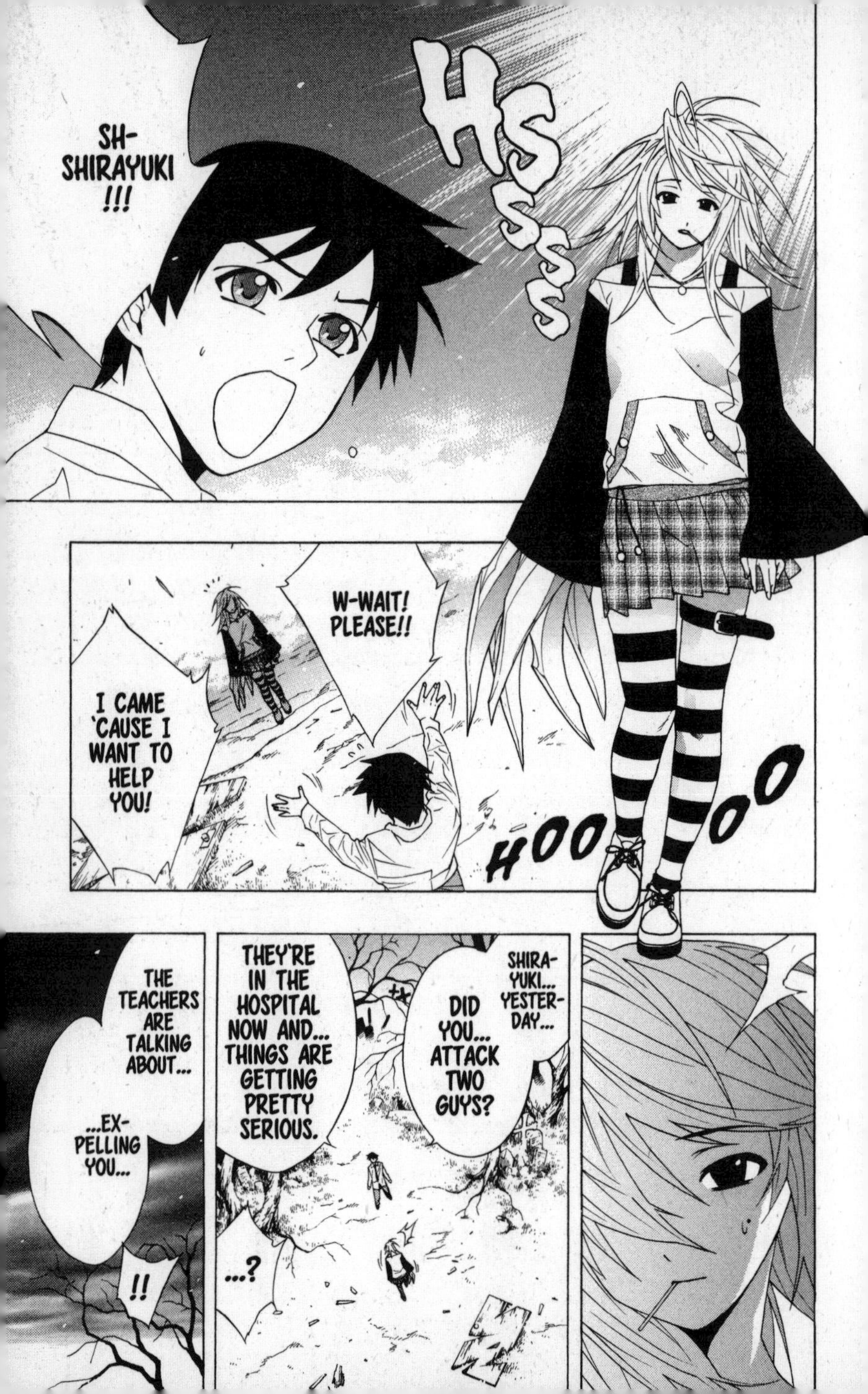
HSSSS
HOOOOO
SH-SHIRAYUKI!!!
W-WAIT! PLEASE!!
I CAME 'CAUSE I WANT TO HELP YOU!
SHIRA-YUKI... YESTER-DAY...
DID YOU... ATTACK TWO GUYS?
THEY'RE IN THE HOSPITAL NOW AND... THINGS ARE GETTING PRETTY SERIOUS.
...?
THE TEACHERS ARE TALKING ABOUT...
...EX-PELLING YOU...
!!

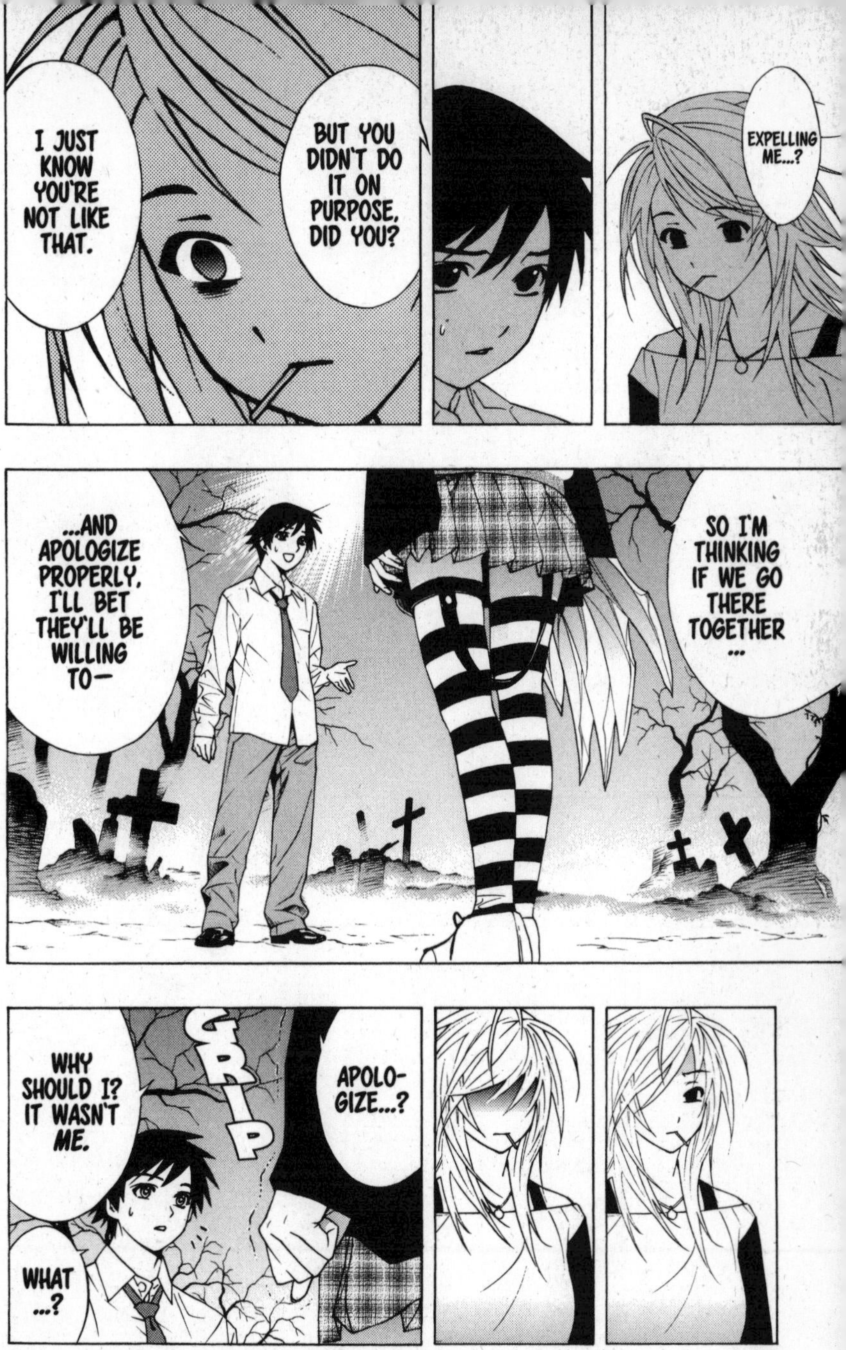
EXPELLING ME...?
BUT YOU DIDN'T DO IT ON PURPOSE, DID YOU?
I JUST KNOW YOU'RE NOT LIKE THAT.
SO I'M THINKING IF WE GO THERE TOGETHER...
...AND APOLOGIZE PROPERLY, I'LL BET THEY'LL BE WILLING TO—
APOLO-GIZE...?
GRIP
WHY SHOULD I? IT WASN'T *ME.*
WHAT...?

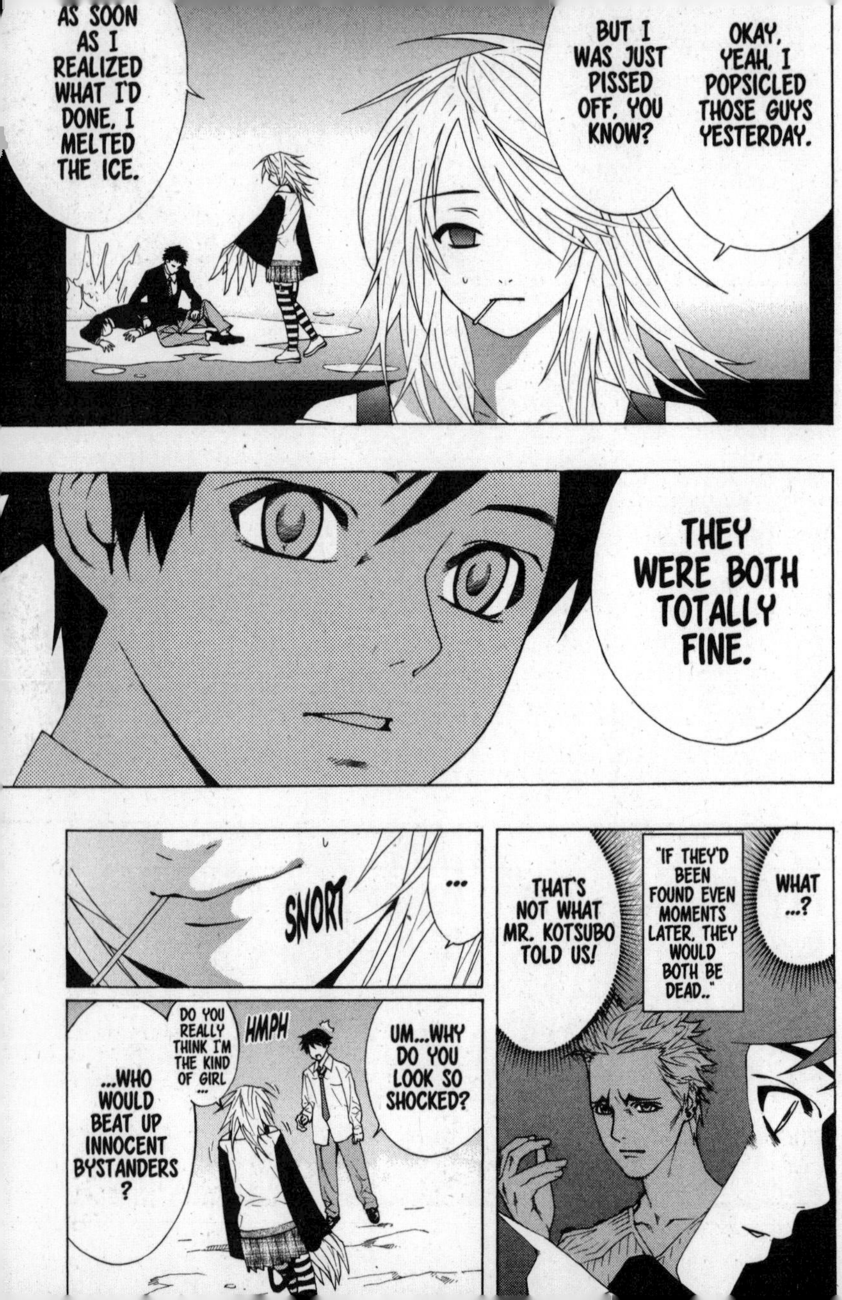
OKAY, YEAH, I POPSICLED THOSE GUYS YESTERDAY.
BUT I WAS JUST PISSED OFF, YOU KNOW?
AS SOON AS I REALIZED WHAT I'D DONE, I MELTED THE ICE.
THEY WERE BOTH TOTALLY FINE.
WHAT ...?
"IF THEY'D BEEN FOUND EVEN MOMENTS LATER, THEY WOULD BOTH BE DEAD.."
THAT'S NOT WHAT MR. KOTSUBO TOLD US!
...
SNORT
UM...WHY DO YOU LOOK SO SHOCKED?
HMPH
DO YOU REALLY THINK I'M THE KIND OF GIRL ...
...WHO WOULD BEAT UP INNOCENT BYSTANDERS ?

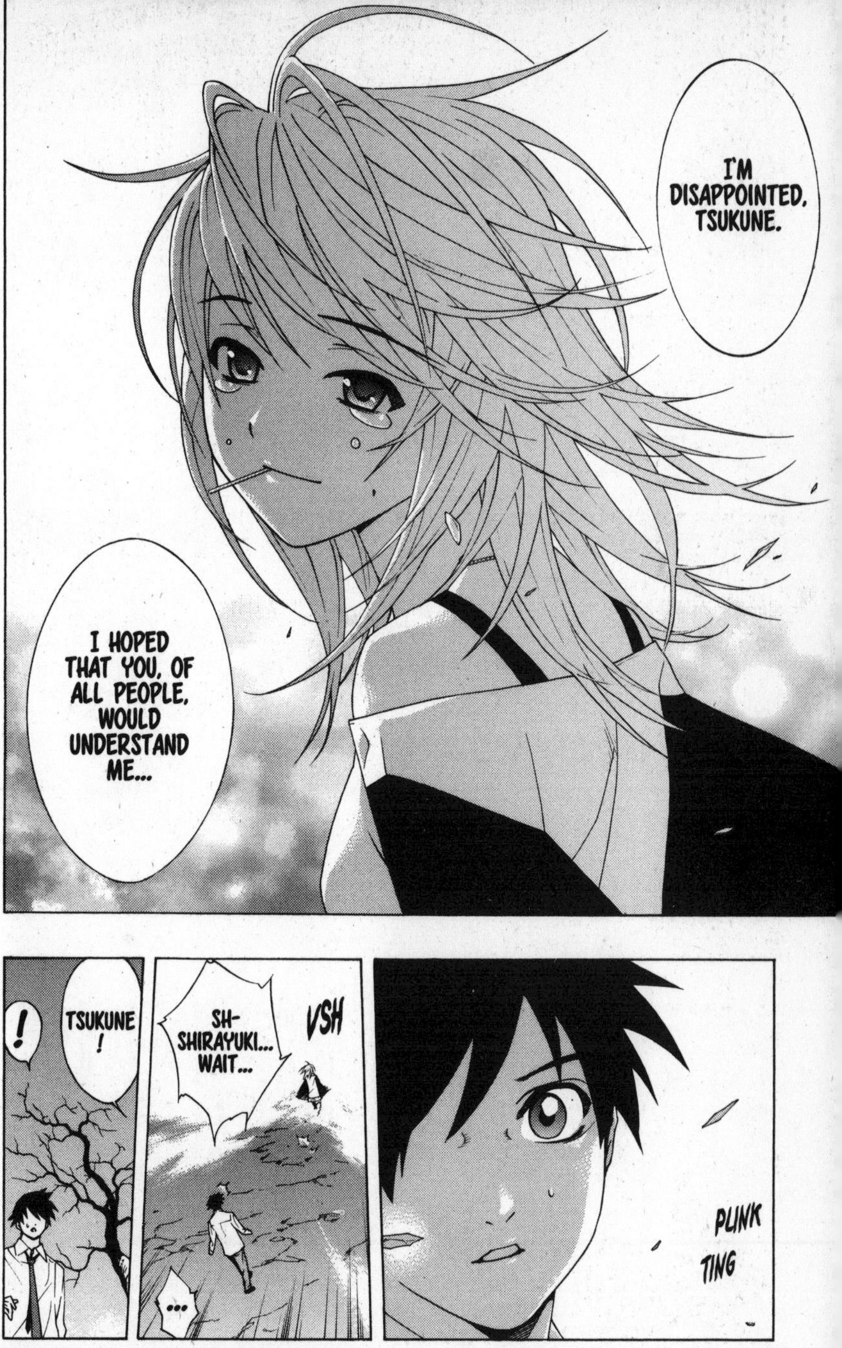
I'M DISAPPOINTED, TSUKUNE.
I HOPED THAT YOU, OF ALL PEOPLE, WOULD UNDERSTAND ME...
PLINK
TING
VSH
SH-SHIRAYUKI... WAIT...
...
TSUKUNE!
!

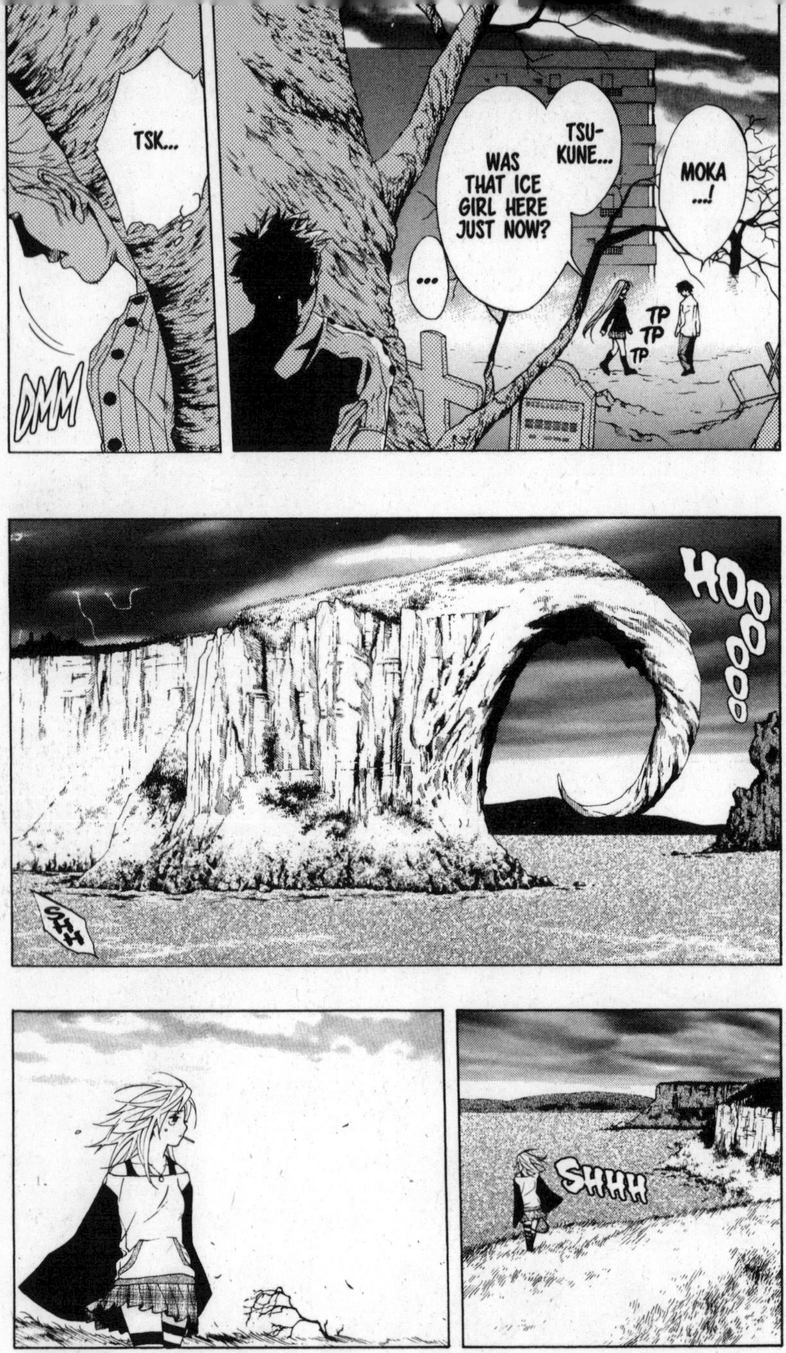
MOKA ...!
TSU-KUNE... WAS THAT ICE GIRL HERE JUST NOW?
TP TP TP
...
TSK...
DMM
HOOOOOOO
SHH
SHHH

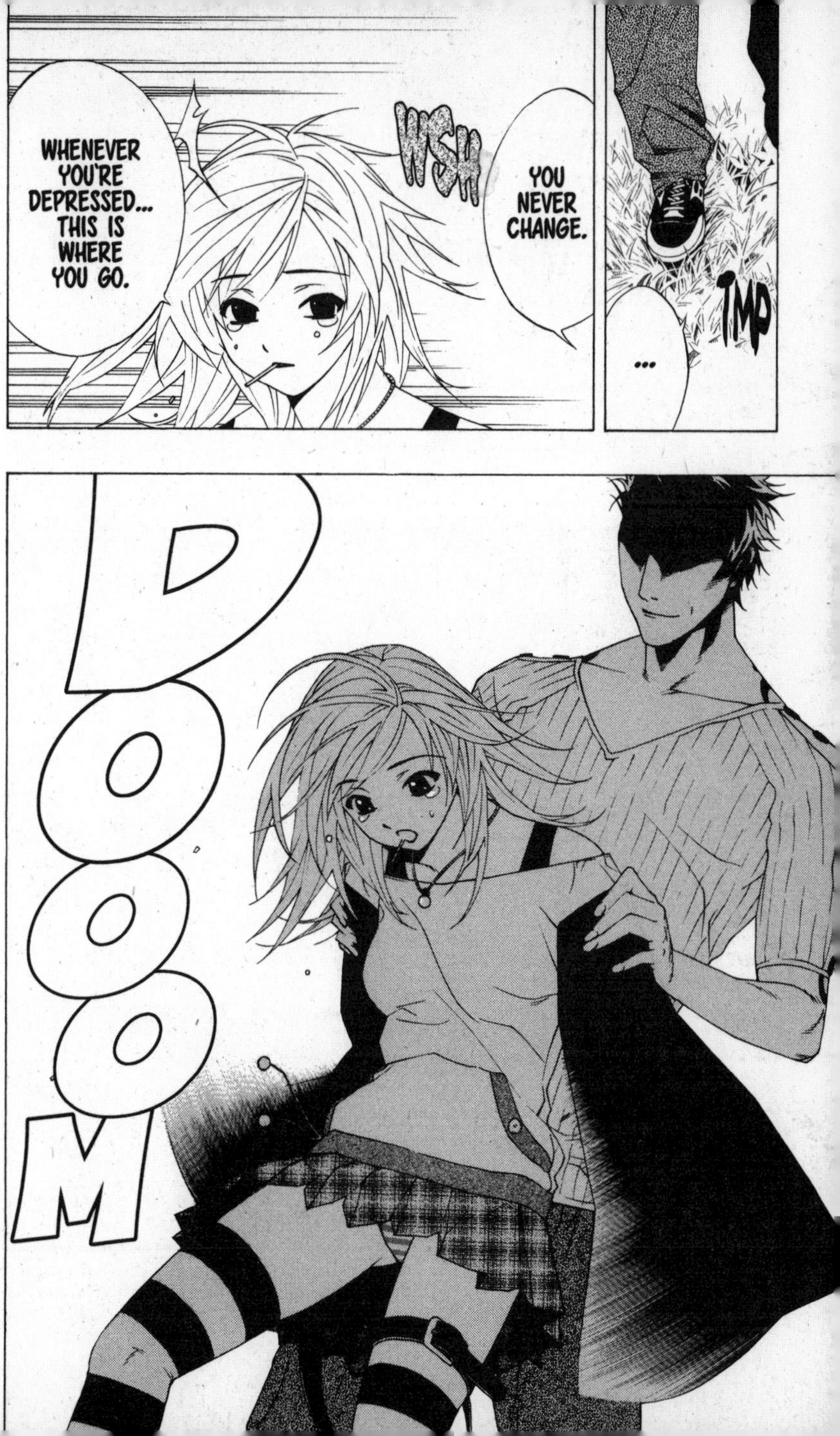
TMP
...
YOU NEVER CHANGE.
WSH
WHENEVER YOU'RE DEPRESSED... THIS IS WHERE YOU GO.
DOOOOM

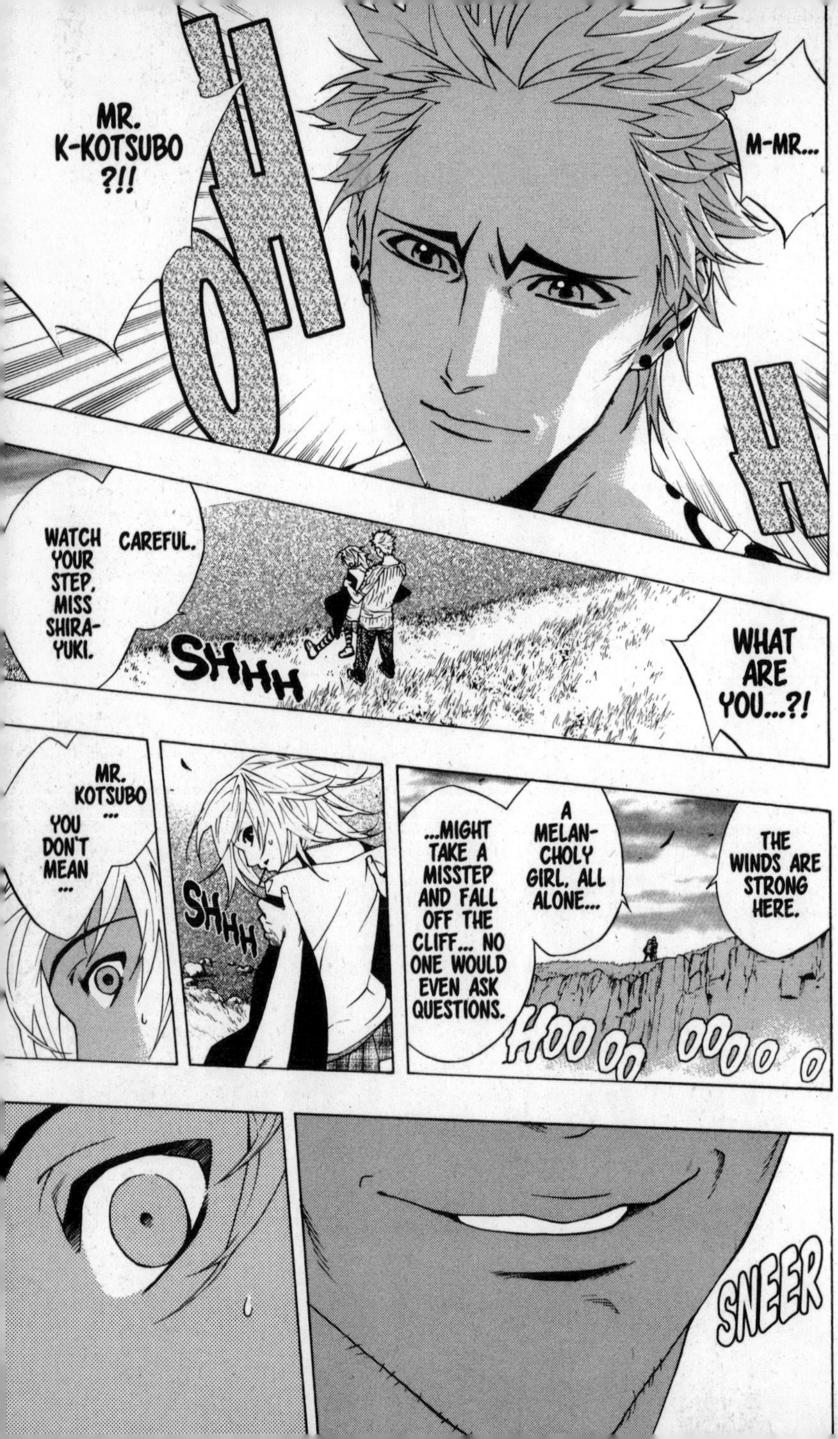
M-MR...
MR. K-KOTSUBO ?!!
WHAT ARE YOU...?!
CAREFUL.
WATCH YOUR STEP, MISS SHIRA-YUKI.
SHHHH
THE WINDS ARE STRONG HERE.
A MELAN-CHOLY GIRL, ALL ALONE...
...MIGHT TAKE A MISSTEP AND FALL OFF THE CLIFF... NO ONE WOULD EVEN ASK QUESTIONS.
HOOOOOOOOO
SHHH
MR. KOTSUBO... YOU DON'T MEAN...
SNEER

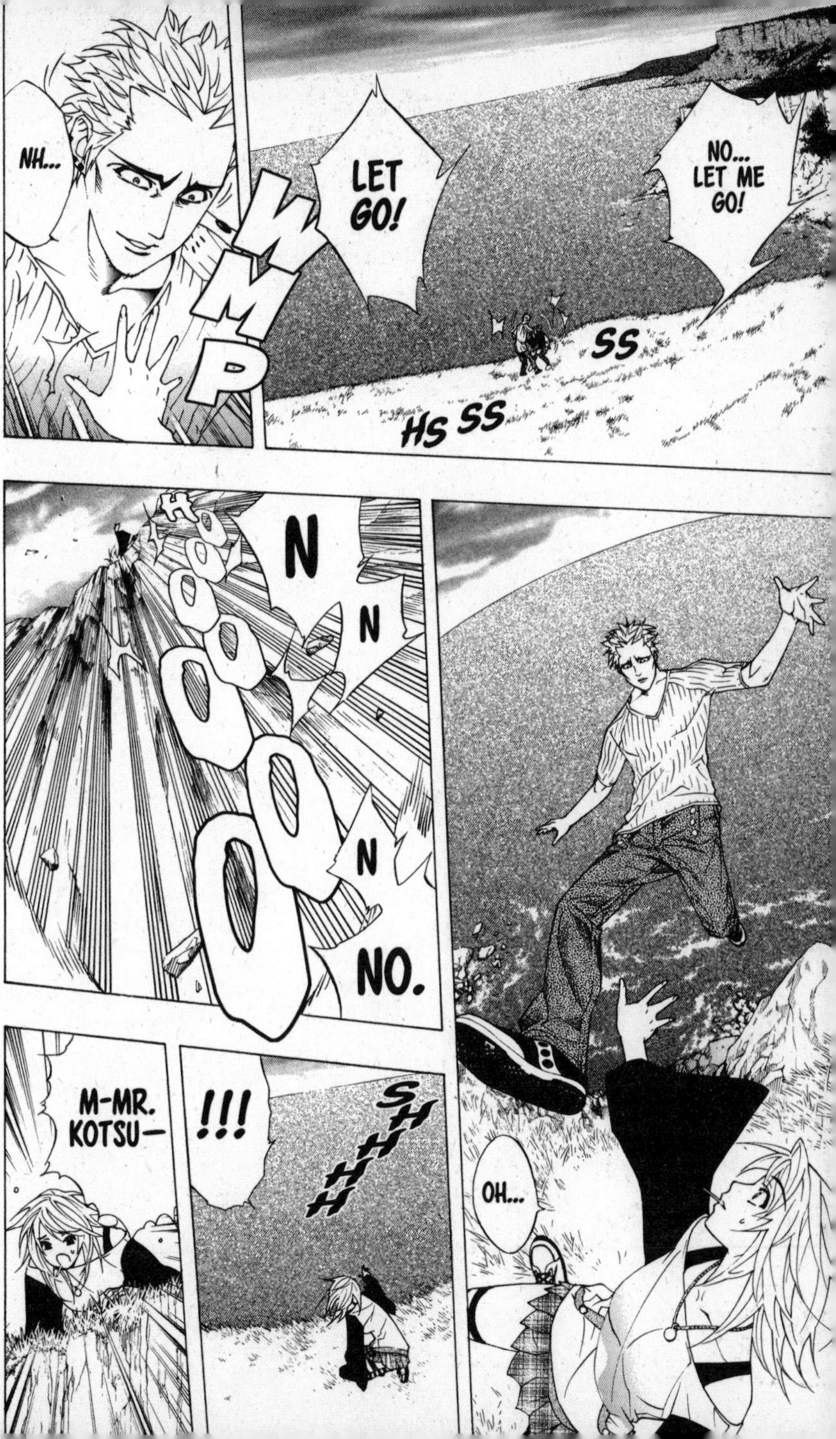
NO... LET ME GO!
LET GO!
SS
HS SS
NH...
WMMP
OH...
HOOOOOOOO
N
N
N
NO.
!!!
SHHHHH
M-MR. KOTSU—

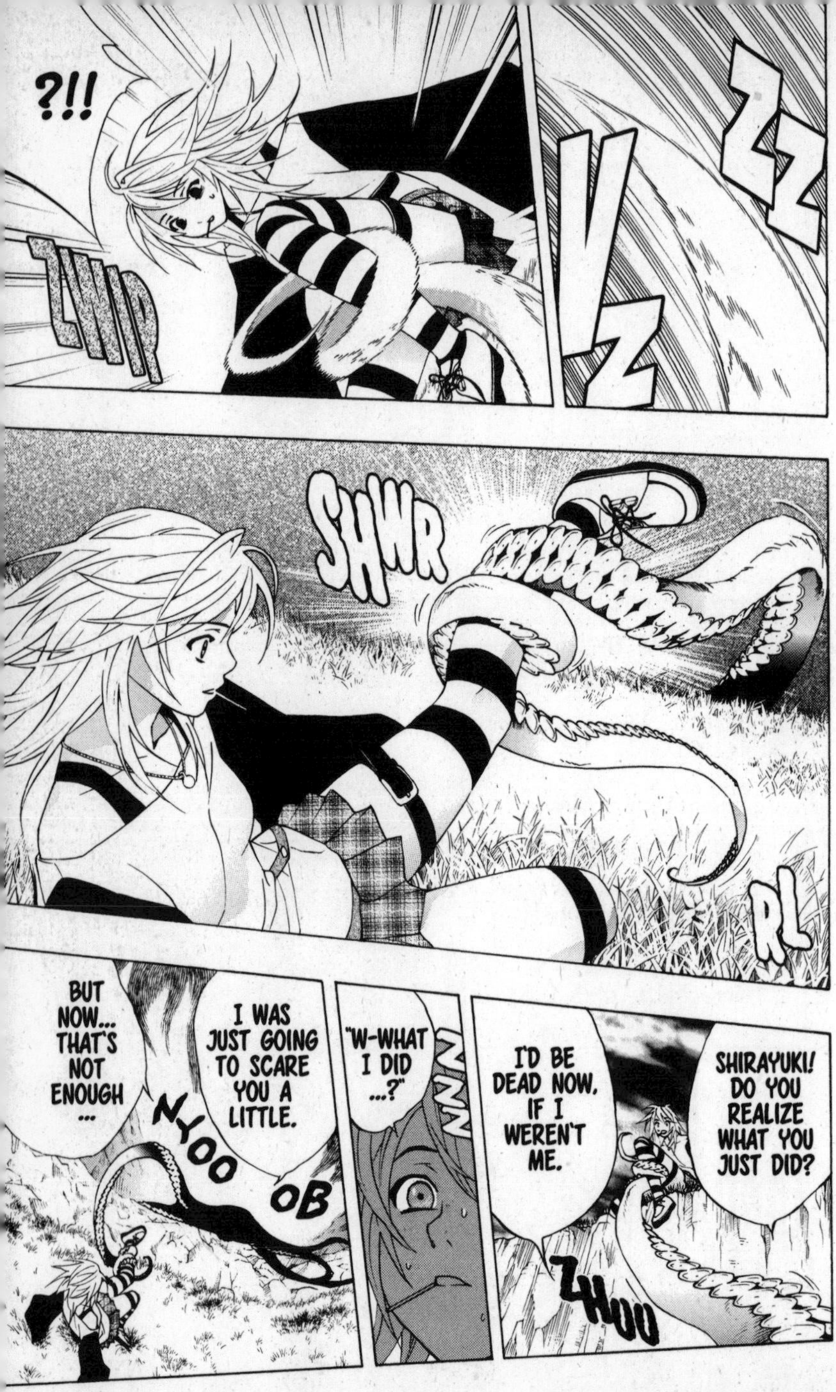
ZZ
VZ
?!!
ZWIP
SHWR
RL
SHIRAYUKI! DO YOU REALIZE WHAT YOU JUST DID?
I'D BE DEAD NOW, IF I WEREN'T ME.
ZHOO
"W-WHAT I DID ...?"
I WAS JUST GOING TO SCARE YOU A LITTLE.
BUT NOW... THAT'S NOT ENOUGH ...
NYOO OB

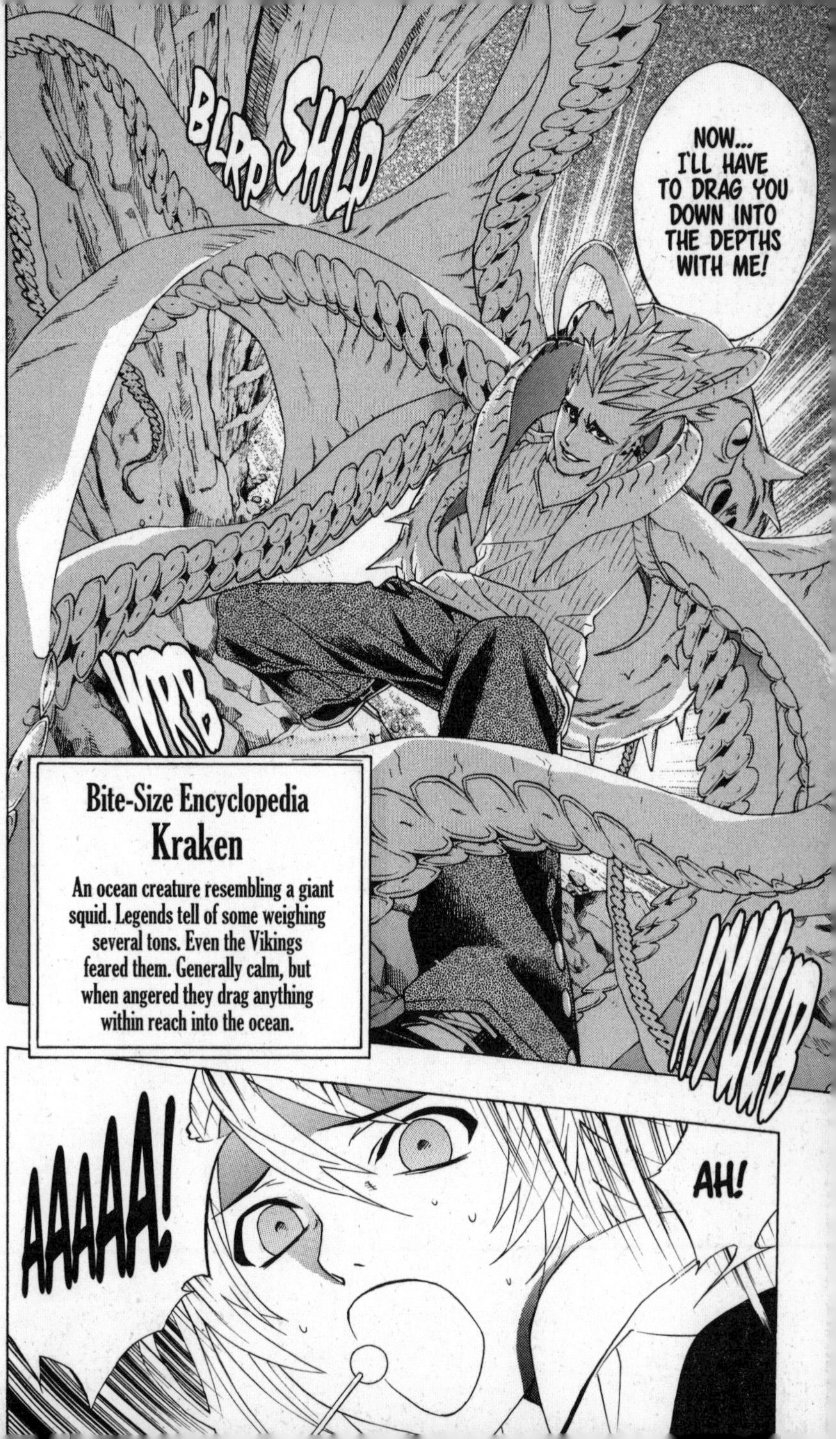
NOW... I'LL HAVE TO DRAG YOU DOWN INTO THE DEPTHS WITH ME!
BLRP SHLP
WRB
Bite-Size Encyclopedia
Kraken
An ocean creature resembling a giant squid. Legends tell of some weighing several tons. Even the Vikings feared them. Generally calm, but when angered they drag anything within reach into the ocean.
AH!
AAAAA!

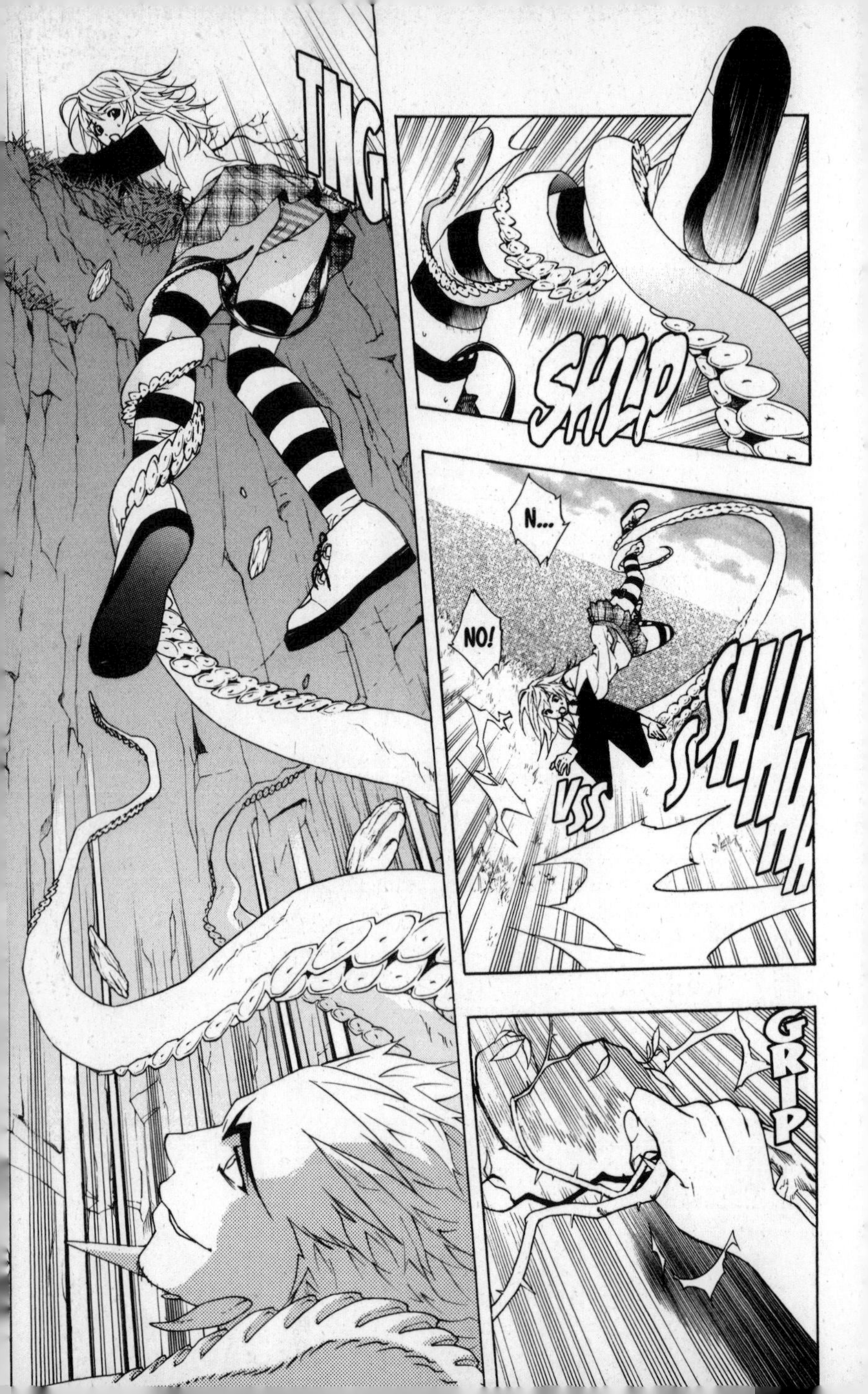
SHLP
N...
NO!
SHH
VSS
GRIP
TING

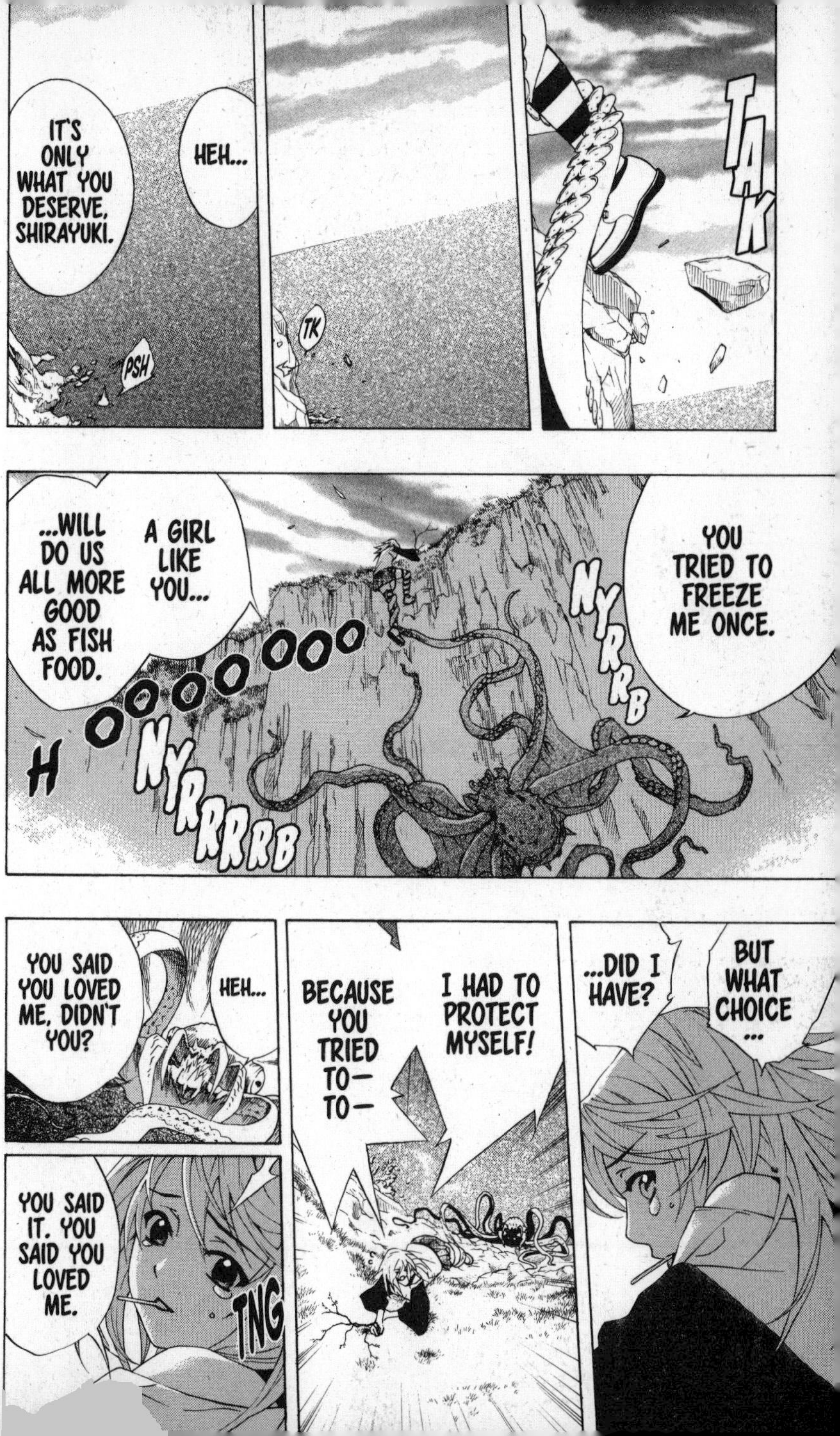
TAK
TK
HEH...
IT'S ONLY WHAT YOU DESERVE, SHIRAYUKI.
PSH
YOU TRIED TO FREEZE ME ONCE.
NYRRB
A GIRL LIKE YOU...
...WILL DO US ALL MORE GOOD AS FISH FOOD.
HOOOOOOOOO
NYRRRRB
BUT WHAT CHOICE...
...DID I HAVE?
I HAD TO PROTECT MYSELF!
BECAUSE YOU TRIED TO— TO—
HEH...
YOU SAID YOU LOVED ME, DIDN'T YOU?
YOU SAID IT. YOU SAID YOU LOVED ME.
TNG

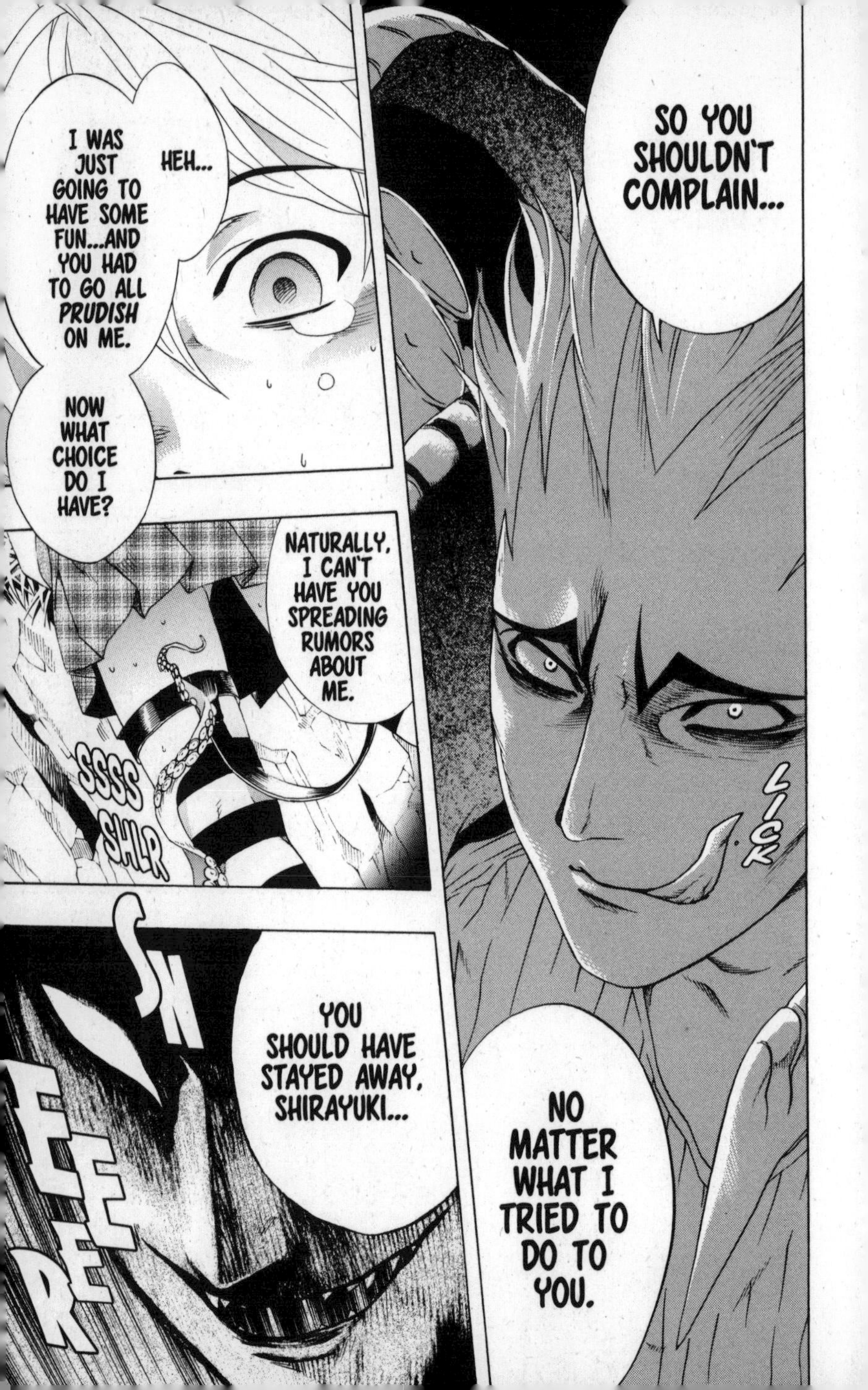
SO YOU SHOULDN'T COMPLAIN...
LICK
NO MATTER WHAT I TRIED TO DO TO YOU.
HEH...
I WAS JUST GOING TO HAVE SOME FUN...AND YOU HAD TO GO ALL *PRUDISH* ON ME.
NOW WHAT CHOICE DO I HAVE?
NATURALLY, I CAN'T HAVE YOU SPREADING RUMORS ABOUT ME.
SSSS SHLR
YOU SHOULD HAVE STAYED AWAY, SHIRAYUKI...
SNEEER

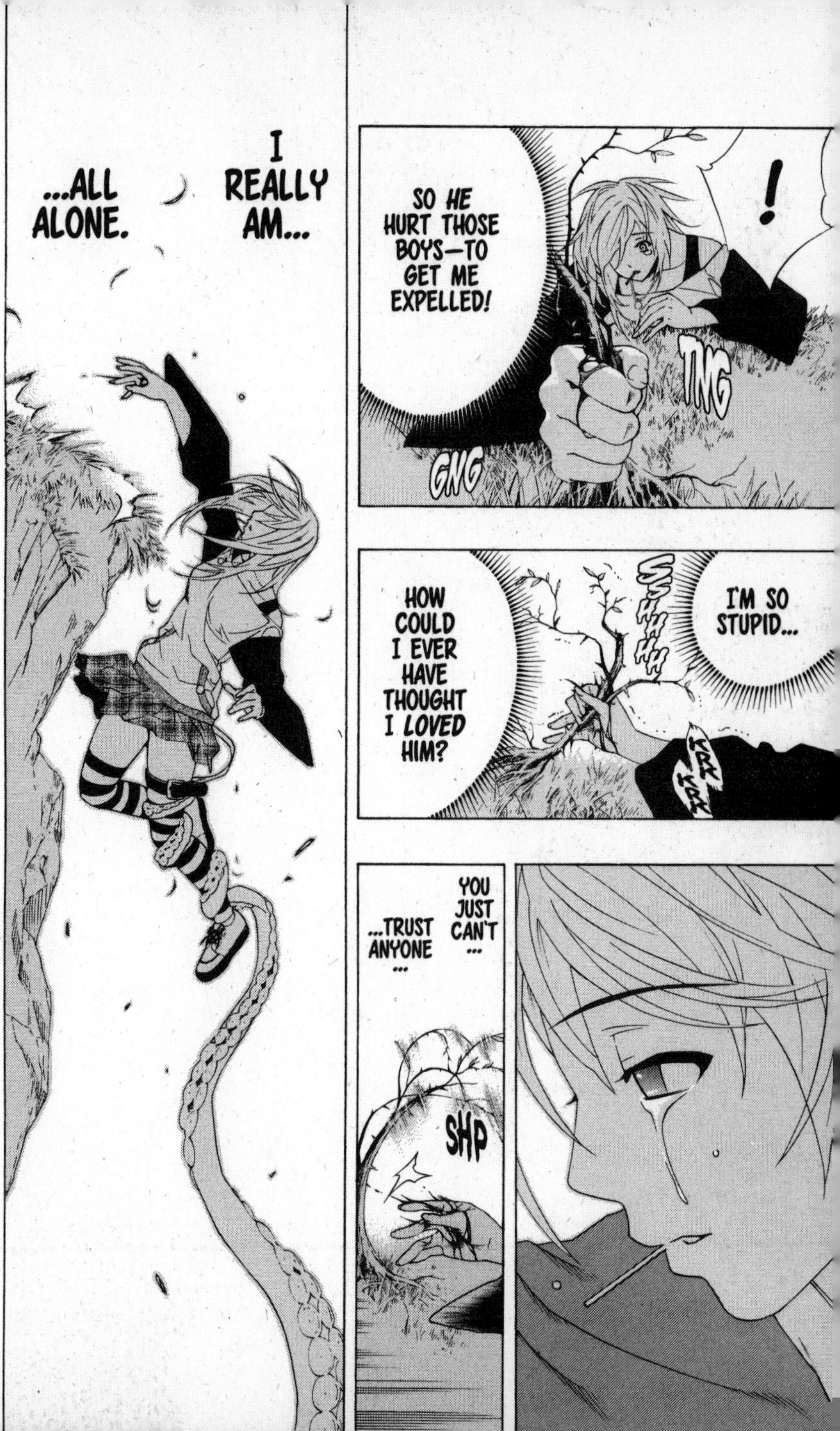
!
SO HE HURT THOSE BOYS—TO GET ME EXPELLED!
TMG
GNG
I'M SO STUPID...
SSSHHHH
HOW COULD I EVER HAVE THOUGHT I *LOVED* HIM?
KRK KRK
YOU JUST CAN'T ...
...TRUST ANYONE ...
SHP
I REALLY AM...
...ALL ALONE.

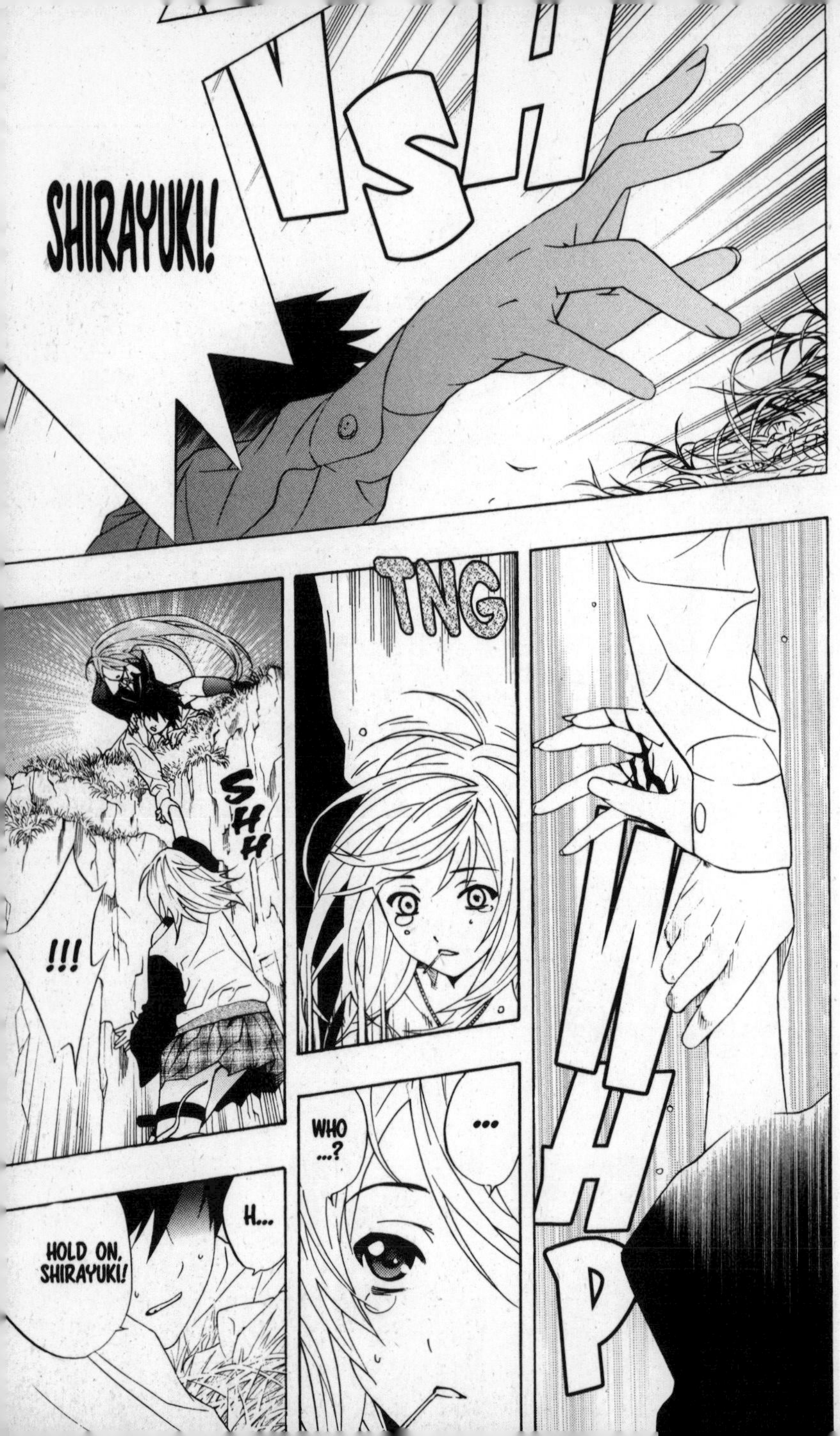
VSH
SHIRAYUKI!
WHAP
TNG
SHH
!!!
WHO ...?
...
H...
HOLD ON, SHIRAYUKI!

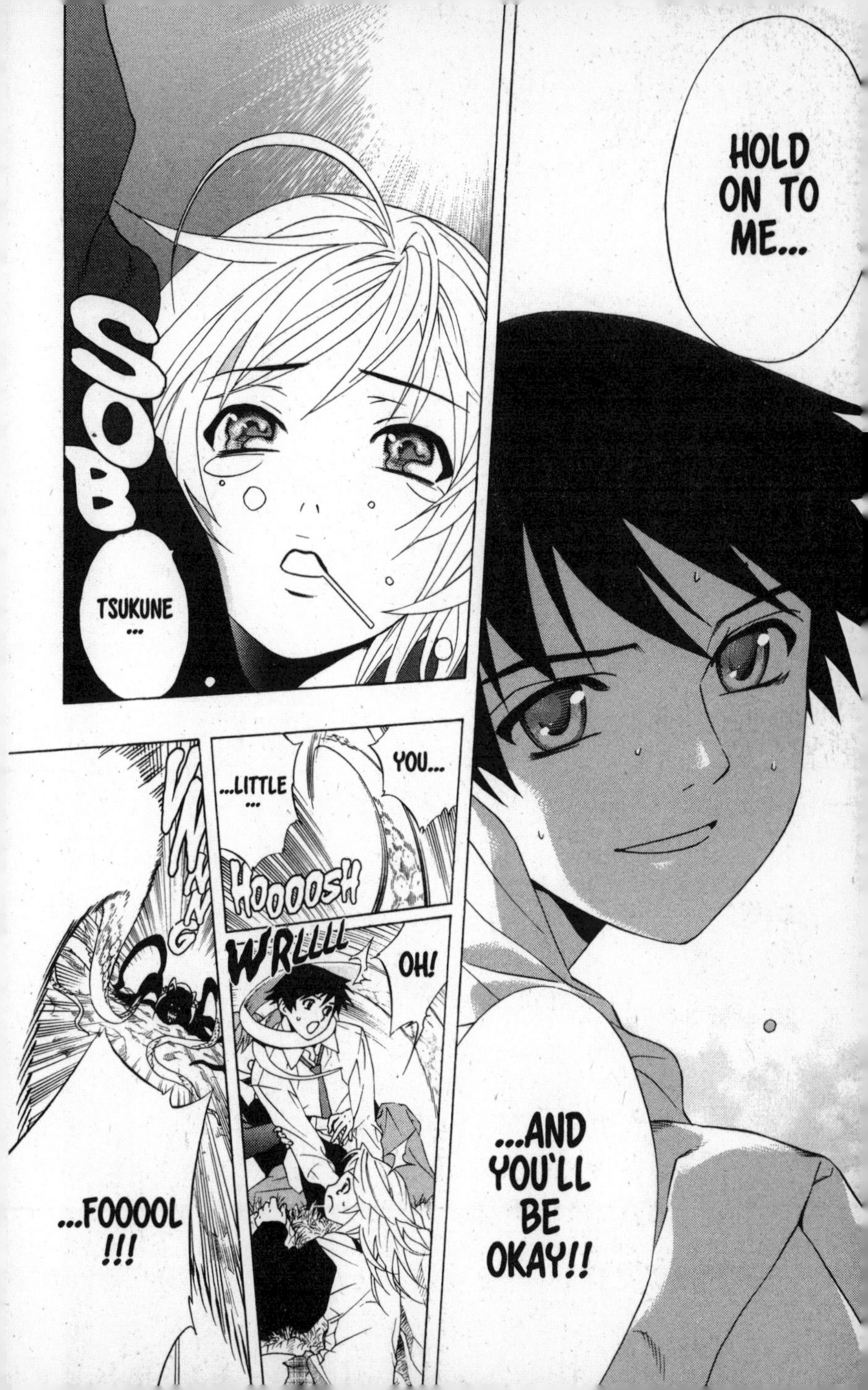
HOLD ON TO ME...
...AND YOU'LL BE OKAY!!
SOB
TSUKUNE ...
YOU...
...LITTLE ...
HOOOOSH
OH!
WRLLL
...FOOOOL !!!

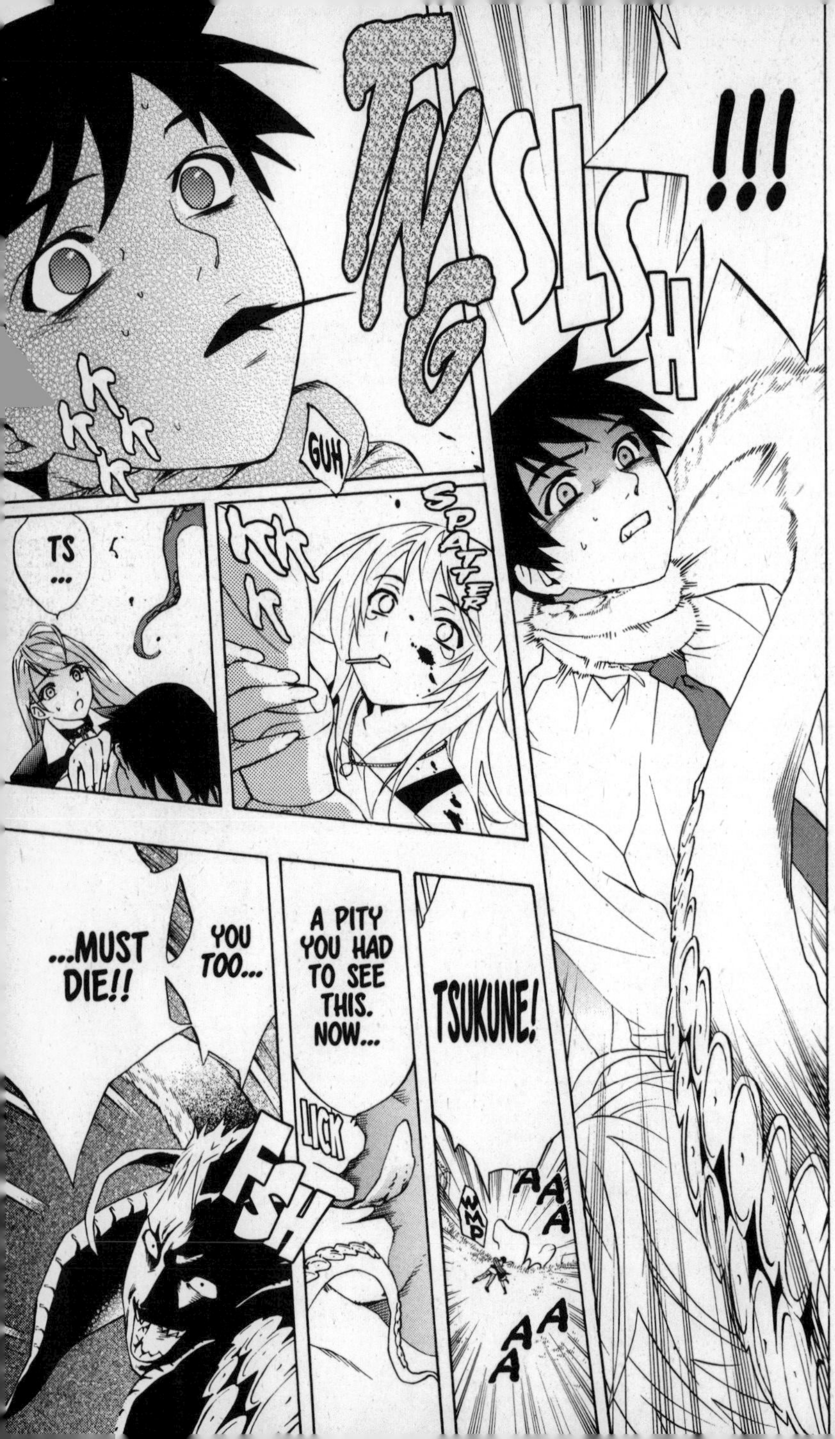
SLISH!!!
TSUKUNE!
WMP
AAAAAA
GUH
KKKKK
SPATTER
KKK
TS...
A PITY YOU HAD TO SEE THIS. NOW...
LICK
YOU TOO...
...MUST DIE!!
FSH

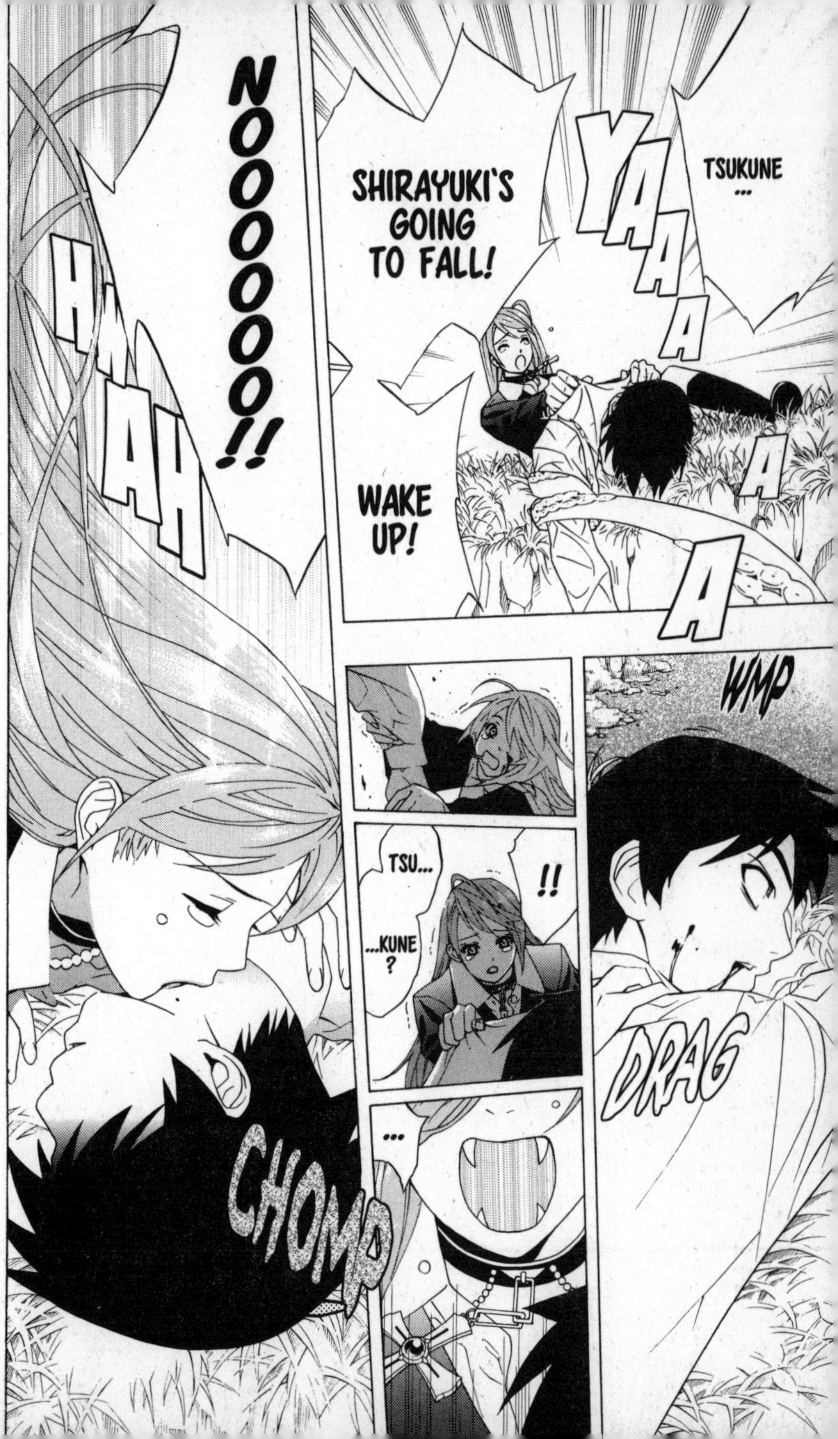
YAAAAAA
TSUKUNE ...
SHIRAYUKI'S GOING TO FALL!
WAKE UP!
WMP
DRAG
TSU...
...KUNE?
!!
...
NOOOOOOO!!
HAH
CHOMP

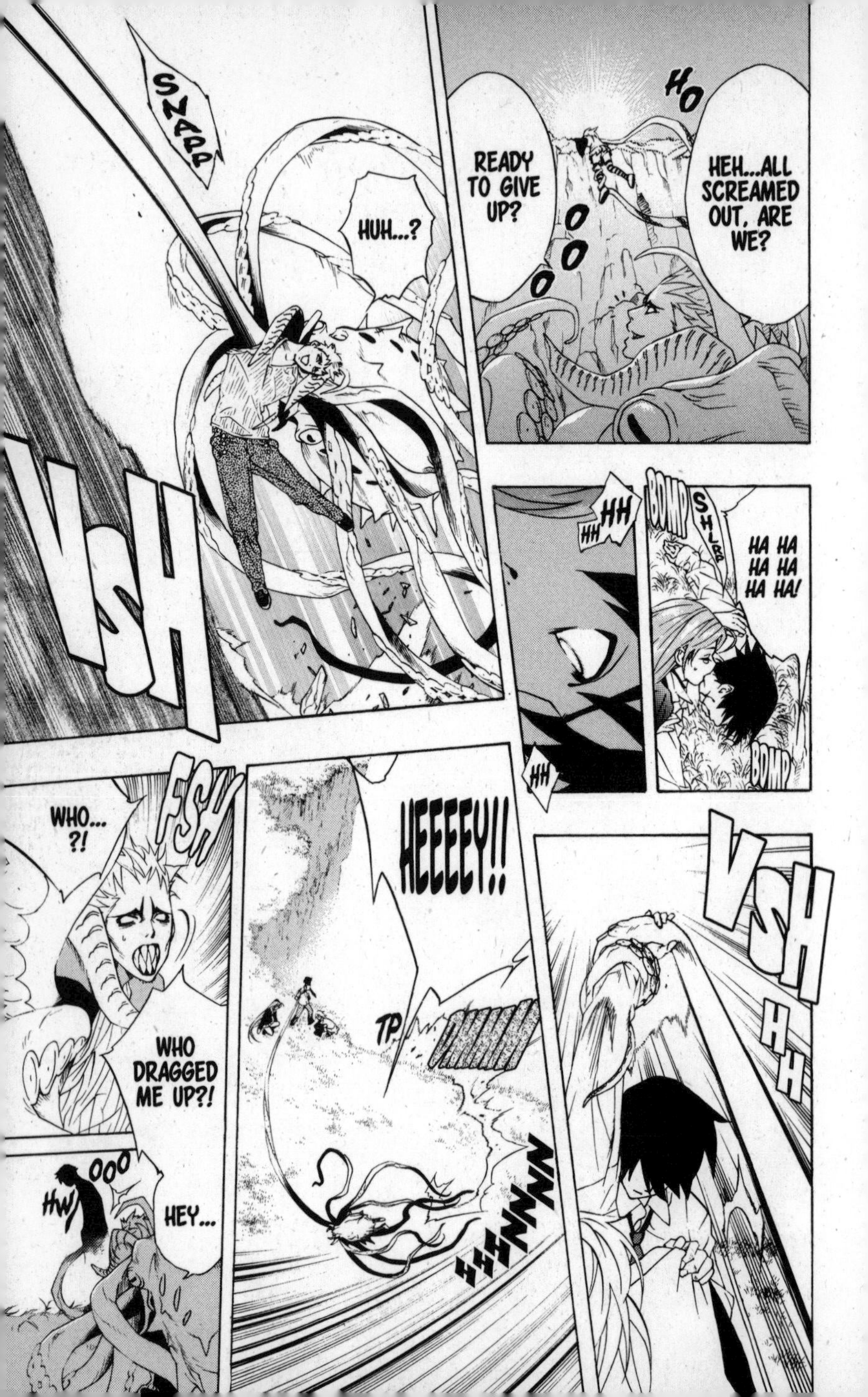
HEH...ALL SCREAMED OUT, ARE WE?
HO
OOO
READY TO GIVE UP?
HA HA HA HA HA HA!
SHLRP
BOMP
BOMP
HHH
HH
HUH...?
SNAPP
VSH
VSH
HH
HEEEEY!!
TP
HHNNNNN
FSH
WHO...?!
WHO DRAGGED ME UP?!
HW
OOO
HEY...

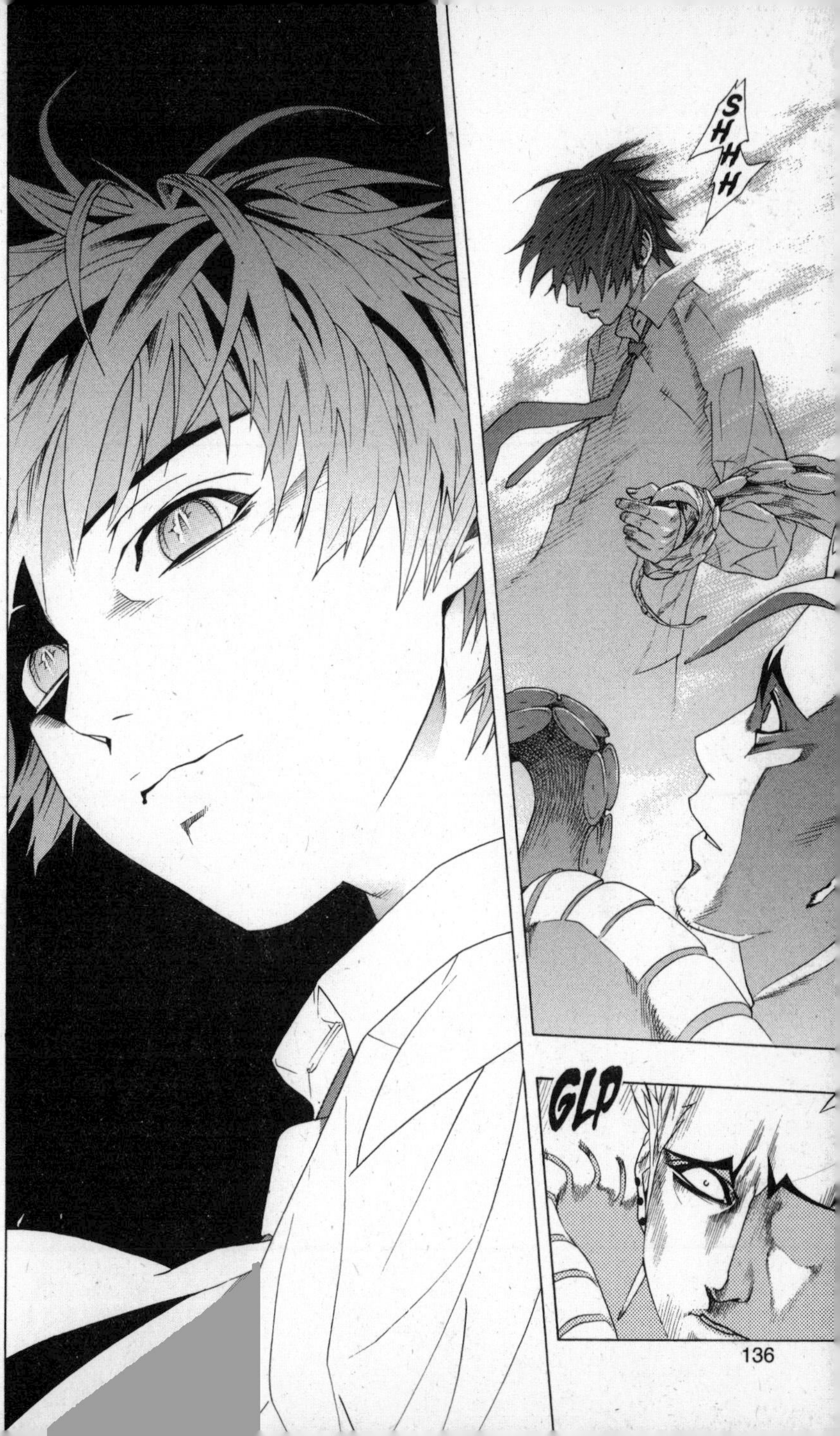
SHHH
GLP

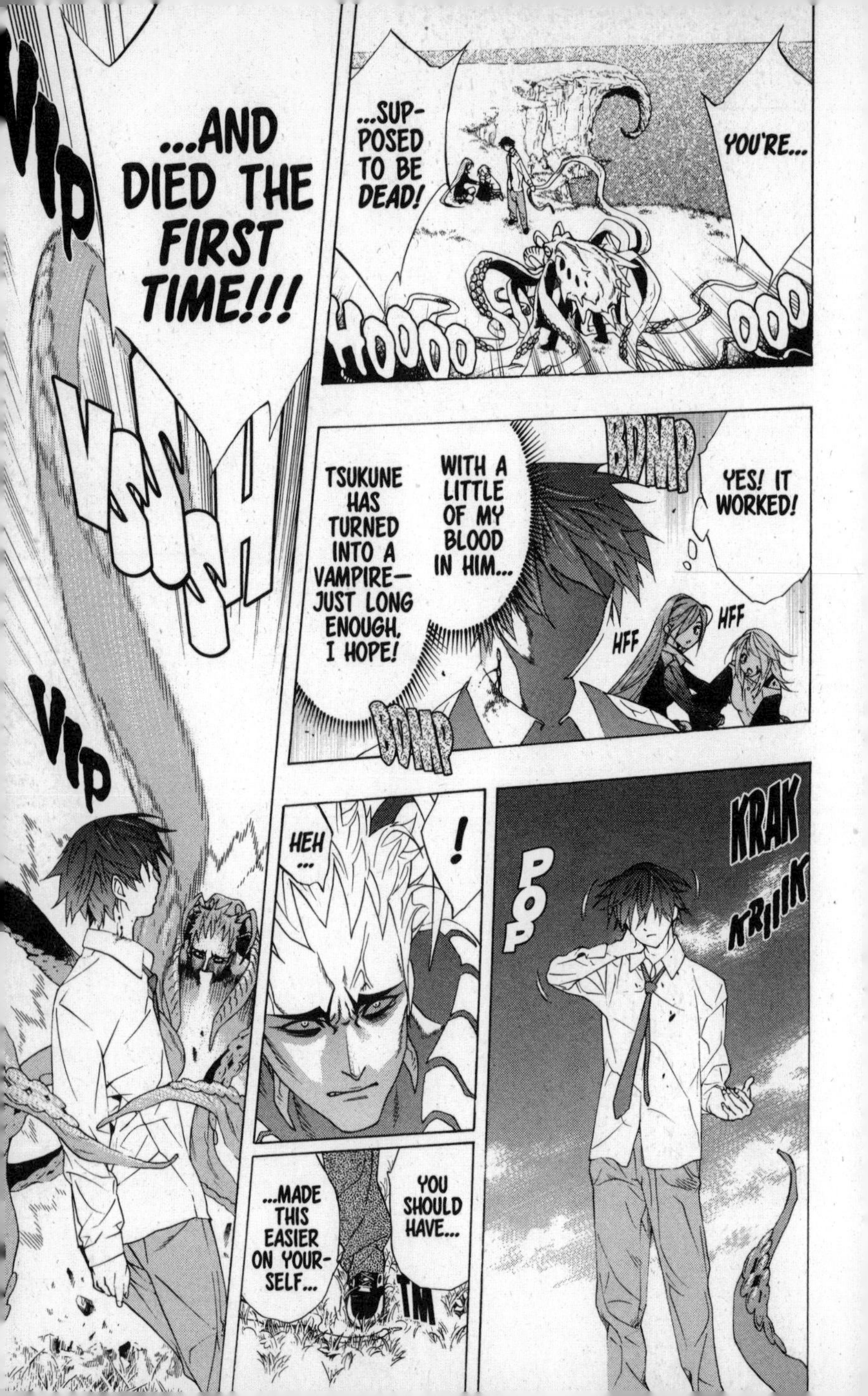
YOU'RE...
...SUP-POSED TO BE DEAD!
HOOOOOOO
YES! IT WORKED!
BDMP
HFF
HFF
WITH A LITTLE OF MY BLOOD IN HIM...
TSUKUNE HAS TURNED INTO A VAMPIRE—JUST LONG ENOUGH, I HOPE!
BDMP
KRAK
KRIIIK
POP
!
HEH...
YOU SHOULD HAVE...
...MADE THIS EASIER ON YOURSELF...
TM
VIIP
...AND DIED THE FIRST TIME!!!
VSSSH
VIIP

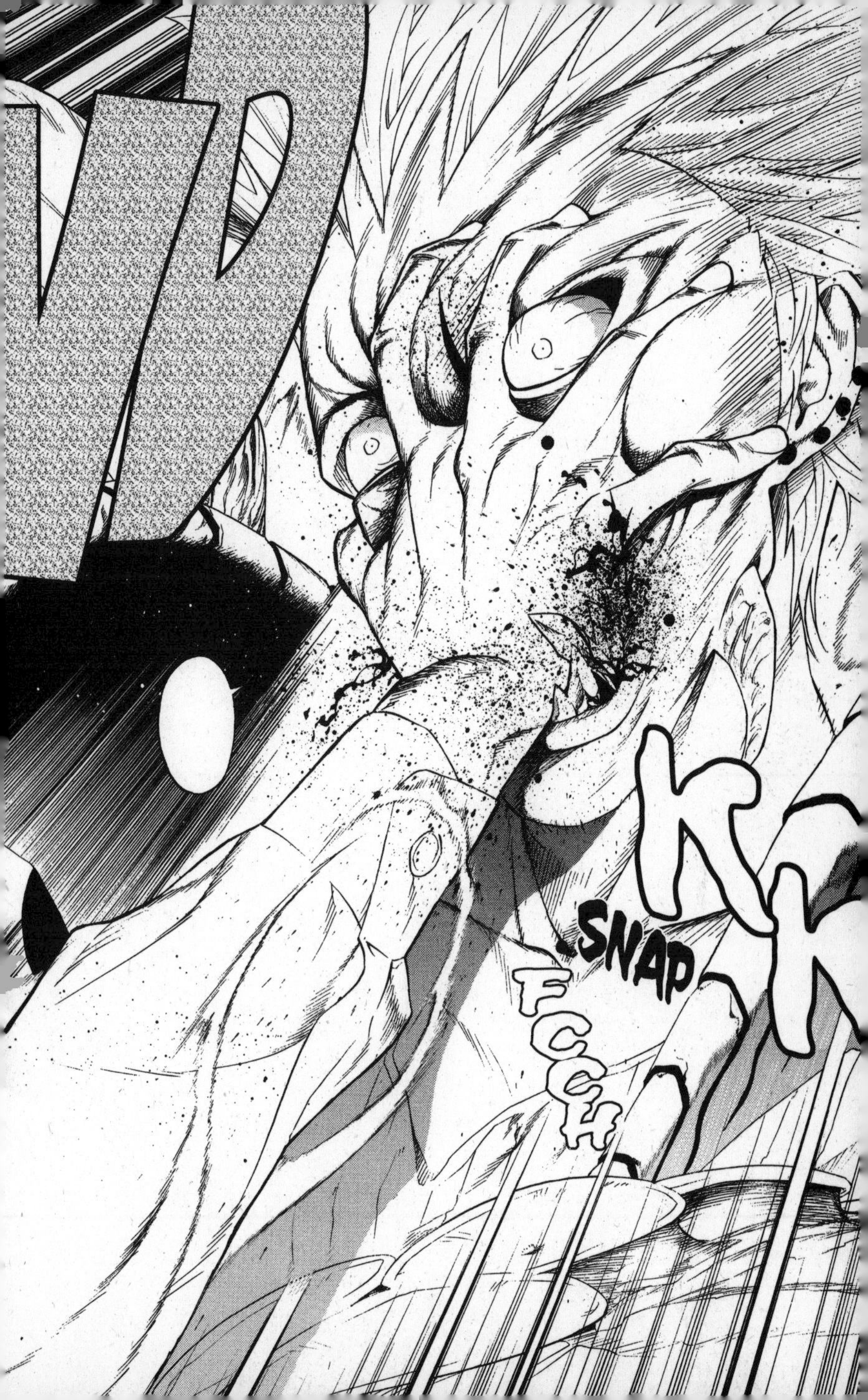
KK
SNAP
FCCH

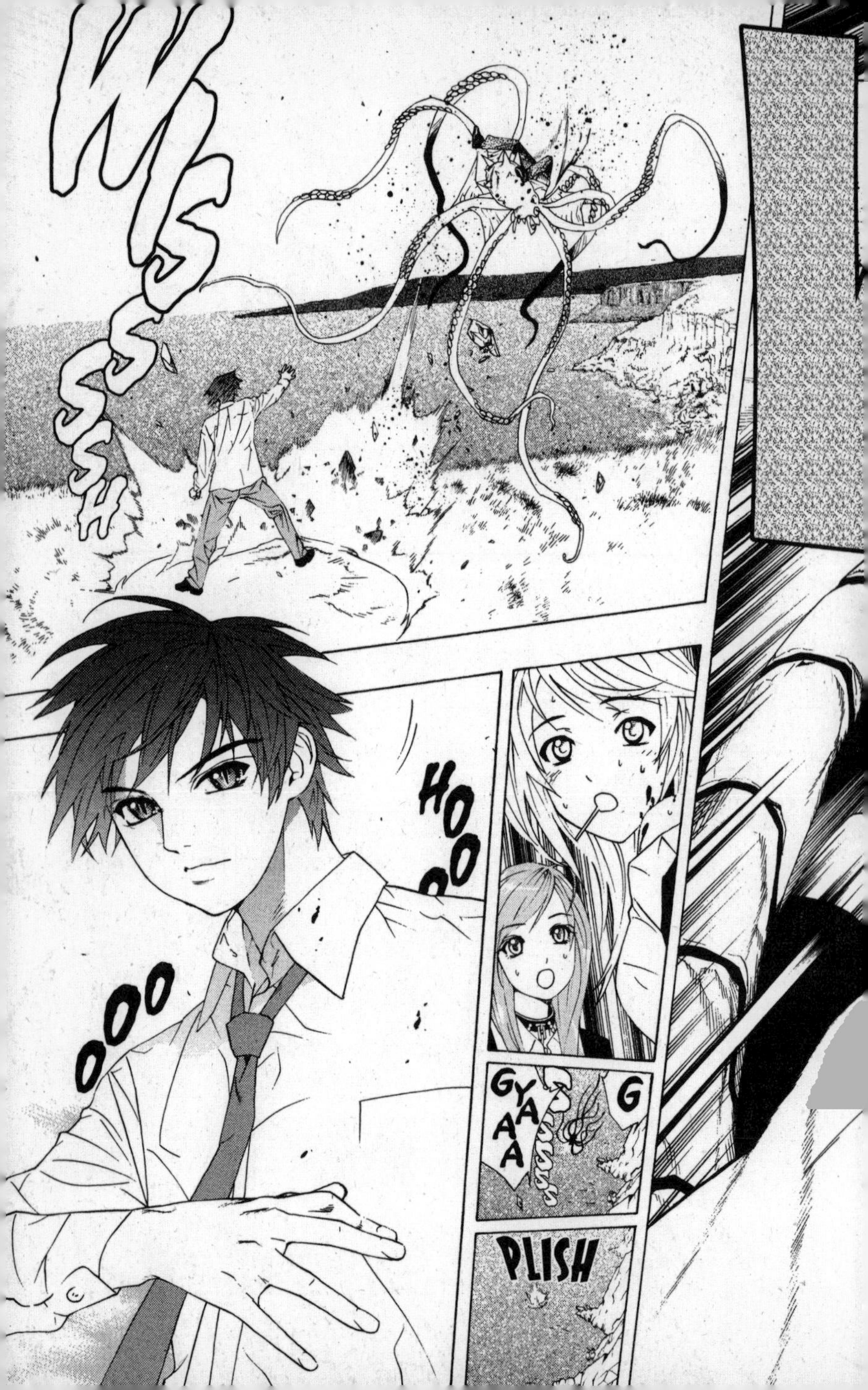
WHSSSSH
G
GYAAA
PLISH
HOOOOOOO

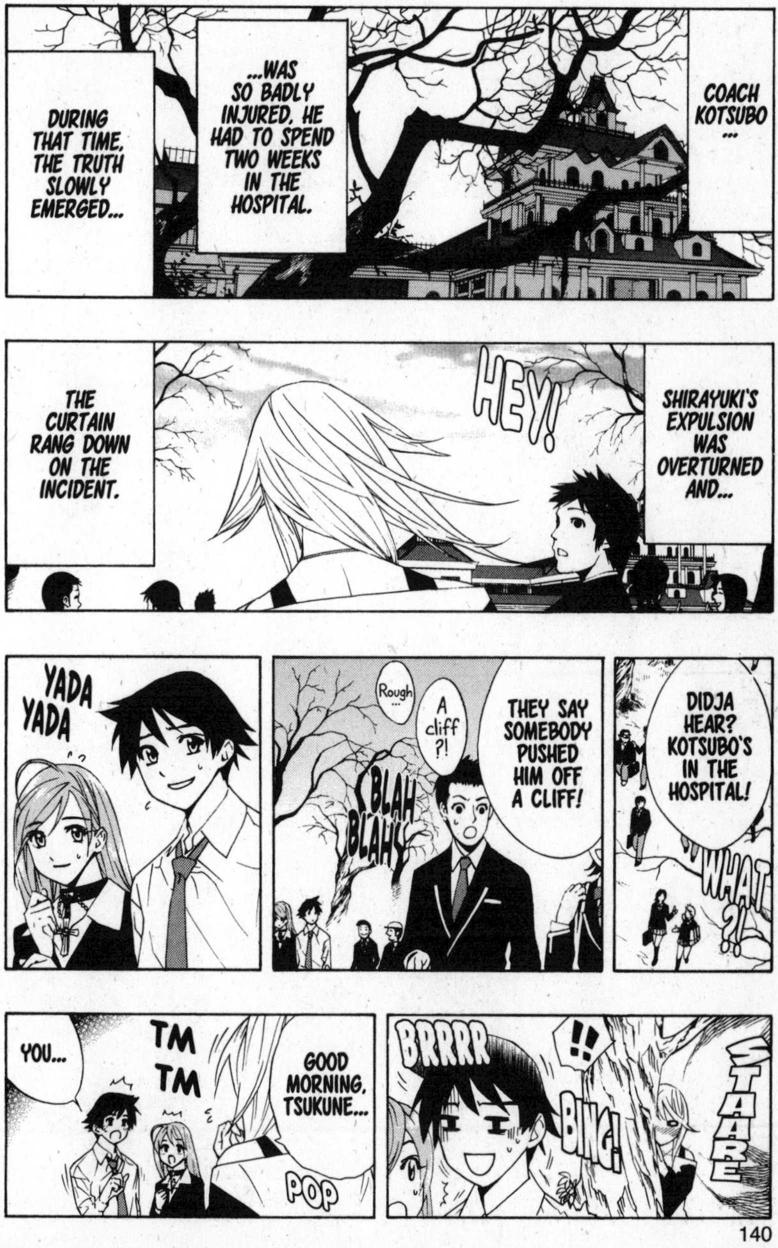
COACH KOTSUBO ...
...WAS SO BADLY INJURED, HE HAD TO SPEND TWO WEEKS IN THE HOSPITAL.
DURING THAT TIME, THE TRUTH SLOWLY EMERGED...
SHIRAYUKI'S EXPULSION WAS OVERTURNED AND...
HEY!
THE CURTAIN RANG DOWN ON THE INCIDENT.
DIDJA HEAR? KOTSUBO'S IN THE HOSPITAL!
WHAT?!
THEY SAY SOMEBODY PUSHED HIM OFF A CLIFF!
A cliff?!
Rough...
BLAH BLAH
YADA YADA
STAARE
!!
BING!
BRRRR
GOOD MORNING, TSUKUNE...
TM TM
YOU...
POP

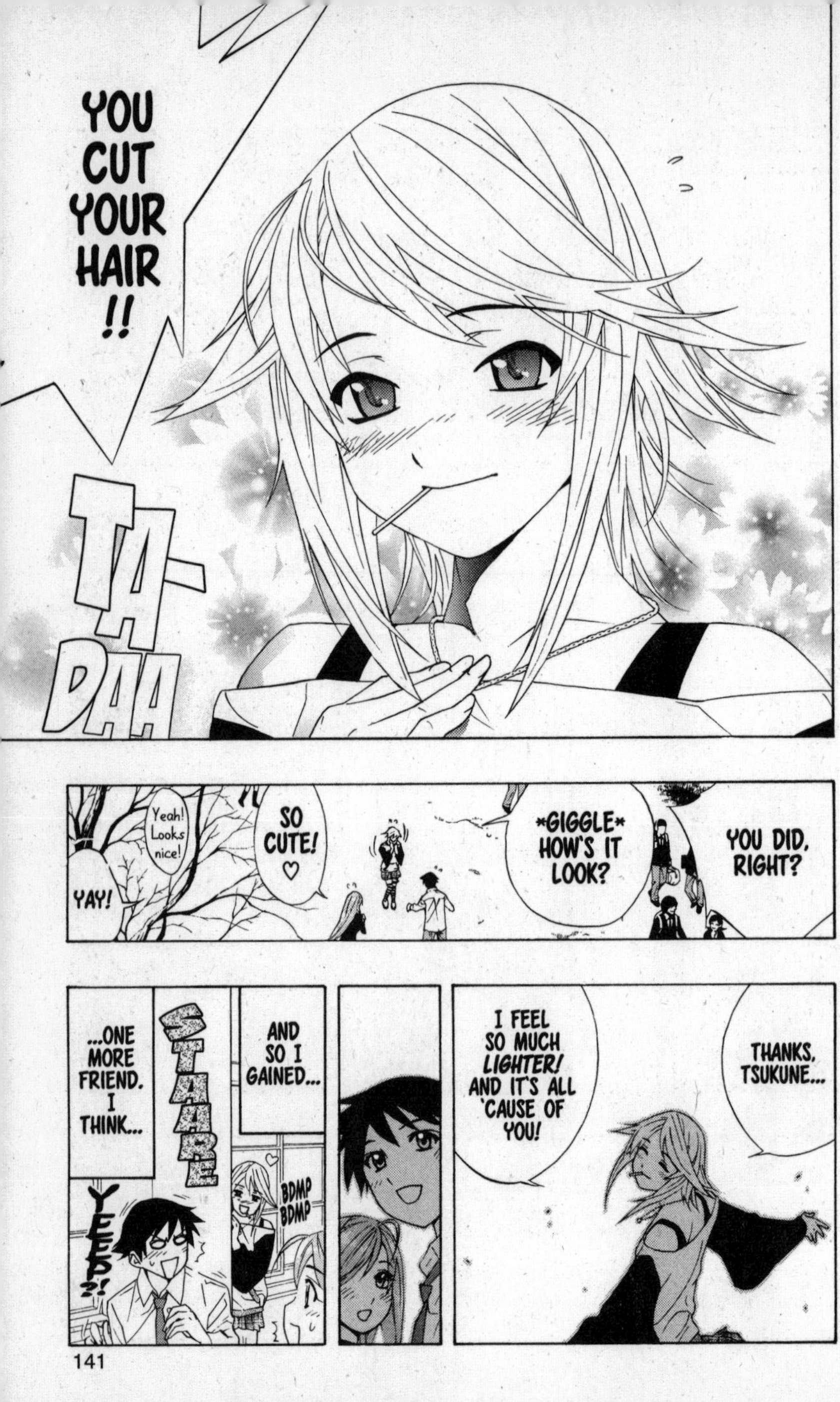
YOU CUT YOUR HAIR!!
TA-DAA
YOU DID, RIGHT?
GIGGLE HOW'S IT LOOK?
SO CUTE! ♡
Yeah! Looks nice!
YAY!
THANKS, TSUKUNE...
I FEEL SO MUCH LIGHTER! AND IT'S ALL 'CAUSE OF YOU!
AND SO I GAINED...
...ONE MORE FRIEND. I THINK...
STAARE
BDMP BDMP
YEEP?!

20: Corrosion

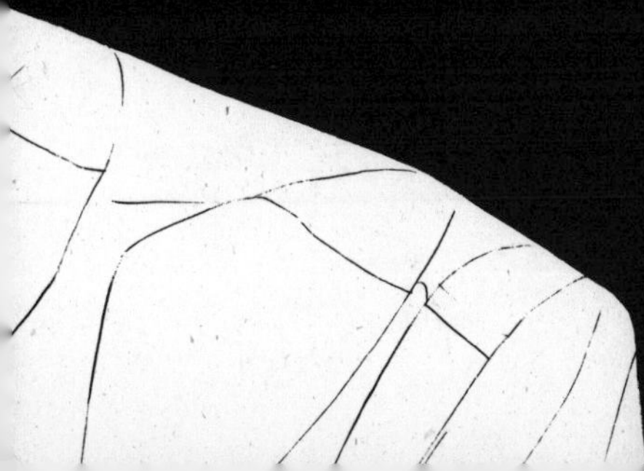

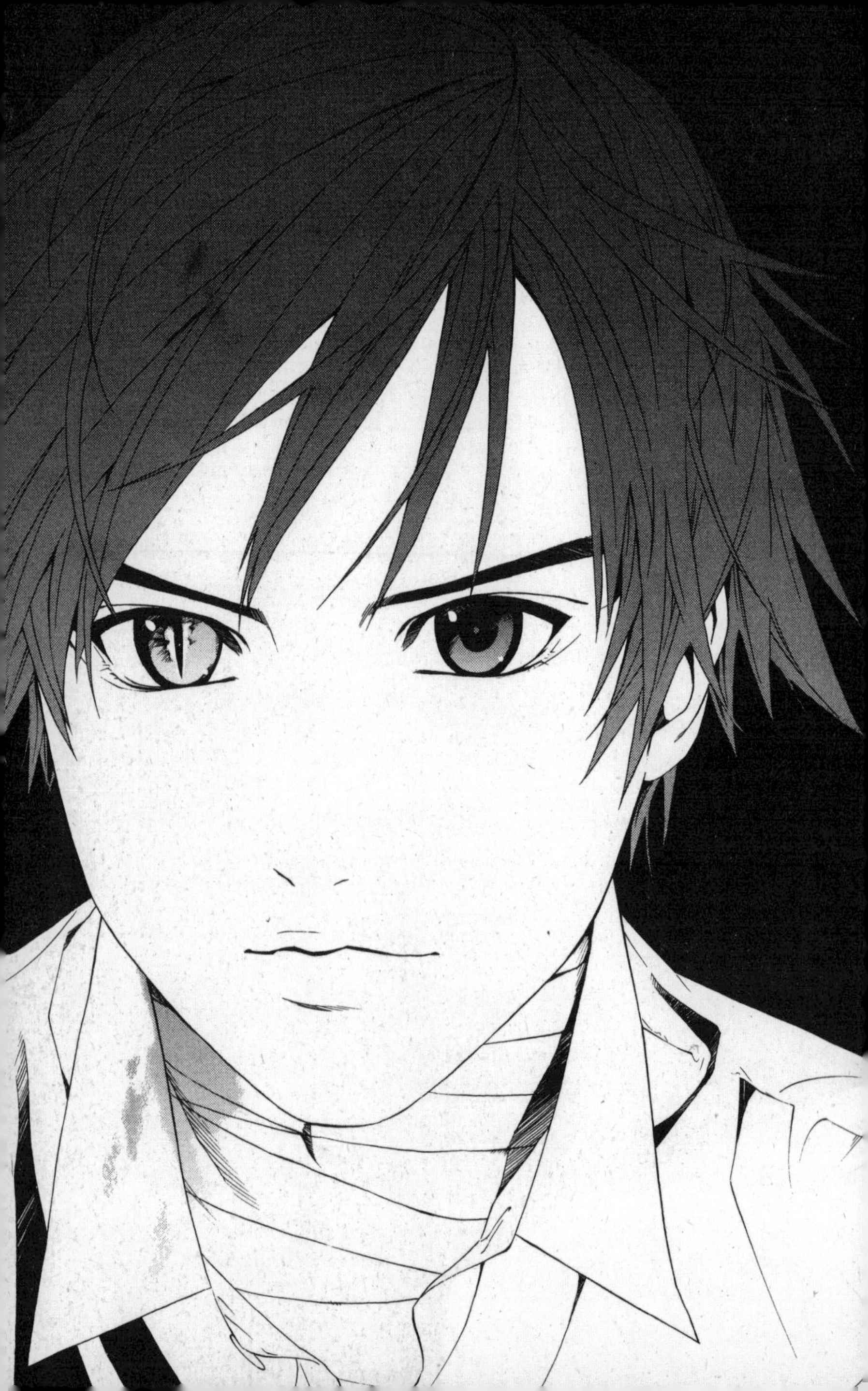

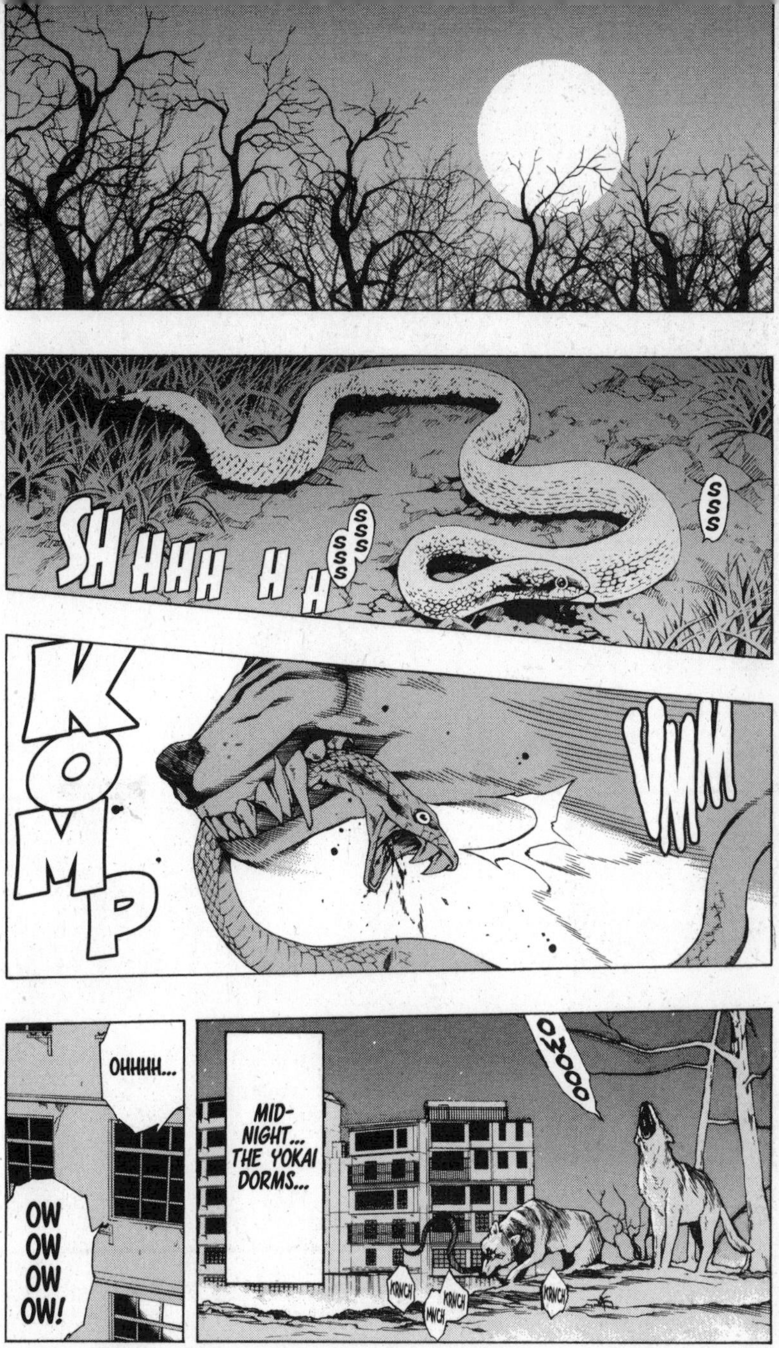
SHHHH H H
VMM
KOMP
OWOOO
MID-NIGHT... THE YOKAI DORMS...
KRNCH
KRNCH
MNCH
KRNCH
OHHHH...
OW OW OW OW!

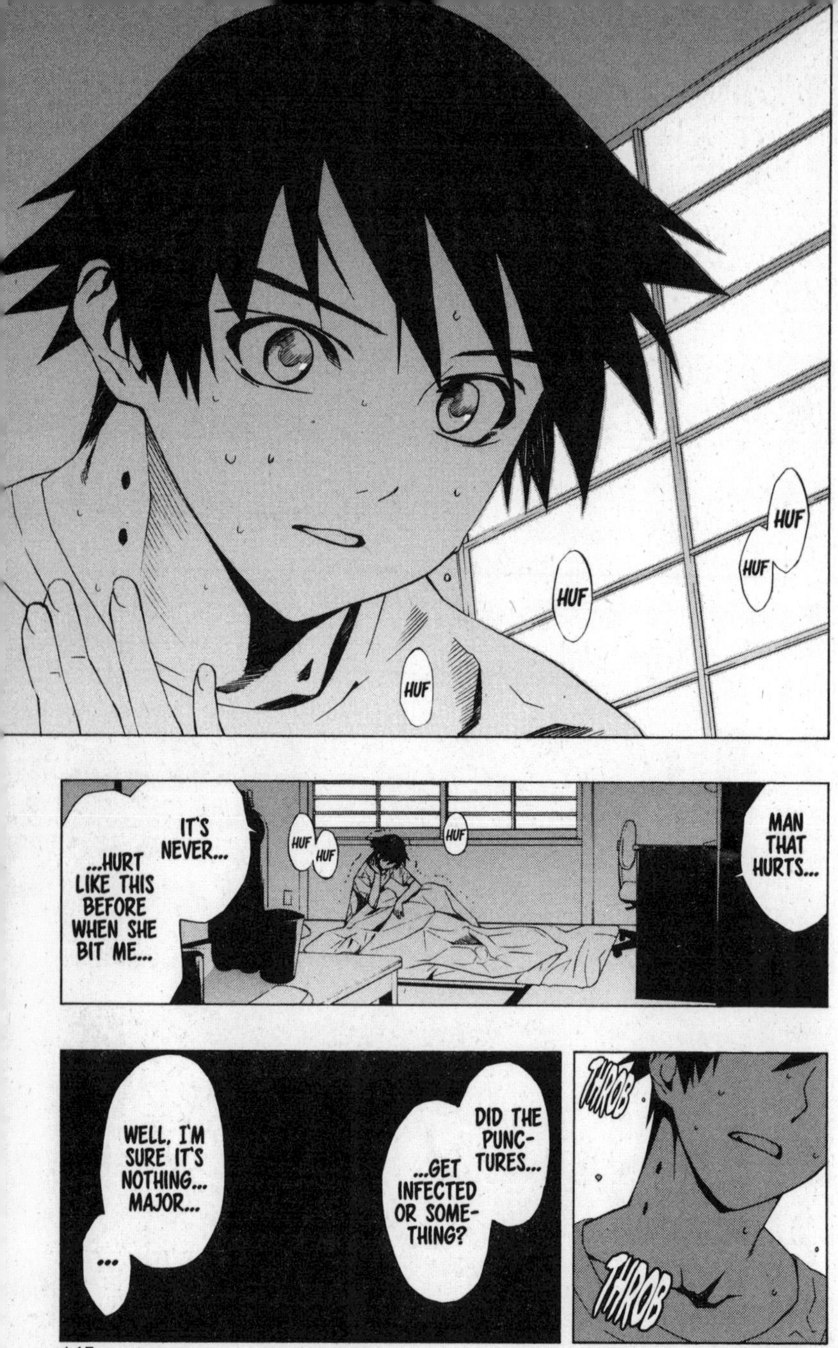
HUF
HUF
HUF
HUF
MAN THAT HURTS...
HUF
HUF
HUF
IT'S NEVER...
...HURT LIKE THIS BEFORE WHEN SHE BIT ME...
THROB
THROB
DID THE PUNC-TURES...
...GET INFECTED OR SOME-THING?
WELL, I'M SURE IT'S NOTHING... MAJOR...
...

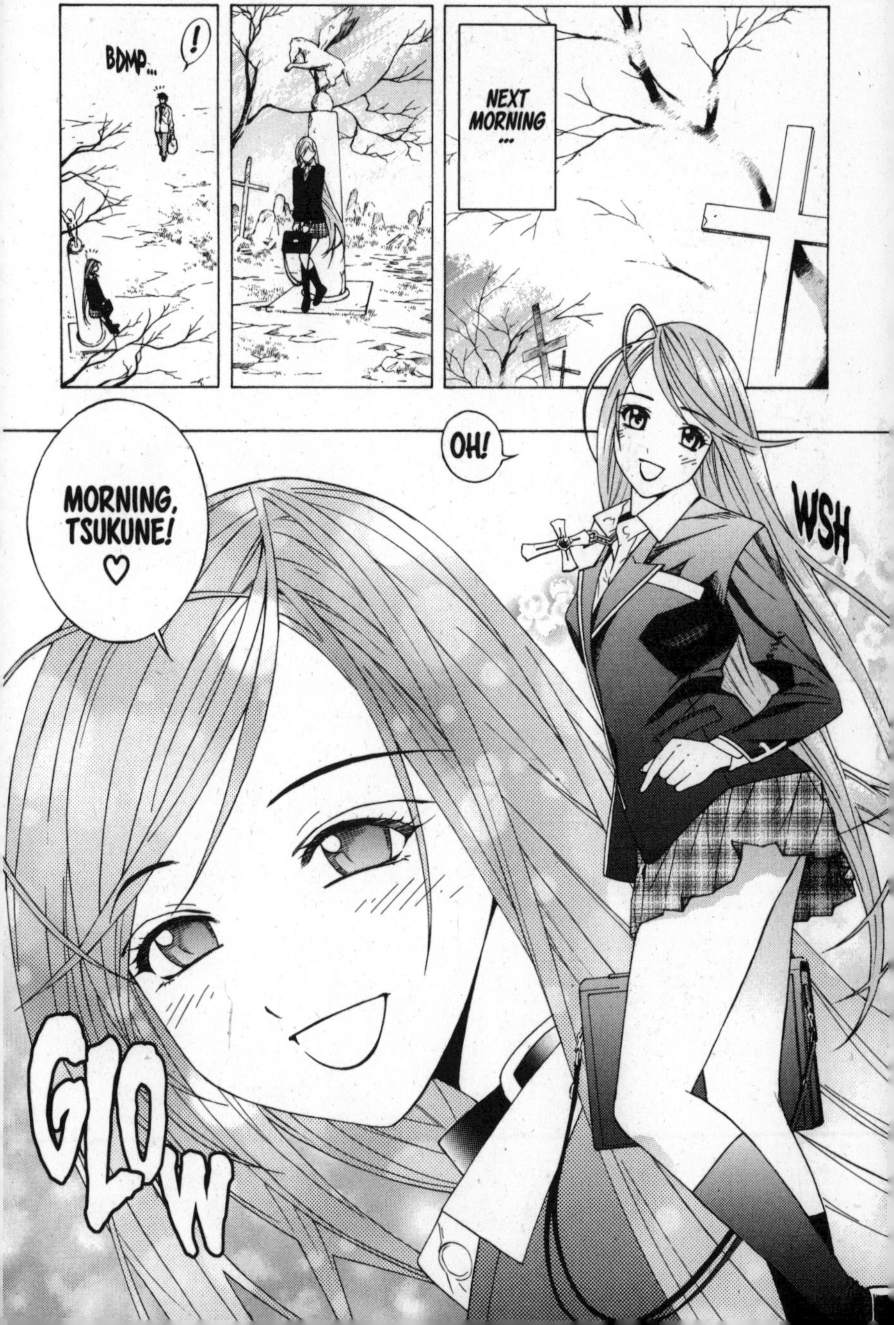
NEXT MORNING...
BDMP...
!
WSH
OH!
MORNING, TSUKUNE! ♡
GLOW

READ THIS WAY

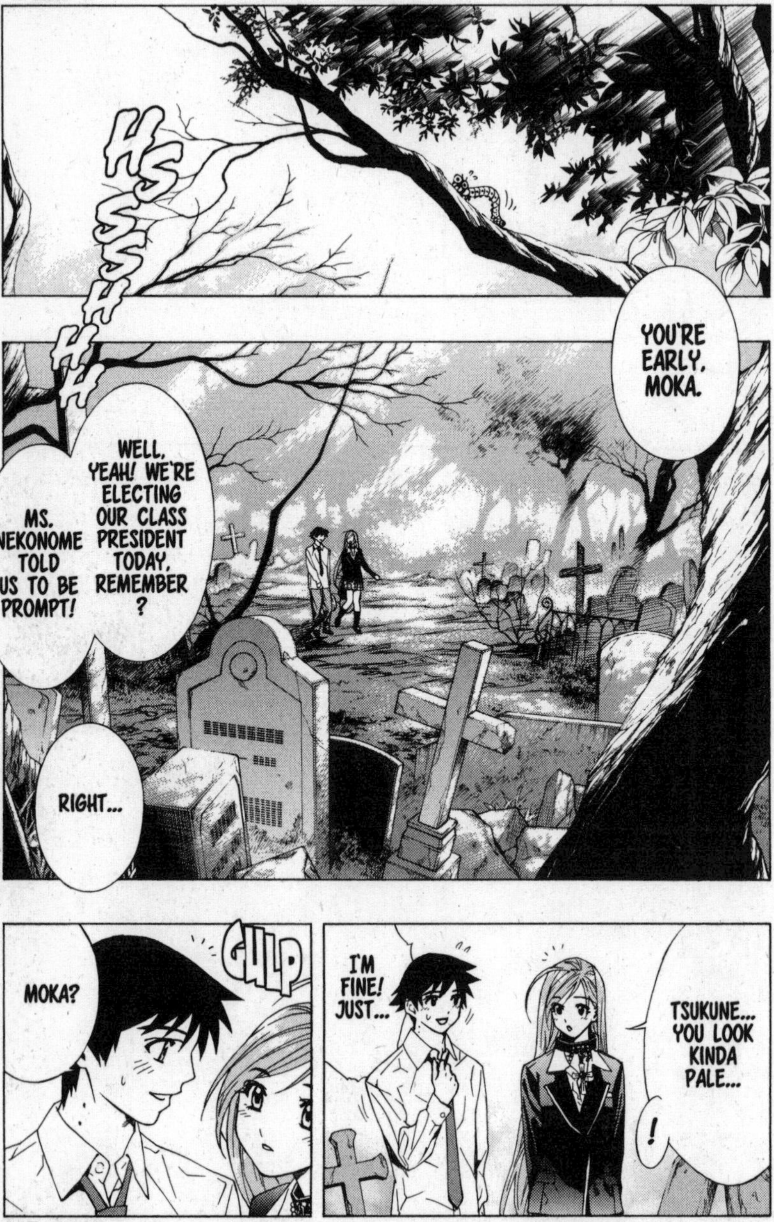
HSSSHHH
YOU'RE EARLY, MOKA.
WELL, YEAH! WE'RE ELECTING OUR CLASS PRESIDENT TODAY, REMEMBER?
MS. NEKONOME TOLD US TO BE PROMPT!
RIGHT...
TSUKUNE... YOU LOOK KINDA PALE...
!
I'M FINE! JUST...
GULP
MOKA?

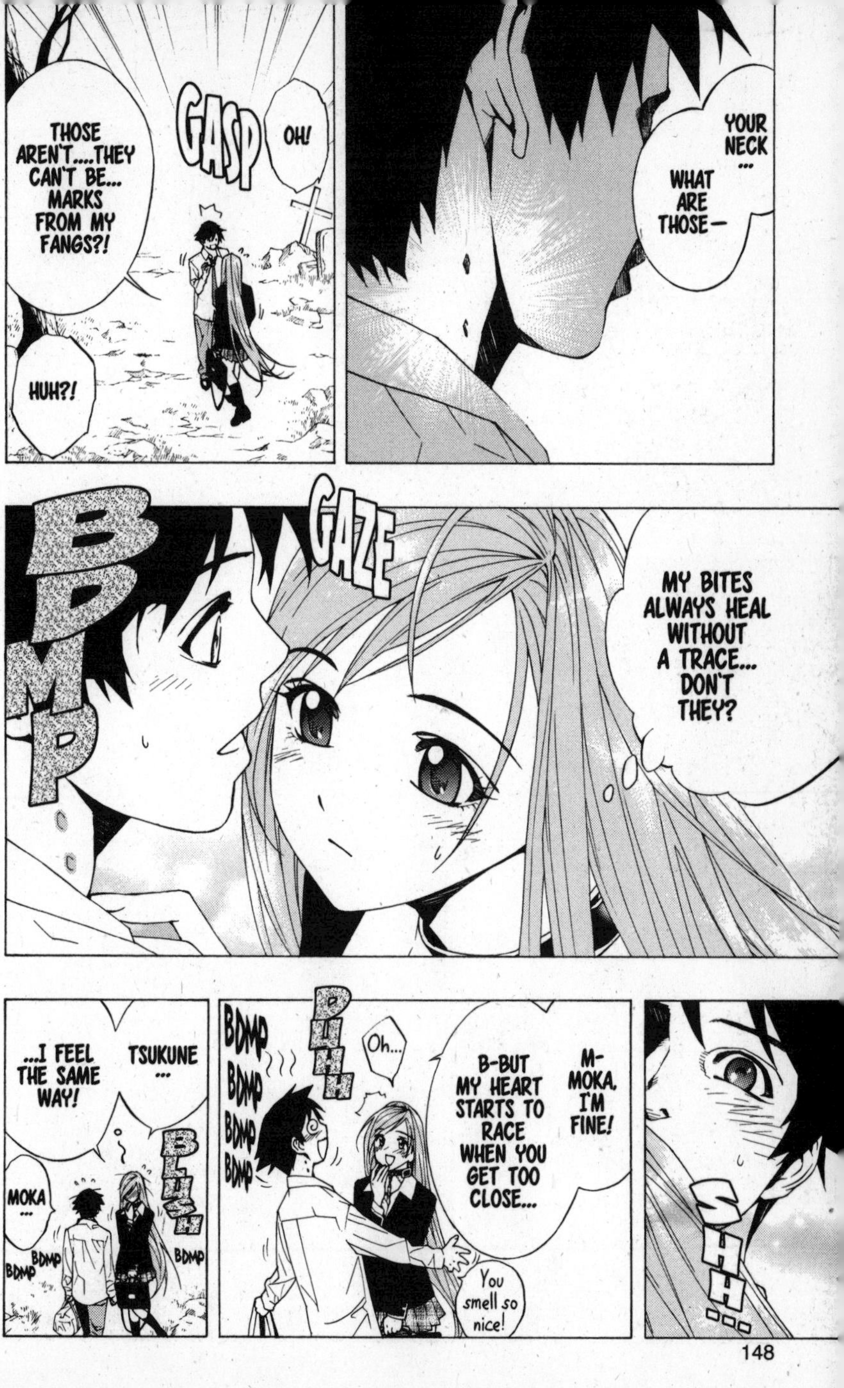
YOUR NECK ... WHAT ARE THOSE—
OH!
GASP
THOSE AREN'T....THEY CAN'T BE... MARKS FROM MY FANGS?!
HUH?!
GAZE
MY BITES ALWAYS HEAL WITHOUT A TRACE... DON'T THEY?
BDMP
SHHH...
M-MOKA, I'M FINE!
B-BUT MY HEART STARTS TO RACE WHEN YOU GET TOO CLOSE...
Oh...
PUHHH
BDMP
BDMP
BDMP
BDMP
You smell so nice!
TSUKUNE ...
...I FEEL THE SAME WAY!
BLUSH
BDMP
MOKA ...
BDMP
BDMP

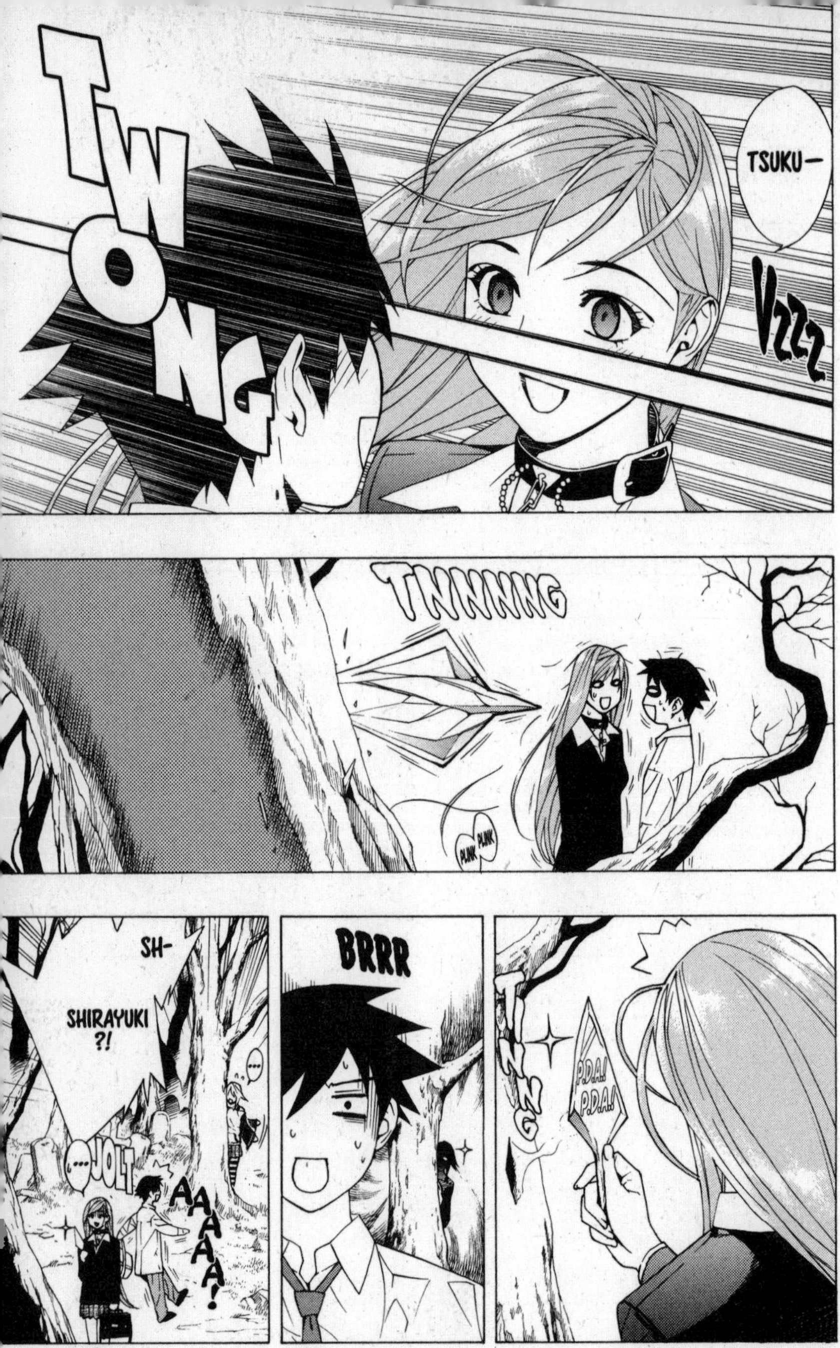
TSUKU—
Vzzz
TWONG
TNNNNG
PLINK PLINK
P.D.A.! P.D.A.!
TNNG
BRRR
SH-
SHIRAYUKI ?!
...
...JOLT
AAAAA!

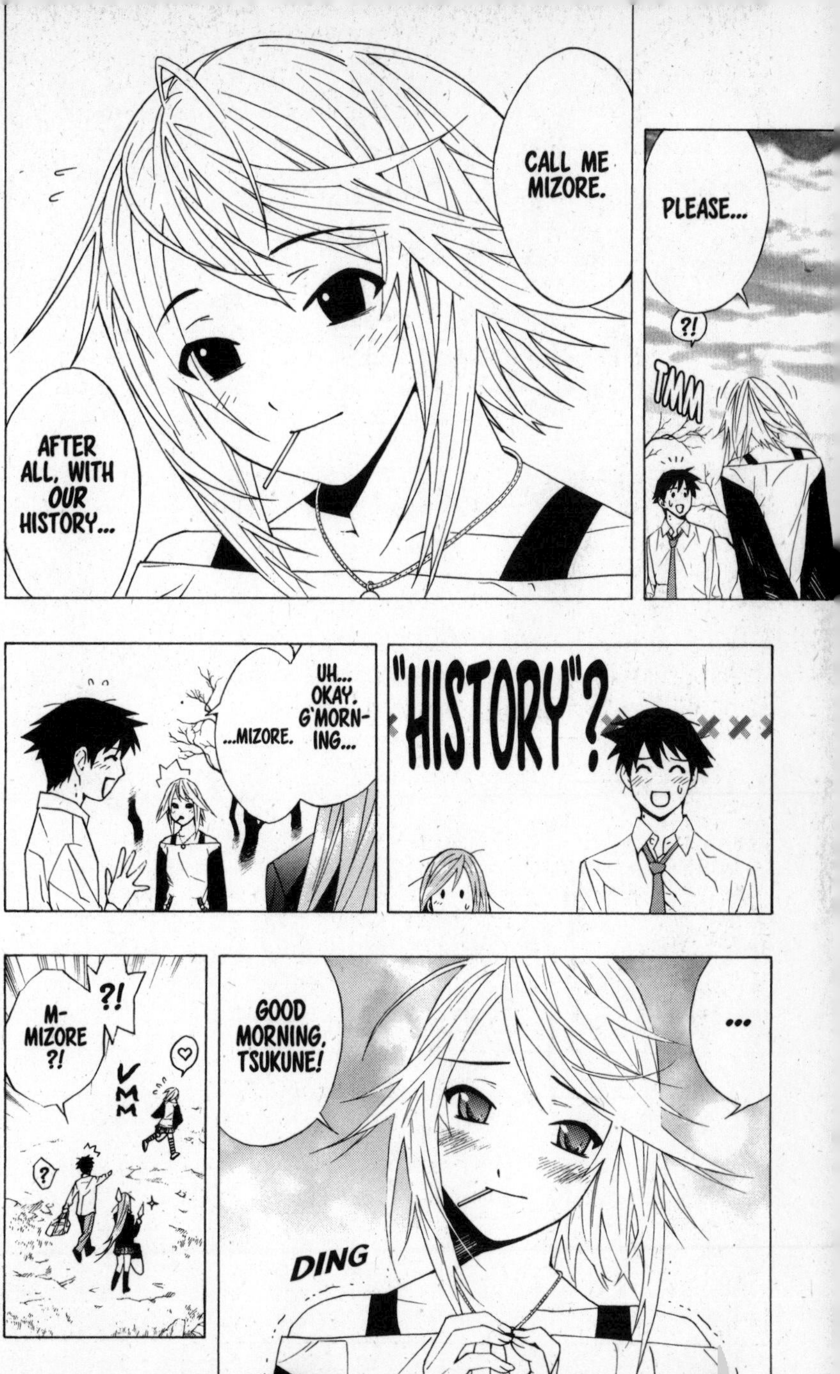
PLEASE...
?!
TMM
CALL ME MIZORE.
AFTER ALL, WITH OUR HISTORY...
"HISTORY"?
UH... OKAY. G'MORN-ING...
...MIZORE.
...
GOOD MORNING, TSUKUNE!
DING
?!
M-MIZORE?!
VMM
?

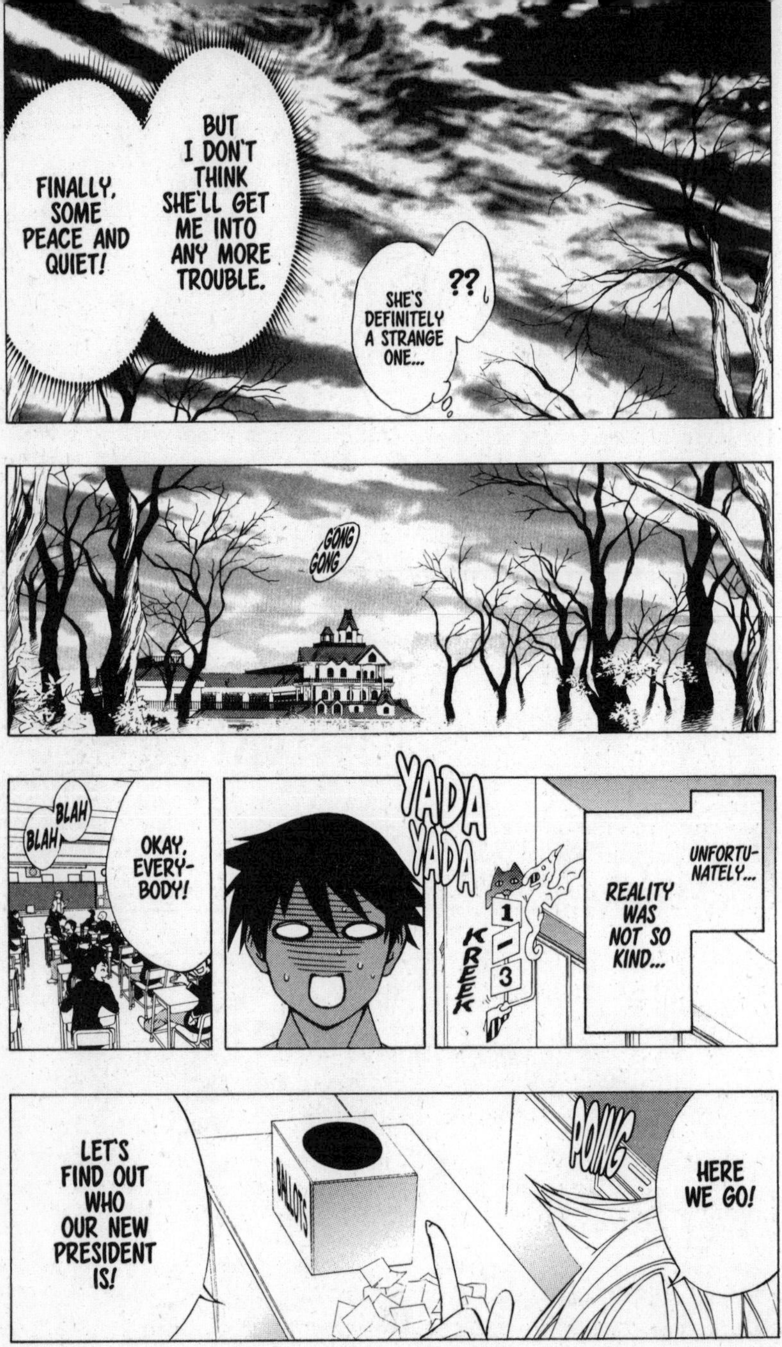
??
SHE'S DEFINITELY A STRANGE ONE...
BUT I DON'T THINK SHE'LL GET ME INTO ANY MORE TROUBLE.
FINALLY, SOME PEACE AND QUIET!
GONG GONG
UNFORTUNATELY...
REALITY WAS NOT SO KIND...
1-3
KREEK
YADA YADA
OKAY, EVERYBODY!
BLAH
BLAH
HERE WE GO!
POING
BALLOTS
LET'S FIND OUT WHO OUR NEW PRESIDENT IS!

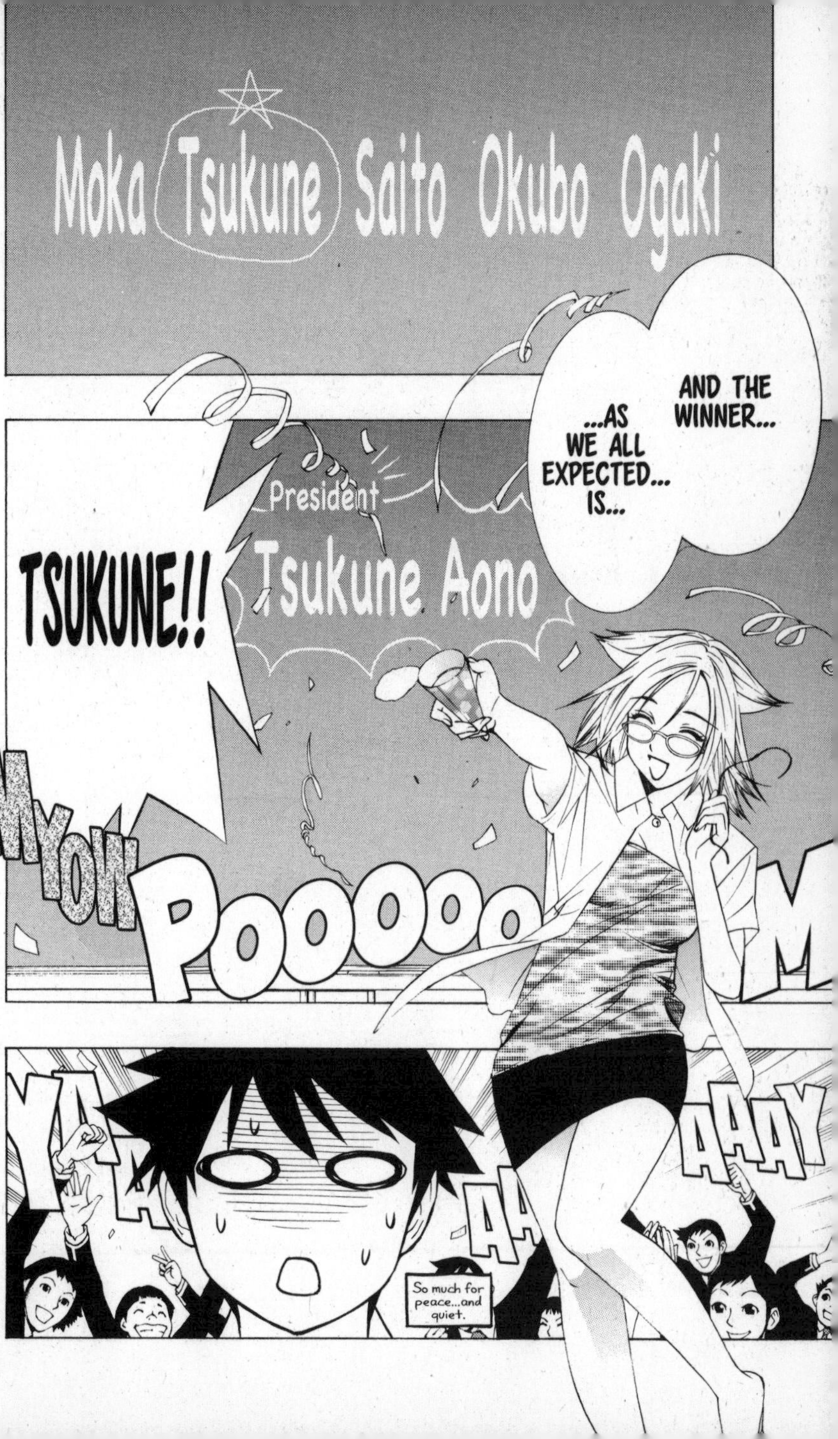
Moka Tsukune Saito Okubo Ogaki
AND THE WINNER...
...AS WE ALL EXPECTED... IS...
President
Tsukune Aono
TSUKUNE!!
POOOOOM
MYOW
AAAY
AA
A
YA
So much for peace...and quiet.

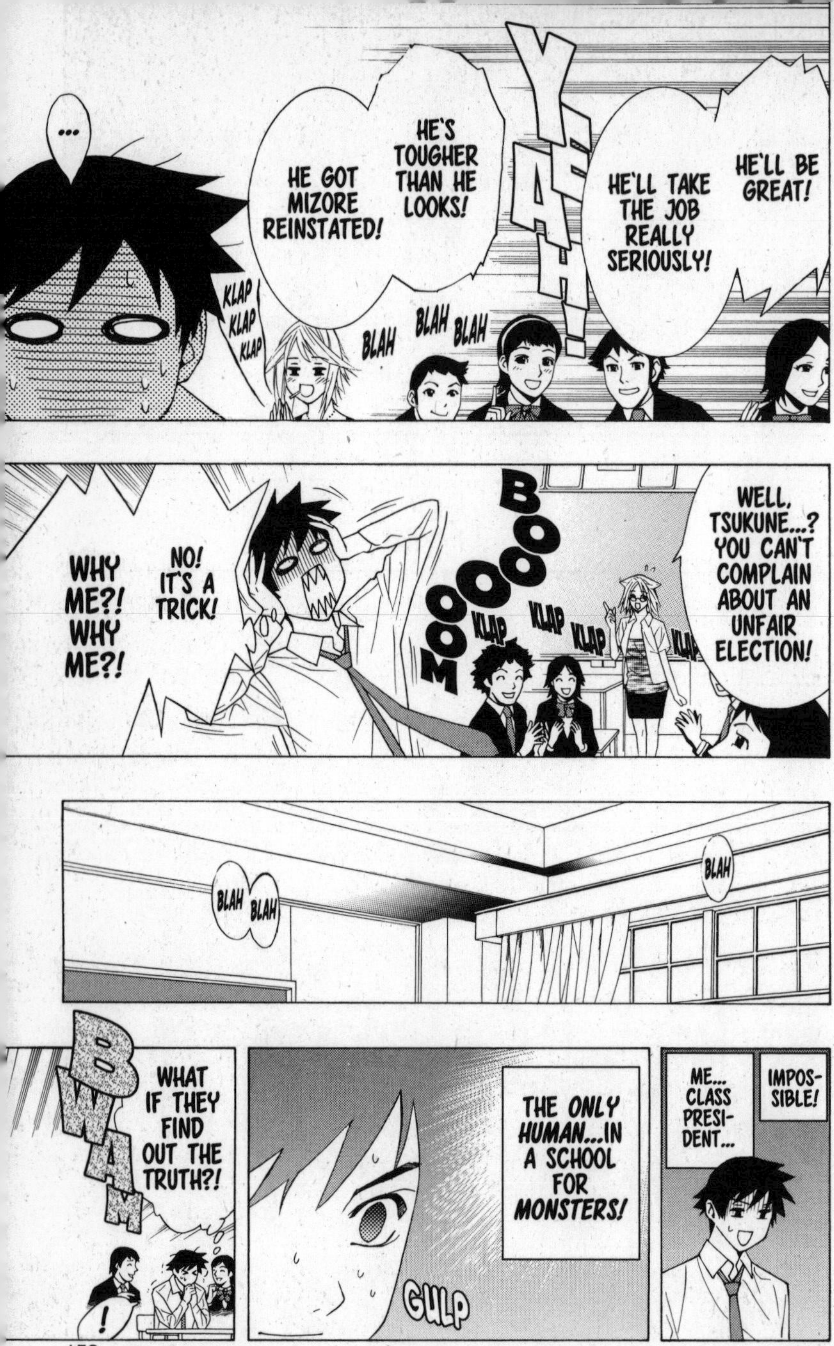
HE'LL BE GREAT!
HE'LL TAKE THE JOB REALLY SERIOUSLY!
YEAH!
HE'S TOUGHER THAN HE LOOKS!
HE GOT MIZORE REINSTATED!
BLAH BLAH
BLAH
KLAP KLAP KLAP
...
WELL, TSUKUNE...? YOU CAN'T COMPLAIN ABOUT AN UNFAIR ELECTION!
KLAP
KLAP
KLAP
KLAP
BOOOOOOM
NO! IT'S A TRICK!
WHY ME?! WHY ME?!
BLAH
BLAH BLAH
IMPOSSIBLE!
ME... CLASS PRESIDENT...
THE ONLY HUMAN...IN A SCHOOL FOR MONSTERS!
GULP
WHAT IF THEY FIND OUT THE TRUTH?!
BWAM
!

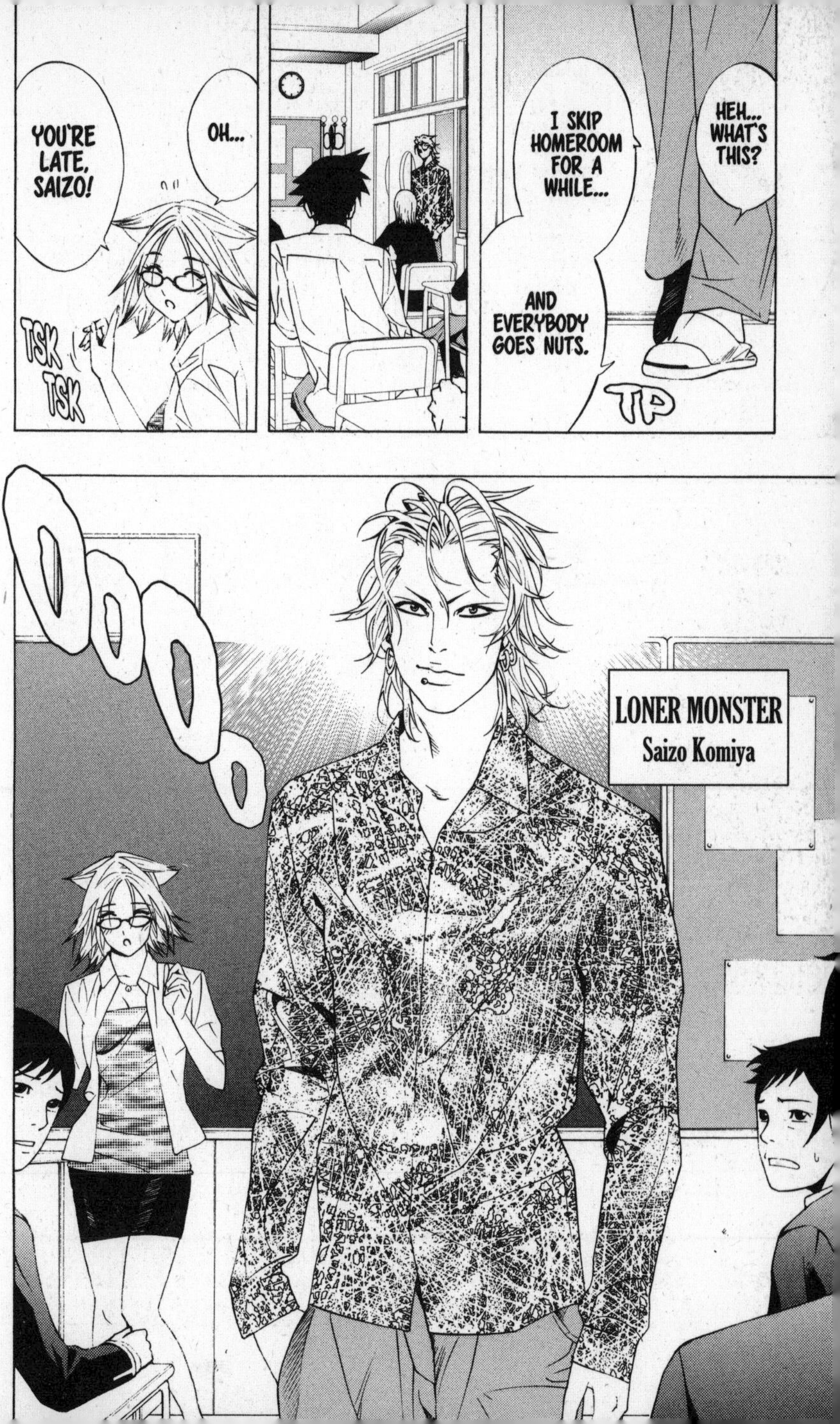
HEH... WHAT'S THIS?
I SKIP HOMEROOM FOR A WHILE...
AND EVERYBODY GOES NUTS.
TP
OH...
YOU'RE LATE, SAIZO!
TSK TSK
OOOOO
LONER MONSTER
Saizo Komiya

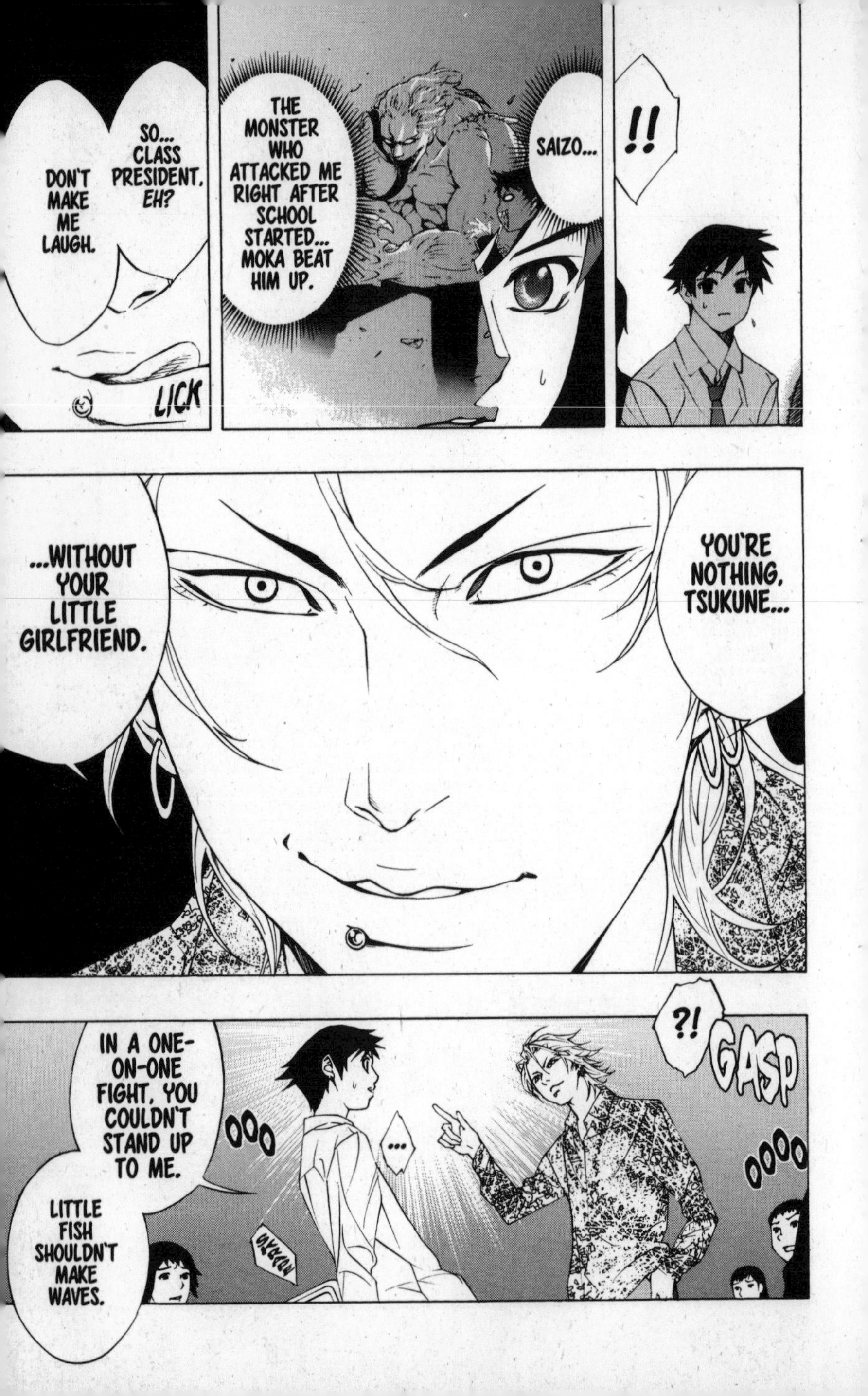
!!
SAIZO...
THE MONSTER WHO ATTACKED ME RIGHT AFTER SCHOOL STARTED... MOKA BEAT HIM UP.
SO... CLASS PRESIDENT, EH?
DON'T MAKE ME LAUGH.
LICK
YOU'RE NOTHING, TSUKUNE...
...WITHOUT YOUR LITTLE GIRLFRIEND.
?!
GASP
OOOO
...
IN A ONE-ON-ONE FIGHT, YOU COULDN'T STAND UP TO ME.
OOO
LITTLE FISH SHOULDN'T MAKE WAVES.

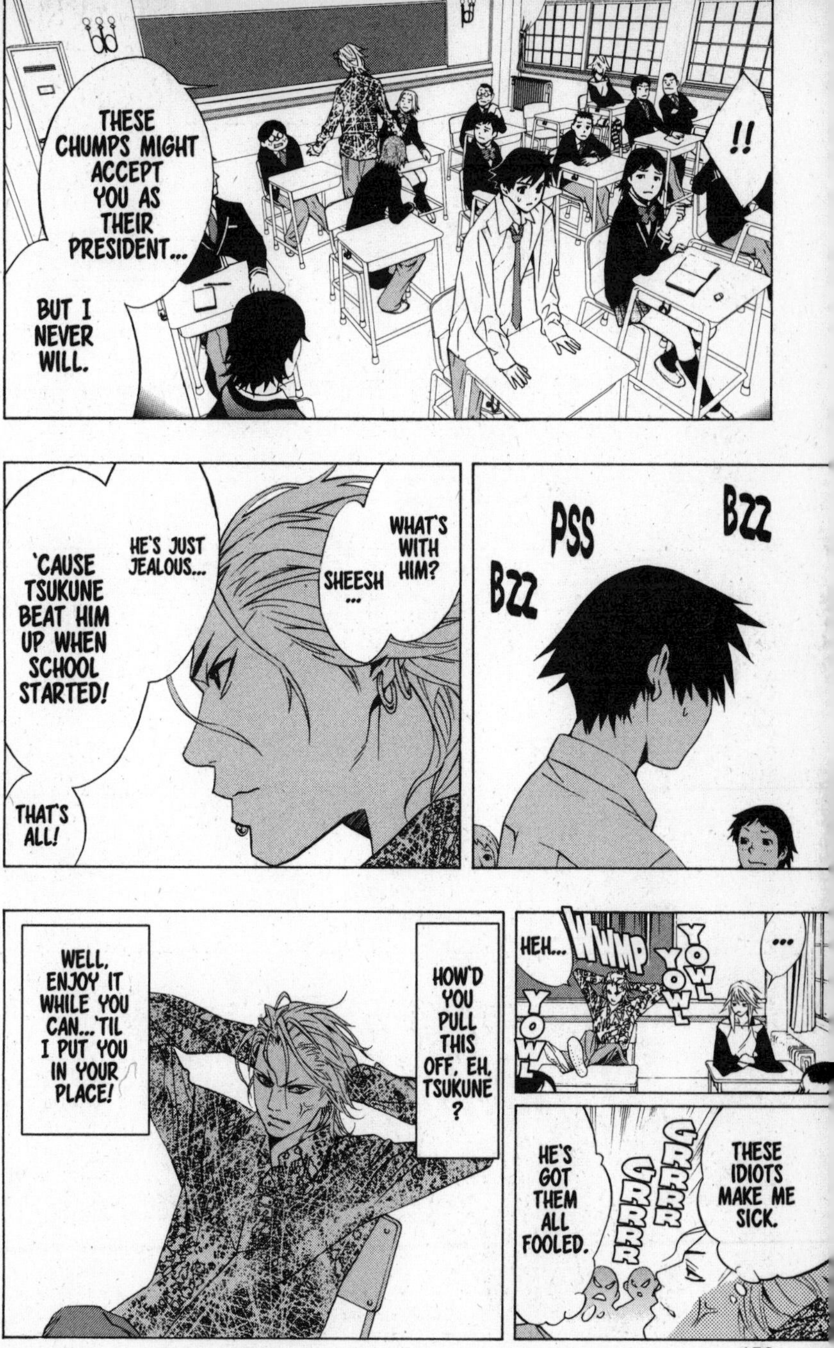
!!
THESE CHUMPS MIGHT ACCEPT YOU AS THEIR PRESIDENT...
BUT I NEVER WILL.
BZZ
PSS
BZZ
WHAT'S WITH HIM?
SHEESH...
HE'S JUST JEALOUS...
'CAUSE TSUKUNE BEAT HIM UP WHEN SCHOOL STARTED!
THAT'S ALL!
...
YOWL
YOWL
WWMP
HEH...
YOWL
THESE IDIOTS MAKE ME SICK.
GRRRR
GRRRR
HE'S GOT THEM ALL FOOLED.
HOW'D YOU PULL THIS OFF, EH, TSUKUNE?
WELL, ENJOY IT WHILE YOU CAN...'TIL I PUT YOU IN YOUR PLACE!

READ THIS WAY

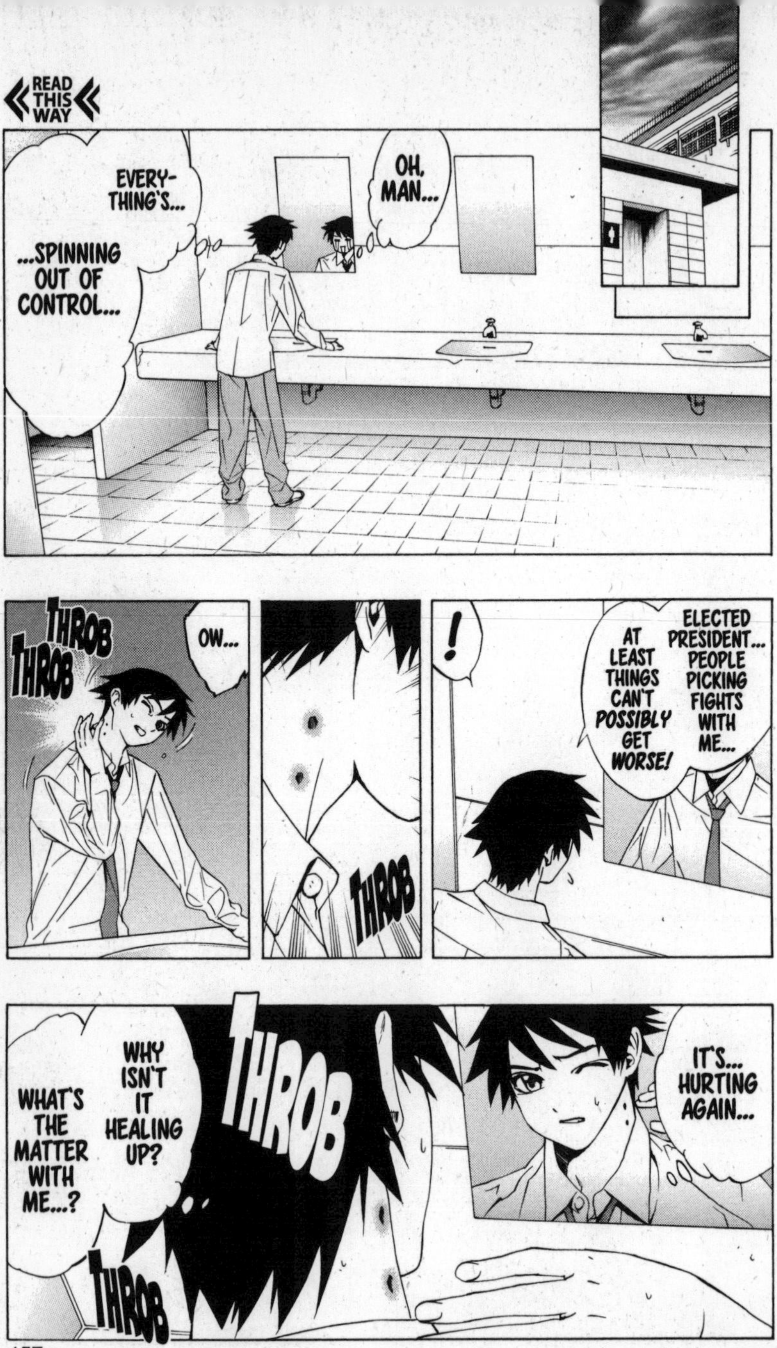

OH, MAN...
EVERY-THING'S...
...SPINNING OUT OF CONTROL...
!
ELECTED PRESIDENT... PEOPLE PICKING FIGHTS WITH ME...
AT LEAST THINGS CAN'T POSSIBLY GET WORSE!
THROB
THROB THROB
OW...
IT'S... HURTING AGAIN...
THROB
WHY ISN'T IT HEALING UP?
WHAT'S THE MATTER WITH ME...?
THROB

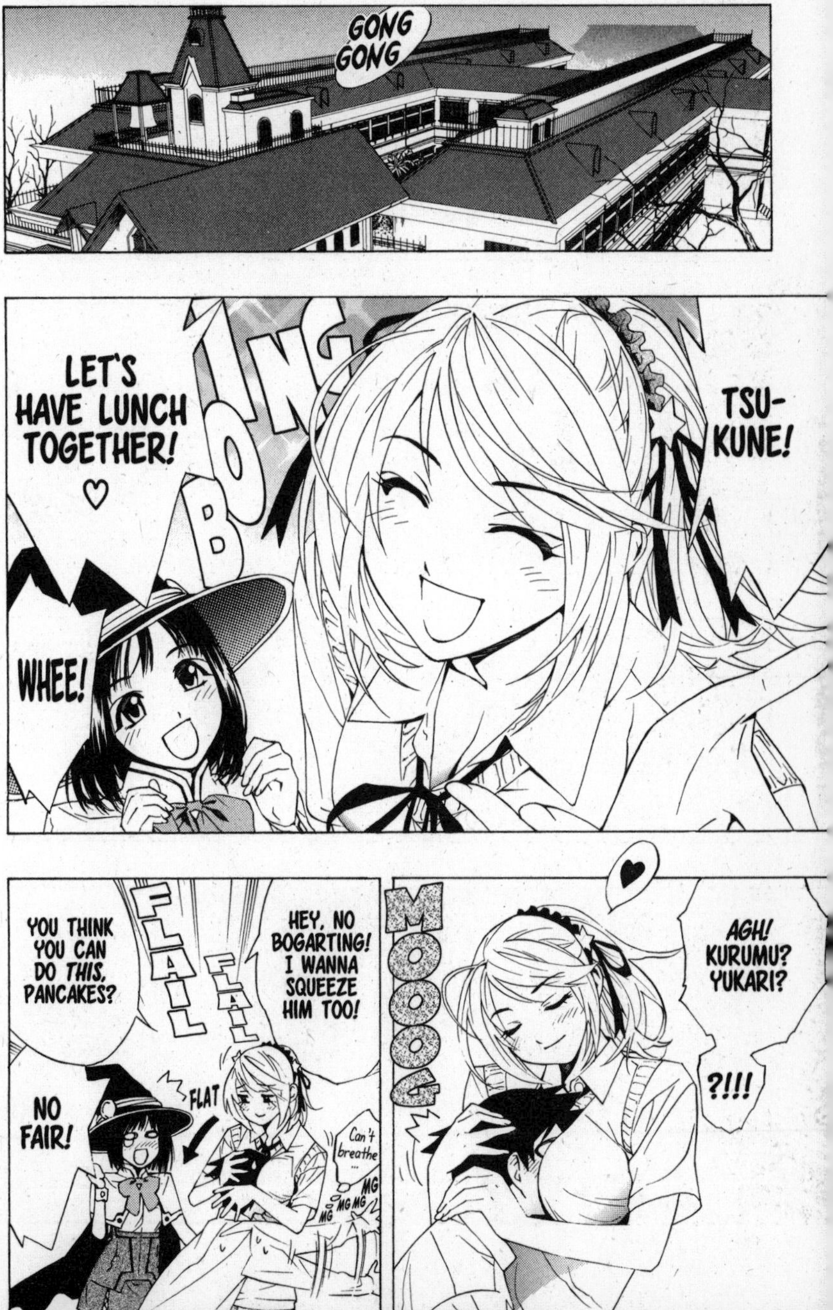

GONG GONG
TSU-KUNE!
BOING
LET'S HAVE LUNCH TOGETHER! ♡
WHEE!
♥
AGH! KURUMU? YUKARI?
?!!!
MOOOG
HEY, NO BOGARTING! I WANNA SQUEEZE HIM TOO!
FLAIL FLAIL
YOU THINK YOU CAN DO *THIS*, PANCAKES?
FLAT
Can't breathe ...
MG MG MG MG
NO FAIR!

READ THIS WAY

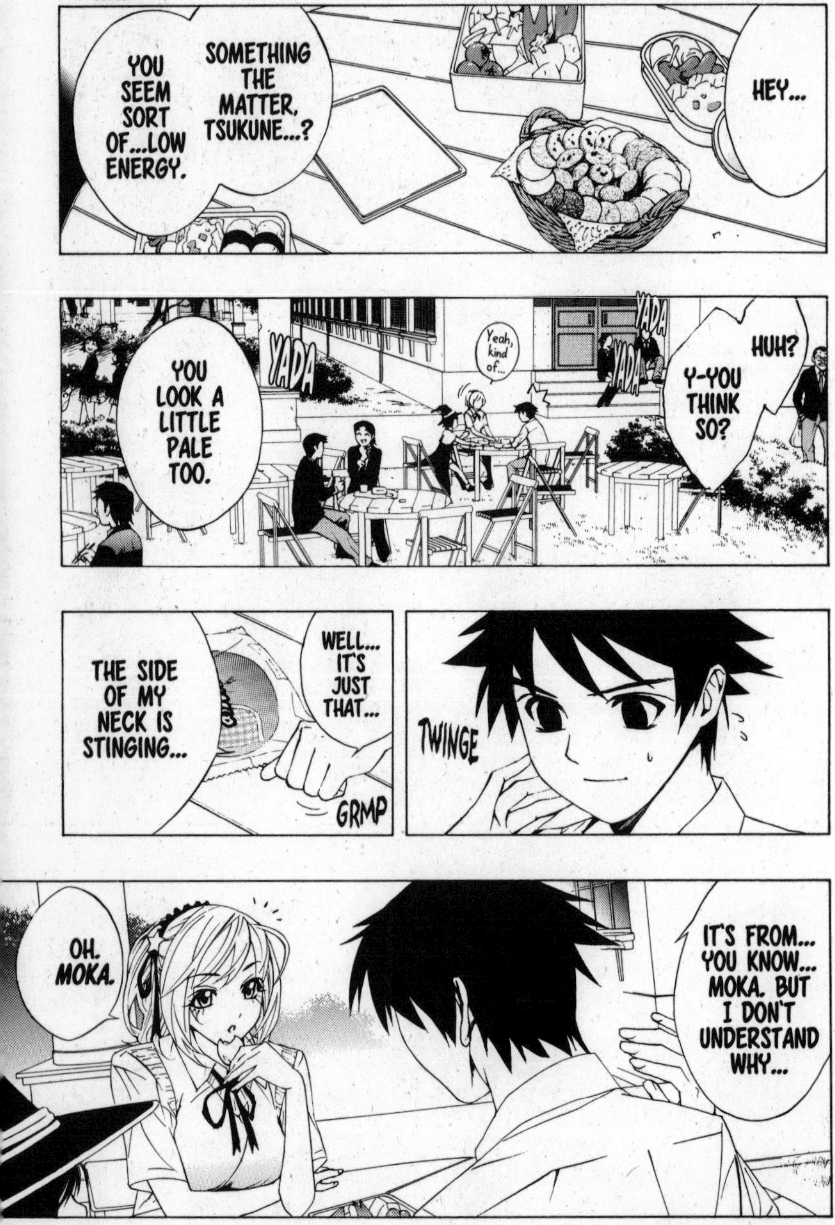
HEY...
SOMETHING THE MATTER, TSUKUNE...?
YOU SEEM SORT OF...LOW ENERGY.
YADA
HUH? Y-YOU THINK SO?
YADA
Yeah, kind of...
YADA
YOU LOOK A LITTLE PALE TOO.
TWINGE
WELL... IT'S JUST THAT...
THE SIDE OF MY NECK IS STINGING...
GRMP
IT'S FROM... YOU KNOW... MOKA. BUT I DON'T UNDERSTAND WHY...
OH. MOKA.

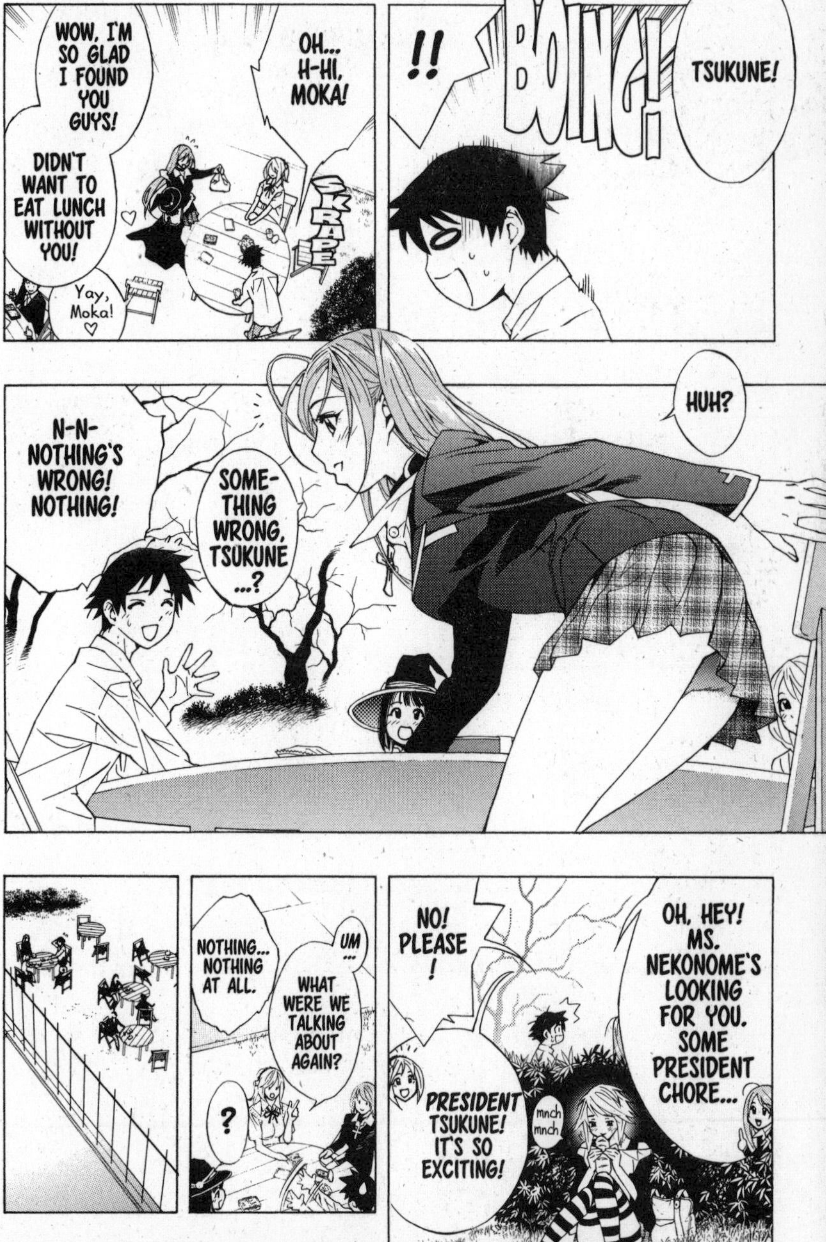
TSUKUNE!
BOING!
!!
OH... H-HI, MOKA!
SKRAPE
WOW, I'M SO GLAD I FOUND YOU GUYS!
DIDN'T WANT TO EAT LUNCH WITHOUT YOU!
Yay, Moka! ♡
HUH?
SOME-THING WRONG, TSUKUNE ...?
N-N-NOTHING'S WRONG! NOTHING!
OH, HEY! MS. NEKONOME'S LOOKING FOR YOU. SOME PRESIDENT CHORE...
NO! PLEASE!
PRESIDENT TSUKUNE! IT'S SO EXCITING!
mnch mnch
UM ...
WHAT WERE WE TALKING ABOUT AGAIN?
NOTHING... NOTHING AT ALL.
?

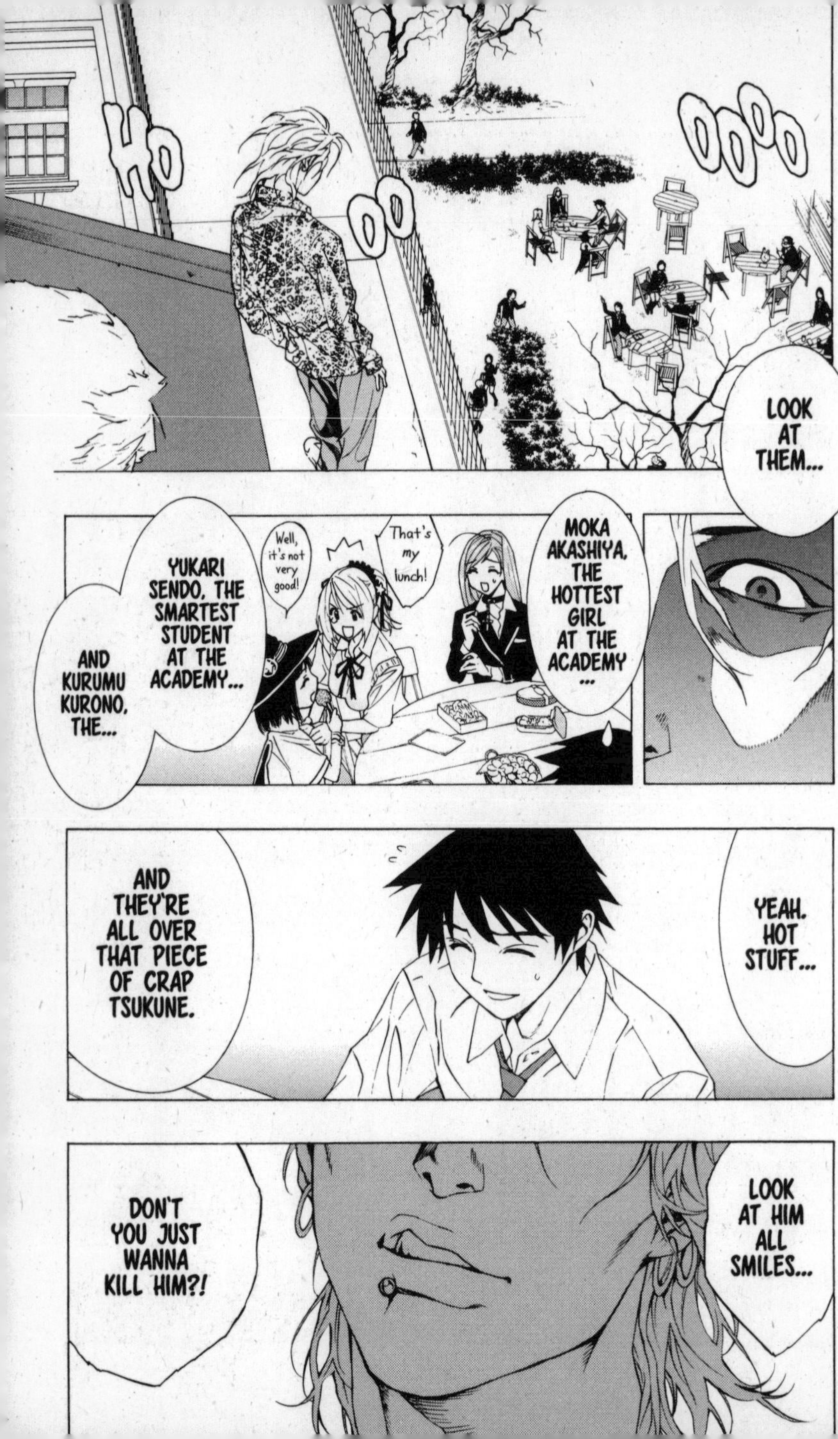
HO OO OOOO
LOOK AT THEM...
MOKA AKASHIYA, THE HOTTEST GIRL AT THE ACADEMY...
That's my lunch!
Well, it's not very good!
YUKARI SENDO, THE SMARTEST STUDENT AT THE ACADEMY...
AND KURUMU KURONO, THE...
YEAH. HOT STUFF...
AND THEY'RE ALL OVER THAT PIECE OF CRAP TSUKUNE.
LOOK AT HIM ALL SMILES...
DON'T YOU JUST WANNA KILL HIM?!

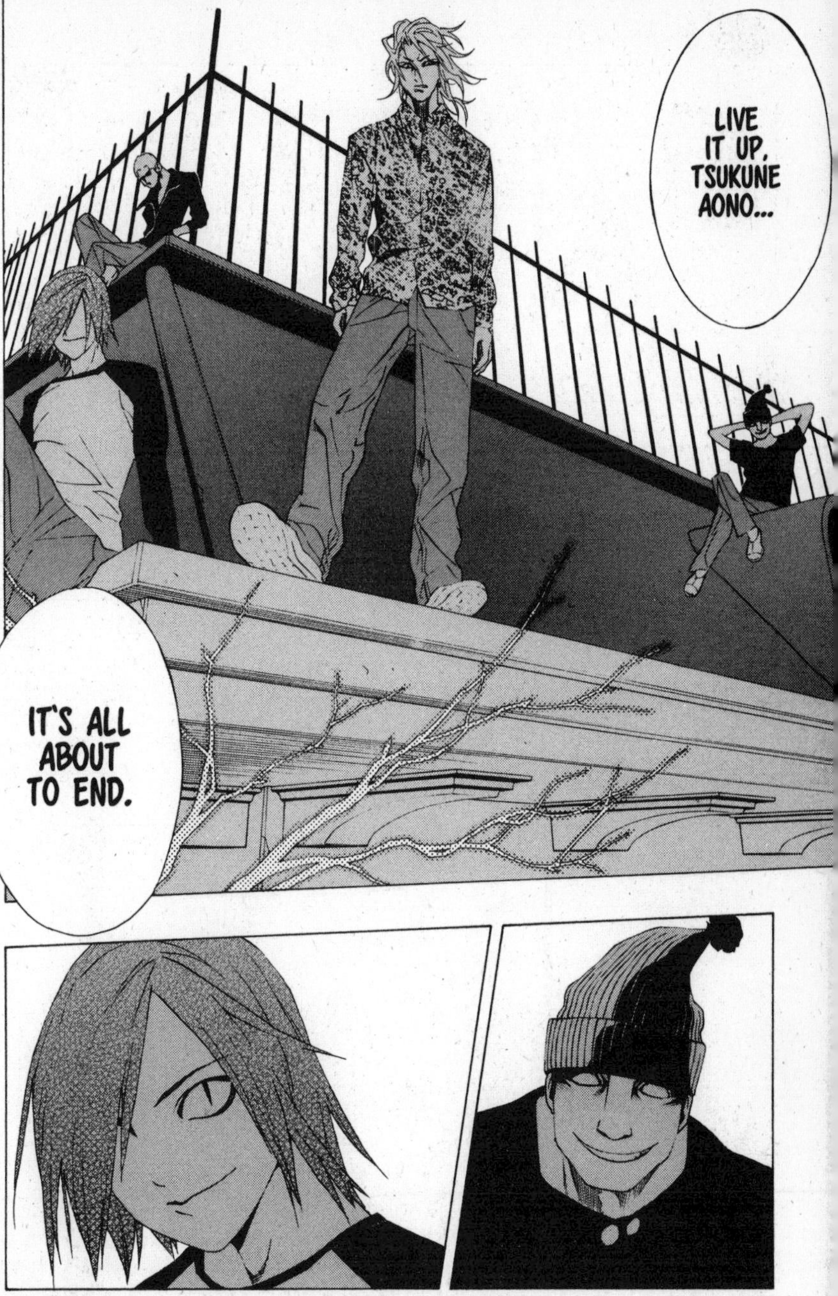
LIVE IT UP, TSUKUNE AONO...
IT'S ALL ABOUT TO END.

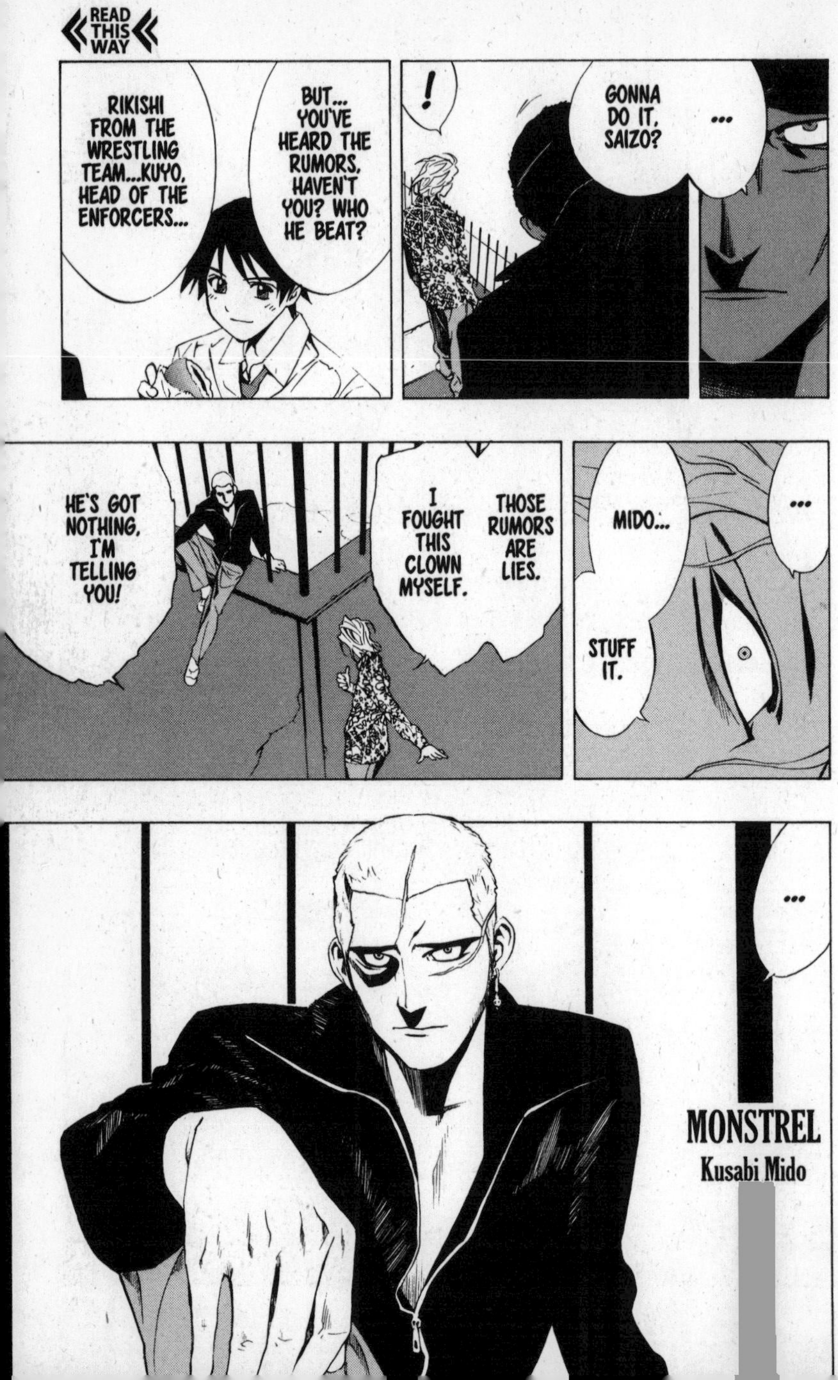
READ THIS WAY
...
GONNA DO IT, SAIZO?
!
BUT... YOU'VE HEARD THE RUMORS, HAVEN'T YOU? WHO HE BEAT?
RIKISHI FROM THE WRESTLING TEAM...KUYO, HEAD OF THE ENFORCERS...
...
MIDO...
STUFF IT.
THOSE RUMORS ARE LIES.
I FOUGHT THIS CLOWN MYSELF.
HE'S GOT NOTHING, I'M TELLING YOU!
...
MONSTREL
Kusabi Mido

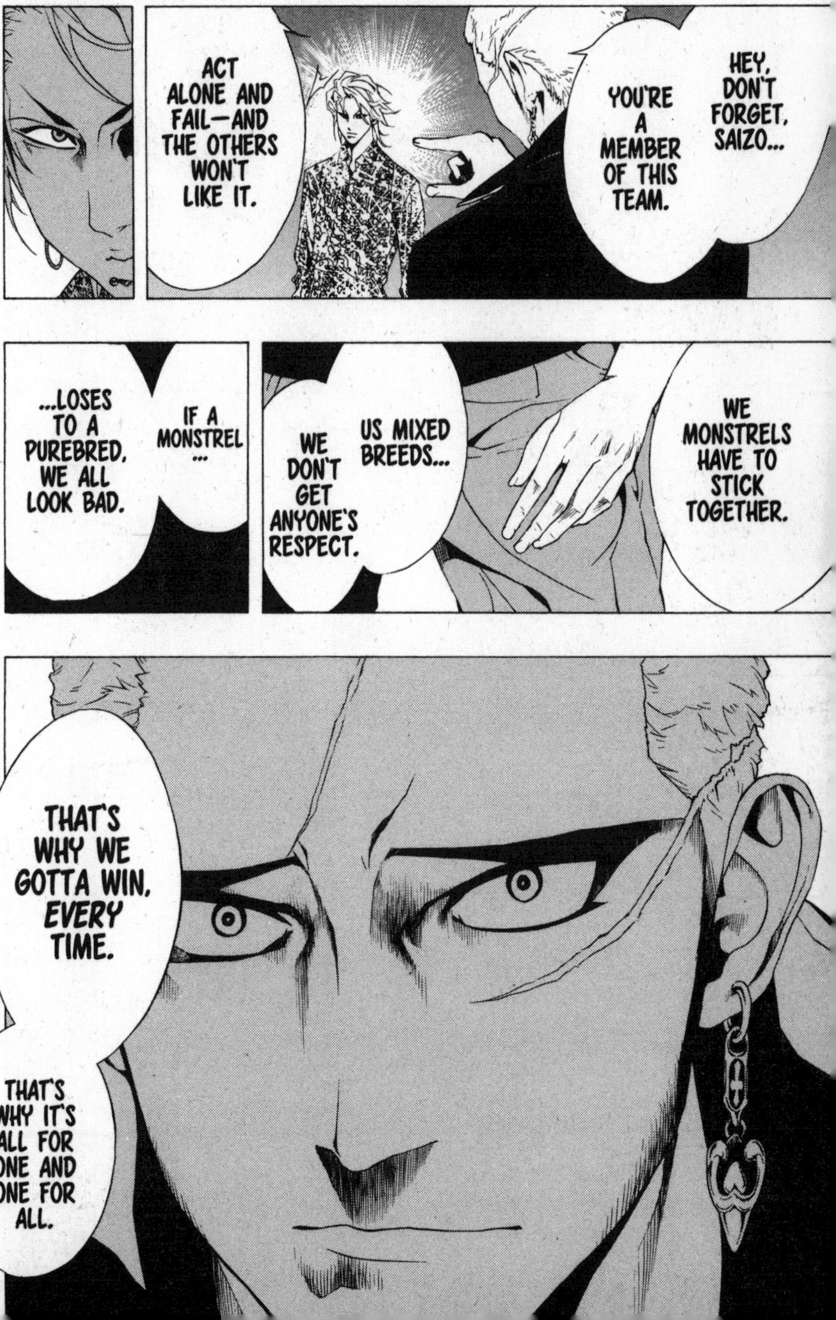
HEY, DON'T FORGET, SAIZO...
YOU'RE A MEMBER OF THIS TEAM.
ACT ALONE AND FAIL—AND THE OTHERS WON'T LIKE IT.
WE MONSTRELS HAVE TO STICK TOGETHER.
US MIXED BREEDS...
WE DON'T GET ANYONE'S RESPECT.
IF A MONSTREL ...
...LOSES TO A PUREBRED, WE ALL LOOK BAD.
THAT'S WHY WE GOTTA WIN, *EVERY* TIME.
THAT'S WHY IT'S ALL FOR ONE AND ONE FOR ALL.

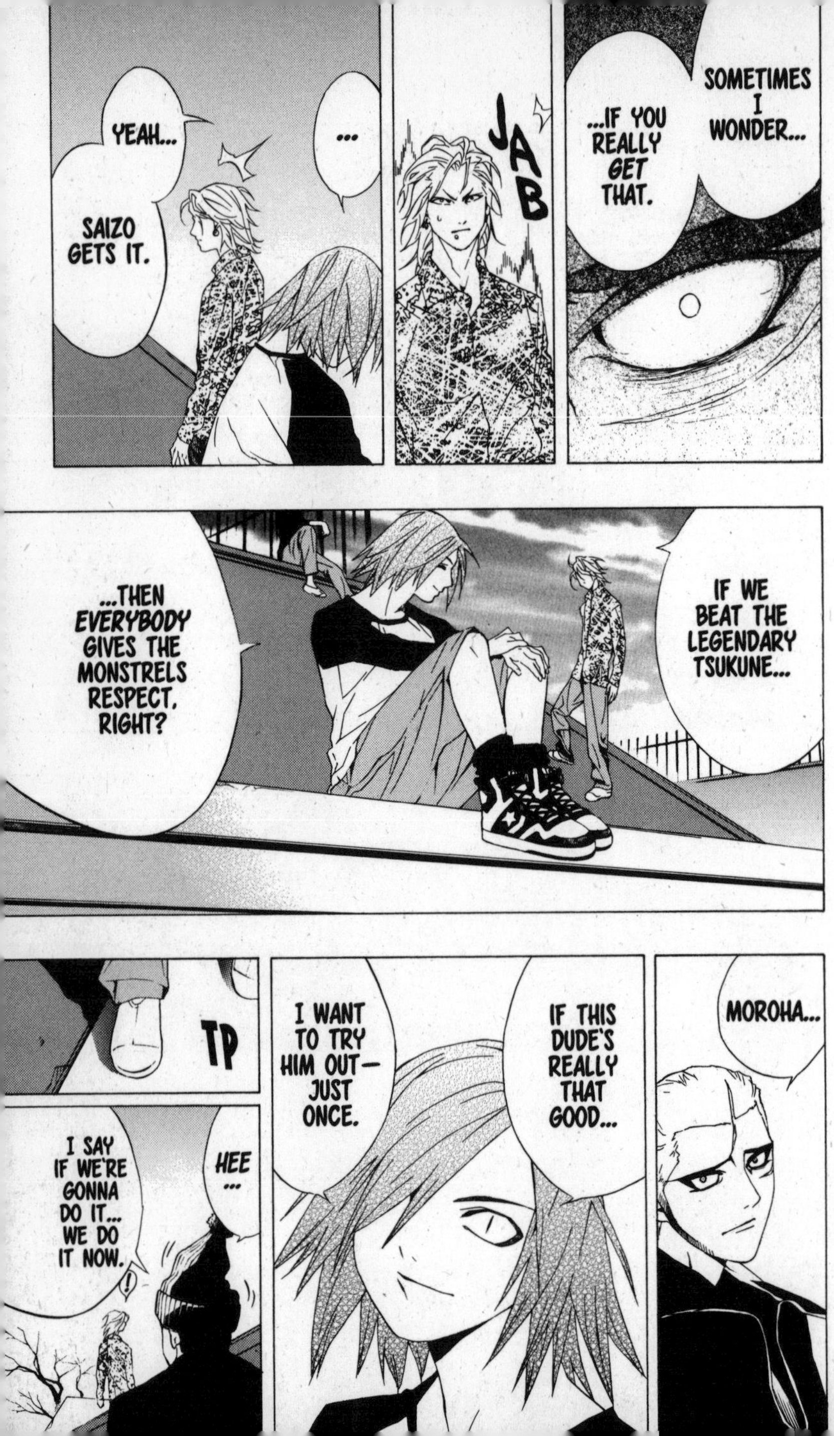
SOMETIMES I WONDER...
...IF YOU REALLY GET THAT.
JAB
...
YEAH...
SAIZO GETS IT.
IF WE BEAT THE LEGENDARY TSUKUNE...
...THEN EVERYBODY GIVES THE MONSTRELS RESPECT, RIGHT?
MOROHA...
IF THIS DUDE'S REALLY THAT GOOD...
I WANT TO TRY HIM OUT—JUST ONCE.
TP
HEE ...
I SAY IF WE'RE GONNA DO IT... WE DO IT NOW.
!

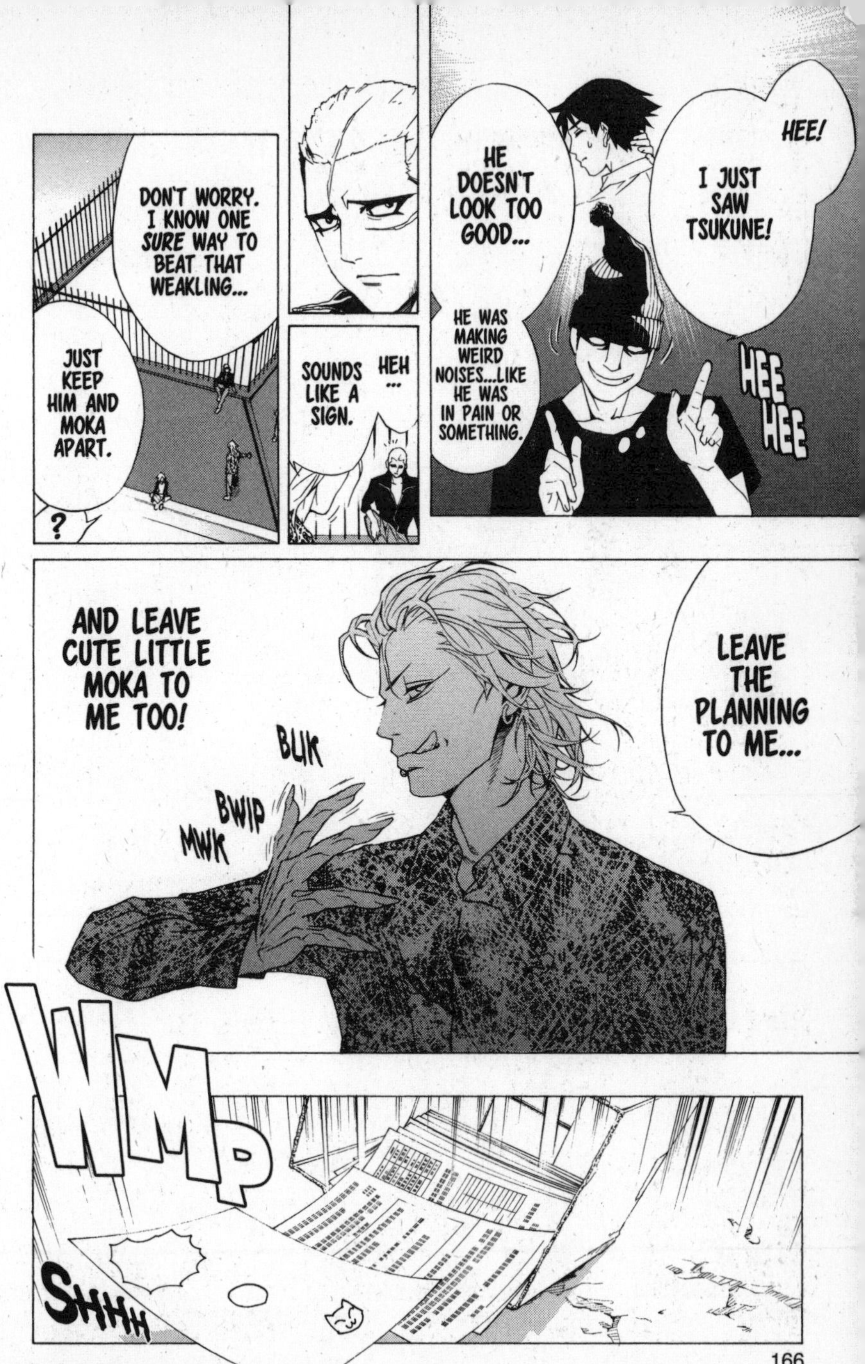
HEE!
I JUST SAW TSUKUNE!
HEE HEE
HE DOESN'T LOOK TOO GOOD...
HE WAS MAKING WEIRD NOISES...LIKE HE WAS IN PAIN OR SOMETHING.
HEH...
SOUNDS LIKE A SIGN.
DON'T WORRY. I KNOW ONE *SURE* WAY TO BEAT THAT WEAKLING...
JUST KEEP HIM AND MOKA APART.
?
LEAVE THE PLANNING TO ME...
AND LEAVE CUTE LITTLE MOKA TO ME TOO!
BUK
BWIP
MWK
WMP
SHHH

READ THIS WAY

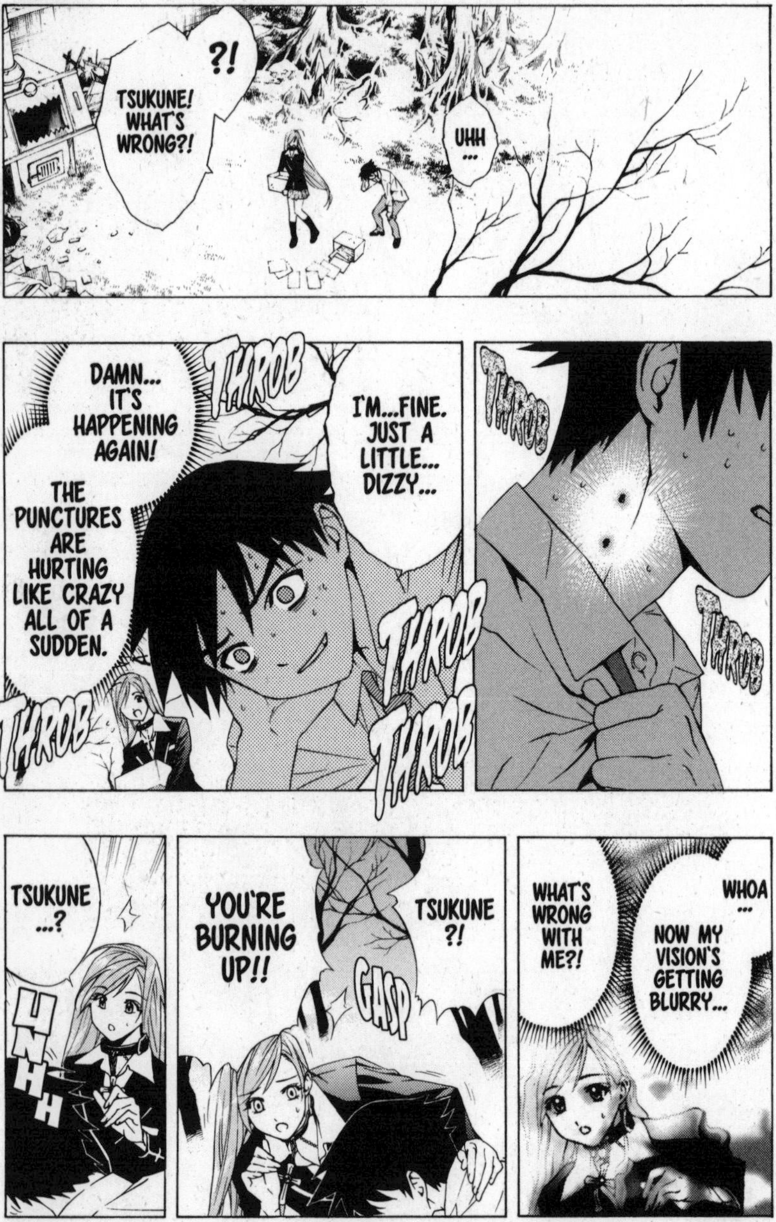

UHH...
?!
TSUKUNE! WHAT'S WRONG?!
THROB
THROB
I'M...FINE. JUST A LITTLE... DIZZY...
THROB
DAMN... IT'S HAPPENING AGAIN!
THE PUNCTURES ARE HURTING LIKE CRAZY ALL OF A SUDDEN.
THROB
THROB
THROB
WHOA...
NOW MY VISION'S GETTING BLURRY...
WHAT'S WRONG WITH ME?!
TSUKUNE ?!
YOU'RE BURNING UP!!
GASP
TSUKUNE...?
UNHH

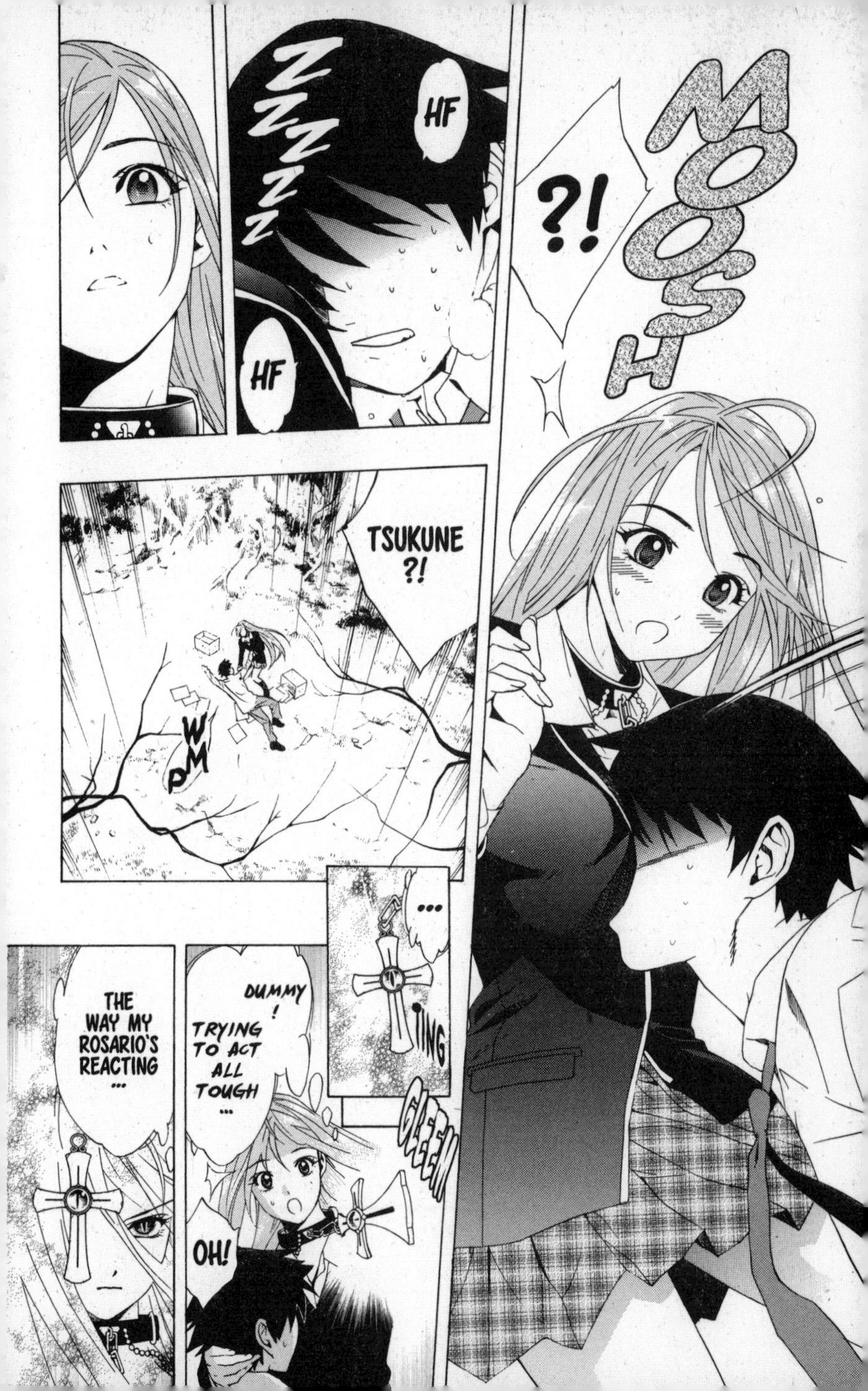
MOOSH
?!
HF
ZZZZZZ
HF
TSUKUNE ?!
WMP
...
TING
GLEEM
DUMMY! TRYING TO ACT ALL TOUGH...
OH!
THE WAY MY ROSARIO'S REACTING...

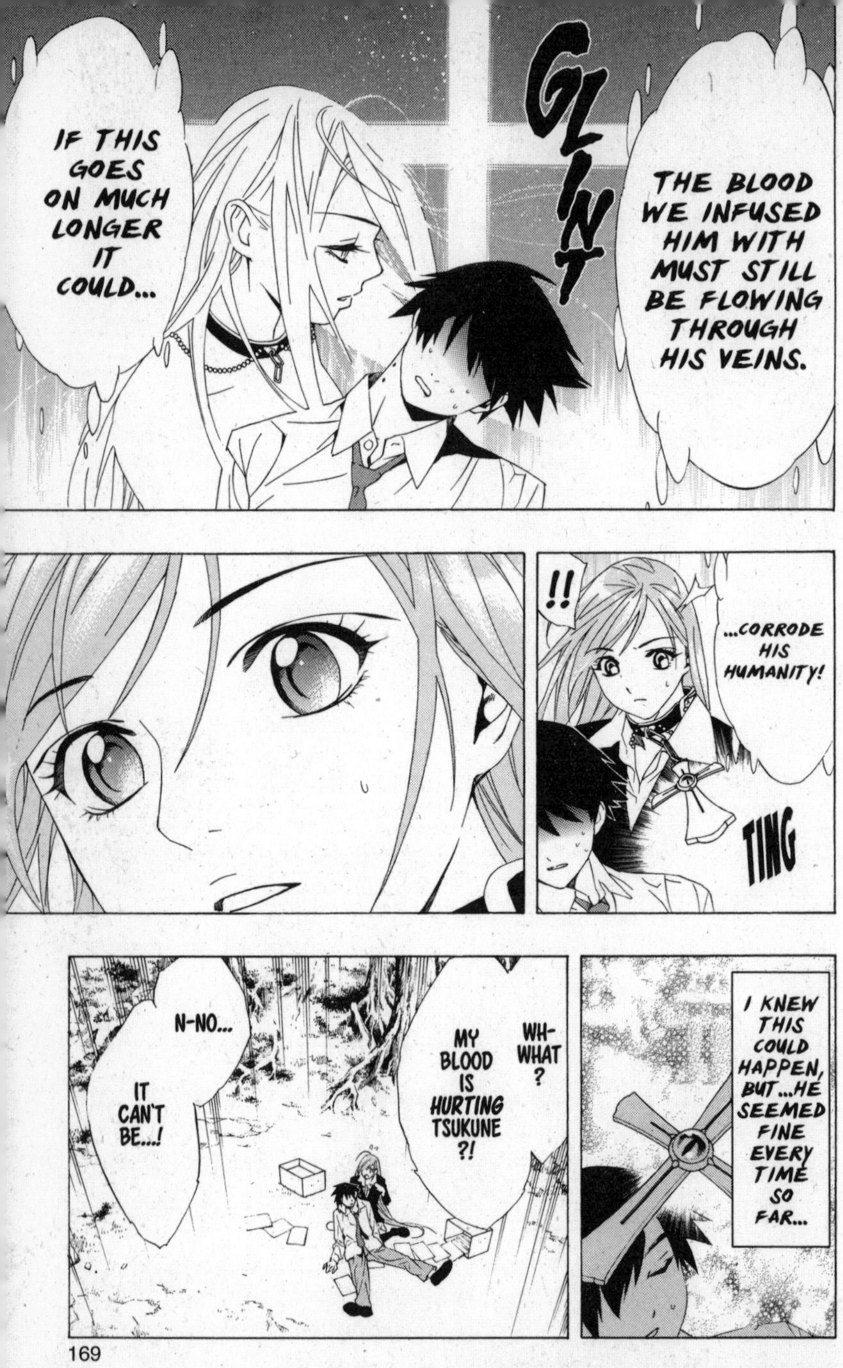
THE BLOOD WE INFUSED HIM WITH MUST STILL BE FLOWING THROUGH HIS VEINS.
GLINT
IF THIS GOES ON MUCH LONGER IT COULD...
!!
...CORRODE HIS HUMANITY!
TING
I KNEW THIS COULD HAPPEN, BUT...HE SEEMED FINE EVERY TIME SO FAR...
WH-WHAT?
MY BLOOD IS HURTING TSUKUNE?!
N-NO...
IT CAN'T BE...!

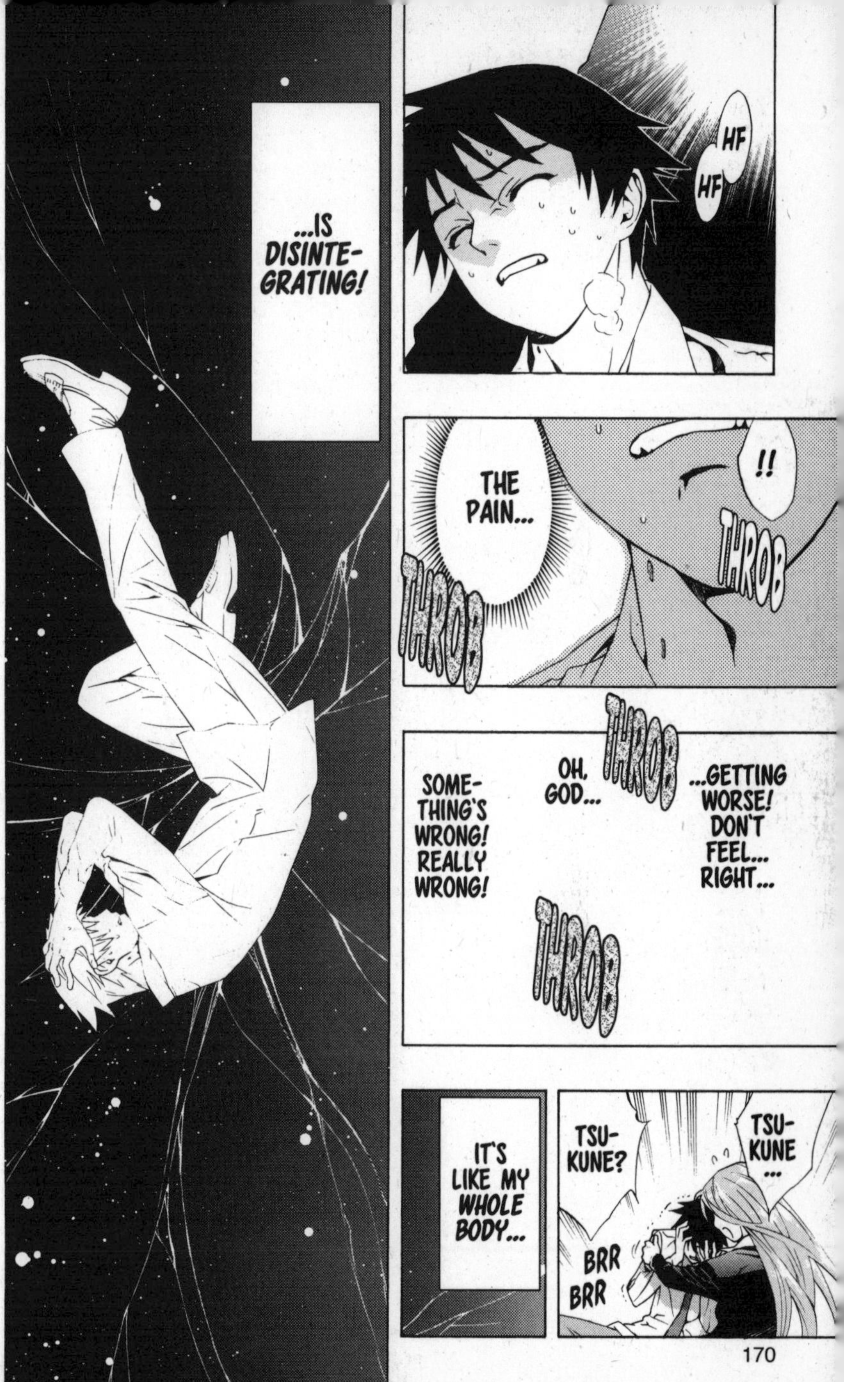
HF
HF
!!
THROB
THE PAIN...
THROB
...GETTING WORSE! DON'T FEEL... RIGHT...
THROB
OH, GOD...
SOME-THING'S WRONG! REALLY WRONG!
THROB
TSU-KUNE...
TSU-KUNE?
BRR
BRR
IT'S LIKE MY WHOLE BODY...
...IS DISINTE-GRATING!

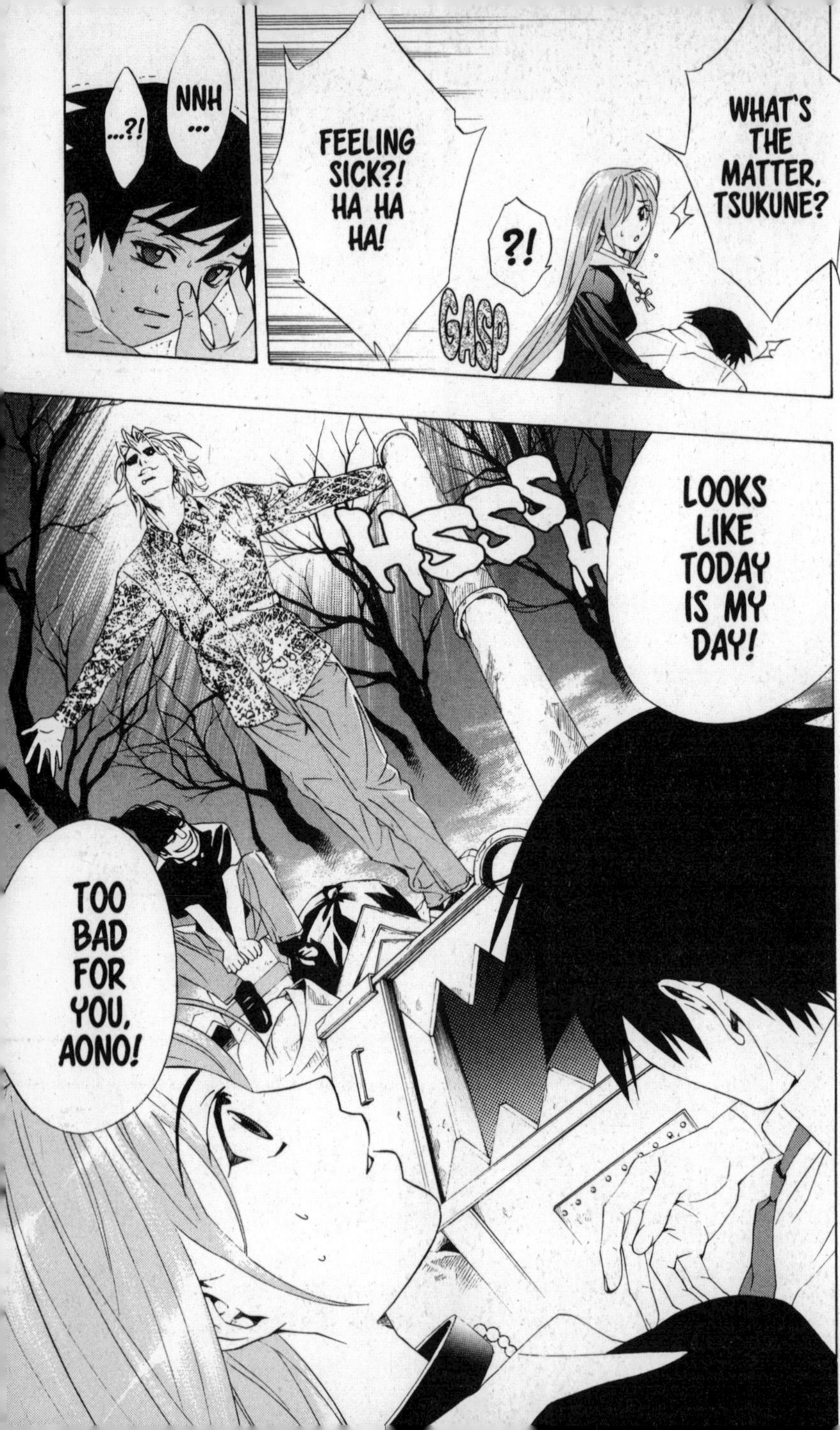
WHAT'S THE MATTER, TSUKUNE?
?!
GASP
FEELING SICK?! HA HA HA!
NNH...
...?!
LOOKS LIKE TODAY IS MY DAY!
HSSSH
TOO BAD FOR YOU, AONO!

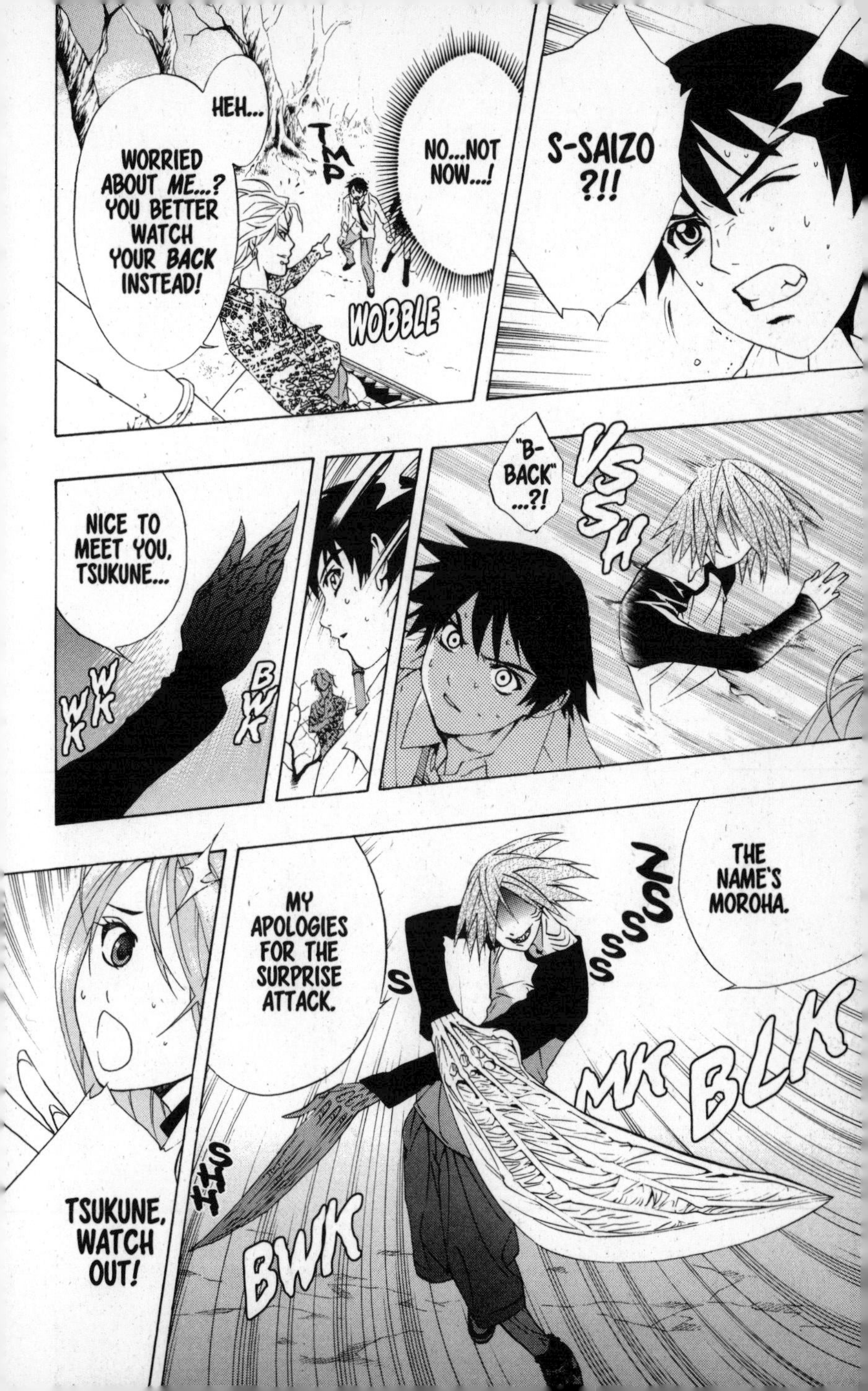
S-SAIZO ?!!
NO...NOT NOW...!
TMP
HEH...
WORRIED ABOUT ME...? YOU BETTER WATCH YOUR BACK INSTEAD!
WOBBLE
"B-BACK" ...?!
VSSH
NICE TO MEET YOU, TSUKUNE...
BWK
WKWK
THE NAME'S MOROHA.
MY APOLOGIES FOR THE SURPRISE ATTACK.
MK BLK
BWK
TSUKUNE, WATCH OUT!

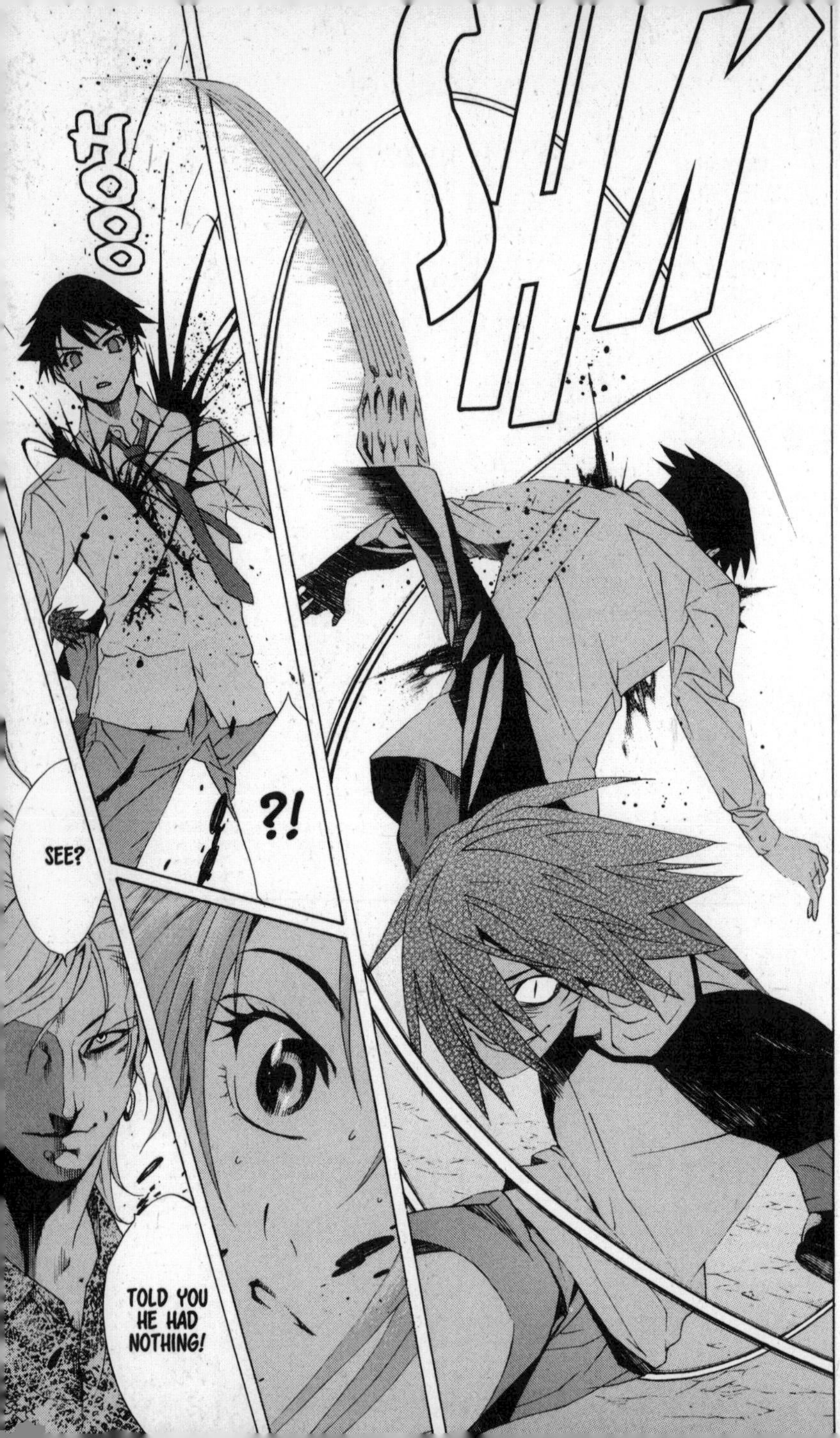
SHK
HOOO
?!
SEE?
TOLD YOU HE HAD NOTHING!

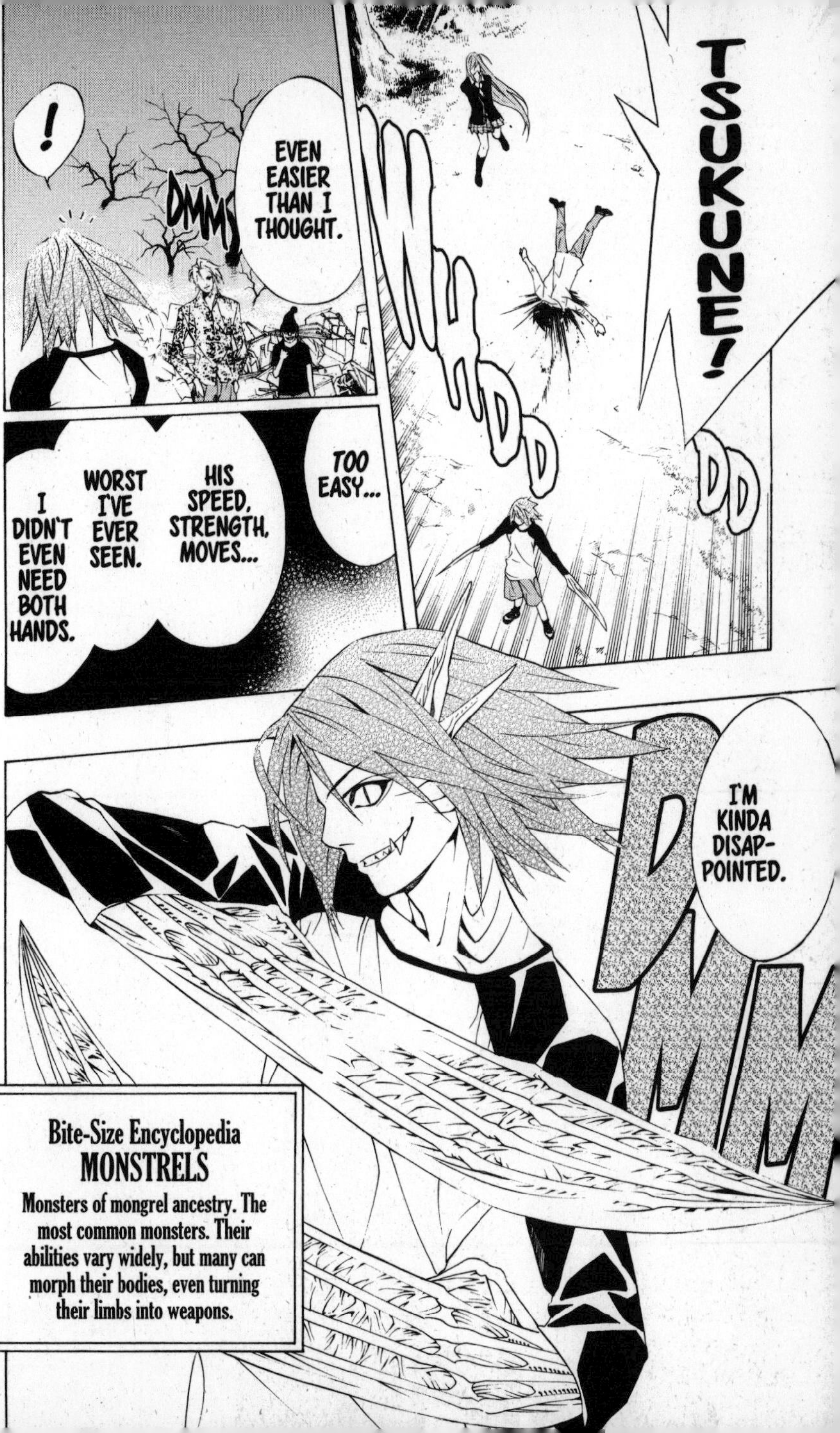
TSUKUNE!
WHUDD
DD
EVEN EASIER THAN I THOUGHT.
DMMS
!
TOO EASY...
HIS SPEED, STRENGTH, MOVES...
WORST I'VE EVER SEEN.
I DIDN'T EVEN NEED BOTH HANDS.
I'M KINDA DISAP-POINTED.
DMMM
Bite-Size Encyclopedia
MONSTRELS
Monsters of mongrel ancestry. The most common monsters. Their abilities vary widely, but many can morph their bodies, even turning their limbs into weapons.

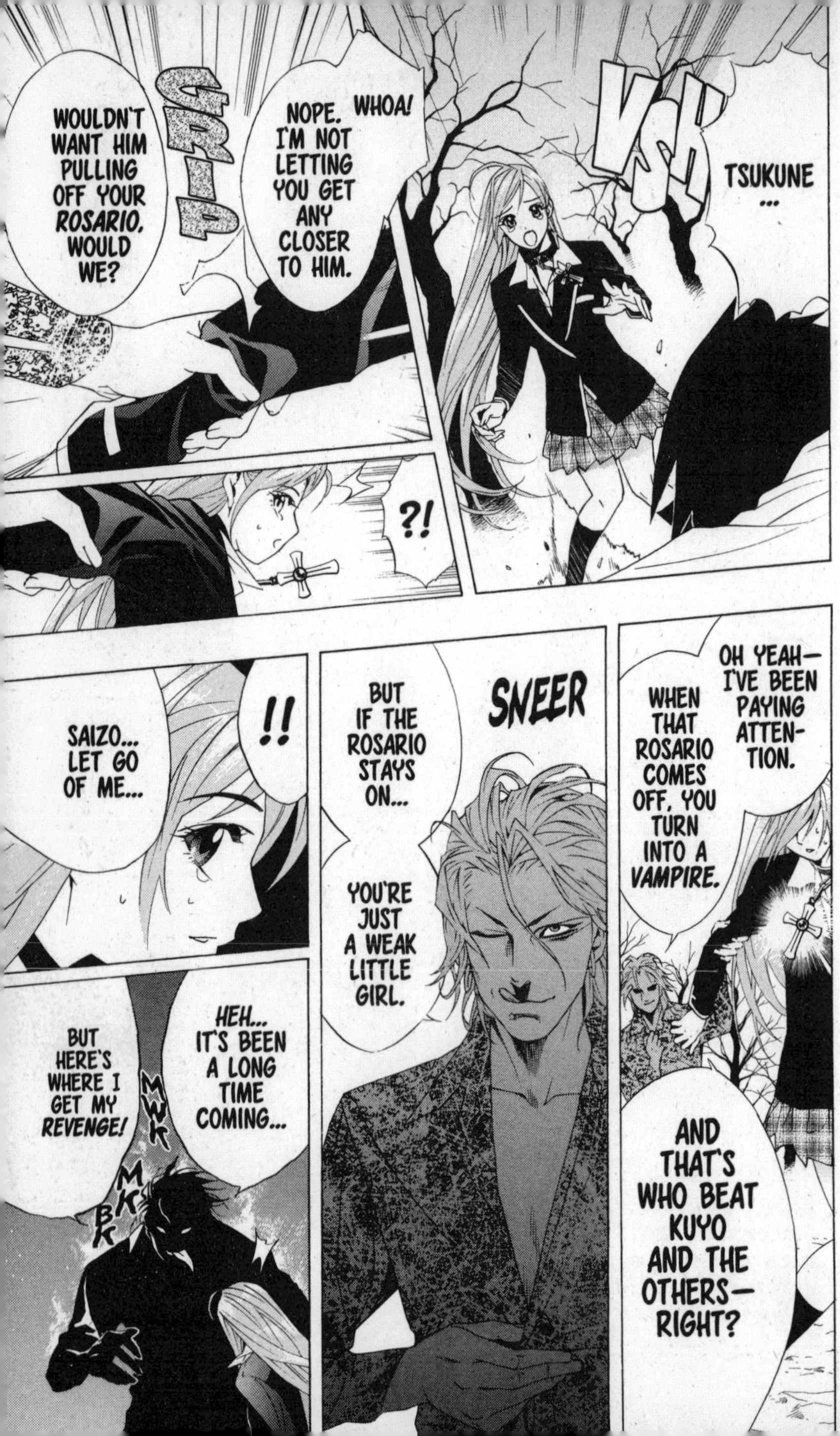
VSH
TSUKUNE...
WHOA!
NOPE. I'M NOT LETTING YOU GET ANY CLOSER TO HIM.
GRIP
WOULDN'T WANT HIM PULLING OFF YOUR *ROSARIO*, WOULD WE?
?!
OH YEAH—I'VE BEEN PAYING ATTENTION.
WHEN THAT ROSARIO COMES OFF, YOU TURN INTO A *VAMPIRE*.
AND THAT'S WHO BEAT KUYO AND THE OTHERS—RIGHT?
SNEER
BUT IF THE ROSARIO STAYS ON...
YOU'RE JUST A WEAK LITTLE GIRL.
!!
SAIZO... LET GO OF ME...
HEH... IT'S BEEN A LONG TIME COMING...
MWK
BUT HERE'S WHERE I GET MY *REVENGE!*
MK BK

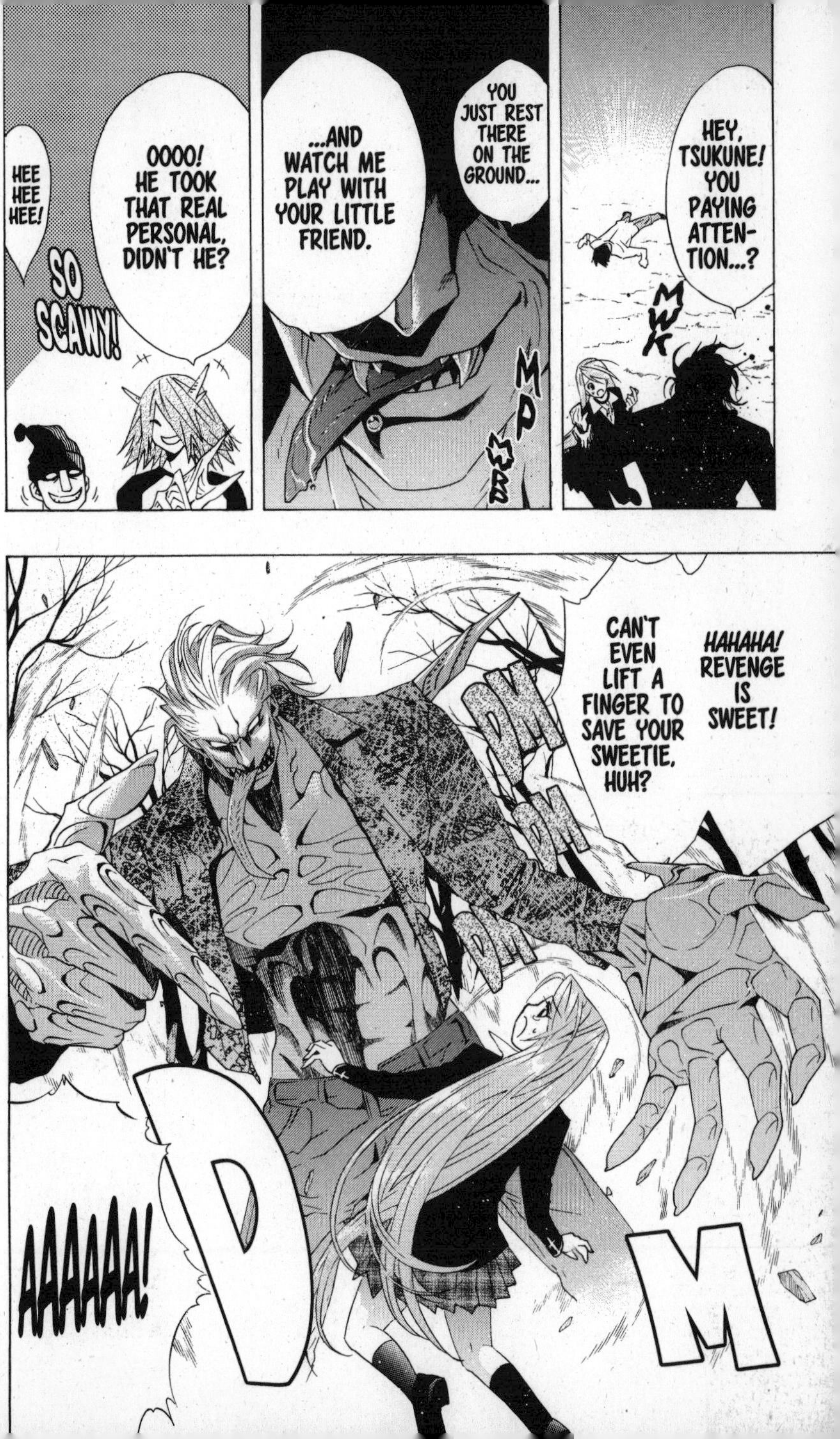
HEY, TSUKUNE! YOU PAYING ATTENTION...?
MWK
YOU JUST REST THERE ON THE GROUND...
...AND WATCH ME PLAY WITH YOUR LITTLE FRIEND.
MP
OOOO! HE TOOK THAT REAL PERSONAL, DIDN'T HE?
HEE HEE HEE!
SO SCAWY!
HAHAHA! REVENGE IS SWEET!
CAN'T EVEN LIFT A FINGER TO SAVE YOUR SWEETIE, HUH?
DM
DM
DM
DM
AAAAAA!

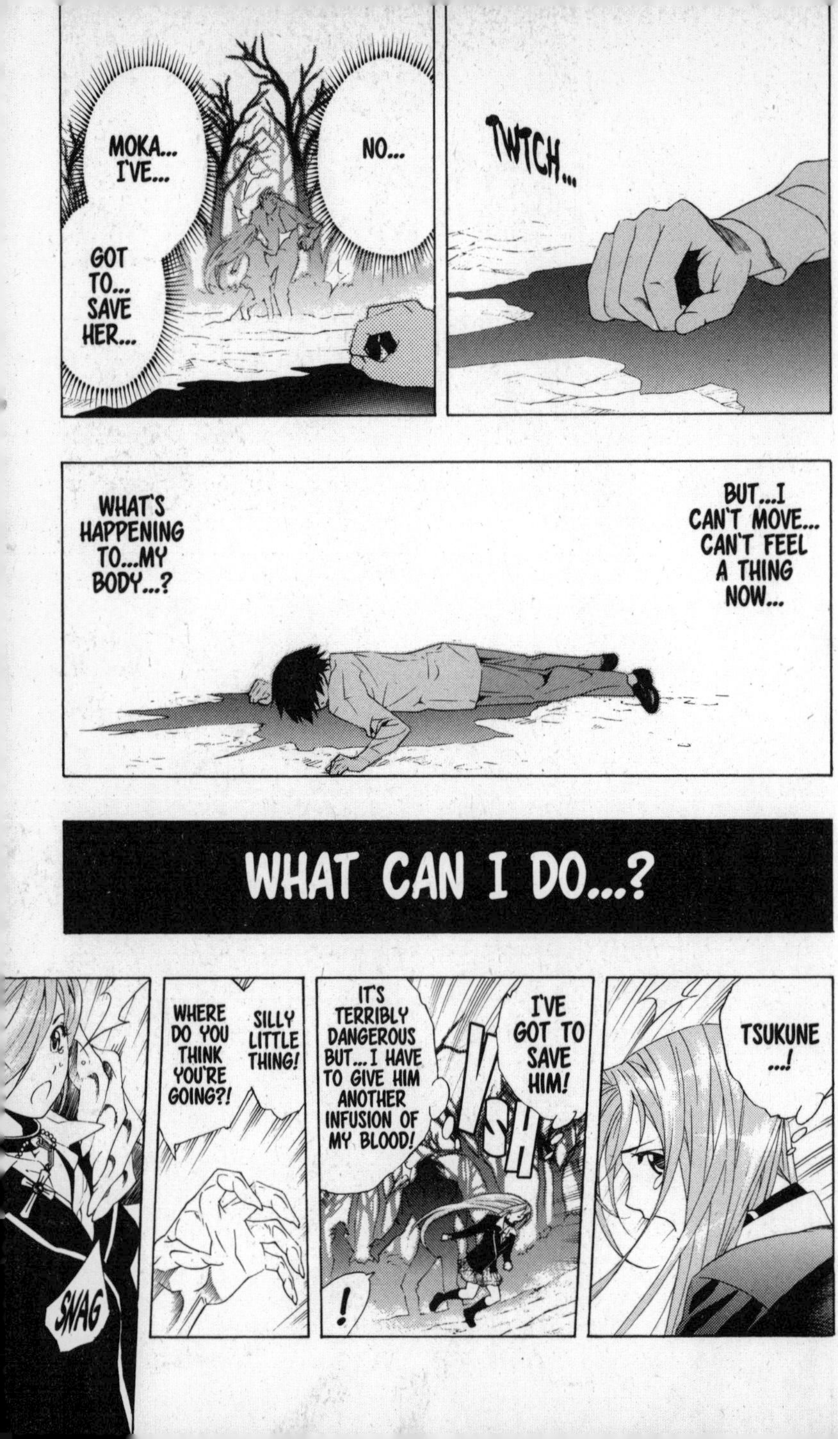
TWITCH...
NO...
MOKA... I'VE...
GOT TO... SAVE HER...
BUT...I CAN'T MOVE... CAN'T FEEL A THING NOW...
WHAT'S HAPPENING TO...MY BODY...?
WHAT CAN I DO...?
TSUKUNE ...!
I'VE GOT TO SAVE HIM!
VSH
IT'S TERRIBLY DANGEROUS BUT...I HAVE TO GIVE HIM ANOTHER INFUSION OF MY BLOOD!
!
SILLY LITTLE THING!
WHERE DO YOU THINK YOU'RE GOING?!
SNAG

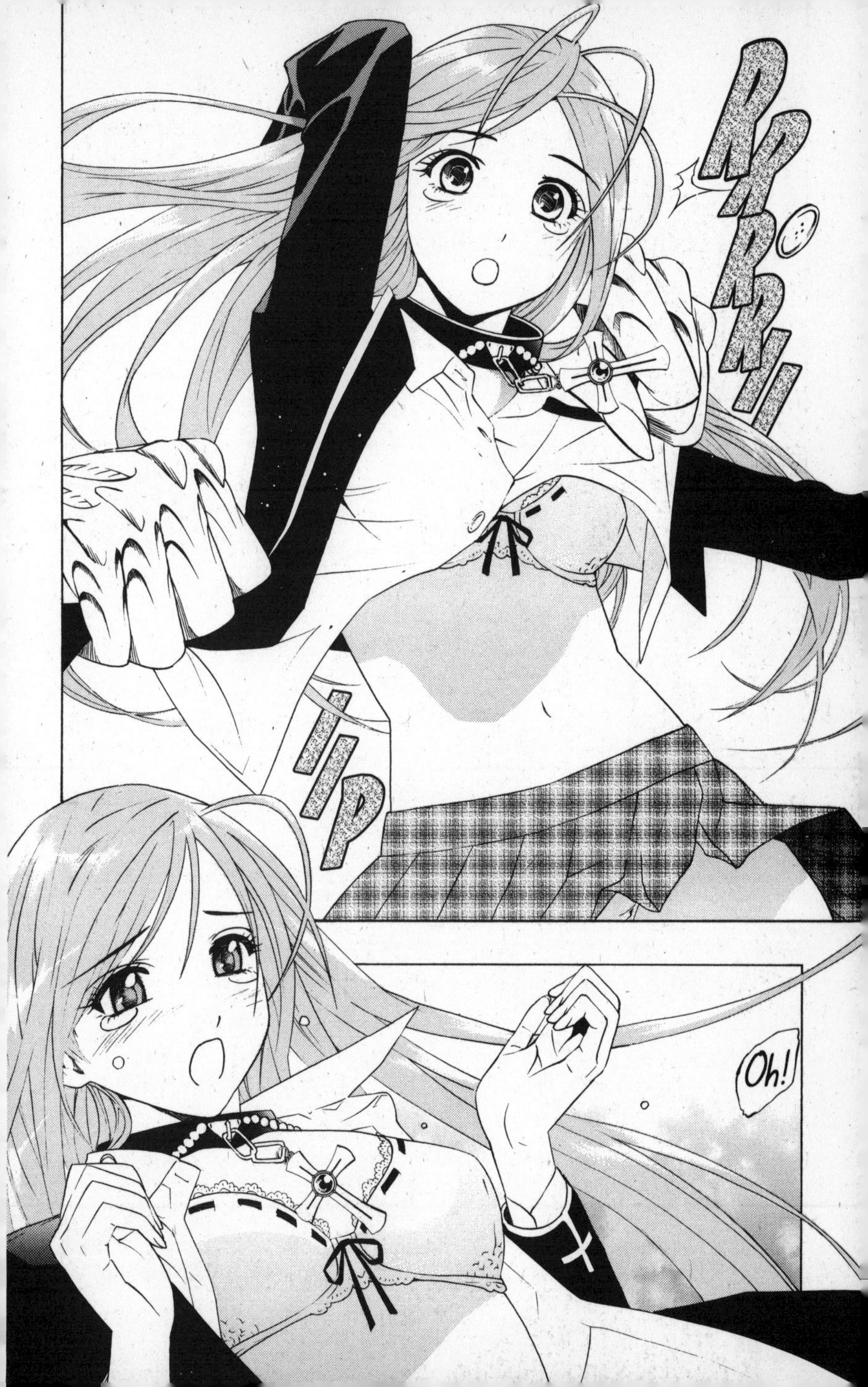
RRRRRII
RIP
Oh!

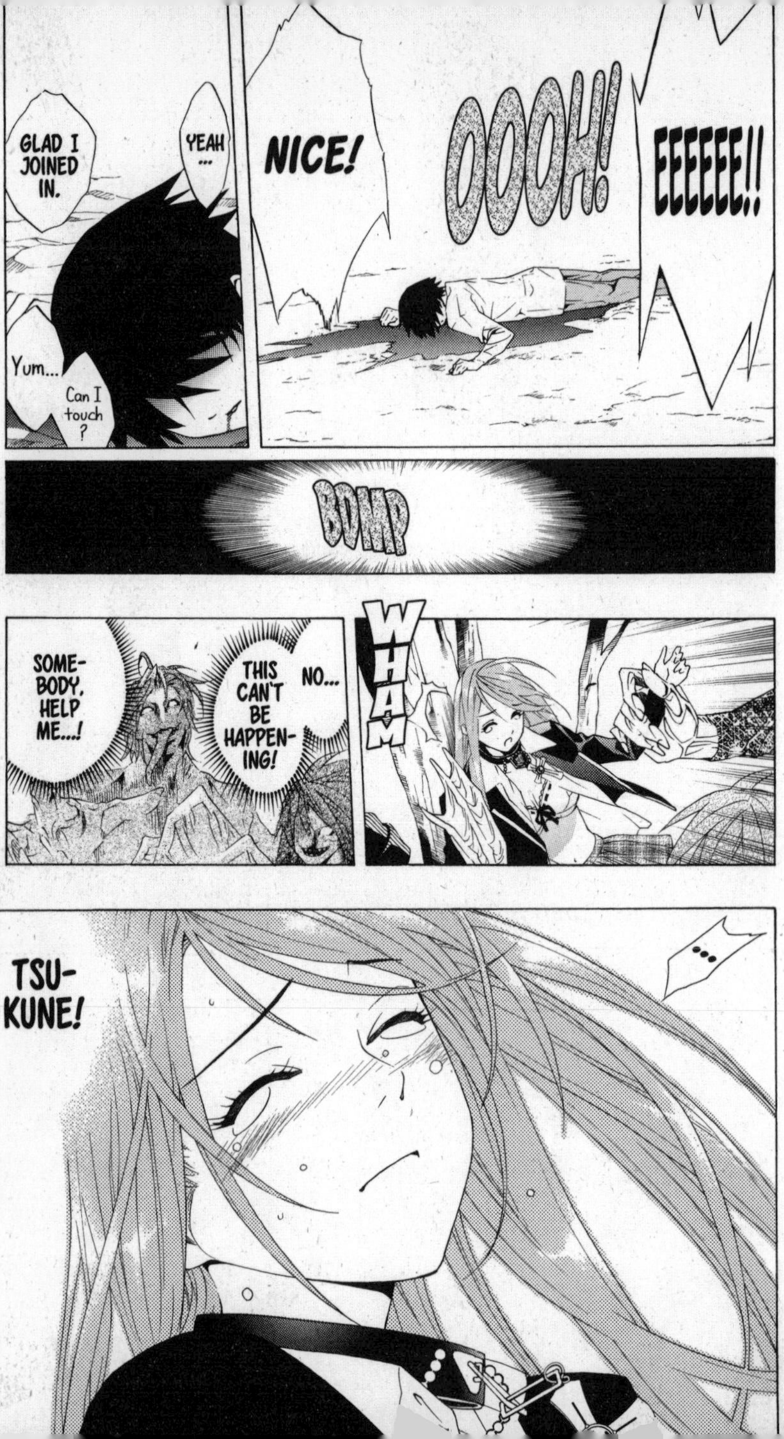
EEEEEE!!
OOOH!
NICE!
YEAH...
GLAD I JOINED IN.
Yum...
Can I touch?
BOMP
WHAM
NO...
THIS CAN'T BE HAPPENING!
SOMEBODY, HELP ME...!
...
TSUKUNE!

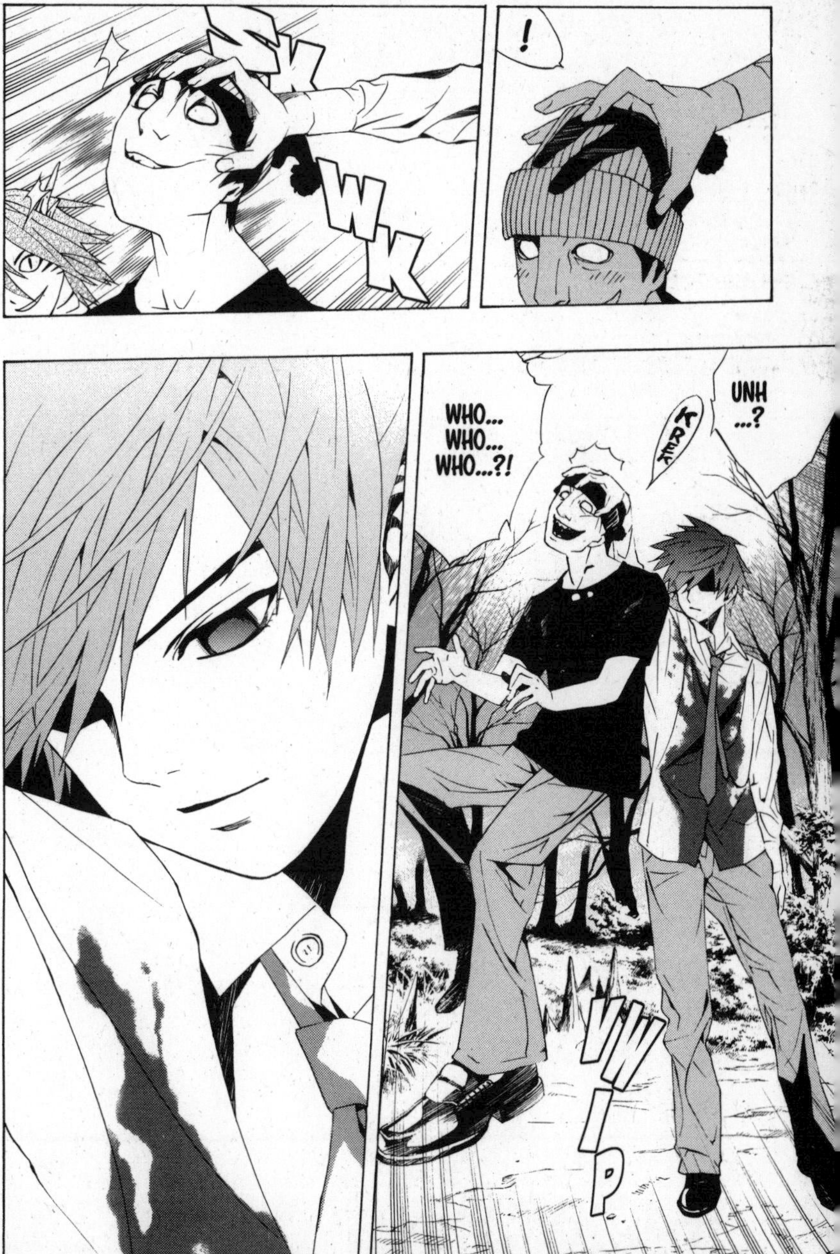
!
K
WK
UNH ...?
KREK
WHO... WHO... WHO...?!
VWIP

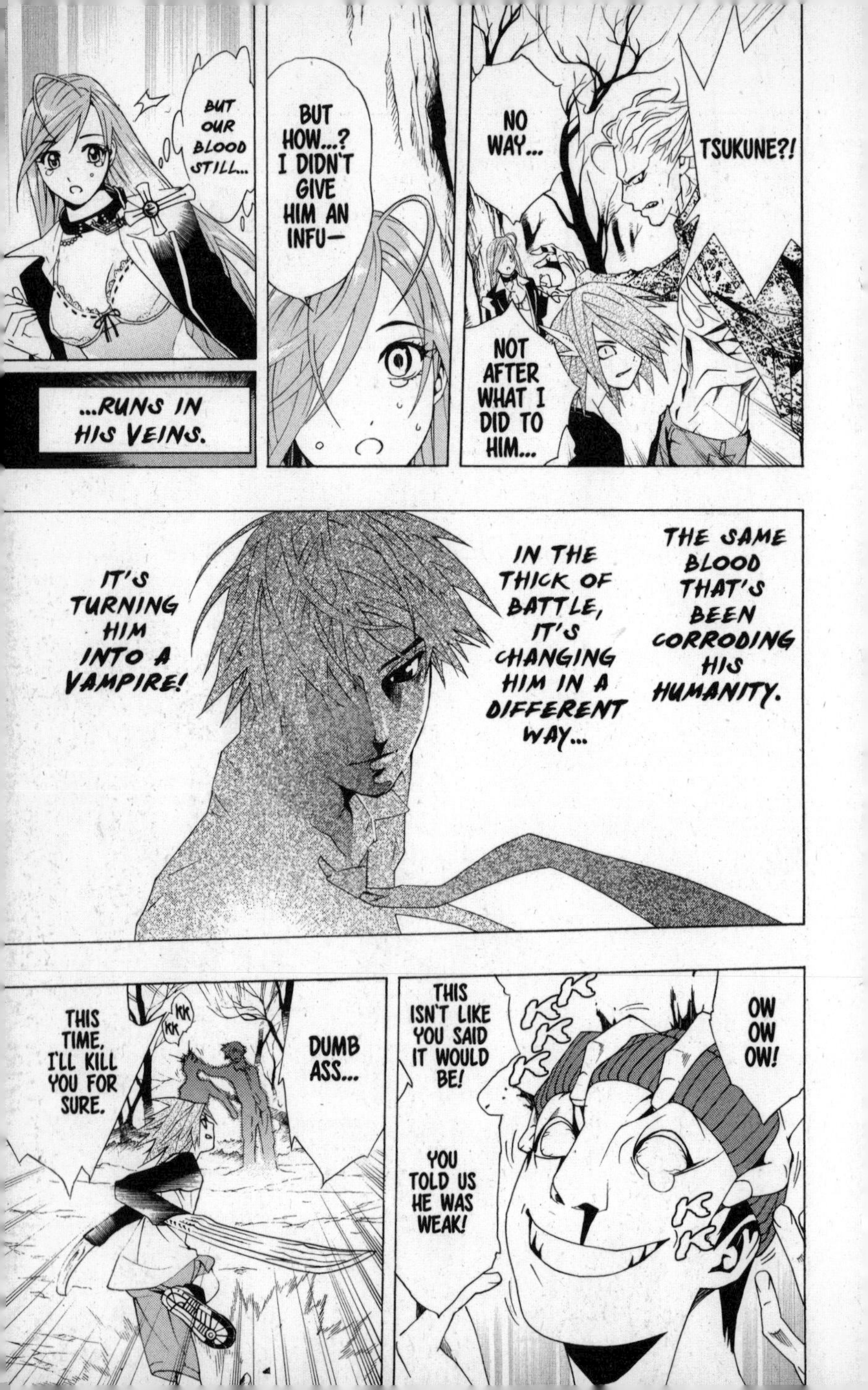
TSUKUNE?!
NO WAY...
NOT AFTER WHAT I DID TO HIM...
BUT HOW...? I DIDN'T GIVE HIM AN INFU—
BUT OUR BLOOD STILL...
...RUNS IN HIS VEINS.
THE SAME BLOOD THAT'S BEEN CORRODING HIS HUMANITY.
IN THE THICK OF BATTLE, IT'S CHANGING HIM IN A DIFFERENT WAY...
IT'S TURNING HIM INTO A VAMPIRE!
OW OW OW!
THIS ISN'T LIKE YOU SAID IT WOULD BE!
YOU TOLD US HE WAS WEAK!
DUMB ASS...
KK KK
THIS TIME, I'LL KILL YOU FOR SURE.

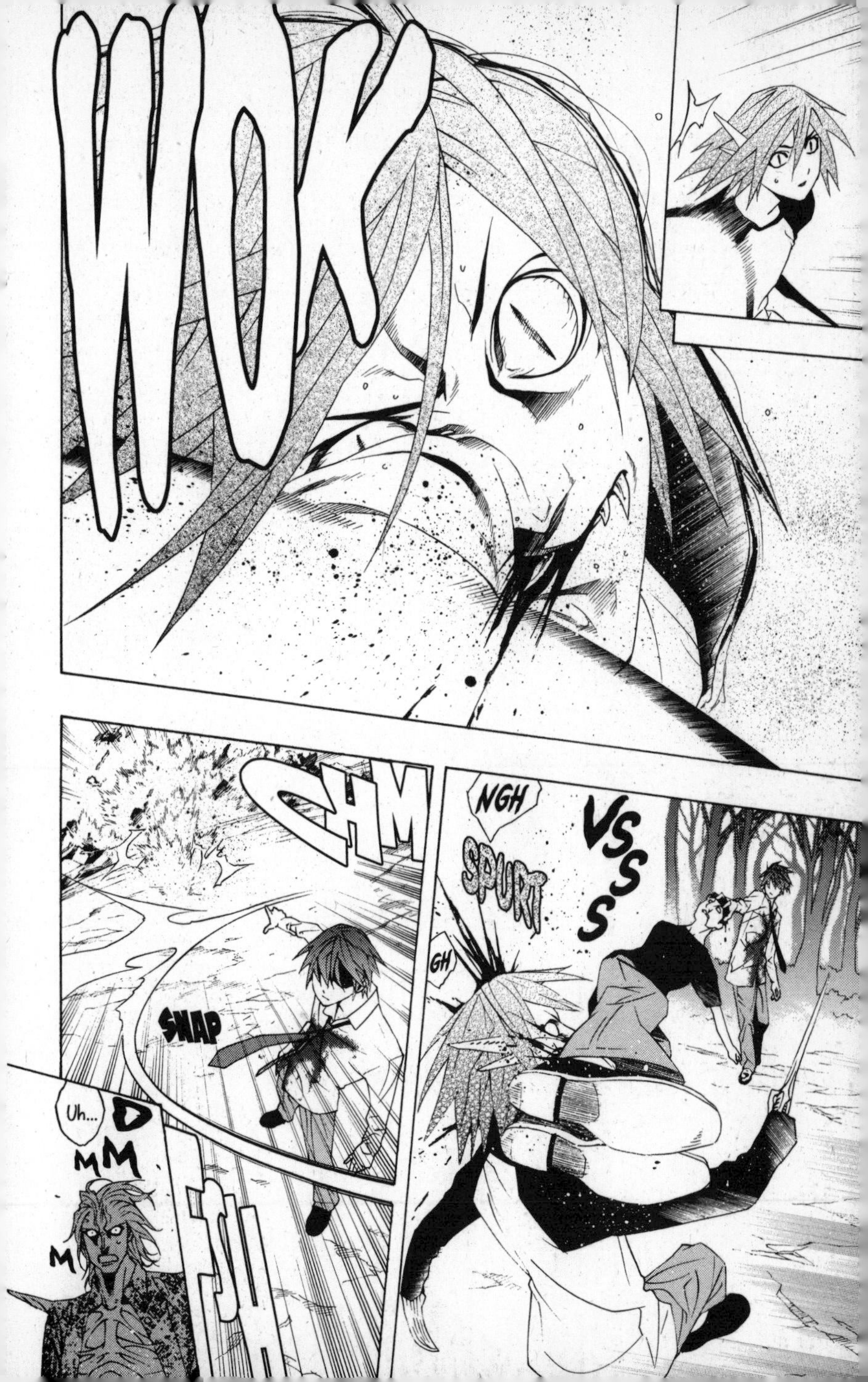
WOK
CHM
NGH
VSSS
SPURT
GH
SNAP
Uh...
DMMM
FSH

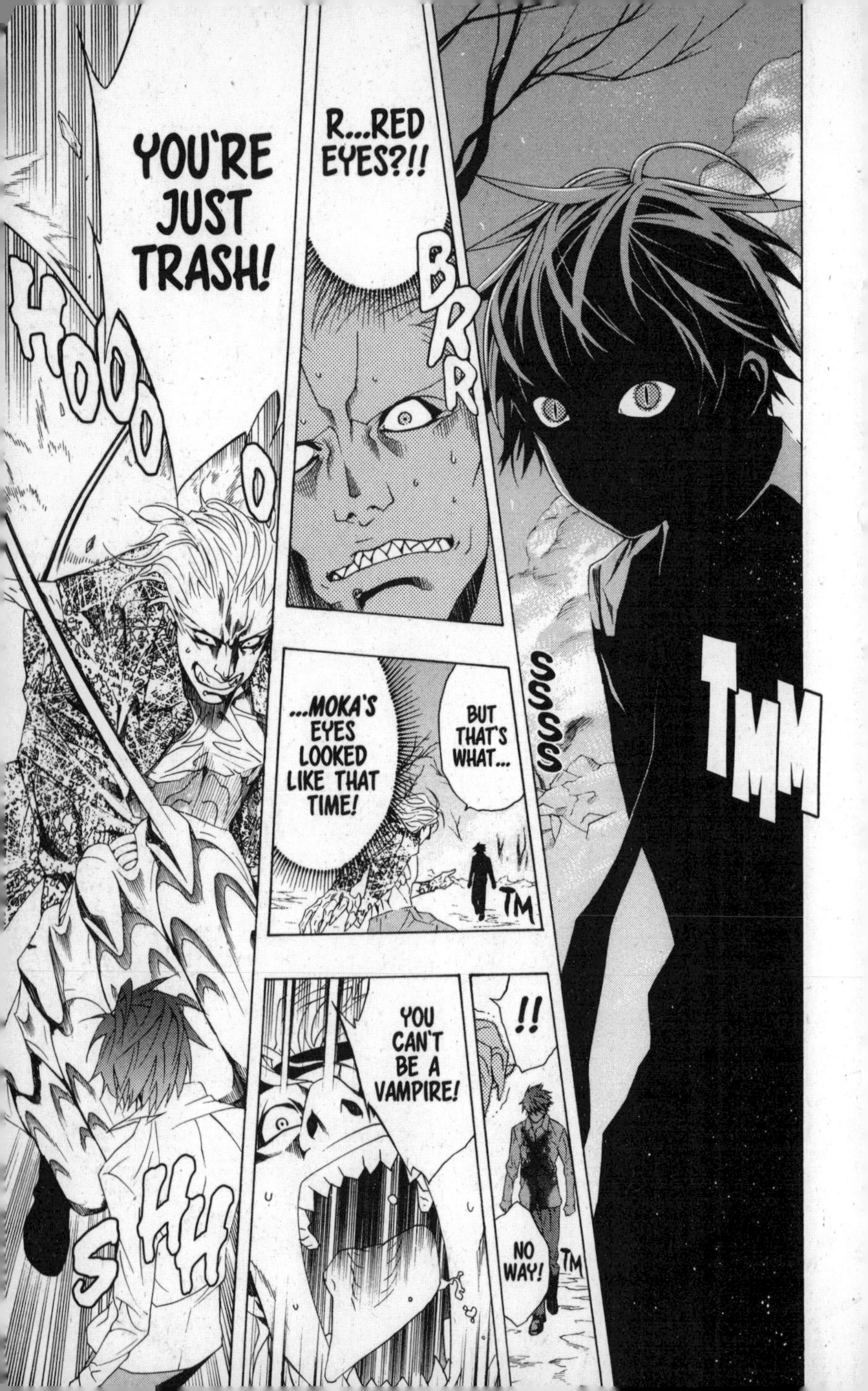
TMM
SSSS
R...RED EYES?!!
BRR
BUT THAT'S WHAT...
...MOKA'S EYES LOOKED LIKE THAT TIME!
TM
!!
NO WAY!
TM
YOU CAN'T BE A VAMPIRE!
YOU'RE JUST TRASH!
HOOOO
SHH

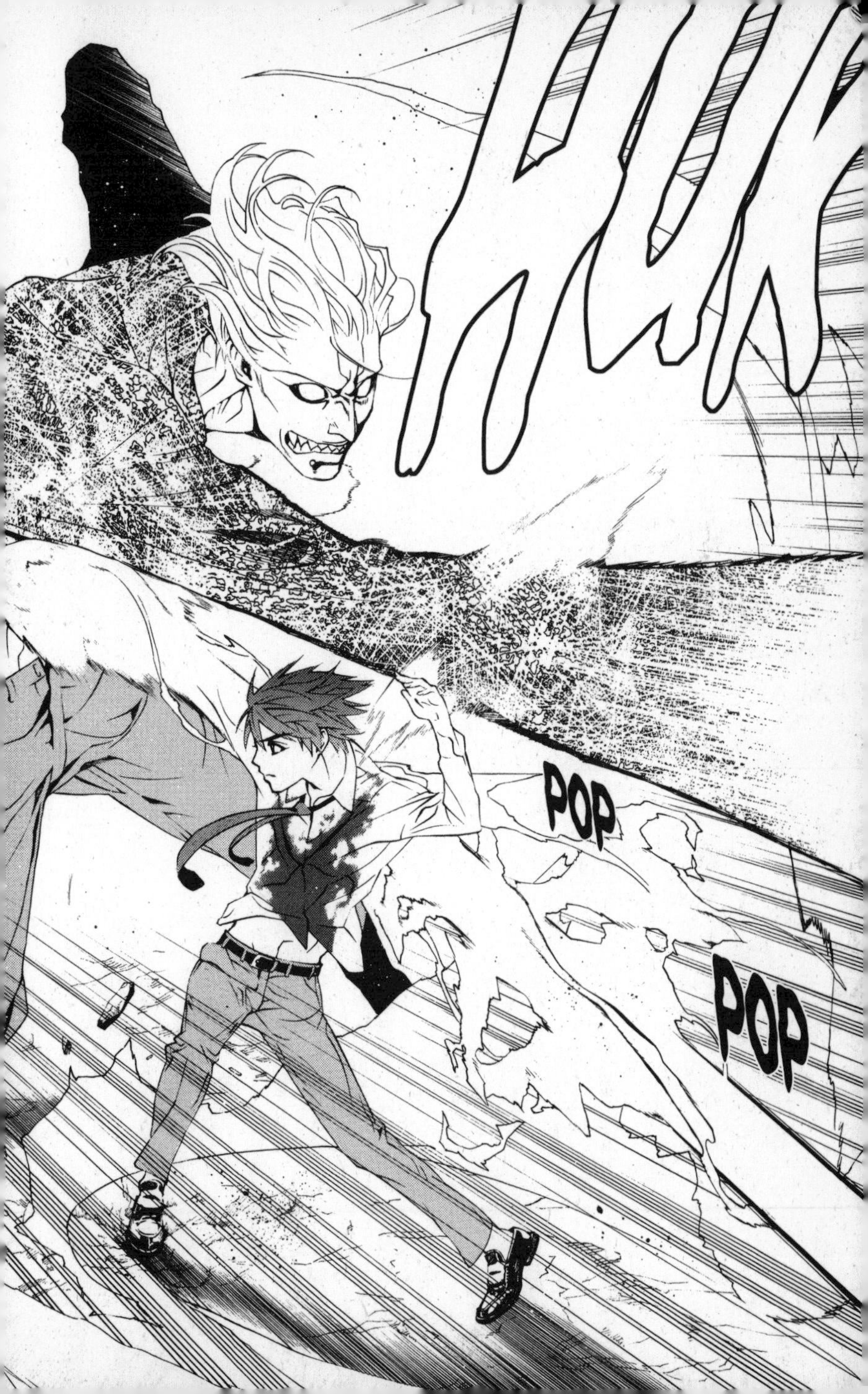
HUK
POP
POP

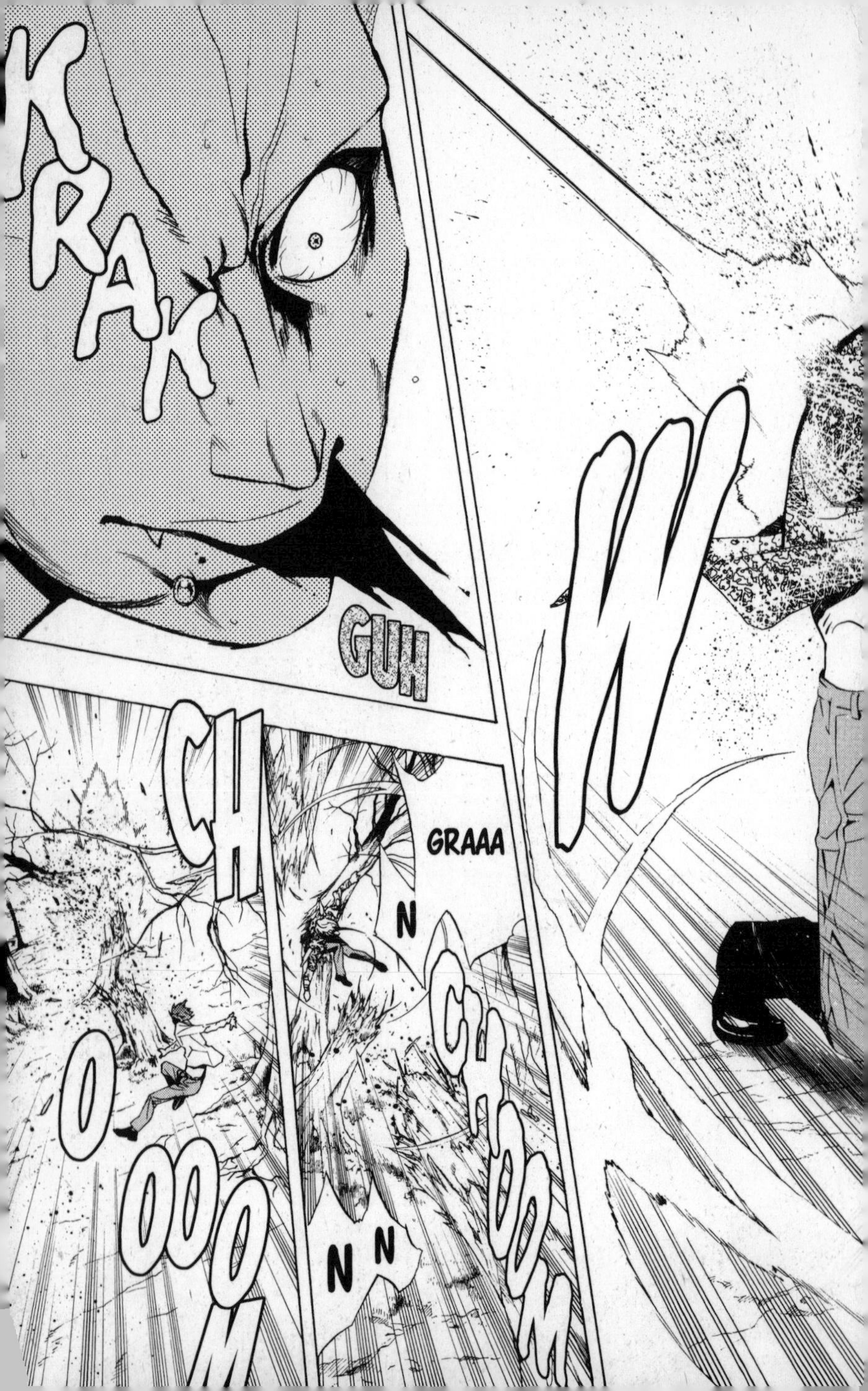
W
KRAK
GUH
GRAAA
N
N N
CHOOOM
CH
OOOOOM

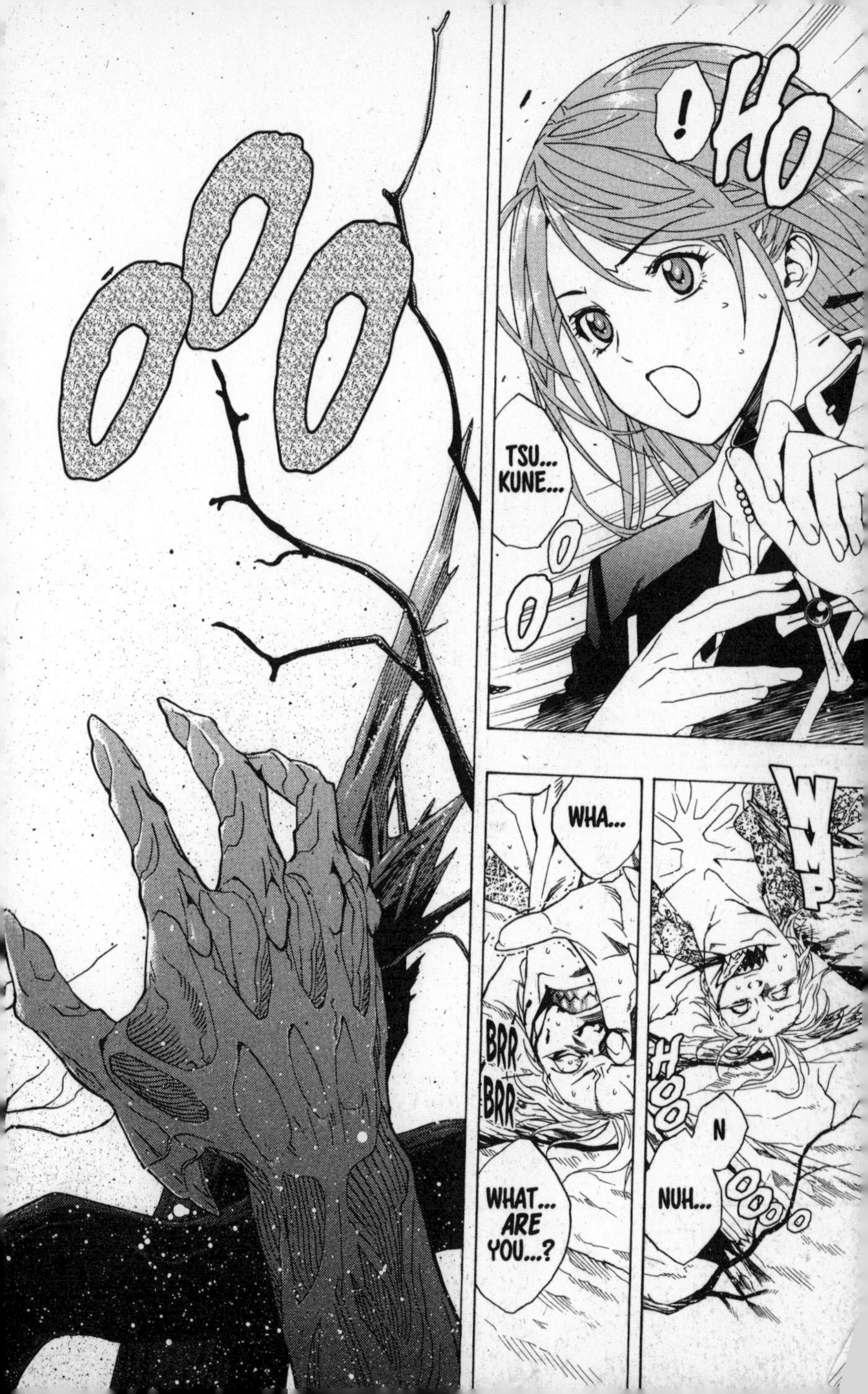

OHO!
TSU... KUNE...
WMP
HOO
N
NUH...
WHA...
BRR BRR
WHAT... ARE YOU...?

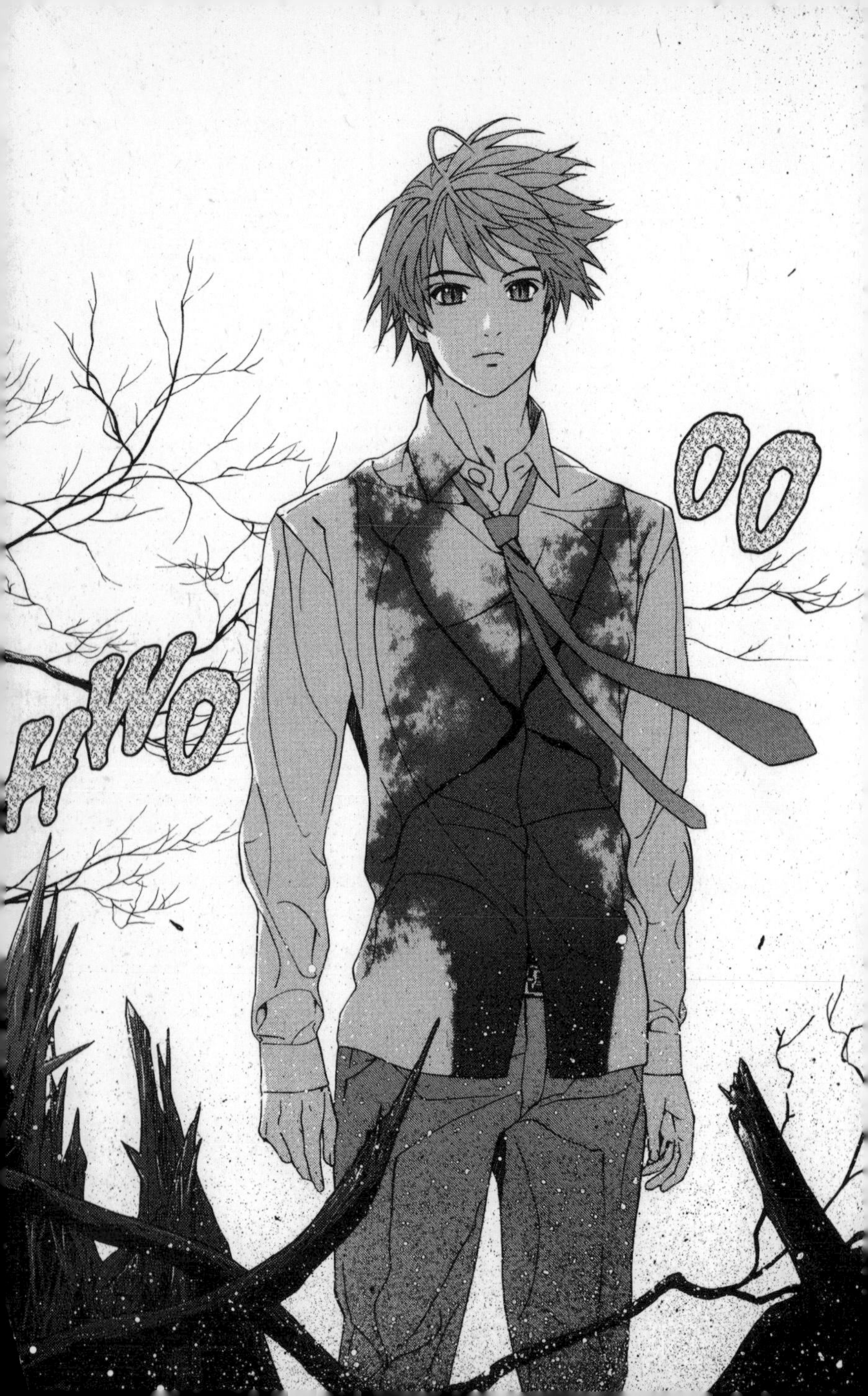
HWO
OO

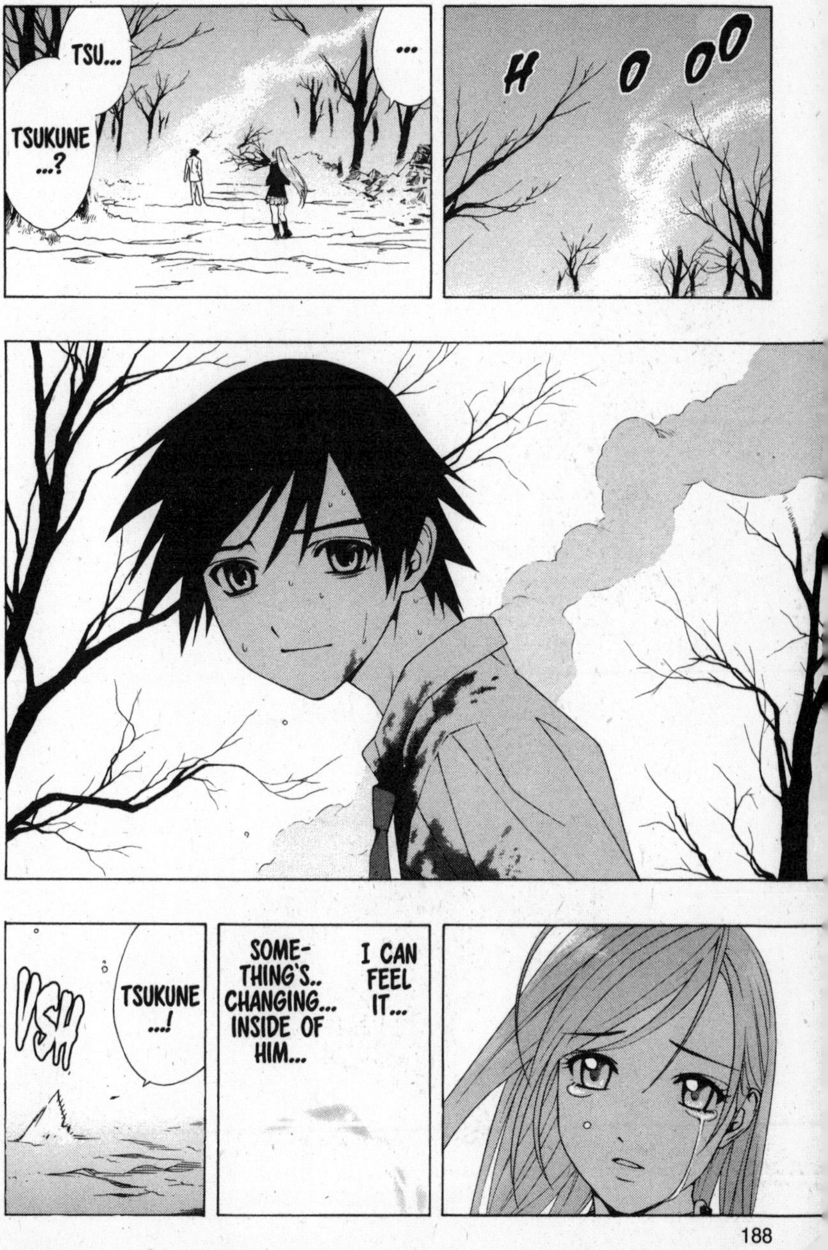
HOOO
...
TSU...
TSUKUNE ...?
I CAN FEEL IT...
SOME-THING'S.. CHANGING... INSIDE OF HIM...
TSUKUNE ...!
VSH

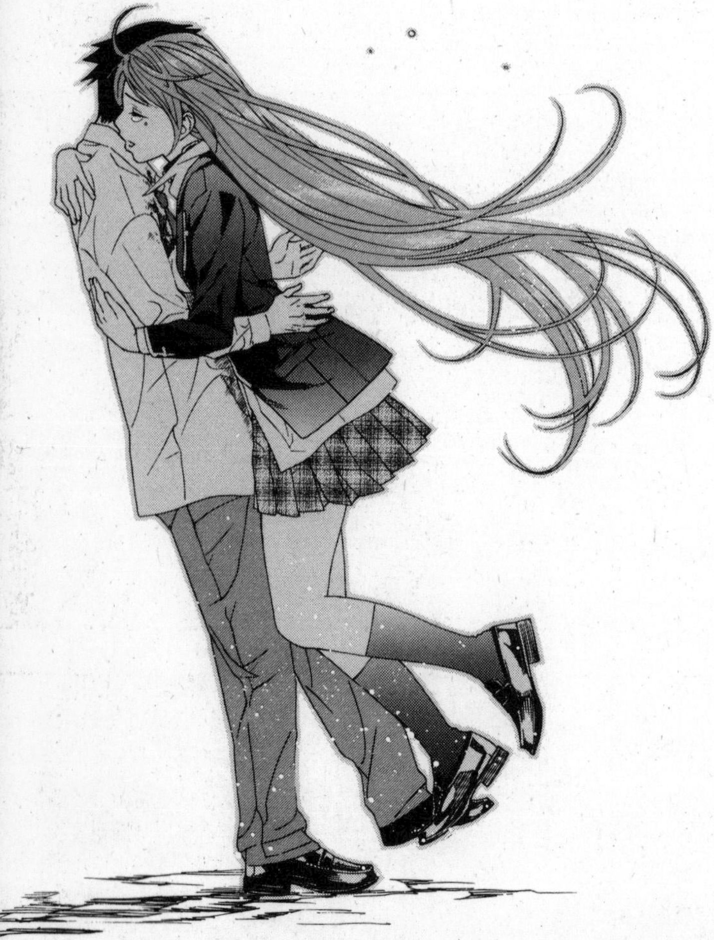

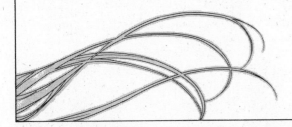

I'M FRIGHTENED... WHAT IF HE ISN'T TSUKUNE ANYMORE...?

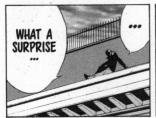

WHAT A SURPRISE ...

...

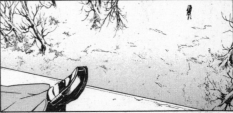

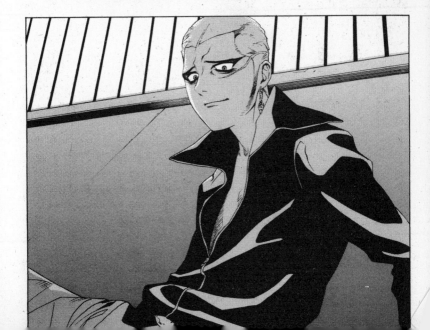

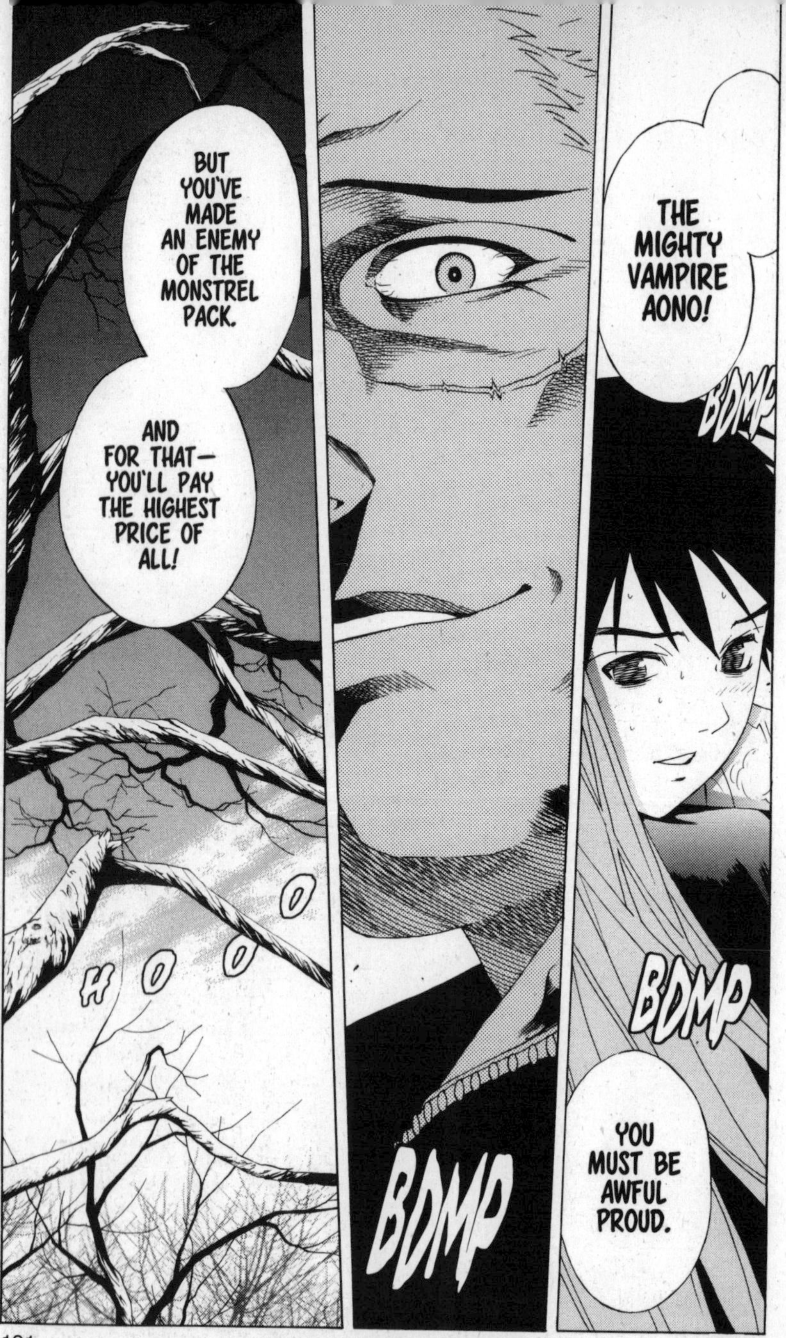
THE MIGHTY VAMPIRE AONO!
BDMP
BDMP
YOU MUST BE AWFUL PROUD.
BDMP
BUT YOU'VE MADE AN ENEMY OF THE MONSTREL PACK.
AND FOR THAT— YOU'LL PAY THE HIGHEST PRICE OF ALL!
HOOOO

ABOMINABLE SNOWGIRL [THE END]

ROSARIO+VAMPIRE

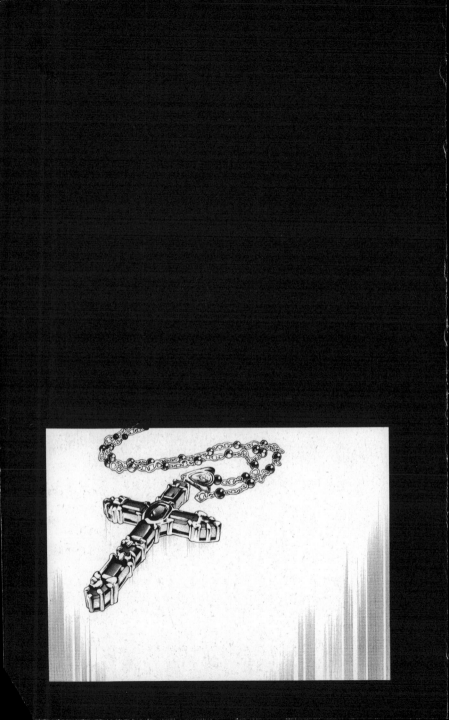

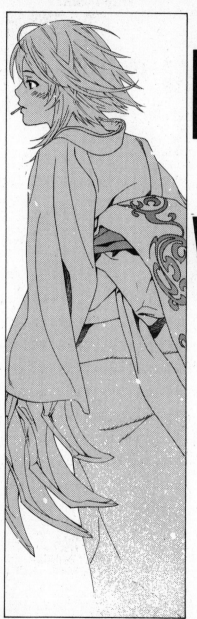

ROSARIO
+
VAMPIRE

Silly
End-of-Volume
Theater

V

Why Stalk?

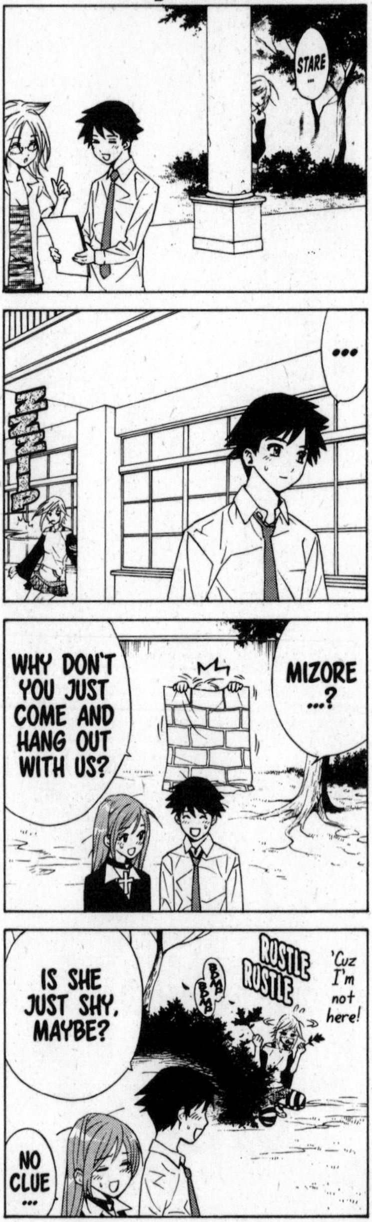
STARE ...
...
ZZIP
MIZORE ...?
WHY DON'T YOU JUST COME AND HANG OUT WITH US?
'Cuz I'm not here!
RUSTLE RUSTLE
IS SHE JUST SHY, MAYBE?
NO CLUE ...

Snow-Colored Romance

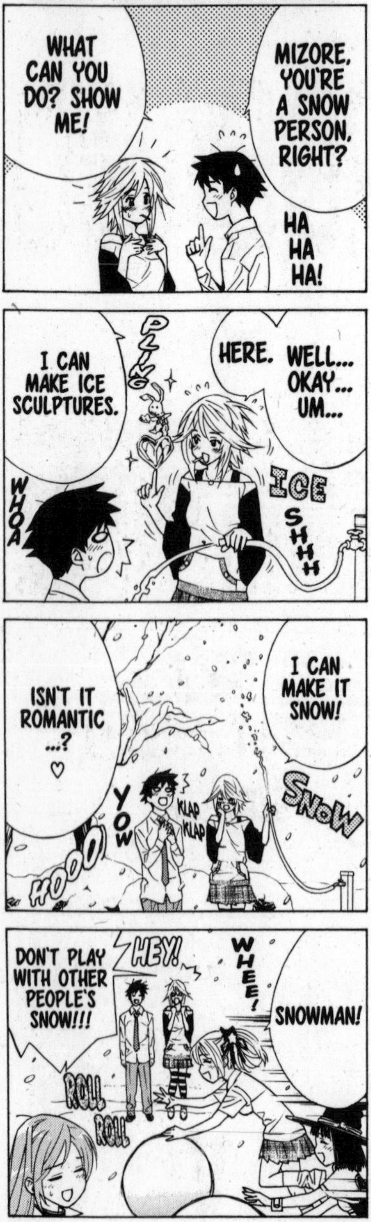
MIZORE, YOU'RE A SNOW PERSON, RIGHT?
HA HA HA!
WHAT CAN YOU DO? SHOW ME!
WELL... OKAY... UM...
HERE.
PLING
I CAN MAKE ICE SCULPTURES.
ICE
SHHH
WHOA
I CAN MAKE IT SNOW!
SNOW
ISN'T IT ROMANTIC ...? ♡
KLAP KLAP
YOW
HOOO
SNOWMAN!
WHEE!
HEY!
DON'T PLAY WITH OTHER PEOPLE'S SNOW!!!
ROLL
ROLL

Making Friends?

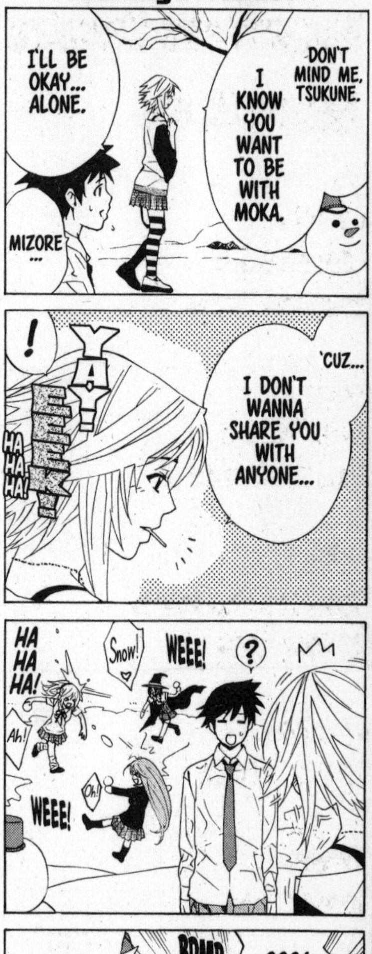
DON'T MIND ME, TSUKUNE.
I KNOW YOU WANT TO BE WITH MOKA.
I'LL BE OKAY... ALONE.
MIZORE...
'CUZ...
I DON'T WANNA SHARE YOU WITH ANYONE...
YAY!
EEEK!
HA HA HA!
!
?
WEEE!
Snow!
HA HA HA!
Ah!
Oh!
WEEE!
OOO!
BDMP BDMP
SNOWBALL FIGHT!
OH BOY!
YAAAY
AAAH!

Teamwork

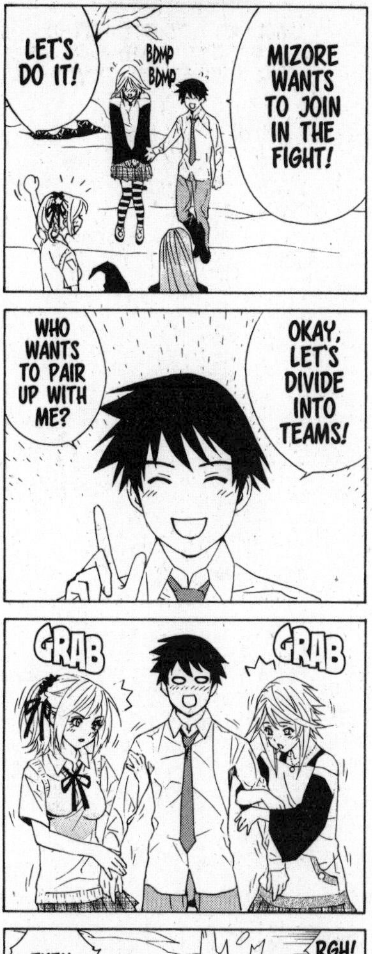
MIZORE WANTS TO JOIN IN THE FIGHT!
BDMP BDMP
LET'S DO IT!
OKAY, LET'S DIVIDE INTO TEAMS!
WHO WANTS TO PAIR UP WITH ME?
GRAB
GRAB
RGH!
VSH
WHY, YOU—!
DIE!
THEY...
...SURE DIDN'T WASTE ANY TIME...
SHHHHH

Send all correspondence to: ROSARIO+VAMPIRE c/o VIZ MEDIA, LLC * P.O. BOX 77010 * SAN FRANCISCO, CA 94107

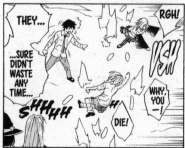

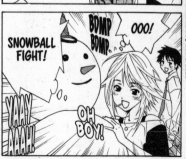

Rosario and Vampire

Akihisa Ikeda

• Staff •
Makoto Saito
Takafumi Okubo

• Help •
Kenji Tashiro
Yuichiro Higuchi

• CG •
Takaharu Yoshizawa
Akihisa Ikeda

• Editing •
Satoshi Adachi

• Comic •
Kenju Noro

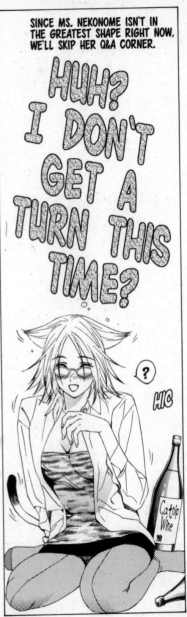

SINCE MS. NEKONOME ISN'T IN THE GREATEST SHAPE RIGHT NOW, WE'LL SKIP HER Q&A CORNER.

HUH? I DON'T GET A TURN THIS TIME?

?

HIC

Catnip Wine

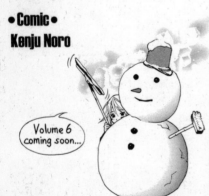

Volume 6 coming soon...

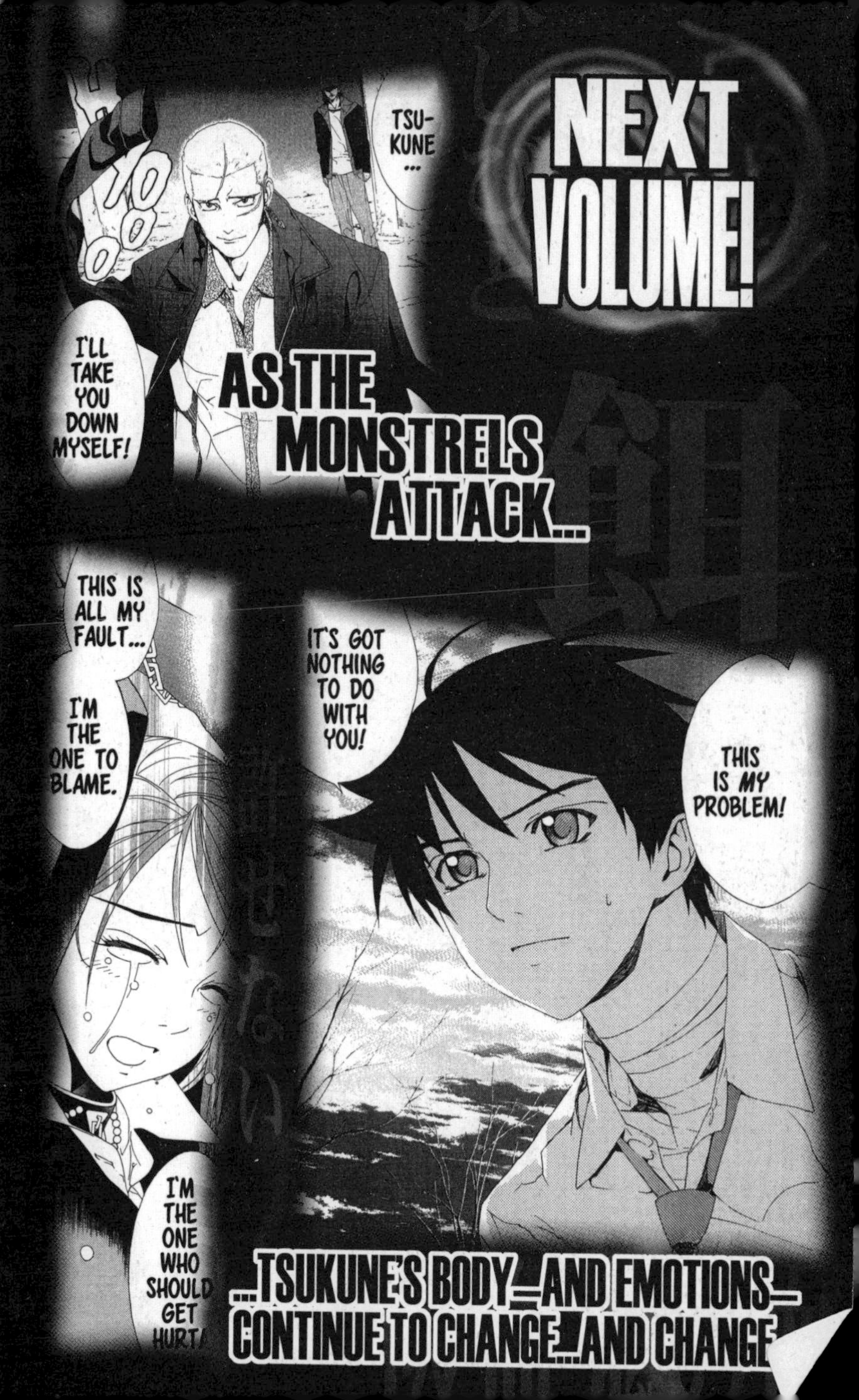
NEXT VOLUME!
TSU-KUNE...
I'LL TAKE YOU DOWN MYSELF!
AS THE MONSTRELS ATTACK...
THIS IS MY PROBLEM!
IT'S GOT NOTHING TO DO WITH YOU!
THIS IS ALL MY FAULT...
I'M THE ONE TO BLAME.
I'M THE ONE WHO SHOULD GET HURT!
...TSUKUNE'S BODY—AND EMOTIONS—CONTINUE TO CHANGE...AND CHANGE

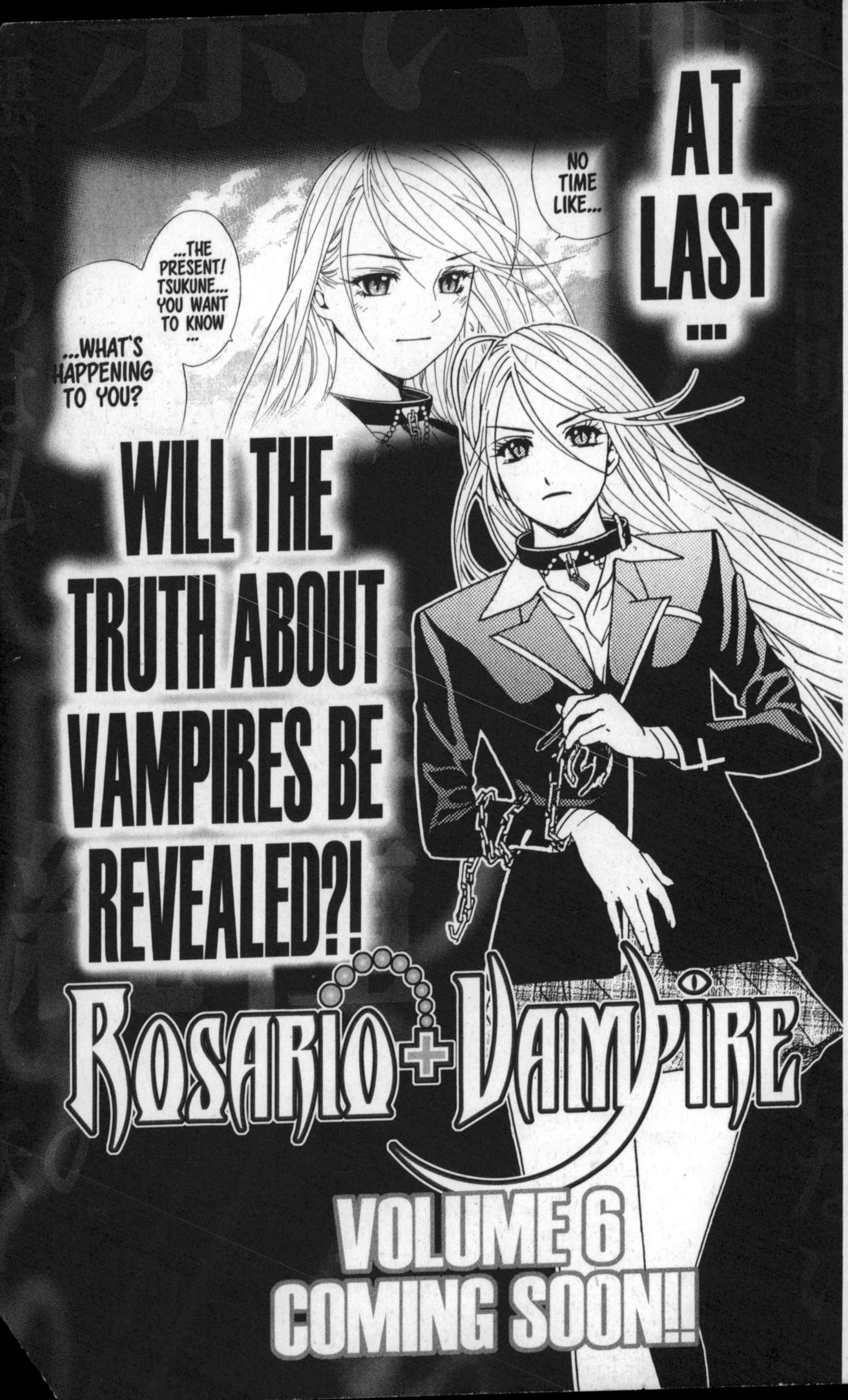
AT LAST ...
NO TIME LIKE...
...THE PRESENT! TSUKUNE... YOU WANT TO KNOW ...
...WHAT'S HAPPENING TO YOU?
WILL THE TRUTH ABOUT VAMPIRES BE REVEALED?!
ROSARIO+VAMPIRE
VOLUME 6 COMING SOON!!

Crypt Sheet for Volume 6: GHOULS

QUIZ 6

THE RECOMMENDED TREATMENT IF YOU FIND YOURSELF TURNING INTO A GHOUL IS...

a. take a relaxing vacation in the human realm

b. drink your vampire girlfriend's blood

c. brains... brains...

TSUKUNE HAS TURNED INTO A GHOUL...
A KILLING MACHINE WHO WANDERS THE WORLD IN SEARCH OF HUMAN FLESH!

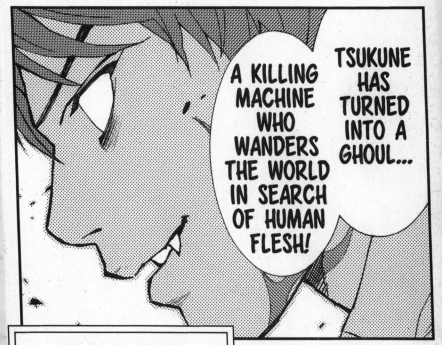

Bite-Size Encyclopedia

Ghoul

When an evil spirit possesses a corpse, it turns into a ghoul. Diet: Human flesh, fresh or well-aged. Ghouls attack helpless children and exhume cadavers from graves to feed. Weakness: The divine and spiritual. Religious symbols repel them.

Available Now!